Energy

Sources, Use, and Role in Human Affairs

Energy

Sources, Use, and Role in Human Affairs

Carol E. Steinhart

John S. Steinhart
University of Wisconsin, Madison

Duxbury Press   North Scituate, Massachusetts
A Division of Wadsworth Publishing Company, Inc.
Belmont, California

Quotations appear in this book from:

The Poetry of Robert Frost edited by Edward Connery Lathem. Copyright 1942 by Robert Frost. Copyright 1947, © 1969 by Holt, Rinehart and Winston, Inc. Copyright 1970 by Lesley Frost Ballantine. Reprinted by permission of Holt, Rinehart and Winston, Inc.

The Grapes of Wrath by John Steinbeck, copyright 1939; copyright renewed 1967 by John Steinbeck. Reprinted by permission of the Viking Press, Inc.

"The Man with the Blue Guitar," from *The Collected Poems of Wallace Stevens*, copyright (1936 by Wallace Stevens and renewed 1964 by Elsie Stevens and Holly Stevens), and Alfred A. Knopf, Inc.

Sonnet CXXXVII by Edna St. Vincent Millay, *Collected Poems*, Harper & Row. Copyright 1939, 1967 by Edna St. Vincent Millay and Norma Millay Ellis. By permission of Norma Millay Ellis.

Duxbury Press
A Division of Wadsworth Publishing Company, Inc.

ISBN-0-87872-069-3
L. C. Cat. Card No. 74-75710
Printed in the United States of America

Energy: Sources, Use, and Role in Human Affairs was edited by Maryellyn Montoro and designed by Duxbury Press.
The cover was designed by Pat Sustendal.
The illustrations were drawn by Christine Kohler and Turner Graphics.

1 2 3 4 5 6 7 8 9 10 – 78 77 76 75 74

**To Gail Steinhart
for her cheerful interest and help**

Contents

Preface

When we began this book in 1971, national concern over environmental deterioration had resulted in the passage of legislation to mitigate these public losses in air and water quality. Yet it seemed to us that many or most of these problems were associated with the increasing energy use in society and there had been no direct policy for energy supplies or use. From teaching courses and reading the earlier writings on energy it became obvious how precariously all industrial societies were balanced on the assumption of endlessly expanding cheap energy supplies. Events since then have provided harsh proof of the consequences of this untested assumption. Availability and prices of energy have changed our lives, have realigned old loyalties and played the key role in foreign policy. The vulnerability of industrial countries is now clear for all to see.

The shortages of fuels and energy will be with us for some time. In order to choose among the options available, a wide range of consequences needs to be examined. To provide broad coverage in a book of modest size, we have treated many complex subjects in a simplified manner. The issue of continued exponential growth, for example is intimately entwined with future energy supply and use, but we have had to be content to treat it only briefly. Many of the choices that must be made depend far more on hopes and dreams than upon objective "facts." For this reason, we have tried to be fair when presenting the evidence, but to make our biases clear. Frankly, it does not appear to us that there is a way out of our present difficulties that is cheap, safe and delightful.

Many people have assisted us by discussing these matters or reading portions of the early drafts of the manuscript. Portions of the book have been read by Dr. Ruth Doell, Dept. of Zoology, San Francisco State University, Dr. Richard Doell, U.S. Geological Survey, Charles Engman and Dr. John Ross, Institute of Environmental Studies, University of Wisconsin, Dr. Charles Stearns, Dept. of Meteorology, University of Wisconsin, Dr. David Pimentel, College of Agriculture, Cornell University, and Thomas Smith, Marine Studies Center, University of Wisconsin. The entire draft manuscript was read by Dr. Richard Cellarius, Evergreen State College, Dr. Laurence G. Hines, Dept. of Economics, Dartmouth College, Dr. Robert Huke, Dept. of Geography,

Dartmouth College, Dr. Marc Ross, Harrison M. Randall, Laboratory of Physics, University of Michigan, and Dr. Alan H. Strahler, Dept. of Environmental Studies, University of Virginia. To all of these, and to other colleagues and students, our sincere thanks. We have profited from their suggestions, and the book has been improved by their efforts. But we have not always taken advice, and we accept responsibility for whatever defects remain.

Carol E. Steinhart
John S. Steinhart

Madison, Wisconsin
December 1973

PART I

Energy in Nature and History

CHAPTER 1

How the Problem Came to Be

If you can look into the seeds of time and say which grain will grow and which will not, speak then to me.

Shakespeare

In the beginning was energy. Through transformations of energy, the universe is evolving, ourselves with it. Whenever anything happens in the universe—anything, anywhere—it is because energy has been transferred from one form to another or from something to something else. Energy makes things happen.

In our speck of the universe, we have energy from the molten interior of the earth, from interactions between earth and other celestial bodies, and most importantly, from the sun. In addition to the familiar cycles of heat and light, the effect of sun on the earth is seen in the winds, the cycle of rainfall and evaporation, the tides, and the energy stored in green plants and, several transformations later, in our own bodies.

When our planet was young, radiation from the sun and from space bombarded a primitive atmosphere, providing energy for the formation of simple organic molecules. These molecules were washed into the growing seas by violent rainstorms. In the lightning that accompanied the rain, still more molecules were born. Eventually, some of the molecules came together into groups, and surface films formed around them. Laboratory experiments simulating postulated conditions on the primitive earth show how this might have happened. Something inherent in the geometry of the atoms and molecules and their distribution of energy makes them behave this way. Thus, a tiny fraction of the radiant

3

energy that reached the earth was stored as chemical energy in associations of organic molecules.

Nature's early molecular experiments were random, but nature has never been conservative with materials. From uncounted failures arose some configurations that grew and reproduced themselves. Improbable? Not really. We know that at some time in the past aggregates of molecules passed through the shadow dividing life from non-life.

Probably these first life forms, 2 or 3 billion years ago, grew, multiplied, and derived their energy at the expense of complex molecules that swam in the "primordial soup." Gradually, however, the large molecules were used up, so that only those organisms could survive that were able to synthesize their own complex molecules from simple ones. Perhaps only a few organisms out of billions achieved the necessary autonomy for the survival of themselves and their descendants. Perhaps—and we will never know—it was only one.

Life's invention of photosynthesis, an energy conversion process, was a key point in evolution. It permitted development of the never-ending variety of life forms that have paraded across the earth in the last 3 billion years. Life is energy conversion.

With photosynthesis came the potential for altering the earth's energy balance ever so slightly and for changing the chemical composition of the atmosphere and the outer skin of the earth itself. Molecules of chlorophyll trapped photons of light, becoming activated and initiating a chain of events leading to the formation of carbohydrates from carbon dioxide and water. Carbohydrates became the fuel of most living cells.

With photosynthesis, larger amounts of solar energy could be diverted to the use of living creatures. For every molecule of carbon dioxide fixed into fuel, a molecule of oxygen was released. Gradually, an oxygen-rich atmosphere evolved through photosynthesis, the photo-decomposition of water, and perhaps through geological and geochemical processes. The new atmosphere permitted the evolution of aerobic respiration, a process much more efficient than anaerobic fermentation in utilizing the stored energy of carbohydrate molecules. In the wake of green plants, animals evolved—first in the water, then in pursuit of plants that invaded the land. With the exception of certain chemo-synthetic bacteria, even microorganisms, as we know them today, are indebted to photosynthetic plants for their existence.

At times the balance must have been delicate between the green energy trappers and the energy eaters. Had the green plants been depleted, the story of life might have ended. But they continued to multiply. They produced enough not only for their own growth and multiplication, but a surplus so large that not all the energy eaters together, from the microscopic decomposers to the mighty dinosaurs, could consume it. The earth began storing unused organic matter in the form of coal, oil, and oil derivatives—the fossil fuels. It would prove to be capital laid away for exploitation by an insatiable energy eater of the future, a creature yet so remote that it was only hinted at by tiny rodent-like beings that scurried around beneath the feet of dinosaurs.

The dependence of energy eaters on green energy trappers is responsible for the pyramidal form of the food web. Approximately 10 kilograms of food are required to produce 1 kilogram of the creature that is fed. Thus, 100 kilos of plants are needed to produce 10 kilos of herbivore which in turn are converted into 1 kilo of carnivore. The pyramid is narrowing rapidly. And the carnivores that prey on the carnivores, and the carnivores that prey on them—all are held parsimoniously in check by their interactions with organisms at other levels of the pyramid.

After perhaps a billion years of evolution, modern man emerged. Until a geologic yesterday, the earth's energy balance sheet came out about even, perhaps a little on the plus side with small amounts of energy being laid away. Each day the sun shone and green plants built energy-rich molecules, more than enough for their own growth and survival into future generations. Much of the remainder was eaten by herbivores that were eaten by carnivores, and everything that died furnished food for scavengers and a host of decomposers. There was a surplus of food. Some of it, buried in mud or at the ocean bottom or otherwise protected from decomposition, became unavailable until yesterday, when modern man discovered fossil fuel.

Only man is able to utilize energy in excess of that necessary to satisfy his nutritional needs. His most recent economic and technological development has been at the expense of that capital energy investment, the fossil fuels. Through clever but heedless manipulation of energy, he has brought himself to an energy crisis. We do not yet know the end of the story, but we do know that when capital is used up a common end is bankruptcy. It is possible that a rich uncle may die opportunely and bequeath a source of unlimited capital. It is possible that technology will tame nuclear fusion or solar energy to fill our real and imagined needs—but we may be appalled by the results.

For the first time in history, man has proposed to dig deeply into the vast sources of physical energy that propel the hurricanes and into the nuclear energy that burns the stars. We have no precedent by which to judge what energy conversions of the contemplated magnitude will do to the earth. Yet we shortsightedly concentrate on overcoming technological problems, asking only "Can we do it?", and never "Should we?" We ponder the consequences of our action superficially, if at all. We are teetering precariously at the top of the ecological pyramid. But our increasing numbers and demands seem to make it imperative that we take our place at the bottom of the pyramid, along with green plants, as primary producers. When we scheme to use solar energy directly we become photosynthesizers in the literal meaning of the word. And we can be certain that if man becomes a photosynthesizer there will be profound consequences on earth.

Our global energy problems—lack of food, surplus of waste energy, uncertainty about future energy supply—are a result of human actions. We need more energy, we are told, so that progress can continue. But can more of the behavior that caused the problems solve them? The best that energy technology can do is make things tidier while we struggle to change our habits. And we must change, not only our habits, but some of our most fundamental assumptions and beliefs. We can no longer deny our evolutionary history and our biological and psychological relationship to the earth.

This book is about energy and change, because energy is the agent of change. We are concerned with energy primarily as it is used by living creatures. With how its availability is crucial to the rise and the threatened fall of civilization. We will consider the nature of energy, its various forms and their interconversion, and the energy technology of man. We will look at the relationship between man and energy, and at some of its implications.

Perhaps you still believe that in our current crisis of crises the energy crisis is less critical than some of the others. We will not run out of fuel for several centuries. The population explosion or pollution or nuclear war may do us in before we need to worry about the depletion of fuels, from which technology may yet save us. But we suggest that the population explosion has come about because of our ability to bend energy to our desires, that pollution is caused by the technology to which energy gave rise, that wars are related to inequitable distribution of energy resources (including food), and that the very degree to which war has become a threat is a function of how we have exploited energy to kill one another. Whenever anything happens in the universe, it is because energy has been transferred from something to something else. Energy makes things happen.

As this book goes to press, the United States is facing a critical energy shortage. The immediate cause of the crisis is a cutoff of oil from the Arab nations, and many people assume that after this political problem has been solved the energy problem will also go away. But the current shortage has been in the making for some time, and the crisis was merely precipitated by the Arab situation. The problem will not go away, as this book attempts to show.

The energy crisis is thought by some to be a blessing in disguise. Sooner or later, something will halt our growth in numbers and our consumption of resources. We can name most of the possibilities: war, disease, famine, depletion of resources, pollution of the environment, lack of space. Perhaps the limit imposed by the availability of energy is the kindest of all these. At least we can foresee our future problems, and we can plan for the kind of future we want, that is, one which is compatible with the realities of our physical and biological world.

CHAPTER 2

Energy, Thespian

We dance round in a ring and suppose,
But the Secret sits in the middle and knows.

Robert Frost

Some of the world's most talented actors have confessed that they don't know who they are, so completely do they become one with the role they are playing. Although they cannot define themselves, we feel that there must be something, or someone, constant behind the shifting manifestations of character. So it is with energy. We feel intuitively that energy is something definable, yet it resists definition. We must be content with the explanation that energy is a capacity, the capacity to do work or to bring about change.

Part of the problem lies in the fact that we persist in thinking of energy as something apart from the objects of everyday life, although twentieth century physics has clearly shown the equivalence of matter and energy, and we can measure, locate, direct—and sometimes even weigh—energy as easily as matter. So while we juggle equations on paper, most of us still have no intuitive feeling for mass-energy.

This lack of feeling is the result of several historical accidents. In our evolutionary development, specialized senses detected particular kinds of energy, while some kinds escaped detection entirely. Light, sound, heat, motion—all were familiar, but without scientific experiment and theory there was no reason to suppose them to be related. As if the evidence of our senses did not confound things enough, our language developed in a way that made it difficult to express certain concepts—concepts that may be a part of the everyday thinking of people whose language structure is different from our own. In some ways, the Hopi Indian language, for example, and consequently the Hopi way of thinking, are better suited to the description of relativistic physics than is English. As a result of our psychological, biological, and linguistic limitations, scientific thought and discovery have sometimes proceeded in a way that obscures unifying principles.

THE FORMS OF ENERGY

The guise taken by energy depends in part on what we are looking for and how we try to measure it. Energy has a variety of forms which are rather freely interconvertible. Table 2–1 shows some familiar examples of the conversion of energy from one form to another.

Different types of energy have customarily been expressed in different units. This makes their equivalence and their relationships difficult to comprehend. In this book we will use the unit watt, or the related megawatt (10^6 watts) or kilowatt (10^3 watts), for power and the kilowatt-hour or calorie for energy. Energy is the quantity that changes form when work is done or when something happens. Power is the rate at which energy does work. Common units for measuring energy and power and the relationships between them are given in Appendix A.

The most abundant form of energy in the universe is gravitational energy. When a mass falls together, as it does in the gravitational collapse of a star, gravitational potential energy is released as a spectacular display of light, heat, and motion. Such celestial events have been noted in the past by astronomers as the sudden appearance of brilliant supernovae, and by fearful observers as harbingers of supernatural events. Because of gravity, an object (for example, a rock on top of a mountain) acquires a certain potential energy that is related to its position. If the rock is shaken loose, its potential energy is converted partly to kinetic energy of motion as it rolls down the mountainside, partly to heat as it strikes against other objects, and partly to sound. The rolling of a rock down a mountain constitutes a local gravitational contraction of the earth.

We use gravity in many ways. For example, although the cycle of water evaporation and rainfall is driven by the sun, it is gravity that makes water run downhill; and as a result it is possible to have a hydroelectric plant at Niagara Falls.

Kinetic energy is associated with motion: with random molecular motion that is heat and an orderly kind of molecular motion that is sound; with wind and windmills, running water and waterwheels, the falling of a weight or the downswing of a pendulum; with the rotation and orbital revolution of planets; and with human and animal muscle power.

Table 2–1. Some Examples of Energy Conversion and Energy Converting Devices

From / To	Mechanical	Thermal	Acoustical	Chemical	Electrical	Light
Mechanical	Oar Sail Jack Bicycle	Steam engine	Barograph Ear	Muscle contraction Bomb Jet engine	Electric motor Piezo-electric crystal	Photoelectric door opener
Thermal	Friction Brake Heat pump	Radiator	Sound absorber	Food Fuel Match	Resistor Spark plug	Solar cooker Greenhouse effect
Acoustical	Bell Violin Wind-up phonograph	Flame tube	Megaphone	Explosion	Telephone receiver Loud speaker Thunder	
Chemical	Impact detonation of nitroglycerine	Endothermic chemical reactions		Growth and metabolism	Electrolysis	Photosynthesis Photochemical reactions
Electrical	Dynamo Piezo-electric crystal	Thermopile	Induction microphone	Battery Fuel cell	Transformer	Solar cell
Light	Friction (sparks)	Thermoluminescence	Rock music light shows	Bioluminescence Candle	Lightbulb Lightning	Fluorescence

Heat is a form of energy which, when absorbed by matter, appears as an increase in the kinetic energy (translational, rotational, and vibrational) of its molecules. As the kinetic energy of molecules increases, they become more reactive chemically, which is why chemical reactions occur more rapidly as the temperature rises.

In the case of muscle power, chemical potential energy of fuel in body cells is converted to mechanical energy by which we perform work. If the products of a chemical reaction contain less energy than the reactants, it is possible to obtain useful work from the reaction. Some of the body's chemical energy is expended in heat, in the slow flameless fire that burns in every organism throughout its life, and some is used to drive still other chemical reactions. Chemical energy is released as heat and light when we burn wood or oil, and chemical energy is discharged explosively when we shoot a gun or detonate a charge of dynamite. While chemical energy is of major importance in the functioning of living organisms and in the affairs of men, it plays a minor role in the energetics of the universe as a whole.

Plants and animals burn chemical fuel. Stars burn nuclear fuel, and man today is attempting to emulate the stars. Because of the equivalence of energy and mass expressed by the relationship $E = mc^2$ (where c is the velocity of light), immense energies are available through nuclear rearrangements in which mass is released as energy. The decrease in mass of the reaction products is so small that it might go unsuspected or ascribed to experimental error, if theory did not predict it. We can measure a change in mass in some violent nuclear reactions, amounting to as much as one part in one thousand. Theory tells us, however, that mass is also lost when a stretched spring relaxes, when water freezes, when a weight falls, or any other time when energy is lost from a system. These changes are far too slight for our most sensitive instruments to record. When mass is converted to energy, the energy may be released in the form of electromagnetic radiation or energetic particles or both.

Electromagnetic radiation is a combination of rapidly alternating electric and magnetic fields between which energy is exchanged. Like the definition of energy this explanation defies intuitive understanding, but the mathematical theory behind it allows us to describe many phenomena that we observe. The electromagnetic spectrum includes types of radiation that are classified, in order of their increasing energy, as radiowaves, microwaves, infrared, visible, ultraviolet, X-rays, and gamma rays (see chapter 12).

Electromagnetic radiation travels through space at a rate of 300,000 kilometers (186,280 miles)* per second. It can be detected only as it interacts with matter, which is why space is black and cold. Before

*We are in a sometimes confusing period of transition from English to metric units. To help establish a "feeling" for the metric system, the more familiar English units are also included throughout this book.

we can detect infrared radiation in the form of heat, something must be warm. Before we can detect light, something must absorb or reflect it. The energy we receive from the sun is in the form of electromagnetic radiation.

Matter itself is electrical in nature. During the early part of the twentieth century, when details of atomic structure were being worked out, matter was thought to consist entirely of **protons** and **electrons** and electrically neutral neutrons composed of one proton and one electron. Now we can identify other charged and neutral particles when an atomic nucleus absorbs or emits energy, but for most practical purposes we still need deal only with protons, electrons, and a few of their combinations.

An electric current is created by charges in motion. The currents most familiar to us are produced by negatively charged electrons moving through a material which permits their relatively free passage—that is, through a conductor. The conductor is usually a metal wire or an **ionic** solution.

LEVELS OF ENERGY

The amount of available energy in a system increases greatly as forces acting at shorter and shorter distances are brought into play.

Physical Energy

Physical interactions over relatively large distances are represented by the falling of an object, the stretching of a spring, or, on a finer scale, by intermolecular forces like those binding water molecules in the crystal lattice of ice. If we use heat as a common denominator for comparing forms of energy, we see that physical energy is quite weak. Water crashing over Niagara Falls converts most of its kinetic energy to heat when it strikes the bottom, yet the temperature of water at the bottom of the Falls is only 0.12° C (.21° F) warmer than at the top!

Dropping a kilogram (2.2 pounds) of water through a distance of 100 meters (328 feet) yields 2.7×10^{-4} * kilowatt-hours of energy, while freezing this kilogram of water so that the molecules arrange

*It is convenient, when dealing with very large or very small numbers, to express them as powers of ten. One convention is to write the actual digits of the number with one digit to the left of the decimal point and the remaining digits to the right. This number is then multiplied by a power of ten to show its actual magnitude. To write out the number in the usual way, move the decimal point to the right as many places as indicated by a positive exponent, or as many places to the left as indicated by a negative one. For example:

themselves in a lower energy state releases 9×10^{-2} kilowatt hours of energy. In the first case, the large distance through which the earth attracted the water was involved. In the second instance, in which more than one hundred times as much energy was released, we were dealing with the much smaller distances through which molecules in a crystal interact.

Chemical Energy

The energies involved in interactions between molecules are many times smaller than intramolecular energies—the energy of the chemical bond. By burning 111 grams (3.9 ounces) of hydrogen with 889 grams (31.1 ounces) of oxygen to get one kilogram of water, we obtain 44 kilowatt-hours of energy. As another example, you can get about 600 times more energy by burning rubber bands than by stretching them.

Nuclear Energy

The greatest energies of all are those which bind particles together in the atomic nucleus. If instead of burning the 111 grams of hydrogen we induced it to undergo nuclear reactions to form the element helium, we would get 2.1×10^7 kilowatt-hours of energy!

Man has learned to use the forms of energy in that order: first physical, then chemical, then nuclear. In war, an art he has mastered well, this is illustrated by successive use of bow, cannon, and nuclear bombs.

ENERGY AS A NATURAL RESOURCE

Energy and matter are natural resources. Eager to exploit material resources, we have often overlooked the role of energy or the fact that energy resources are limited as surely as are copper and gold. We forget that only energy makes things happen. In the days when men struggled to realize grandiose dreams with primitive machines and slave

$$2.3 \times 10^{-10} \quad = \quad 0.00000000023$$
$$2.3 \times 10^{-3} \quad = \quad 0.0023$$
$$2.3 \times 10^{-1} \quad = \quad 0.23$$
$$2.3 \times 10^0 = 2.3 \times 1 = \quad 2.3$$
$$2.3 \times 10^1 \quad = \quad 23$$
$$2.3 \times 10^3 \quad = 2300$$

We often speak of an order of magnitude. An order of magnitude is a factor of ten. The number 230 is greater than 23 by one order of magnitude and greater than 0.23 by three orders of magnitude. (You would have to multiply 0.23 by 1000, or 10^3, to get 230.)

labor, they understood that energy was a precious commodity. But today in the United States we try to deny our limitations and talk of going to the stars. At the same time we curse the bungling power company for brownouts, blackouts, and pollution.

We are using up our energy supplies as surely as we are using up our metals. Of course we are not actually using up either commodity, in the sense that there is less than there once was. There is as much iron as ever, and about as much energy, too. But we have changed the form of these resources and spread them around so that they are no longer useful. In the case of metals, it eventually becomes technically, economically, and energetically infeasible to reclaim them from garbage or to mine low-grade ores. As for energy, the inexorable laws of thermodynamics take over as we perpetually degrade concentrated energy to diffuse, useless heat. Our planet will not remain indifferent to our escalating efforts to unbalance its energy balance. We must look at the energy resources of the earth and at how they stay in balance, so that we might use them today without mortgaging tomorrow.

THE ENERGY BUDGET OF THE EARTH

Energy flows constantly to and from the earth. This flow shows local and short-term imbalance — warm days and cool nights, heat waves and cold snaps. However, it is in long-term equilibrium, and thus we have nearly constant mean annual temperatures. And it exhibits very long term changes: a subtropical global climate gave way to the glaciers. The earth's energy is derived from solar radiation, the tides, and her own heat.

Of the 1.5×10^{20} kilowatt-hours of solar energy intercepted by the earth each year, as much as 35 percent is reflected back into space without affecting anything at all. This fraction of reflected energy is called the albedo. Most of the energy is reflected from atmospheric clouds and dust, but some is from the surface of the earth as well. The albedo of the oceans averages around 2 percent; it varies with the size of waves and ripples and with the angle of the incoming radiation. The albedo of forested land ranges between 3 and 10 percent while that of snow or ice can surpass 90 percent. A succession of unusually snowy seasons increases the earth's albedo and decreases the energy available for melting snow and ice, thereby shortening the snow-free season, lowering the mean annual temperature, and leading to more snow, more ice, and less melting. In this way long-term cooling trends or glacial periods might begin and perpetuate themselves, although these processes are much more complex than we have indicated here.

While clouds and dust scatter almost a third of our incoming energy back into space, carbon dioxide, water vapor, and ozone in the atmosphere absorb another 10 to 15 percent of it. This absorption is not uniform across the spectrum, but is concentrated at certain wavelengths. Ozone, an uncommon molecular form of oxygen (O_3), selectively absorbs most of the ultraviolet light that otherwise would reach the earth at life-destroying intensities.

About half of the solar energy intercepted by the earth reaches its surface, where most of it is absorbed. Here it drives a number of processes before it is degraded and reradiated at longer wavelengths than those originally received. Figure 2–1 shows the fate of the solar energy that reaches the earth.

Figure 2–1. What happens to solar energy intercepted by the earth.

BOX 2-1   THERMAL PROPERTIES OF WATER

A great deal of heat is required to melt, boil, or raise the temperature of water. The amount of heat required to melt one gram (.035 ounce) of ice at 0°C (32°F) (its heat of fusion) is 80 calories. One additional calorie is needed to raise the temperature of the resulting gram of water 1°C. (The specific heat of water is one calorie per gram.) At 100°C, 540 calories are required to convert the water from liquid form to water vapor. In other words, the heat of vaporization is 540 calories per gram. To see why so much solar energy is used to melt, heat, and evaporate water, we can compare the thermal properties of water with those of some other common substances:

Substance	Specific Heat at 0°C (cal/g/°C)	Heat of Fusion (cal/g at freezing point)	Heat of Vaporization (cal/g at boiling point)
Water	1.00	79.7	539.6*
Mercury	0.03	2.8	70.6
Lead	0.03	5.9	–
Ethyl alcohol	0.54	24.9	204.0
Oxygen	0.22	3.3	50.9
Carbon monoxide	0.26	8.0	50.4

*At 20° the heat of vaporization is 585 cal/g

When we melt, heat, or vaporize something we are adding energy to it. Because of the equivalence of mass and energy, this energy increases the mass. If balances were sensitive enough, we would find that 1 gram of ice, when melted, would weigh more than a gram—by an amount equal to the energy acquired during melting divided by the square of the velocity of light. When heated to the boiling point it would weigh still more, and the water vapor would weigh most of all. It would weigh 1.000,000,000,000,002 grams.

Most incoming radiation is in the visible portion of the spectrum. What is reradiated is largely infrared. This results in the greenhouse effect. Although the atmosphere is transparent to light in the visible range, it is opaque to radiation of longer wavelengths. Visible light passes freely to the earth's surface, does its work, and is reradiated toward space. But having been changed by its stay on earth, it cannot pass back through the atmosphere as freely as it came. It is trapped by the water vapor and carbon dioxide of the air, where it remains to warm the lower layers of the atmosphere and the surface of the earth.

A large percentage of the energy absorbed at the earth's surface is used to evaporate water (see Box 2–1). To evaporate the annual rainfall at an average rate of more than a billion gallons per second requires 2.6×10^{19} kilowatt-hours of energy, about one-third the amount reaching the earth's surface. This heat is eventually released when rain condenses. Much of it is lost to space. Some remains to warm the air and earth, and some powers winds and convection currents.

If we add up the fractions of solar radiation that are reflected (35 percent), absorbed and converted to heat (45 percent), and involved in the evaporation of water (20 percent), we get a total of 100 percent. Something very important seems to be missing. We have not mentioned the energy used in photosynthesis. About one-fiftieth of 1 percent of the solar energy reaching the earth supports all of life. The energies that maintain the biosphere are pathetically puny in comparison to the formidable forces that drive the physical processes of land, sea, and sky. Perhaps they achieve significance only in, or through, the mind of man.

Tidal and geothermal energy sources provide very little energy relative to that provided by the sun. Together they contribute less to the energy budget than is used by plants in photosynthesis. Each year about 2.8×10^{14} kilowatt-hours of energy is carried by conduction and convection and by hot springs and volcanoes from the interior of the earth to its surface. Tidal energy provides about 2.6×10^{13} kilowatt-hours per year. The shifting, rising, settling, and rearrangements of the earth's crust that we call earthquakes, violent as they may be, release only 3×10^{12} kilowatt-hours per year.

SUGGESTED READING

Dyson, F. "Energy in the Universe." *Scientific American* 224, 3 (1971): 50–59.

Harte, J., and R. Socolow. 1971. Energy. In *Patient Earth,* ed. J. Harte and R. Socolow, pp. 276–294. New York: Holt, Rinehart and Winston, Inc.

Hubbert, M. K. "The Energy Resources of the Earth." *Scientific American,* 224, 3 (1971); 60–70.

Oort, A. "The Energy Cycle of the Earth." *Scientific American* 223, 3 (1970): 54–63.

CHAPTER 3

Cycles, Spirals, and Lines

The sun at noon is the sun declining.
The creature born is the creature dying.

Chinese Proverb

The earth's energy balance involves many dynamic, interrelated processes. Daily, monthly, annual, and longer-range cycles interact to yield a high degree of environmental predictability and short-term stability. This predictability rests upon a precarious and delicate foundation in nature, which gives the illusion of invulnerability because of the vast forces and amounts of material involved. Among the cycles of concern are the seasonal cycles that provide our crops, the biological cycles that govern reproduction and growth, and the chemical cycles that convert inorganic carbon dioxide, nitrogen, phosphorus, and sulfur into the materials of human life. We are now able to interfere with most of these cycles, as will be shown in this and in later chapters. Our interference is not due so much to the sheer magnitude of our activities as to subtle inputs of energy or materials at critical leverage points. For example, it seems unlikely at the present time that we can change the temperature of our planet by rejecting large amounts of waste heat into the atmosphere, but entirely possible that we will achieve this effect by a slight alteration of the atmospheric concentration of carbon dioxide. Similarly, it is difficult (but, as the passenger pigeon proves, not impossible) to hunt a species to extinction; yet small amounts of poison or other subtle environmental changes are driving many species to the brink of extinction.

In Western civilization there has been little perception of the fact that, in nature, cycle is superimposed upon cycle, beginning in our own minds and bodies and extending throughout the universe. This denial of cycles is expressed in our concept of time, which is linear. To the Biblical fundamentalist, time began on October 16, 4004 B.C., with the creation of the universe. It has proceeded linearly since then.

The ancient Greeks and Romans conceived of time as a cyclical phenomenon. Similarly, Chinese astronomers of the eleventh and twelfth centuries were calculating astronomical periods in millions of years. In addition to cycles, the Chinese recognized a series of evolutionary unfoldings; cycles became more like spirals, and history was possible. The people melded peacefully with nature and history. In Indian philosophy, life itself is endlessly recycled through rebirth and transmigration of the soul. For these cultures, the cycles of nature are perceived as easily as the cycles of time.

Contrast Western man, rushing pell-mell down his one-way superhighway. Not only does he no longer heed messages from his own body, but he can no longer understand nor even detect them. He drives himself at a peak rate through the winter, when good sense might advise him to slow down as most creatures do. Perhaps as a result, January is a peak month for deaths. He jet commutes half way around the world and wonders why his digestion, as well as his sleep, is upset. Eating on a schedule of habit or convenience, he does not even recognize a feeling of hunger. For more than two million years man and his immediate ancestors evolved in harmony with the periodicities of the earth. Modern man ignores these relationships to his sorrow.

Loren Eiseley has called Western man a world eater and a time effacer.[1] It is as if he would erase the record of the past, disdain the present, and only dream frantically of possible futures. Where progress is a byword and some utopian goal—if anyone can remember what it was—justifies any means, there is no other way. But at last we are coming to know that we must deal with both cycles and linear evolution—that even while the seasons rotate, irreversible changes are underway. We fear that we may unwittingly set some of these changes into motion and that they will bode ill for us; for while we have ample power to change the history of earth, we lack both the power and the wisdom to control the change we effect.

CYCLICAL PHENOMENA OF THE EARTH-MOON-SUN SYSTEM

Some cyclic phenomena are so striking that men described and predicted them several thousands of years before they could be scientifically explained. The earth rotates around her axis in a period we call a day. In addition to the obvious alternation of light and dark, a host of subtler patterns are geared to the earth's rotation. During the night, the photosynthetic apparatus of green plants sits idle as plants carry on the same combustion reactions (respiration) that are common to animals. Energy is released. Oxygen is removed from the air. During the day, specialized pores in the leaves open to facilitate gas exchange, photosynthesis proceeds at a rate several times that of respiration, and there is a net storage of energy and oxygen release into the atmosphere. At the same time, water is drawn through the conductive tissue of the plant and is evaporated from the open pores. This process is called transpiration, and accounts for the enormous water requirements of plants and for about half of the evaporation of water that takes place over land.

Most animals also set their clocks by the sun. Scientists have observed daily activity cycles in their laboratory animals for many years. They are only now beginning to discover a myriad of circadian rhythms in animals and man. Almost anything they measure—body temperature, hormone levels, rates of physiological processes—shows a rhythm, so it is tempting to postulate that these many rhythms are merely different expressions of one or a few basic rhythms which remain unidentified. Daily cycles, from the succession of days and nights to the periods of sleep and running of a laboratory mouse, are expressions of energy flow. Something has gained energy and something has lost it, or energy has been changed from one form to another.

Another basic cyclical phenomenon is the revolution of the earth and moon around their mutual gravitational center once in 28 days. The progression of the moon from new to full and back to new has been familiar to man since he first gazed into the sky and wondered. Gravitational interaction between the earth and moon causes mutual tidal effects. Data from the Apollo moon flights show that there are occasional small moonquakes. One theory postulates that the moon's seismic activity is due to tidal forces caused by the earth.

A day with respect to the moon is 24 hours and 51 minutes, slightly longer than the time required for one rotation of the earth with respect to the sun, because while the earth is turning once on its axis, the earth and moon have completed one twenty-eighth of their revolution around each other. A double bulge in the atmosphere, sea, and solid earth moves around the earth once in each lunar day. This deformation is symmetrical because of the earth's elasticity. We are not aware of the distortion in the atmosphere or land, although instruments can measure it; but the distortion in the sea cannot escape notice. We call it the tide. High tides occur at intervals of approximately 12 hours and 25 minutes, near the times when the moon crosses the local meridian. Low tides occur when the moon is near the horizon.

The tides affect the distribution of creatures living in the intertidal zones along the seashore. Their lives are tuned to the number and duration of their monthly baths. Some species live just beyond the reach of the highest high tides, moistened only by sea spray. Others inhabit the narrow strip between the highest high tide and the lowest high tide, where they are submerged for only a few hours two or three times a month. The richest variety of life is found in the permanent tide pools which are exposed but a few times each month at the very lowest tides.

Once every 29½ days, at the time of the new moon, the sun and moon rise and set together. The changing relationships between earth, sun, and moon during this cycle govern the reproductive behavior of many sea creatures, some insects and perhaps higher land animals as well. It is probably no accident that the average length of the menstrual cycle in the human female is 29½ days, and no accident that the moon and fertility are connected in many ancient rites. The date of Easter is set by the first full moon after the spring equinox. A number of 28- to 30-day rhythms have been found in man, and we will probably find more if we look for them.

The sun also causes tides in the earth, with a period of 12 hours, but because of its great distance (gravitational attraction decreases with the square of the distance between objects) its effects are detectable mainly as they modify lunar tides.

The tides represent an energy flow which must come from the kinetic energy of the earth. If the earth is losing rotational energy, the days should be getting longer. Astronomical and geological evidence suggests that the period of the earth's rotation is in fact lengthening at the rate of 1.8 milliseconds per century. With days of the current length, eclipses recorded by astronomers in antiquity would have been observed at different times and in different places. Variation from the predicted times of occultation of heavenly bodies by the moon also indicates that day length is changing as expected. Rocks tell the same story. Corals exhibit both daily and yearly cycles of growth, and these growth lines may be preserved in fossils. All fossils in which growth lines can be counted contain well over 365 lines in a year's growth. Two fossil corals from almost 300 million years ago showed 390 and 385 growth lines per year. So the day is lengthening as energy flows—about 2.6×10^{13} kilowatt-hours per year—with the ebb and flow of the tides.

The earth's revolution around the sun creates the seasons as, her axis of rotation tipped with respect to her orbit, the earth presents ever changing faces to the full rays of the sun. Life cycles of plants and animals are finely adjusted to patterns of heat and cold, long days and short. Even near the equator, where temperature and day length remain almost constant, recurrent seasons of tropical storms may mark the progress of the earth along her orbit. Polar ice caps shrink during summer and creep forward during winter. Permanent and temporary heat deficits or excesses are partially compensated by circulating winds and ocean currents, which themselves are powered by cyclic changes. Together, these phenomena produce the climates of the earth. Chapter 12 describes how man's use of energy may change the very winds.

SOME PHYSICAL AND BIOGEOCHEMICAL CYCLES

Land, sea, and atmosphere form a dynamic union through which matter, energy, and momentum are exchanged. Most of the action takes place in the sea, while the atmosphere, because of its great mobility, acts as an integrating agent between sea and land.

Water and the Hydrologic Cycle

About one-third of the solar energy reaching the surface of the earth, some 2.6×10^{19} kilowatt-hours per year, is used to evaporate water. This water returns to earth as precipitation, releasing its latent heat of vaporization as it condenses. Figure 3–1 shows the basic features of the hydrologic cycle.

Although 86 percent of evaporation takes place over the sea, only 77 percent of the annual precipitation falls onto the sea. Therefore, more than a third of the rain falling on land, 3.7×10^{16} liters (9.8×10^{15} gallons) per year, originated in the sea. This represents a colossal world-wide desalination program: 28,500 liters (7500 gallons) per day for every living person.

All forms of water play key roles in the earth's energy budget. Ice and snow reflect radiation. Clouds reflect incoming radiation, so that a dense cloud cover, like a blanket of snow, increases the earth's albedo. Clouds also slow down the earth's back radiation of heat into space by re-reflecting it to the surface. Cloudy days are cooler than clear ones because incoming solar radiation is intercepted and turned back; but cloudy nights are warmer than clear ones because, as the dark earth loses heat, the clouds prevent its escape.

Atmospheric water vapor strongly absorbs energy in the infrared region of the spectrum. In fact, water vapor is the chief insulating ingredient of the atmosphere, preventing the extremes of daytime and nighttime temperature that occur, for example, on the moon.

Liquid water absorbs most of the radiation that strikes it, re-radiates this energy back into the atmosphere, and transfers tremendous amounts of potential energy to the atmosphere when it evaporates. Evaporation contributes about two-thirds of all energy transferred from surface to atmosphere.

One other energy transfer is related to the hydrologic cycle: lightning, a discharge of electrical energy in a display of heat, light, and

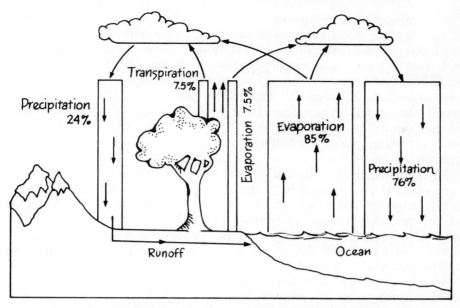

Figure 3-1. About 1.1×10^{17} gallons of water evaporates each year from the continents and oceans. Of this, 85 percent comes from the oceans, 7.5 percent from the soil and fresh water, and 7.5 percent from transpiration of plants. Seventy-six percent of the annual precipitation falls on the ocean and 24 percent on land. More than a third of the water falling on land runs back to the sea.

sound. About 50,000 thunderstorms occur each day, 2000 at any given moment. They hurl thunderbolts at a rate of 100 per second. Each stroke discharges about 3 million kilowatt-hours of energy, for a total of 8×10^{15} kilowatt-hours per year. This is 1000 times more energy than the largest nuclear power plant puts out. With due respect to Smokey Bear, lightning has kindled many more prairie and forest fires than man. Perhaps lightning started man on his energy binge by giving him fire.

There is plenty of water for all our purposes, but it is not always distributed according to our needs. Through irrigation of crops, the discharge of waste heat from industry and power plants, the creation of artificial lakes, and the cutting of forests and destruction of grasslands, we are altering local balances between precipitation and evaporation. This, too, as chapter 12 will show, may alter the climate on a global scale.

Winds and Ocean Currents

So far, the earth's energy balance has been represented as a varying input of solar radiation with its subsequent degradation and re-radiation to space, an essentially vertical exchange. There is also a large-scale horizontal transfer of heat, due to the extreme mobility of the atmosphere and the relatively high mobility of the sea. If the land is moist, the air will be quiet, and most incoming energy will be consumed in the evaporation and transpiration of water. If the land is dry, however, incoming energy will be largely directed to causing turbulence in the air.

Both air and water are set into motion by small imbalances in temperature. The consequent global circulation patterns moderate climatic extremes. About one quarter of this is accomplished by circulating ocean currents and three quarters by winds. The latitudes between 40° N and 40° S provide an annual heat surplus; poleward of 40° is a heat deficit. Were it not for the energy flowing with winds and ocean currents, the tropics would be much hotter and the polar regions much colder than they are. Even so, global circulation is less complete now than it once was, for geological evidence testifies that in times past the earth's climate was uniformly milder (see chapter 12).

The Carbon Cycle

Carbon is a remarkable element in all its forms and combinations, from diamond to DNA. If water is largely responsible for creating an environment that permits life, it is carbon, with its unique chemistry, that is the key to life. Structures of about half a million different compounds of carbon are known; astronomical numbers of structures are possible.

The phenomenon called life is the capture of radiant energy, its conversion to the chemical energy of the carbon bond, and its flow from molecule to molecule, cell to cell, organism to organism, and generation to generation. The carbon cycle of the biosphere is illustrated in figure 3–2 and the cycles of photosynthesis and respiration are discussed in Appendix B. The cycling of carbon in the biosphere represents but a tiny gear in the total carbon cycle (table 3–1), but it achieves a rate, complexity, and significance far out of proportion to its size. The amount of carbon tied up in living organisms and undecayed organic matter is a miniscule 0.02 percent of the total carbon reservoir, although about 15 percent of atmospheric carbon is cycled through the biosphere each year. The rest of the cycle moves on a much grander, if slower and less intricate, scale.

Carbon occurs in the atmosphere primarily as carbon dioxide (CO_2). It is constantly removed by photosynthesis, by solution in the sea or fresh water, or by raindrops. The first step in the weathering of

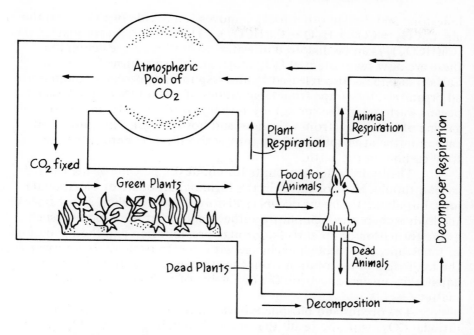

Figure 3-2. This is a simplified scheme of the carbon cycle as it occurs on land. The widths of the paths correspond roughly to the proportions of carbon involved at each step, although in a particular system the values may be very different from these. A similar cycle operates in the sea.

Table 3-1. Distribution of Carbon in the Earth

Site		10^{14} kg Carbon
Atmosphere		7
Hydrosphere (oceans, fresh water)		390
Biosphere (living organisms and undecayed organic matter)		44
Lithosphere total (rocks, fossil fuels, and interstitial water)		276,000
Fossil fuels	(81)	
All other lithosphere	(275,919)	
Total carbon		276,441

These numbers are derived from data on carbon collected from various sources by W. Rubey. They are rough approximations because of the difficulties in obtaining accurate global data of this nature.

limestone and certain other rocks removes a molecule of CO_2 from the air: $CaCO_3 + CO_2 + H_2O \rightarrow Ca(HCO_3)_2$. The calcium bicarbonate ($Ca(HCO_3)_2$) can be dissolved in water, where for each calcium ion there are now two potential CO_2 molecules to be returned to the air. Carbon dioxide is also released by the respiratory processes common to all organisms, by escape from large bodies of water (as when lakes and oceans warm up in the spring), by burning of fossil fuels, and by outgassing of the earth (from volcanoes and hot springs). The amount of carbon in the atmosphere at any time is about 0.003 percent of the total carbon on the earth.

The hydrosphere accounts for about 0.1 percent of the earth's carbon supply. Most of this is in the form of carbonate or bicarbonate ions, but about 1 percent occurs as dissolved CO_2. Carbon is lost from the hydrosphere through photosynthesis and other life processes such as the formation of coral reefs, through precipitation and the formation of limestone, and through exchange with the atmosphere. It returns to the hydrosphere by solution from the atmosphere, from respiration of aquatic organisms, and from the dissolving of carbonates and organic matter.

The oceans and biosphere have a limited ability to take up additional CO_2, with the result that more than half of all the CO_2 added to the atmosphere from the burning of fossil fuels is still where we put it—in the atmosphere. Although a 10 percent increase in atmospheric CO_2 can yield a 5 to 8 percent increase in the rate of photosynthesis if other requirements are satisfied, the actual effect of additional CO_2 on the biomass is difficult if not impossible to determine. The ocean may seem at first to be an enormous sink for excess CO_2, but in reality only the surface layer of seawater is involved. The effective ocean reservoir contains only 3 to 8 times the amount of CO_2 found in the atmosphere. Overturning of deeper waters is exceedingly slow: exchange of surface water with water below 1 kilometer requires 500 to 1000 years or more.

Most of the action involves the 0.1 percent of carbon that cycles through the atmosphere, hydrosphere, and biosphere; it is on this portion of the cycle that human activity can have an impact. The remaining 99.9 percent sits sluggishly in the lithosphere where time is reckoned in eons, not in seasons. An amount of carbon roughly equal to or perhaps up to twice as great as that in the biosphere is tied up in the fossil fuels. The rest occurs as rocks, chiefly limestone, or dissolved in the interstitial water of the rocks. New fossil fuel is constantly being formed; rocks weather continuously and new sedimentary rocks are deposited. However, these processes are glacially slow in comparison to the rhythmic breathing of the biosphere and the exchange between atmosphere and surface waters.

Other Cycles

The Nitrogen Cycle
Nitrogen cycles so rapidly through the atmosphere and bio-sphere that the geologic nitrogen cycle is trivial by comparison. The nitrogen that makes up 78 percent of our present atmosphere by volume (75 percent by weight) probably came originally from outgassing of the earth through volcanic activity.

The chemical combination of nitrogen with other elements is called **fixation**. Nitrogen fixation requires energy, whether it is accom-plished by an electrical discharge, by microorganisms, by a photochem-ical reaction, or by an industrial process. The activities of man have roughly doubled the rate of nitrogen fixation, and another doubling is expected by the end of the century. This increase will not cause a detectable change in the amount of atmospheric nitrogen, but it may affect other parts of the nitrogen cycle. For example, application of nitrate fertilizer to agricultural land has increased the amount of nitrate in groundwater and bodies of fresh water.

The basic features of the nitrogen cycle are shown in figure 3–3. Higher plants require most of their nitrogen in the form of nitrate, although part of their requirement can be satisfied by ammonia. This inorganic nitrogen is incorporated into amino acids, protein, and other organic compounds which are subsequently utilized by animals and many microorganisms. The nitrates used by plants are supplied in many ways: by lightning and photochemical reactions, inorganic sources in soil and soil water, nitrogen fertilizers applied by man, fixation of mole-cular nitrogen by free-living or symbiotic microorganisms, the activities of decomposer organisms, and manmade nitrogen oxides dissolved and washed from the sky in rain. Nitrate released by decomposers forms a special loop of the nitrogen cycle that bypasses the atmosphere.

Some bacteria, known as nitrifying bacteria, obtain their energy by burning reduced nitrogen compounds much as other organisms burn carbohydrates. Another group of bacteria, the denitrifying bacteria, liberate free nitrogen by reducing nitrites and nitrates. They do this in the absence of free oxygen, using the oxygen derived from the process in various energy-yielding reactions. Box 3–1 shows the unusual ways in which some little-known but very important bacteria obtain energy and, in the process, maintain the biogeochemical cycles that support life.

The Sulfur Cycle
For some organisms, sulfur plays a key role in providing energy for chemosynthesis (box 3–1). Just as some bacteria burn nitrites or ammonia for energy, others burn sulfides or elemental sulfur. Again,

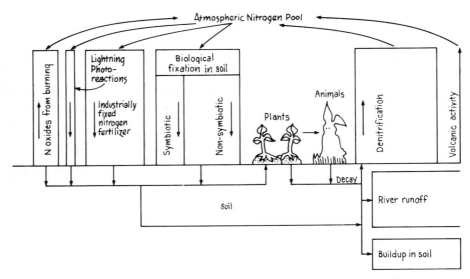

Figure 3–3. The widths of the bars indicate relative contributions of the various processes. Biological denitrification is thought to be roughly in balance with biological fixation. The activities of man contribute an amount of fixed nitrogen that may equal the amount fixed biologically; this nitrogen, primarily from agricultural runoff and the burning of fuels, is accumulating in water and soil. A similar nitrogen cycle operates in the sea, with the exception that "fertilizer" is in the form of runoff from land, and there is no symbiotic fixation comparable to that which occurs on land.

analogous to the denitrifying bacteria, some bacteria reduce sulfate to sulfide or pure sulfur, using the oxygen derived in the process in respiration. Plants and microorganisms can reduce sulfate for use in synthesizing organic compounds containing sulfur, but animals depend on their food for sulfur in organic form. When plants and animals die, their decay returns sulfur to the environment in reduced form, useless to both higher plants and animals. The activity of the sulfur oxidizing bacteria is thus essential to the maintenance of the sulfur cycle and life (figure 3–4). Sulfur bacteria also produce sulfuric acid in water contaminated with sulfur from coal mines; and they contribute to deterioration of stonework in cities by oxidizing sulfides and sulfites dissolved in films of water on buildings and other structures.

Although it is difficult to estimate the amount of sulfur that flows through the atmosphere, biosphere, and hydrosphere, and although the mechanisms by which it flows are incompletely understood, it is thought that the activities of man may have increased the amount of sulfur in the atmosphere by a factor of almost two.[2] The largest reservoir of sulfur is in the ocean. It is almost inconceivable that man will have a significant effect on that.

BOX 3-1   NON-PHOTOSYNTHETIC ENERGY-YIELDING PROCESSES

Except for photosynthetic organisms which get their energy from the sun, all organisms depend on chemical transformations for their energy. Most of them live at the expense of photosynthetic plants. A few groups of bacteria, however, build their own organic compounds using energy derived from oxidation of inorganic substances. Many of these organisms live in soil, mud, or sewage. Some live in the effluent from mines or in films of dirty water on buildings and bridges. Two genera, Nitrosomonas *and* Nitrobacter, *play important roles in the nitrogen cycle. Many organisms besides the chemosynthetic bacteria can carry out the reactions shown below, but the energy is lost because it is not coupled to other synthetic processes. The energy made available is not extravagant. For comparison, we might note that complete oxidation of one mole of glucose yields 690,000 calories (see Appendix B).*

Nitrosomonas:	$NH_3 + 1\frac{1}{2}O_2 \rightarrow HNO_2 + H_2O + 66,000$ cal
Nitrobacter:	$NO_2^- + \frac{1}{2}O_2 \rightarrow NO_3^- + 17,500$ cal
Thiobacillus denitrificans:	$6KNO_3 + 5S + 2CaCO_3 \rightarrow 3K_2SO_4 + 2CaSO_4 + 2CO_2 + 3N_2 + 132,000$ cal/mol S
Other chemosynthetic bacteria:	$H_2S + \frac{1}{2}O_2 \rightarrow H_2O + S + 41,000$ cal
	$H_2O + 1\frac{1}{2}O_2 + S \rightarrow H_2SO_4 + 118,000$ cal
	$H_2 + \frac{1}{2}O_2 \rightarrow H_2O + 56,000$ cal
	$CNS^- + 2O_2 + 2H_2O \rightarrow SO_4^= + NH_4^+ + CO_2 + 220,000$ cal
	$Fe^{++} \rightarrow Fe^{+++} + e^- + 11,300$ cal
	$4H_2 + H_2SO_4 \rightarrow H_2S + 4H_2O + 60,000$ cal
	$CO + \frac{1}{2}O_2 \rightarrow CO_2 + 74,000$ cal

The Phosphorus Cycle

The major reservoir of phosphorus is in rocks, which makes its natural movement very slow. In soil, rocks, and living matter it occurs almost exclusively as phosphates. The phosphorus cycle is thus quite simple, chemically. Phosphate is absorbed by plants, converted into organic compounds which are eaten by animals, and returned to the soil in inorganic form when plants and animals decay. Phosphate which is dissolved or eroded from the land finds its way to streams and lakes and

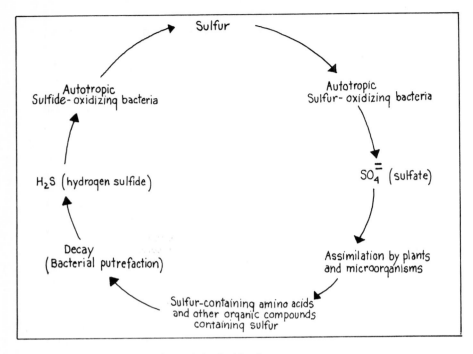

Figure 3-4.   The sulfur cycle in the biosphere.

eventually to the sea. In the sea, some of it is used by marine organisms but most of it is precipitated at the sea floor. Here it is lost to the biosphere until the geologic process that imperceptibly remold continents and oceans lift up new areas of dry land. The only significant return of phosphate from sea to land is in the excrement of sea birds and in food harvested from the sea.

Mining activities of man have greatly accelerated the movement of phosphates to the sea. Large amounts of low grade phosphate ore are left exposed to erosion by wind and water during the process of mining the higher grade deposits. As much as half of what is recovered may be lost in washing and concentrating operations. Worldwide, between 80 and 90 percent of the phosphate mined is destined for use as fertilizer which also ends up—as runoff from agricultural land—in the sea. We are running out of phosphate at the same time that we are flooding the environment with it.

The Energy Non-Cycle

Nature cycles materials again and again, but energy flows through a system only once and in one invariable direction: toward dis-

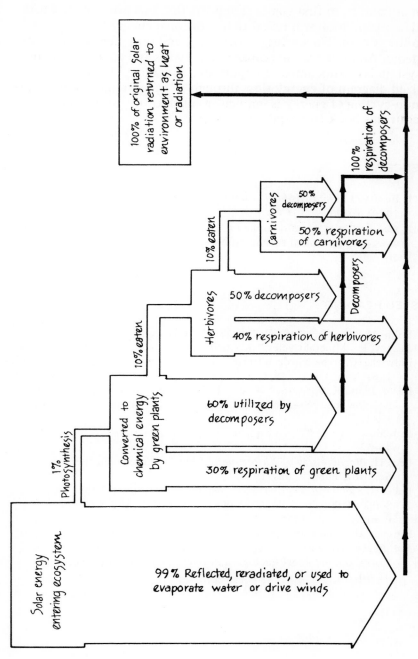

Figure 3-5. Energy flow through an ecosystem. Simplified diagram showing energy flow through an ecosystem. The actual percentages of energy flowing along the various pathways vary from system to system; those given here are representative but several energy pathways have been omitted from the diagram, for simplicity. In an actual ecosystem, for example a lake, some energy in the form of organic matter may be imported via a river that feeds the lake or exported via a river that drains it. In any system, a small amount of organic matter may remain in the earth to undergo conversion to fossil fuels. Finally, decomposers may be eaten by other soil-dwelling organisms, creating a small energy shunt leading back to carnivores.

sipation as heat. If on first glance it appears that this principle has been violated, a second look will reveal that additional energy has been supplied to the system. The cycles of nature depend on a steady supply of solar energy. An understanding of material cycles and energy flows in an ecosystem is of fundamental importance in ecology. Figure 3–5 is a generalized diagram of energy flow through an ecosystem. The principle of the non-cycling of energy is implicit in much of the discussion throughout this book (see especially chapter 5).

REFERENCES

1. Eiseley, L. *The Invisible Pyramid.* (New York: Charles Scribner's Sons, 1970) p. 000.
2. *Man in The Living Environment.* The Institute of Ecology Report of the Workshop on Global Ecological Problems. Cycles of Elements. Pp. 41–90.

SUGGESTED READING

Bolin, V. "The Carbon Cycle." *Scientific American* 223, 3 (1970): 124–132.

Deevey, E. "Mineral Cycles." *Scientific American* 223, 3 (1970): 148–158.

Delwiche, C. "The Nitrogen Cycle." *Scientific American* 223, 3 (1970): 136–146.

Harte, J. and R. Socolow. "Water." In *Patient Earth,* ed. J. Harte and R. Socolow, pp. 261–275. New York: Holt, Rinehart and Winston, Inc., 1971.

Hutchinson, G. E. "The Biosphere." *Scientific American* 223, 3 (1970): 44–53.

Lees, H. *Biochemistry of Autotrophic Bacteria.* London: Butterworths Scientific Publications, 1955.

Luce, G. *Biological Rhythms in Psychiatry and Medicine.* Public Health Service Publication No. 2088. Washington, D.C.: U.S. Government Printing Office, 1970.

Penman, H. "The Water Cycle." *Scientific American* 223, 3 (1970): 98–108.

Man In the Living Environment. The Institute of Ecology Report of the Workshop on Global Ecological Problems. Cycles of Elements. Pp. 41–90.

CHAPTER 4

Energy and History: Two Tales of Prometheus

. . . they were running hand in hand, and the Queen went so fast that it was all (Alice) could do to keep up with her: and still the Queen kept crying "Faster! Faster!" The most curious part of the thing was, that . . . however fast they went, they never seemed to pass anything.

". . . in our *country," said Alice, . . . "you'd generally get to somewhere else—if you ran very fast for a long time as we've been doing."*

"A slow sort of country!" said the Queen. "Now here, *you see, it takes all the running you can do, to keep in the same place. If you want to get somewhere else, you must run at least twice as fast as that."*

"I'd rather not try, please!" said Alice. "I'm quite content to stay here."

Lewis Carroll

In the beginning man, like other animals, had only his own energy to use in the struggle for life. This came from the food he ate, about 2200 kilocalories per day averaged over his lifetime, or 843,000 kilocalories per year. That is not very much. It represents a power output about equal to one 100 watt light bulb. Today, many of the world's people still exist at or below this level, for they are starving. But in the United States, the per capita energy consumption is roughly 87,000,000 kilocalories per year,* more than 100 times the energy that operates a human body.

*This number is higher than the number sometimes quoted, because it represents primary sources of energy: wood, water, coal, petroleum, nuclear energy. Electricity must be produced from one of the primary sources of energy. Since the conversion

What do we have to show for this incredible use of energy? We convert it to heat, light, motion, sound, and things. We have passed the point of diminishing returns, however, for our per capita energy consumption is rising faster than the standard of living, and our life expectancy and other tangible measures of well-being are below those of some less consumptive societies. This is partly because it takes an increasing amount of energy just to stay where we are. Alice's lament seems so sensible, compared to the obsessive demands of the Queen. Why are we running? Where are we trying to go? Are we unable to see where we are really headed?[†]

We did not always run in order to stand still. Look at the road we have traveled in a few tens of thousands of years. In agriculture we have gone from manpower to oxen to tractors. In transportation, human feet and backs yielded first to dogs, then to oxen, pack mules, horses, camels, and elephants, which were sometimes attached to mechanical contraptions; now we have jets and spaceships. The tools of war evolved from stones through gunpowder to hydrogen bombs. In medicine, magic grudgingly gave way to vaccines and antiseptics; today we boast of laser machines and artificial kidneys. Leaves were abandoned when we learned to make paper fans; now we have central air conditioning. Communication began as spontaneous information exchange between people; it was revolutionized by writing, again by the printing press, and most recently by satellite TV. The common denominator is the exploitation of energy.

The history of mankind, and of Western man in particular, could be written in terms of the conquest of energy. Appendix C gives a chronology of events in this history. In timeless cultures where tradition rules, there has been until recently either no desire for or no way to obtain the extra energy that makes things happen.

Much "progress" is clearly misdirected. But you are physically comfortable and well fed, and through most of time your ancestors were not. They were often cold and fearful. They had miscellaneous parasites and infections and broken bones. Many died at birth or giving birth. Few lived past their reproductive period. Many—of all races, in all lands—were slaves, whether or not they were called by that name. That

---

of one form of energy to another is less than perfectly efficient (it averages around 33 percent for conversion of fossil fuels to electricity), any figure based on electrical power use will be lower than the one quoted above. Even after we go back to the primary source, it is difficult to know what value to use. Should it be the total theoretical energy of the fuel, for example, or should we subtract what goes up the smokestack? For our purposes, the exact numbers are not as important as the scale of the phenomenon.

[†] In economic terms, the marginal benefits from equal increments of output are decreasing and the marginal costs of equal increments of output are increasing. At some point, extra output costs more than it is worth.

is why they invented Paradise. And no wonder, when they began to see what energy could do for them, that they believed energy would bring Paradise to earth if only they could tame enough of it!

Now, man has walked on the moon. Artificial moons gather data about the weather and beam the latest news onto television screens in India and America, alike. Nations vie with one another to build faster-than-sound aircraft to carry businessmen from breakfast in Moscow to lunch in London.

The people of the world today use energy at a rate of about 5.7×10^9 kilowatts, not including food. With the population approaching 4 billion, this is about 1.4 kilowatts per person. If food is included, every person in the world can be imagined as radiating the energy of fifteen 100 watt light bulbs. In the United States, about 200 million people glow at the per capita rate of one hundred and sixteen 100 watt light bulbs.

A BACKWARD GLANCE—100 YEARS

Forty or fifty years ago, world population was approaching 2 billion. Each of these people was using energy at a rate of about ten 100 watt light bulbs. The United States even then led the pack in power consumption by a factor of ten. Radio was revolutionizing home entertainment. A war which killed five and a half million people seemed so terrible that another war was unthinkable. The number of cars in America had grown to more than 8 million. One out of eight adults now had an automobile which carried him bumpily and uncertainly over rudimentary highways. On the farms, mules and horses outnumbered tractors 45 to 1. One-quarter of America's farmland was planted in crops to feed her 25 million draft animals. In the 1920s most homes were heated with coal. Wood was on the way out and petroleum products were on the way in. The first electric refrigerators were beginning to displace the ice box, and electricity was already supplying substantial power to industry.

If we go back a few more decades, to the end of the nineteenth century, we will find that the world was darker then. Homes could not be flooded with light to make midnight rival noon. The first oil booms, which led to frantic search for new markets, had permitted petroleum products to replace scarce and expensive whale oil for illumination. On September 4, 1882, the Pearl Street Station in Manhattan first switched on to furnish power for 400 light bulbs of 83 watts each. It was a sign of things to come.

After a 300-year gestation period, a practical internal combustion engine had been born. The 1890s witnessed the first cars in both

Europe and America and the first flying machine with an internal combustion engine—a fatal experiment for its inventor. Further hastened by the evolution of electric motors, the end of the steam engine was in sight even as it was achieving its most remarkable feats.

Animals provided man's extra power for agriculture, as well as much of his transportation. Wood heated his home and cooked his food. Coal, wind, and water—but by now mostly coal—drove his industrial machines. There were a billion and a half people in the world using power at the rate of about 700 watts per person. Becquerel discovered radioactivity in 1896, but it would be half a century before people would comprehend the full meaning of his discovery.

During the eighteenth and nineteenth centuries, the Western world was convulsed by the Industrial Revolution, while the rest of the world went on much as it had for thousands of years. The Industrial Revolution came late to America, sparing her some of Europe's agony. The new continent offered abundant opportunities in agriculture and a challenge to exploration. Population density was low, distances enormous, and transportation primitive. The predominant pattern in the colonial and early national period was one of skilled home and local industries, run by master craftsmen with a few apprentices who themselves hoped to be master craftsmen one day. All but the newest and most isolated communities had mechanical power, chiefly water, sometimes wind, for specialized heavy tasks. In fact, the mill often came first, and the town huddled around it. Riverside gristmills and sawmills were small but thickly scattered across the land, for a round trip of 40 kilometers (25 miles) to the mill and back was as much as most farmers could negotiate in a day. Local iron works, paper mills, brickyards, breweries, and other small industries were common. Communities had to be self-sufficient.

In the last half of the nineteenth century, many things led to the industrial development of America: creation of vast private fortunes; new waves of immigration providing, for the first time, abundant labor; the development of marketing techniques and the market system; the expanding network of railroads; and a burst of inventions. With energy from the steam engine for transportation and heat-requiring industries, and energy from further refinement of the waterwheel and the first hydraulic turbines for manufacturing, craft after craft gave way to mass production.

In 1850, energy consumption in the United States was already at a rate of 4.5 kilowatts per capita, but the average for the world's billion people was only 0.4 kilowatts. Of the energy used in the United States, two-thirds was supplied by draft animals and by man himself. Of the remaining third, two-thirds was supplied by wind and water and one-third by fuels. Ninety percent of this fuel was wood; 10 percent, coal.

The first oil well was yet to be drilled. In Europe the story was much the same, except that some countries burned more coal because they had depleted their forests.

THE INDUSTRIAL REVOLUTION

The Industrial Revolution was born in England in the eighteenth century, amidst a flurry of mechanical inventions and technological advances whose names are familiar and will not be documented here. Of the inventions, the steam engine was king. Improved iron and steel technology stood behind much of the industrial development.

Social and economic changes had been preparing the way for the revolution for five hundred years. Most people bitterly opposed the changes imposed by the Industrial Revolution. Innovation had been fought for centuries, by individuals, craft and trade guilds, and governments. New patent applications were routinely denied when they threatened old ways, and people were put to death for defying convention. But invention became an obsession. Even when temporarily defeated, it rose again like the phoenix, stronger than before.

Eighteenth century England reeled under rampant poverty and unemployment, resulting largely from an unprecedented land grab (which also took place on the continent) begun by sheep-raising noblemen a hundred years before. It threw many tens of thousands of agricultural workers off what had been the common land. At first, a dismayed government restricted the paupers to their local parishes, on poor relief. Later, when factories grew, paupers flocked to the cities, even as the agricultural poor do today. All over England, humanity rebelled against the tyranny of the machine and against the conditions of crowding and poverty that were laid to it. The situation was very like that of recent years, with the affluent calling for law and order, feeling that not only their security but their lives were in danger. The mobs of rioting poor were protesting their alienation as much as their poverty. Rumor spread that a General Ludd or King Ludd was masterminding the rebellion. His followers were called Luddites. The Luddites wanted to blot out all social, economic, and technological change and to return to some mythical utopia of the past. They were not successful. History cannot be erased and rewritten; time cannot be reversed. Nothing can be accomplished unless we accept the fact of where we are, and begin from there.

Lewis Mumford argues persuasively that the technological ingredients of the Industrial Revolution had lain around for centuries, waiting to be blended with the right social, political, and economic conditions in the eighteenth century.[1] Man had mastered the principles of machines a thousand years before the Industrial Revolution and could use wheels, gears, levers, and pulleys to his advantage. Prototype machines of many descriptions had been invented by the Egyptians, the Chinese, the Arabs, the Cretans, and later the Greeks and Romans. Many of these machines seemed to be but toys, created for amusement.

There was also plenty of power. Despite the excitement about the steam engine, the early Industrial Revolution was based on water-wheels and windmills. The first windmills had appeared in the Moslem world about A.D. 650, they were used in China from the year 1000 on, and by the fourteenth century they had spread throughout Europe. The gigantic land reclamation projects of the Netherlands were accomplished by means of windpower during the sixteenth century. Waterwheels had been in existence still longer. They probably originated in the Near East in the fourth or third century B.C. and spread through Rome to Europe. By the twelfth century there were thousands of waterwheels through-out western Europe. It is difficult to estimate the total power that was available at any particular time, but we do know the approximate power output of the most common machines. Box 4–1 shows the power avail-able from basic machines, from primitive to contemporary times.

With power and machines widely available in the Middle Ages, why did the Industrial Revolution wait until 1700 to begin? Mumford believes that the probable explanation involves a breakdown in European society, the substitution of competition and personal gain for the medi-eval traditions that had prevailed, the substitution of abstract values for life values, and preoccupation with insignificant luxuries. Certainly social and economic conditions were at the root of the change. Tech-nically, it could have begun centuries earlier. It could have begun in China or somewhere else. But it began in England about 1700 and still reverberates around the world, and we are left to deal with the conse-quences as best we can.

Heralds of the Revolution included both technological optimists and technological pessimists, much as our forecasters do today. Environ-mental problems and the bleak realities of life contrasted shockingly with what people thought could and should be. Here is a commentary on mining, written early in the sixteenth century:

The critics say further that mining is a perilous occupation to pursue because the miners are sometimes killed by the pestilential air which they breathe; sometimes their lungs rot away; sometimes the men perish by being crushed in masses of rock; sometimes falling from ladders into the shafts, they break their ams, legs, or necks. . . . Besides this the strongest argument of the detractors is that the fields are devastated by mining operations, for which reason formerly Italians were warned by law that no one should dig the earth for metals and so injure their very fertile fields, their vineyards, and their olive groves. Also they argue that the woods and groves are cut down, for there is need of endless amount of wood for timbers,

---

BOX 4-1   POWER OUTPUT OF SOME BASIC MACHINES

A machine does not produce energy, but merely transforms or redirects it. If the machine converts food, fuel, or force to work or power it is a "prime mover." An electric motor is not a prime mover because it does not convert food, fuel, or force; and your home furnace is not a prime mover because it produces only heat, not work or power.

Power is the rate at which energy flows. A machine with a low power rating can often do the same job as one with a high power rating, but it will take a longer time. A woman, a horse, or a tractor can plow a field, but the tractor will do it in the least time. The energy in a gallon of gasoline can operate your car for half an hour with a power output of 38 kilowatts. It would run a jet airplane, at 45,000 kilowatts, for a second and a half.

The typical power output of some prime movers is shown below, in kilowatts. Listed in order of increasing power output, these machines are also in approximate order of their invention or exploitation by man. The power output of prime movers has increased by 8 orders of magnitude in the last ten thousand years.

man	*0.1*
ox	*0.2*
horse	*0.5*
windmill	*15*
waterwheel	*300*
steam engine	*2,000*
internal combustion engine	*10,000*
gas turbine	*80,000*
water turbine	*100,000*
steam turbine	*1,000,000*
liquid fuel rocket	*16,000,000*

---

machines, and the smelting of metals. And when the woods and groves are felled, there are exterminate the beasts and birds. . . . Further, when the ores are washed, the water which has been used poisons the brooks and streams, and either destroys the fish or drives them away.[2]

Contrast this prophecy, written in the seventeenth century:

I doubt not posterity will find many things that are now but rumors verified into practical realities. It may be that, some ages hence, a voyage to the Southern tracts, yea, possibly to the moon, will not be more strange than one to America. . . . The restoration of grey hairs to juvenility and the renewing the exhausted marrow may at length be effected without a miracle; and the turning of the now comparatively desert world into a paradise may not improbably be effected from late agriculture.[3]

Led by Francis Bacon, the greatest thinkers of the Renaissance and early seventeenth century wrote a prescription for the course that science and technology would pursue into the twenty-first century. They wrote it at a time when technology in the modern sense had barely been conceived, when scientific imagination was hundreds of years ahead of technical ability. Yet the predictions were accurate and the prophecies self-fulfilling, except for one detail: the place to which energy and the machine would lead man was supposed to be utopia.

One of the many causes of utopia's eluding us was our inclination toward warfare. Man has always pursued the technology of weapons with vigor—the first tools were also weapons. Developments in energy use, iron technology, and explosives were united in Austria in 1404 to produce the first giant cannon on record. It weighed almost five tons. In 1450, near Caen, in Normandy, 4000 Frenchmen and two cannons faced 7000 Englishmen and demolished them. The body count: 12 French, 5600 English. Two years later, with cannon, the Turks conquered Constantinople.

France built her first blast furnaces around 1500. By 1600, there were thirteen foundries in France, all of them manufacturing cannons. Sweden and Russia also had arms factories. When the sewing machine was invented in 1829, the French War Department was the first to try it, for mass producing uniforms. An army is a wonderful thing for the economy.

A PRE-INDUSTRIAL WORLD

What of life before Europe's surrender to the machine? History, as it is often written, suggests that the Middle Ages—the period between A.D. 400 and 1400 (1300, in Italy)—were a time of dismal stagnation. Curiosity was absent, if not dead, and there was no concern with progress. After this deep and dreamless sleep, people awoke in the bright morning of the Renaissance and shook themselves back to reality. One of the major events that occurred in the dawn was the rise of capitalism. It is interesting to ponder whether the goals and abstractions of capitalism were more real as a guide for life than the saints, angels, and demons that cast their shadows on the medieval world. Capitalism was the ultimate alchemy. It transmuted everything into gold.

The energy of the Middle Ages did not grossly pollute air, soil, and water. Wind and water power were clean and free; wood, if judiciously managed, was replaceable; and animals were not yet in competition with man for food. Although life was not easy, men of the Middle Ages created a panorama of farms, towns, cities, gardens, canals, and harbors that in many ways shamed the squalid scenes to follow. The beauty of the towns and country contrasted cruelly, however, with the primitive medical and sanitary practices that led to periodic pandemics of the Black Death, in which an estimated quarter of the population perished.

It is difficult to estimate how much power was available during the Middle Ages. The use of power was low, only a few hundred watts per person. There was a literal increase in horsepower, made possible by the invention of iron horseshoes and the modern harness. (The Chinese had this harness in 200 B.C.; Europeans re-invented it 1100 years later.) Another new source of energy was coal. The earliest recorded use of coal as a fuel was at the Abbey of Peterborough, England, in 852. From that obscure time when monks first gathered "sea coales" from England's rocky shores, the demand for coal would grow until, at the turn of the twentieth century, coal would become the number one source of energy in the world. In 852, sea coales were mostly a curiosity. Two hundred years later they had begun to take pressure off Europe's vanishing forests, and through their mining and use man embarked on a new phase of the exploitation of his planet.

Water power was rapidly developed along the Rhine, the Danube, Italy's swift streams, and in North Sea and Baltic lands. Water mills ground grain, sawed wood, pulped rags for paper, pumped water, crushed ore and otherwise furthered mining and metal working, and fostered the development of Europe's textile industry. Wind was more difficult to harness, although where conditions were favorable it was the main source of power. Wind had driven sailboats since Stone Age times. The close of the Middle Ages saw the opening of an era of sailing and discovery that lasted for hundreds of years, an age that came to a dramatic end in 1929 when the oceanographic research vessel *Carnegie* burned in Pago Pago.

The Beginnings of Metallurgy

The technology of the Middle Ages depended on the smelting and working of iron, with wood for fuel. But the foundations of mining and metallurgy had been laid thousands of years before, when man's glance was first arrested by the glitter of gold. In prehistory men found chunks of native metal and pounded them into various utilitarian objects. But they could not get very far with this technique. It was difficult to find metal in useful amounts, and there was a limit to what could be accomplished by brute force pounding. Sometime around 3000 B.C. came a dramatic moment when someone observed that pure liquid melted from certain rocks when they were heated, and this metal was much easier to work than that obtained in the old way. Thus, the period commonly called the Bronze Age signified the discovery of a brand new use of energy and the beginning of mining and metalworking.

Copper, silver, gold, and meteoritic iron were found in their native metallic state in prehistoric times, but man knew other metals as well, including lead and tin. Lead and tin, and also copper and silver, occur most abundantly in chemical combination with oxygen (as oxides) and sulfur (as sulfides); they are also found as carbonates, sulfates, and more complex minerals. To obtain useful metal from these minerals required more than simply heating a rock. By accident or experiment, man learned to smelt these ores in combination with charred wood, which reduced the combined metal to its elemental state. He developed the forced-draft charcoal-fed furnace which produced temperatures up to 1200° C (2100° F). He learned to fracture rocks by building fires against them and splashing them with cold water. He added a new dimension to his exploitation of energy and the earth.

Before metalworking began, the only division of labor was according to age and sex. In the later Stone Age, it is likely that certain people, perhaps the older men, produced many of the common flint tools and taught their art to others. But anyone could make his own ax or knife or arrowhead if he had to. Not so, with the strenuous and exacting art of the smith. Smiths were probably the first specialized craftsmen, and their appearance marks the beginning of far-reaching social change. The change was resisted, as change always is. Stone tools persisted in Egyptian agriculture for 2000 years after the superiority of metal products had been demonstrated. This may be partly a sign of the failure of supply to meet demand, but it must also result from the farmer's balkiness in accepting innovation. There may be a parallel in American history, when the white man tried to pawn his culture off on the Indian:

Then the Chief . . . took his stone knife and skinned the heifer, and cut off a piece of fat meat. When he had done this, he said, "Why should I take your knives? The Ruler has given me something to cut with."[4]

There were about 100 million people in the eleventh century B.C., a century that witnessed the entry of iron, camels, large riding horses, dwindling forests, soil erosion, simplified writing, and coined money into the affairs of men. Camels and goats gave man mobility and high quality protein. They permitted him to live in areas where he could not support himself by agriculture. They also girdled trees and bushes and cropped the grazing lands too close and helped to expand the deserts.

The price of improvement everywhere was increasing degradation of the earth's resources. The result of improvement was specialization and growth in the size and complexity of social institutions. Energy was increasingly diverted away from life support and into the building and maintenance of social structure. And when society began to grow complex, man domesticated yet another animal to provide more energy: man. Slaves built the pyramid of Cheops and slaves supported Greek civilization.

Agriculture

Individual hand technology and simple human relations could not give way to specialization, group production, machines, and a complicated social structure until centers of high population density were formed. As long as man obtained his food by hunting and gathering, no permanent social grouping larger than an extended family or tribe was possible because so much territory was needed to supply each person's food. Without agriculture or industry, the earth might support between 20 and 40 million people—hunting, fishing, collecting fruits and nuts, digging for roots, and catching whatever worms, insects, frogs, snakes, and turtles they could find. At present, instead of 40 million, our numbers are rapidly approaching 100 times that figure. Only one thing makes this possible: agriculture.

At the dawn of agriculture there were about 5 million people on the earth, spread thinly over the 52 million square kilometers (20 million square miles) that were hospitable enough to support them. Observations of hunting and gathering cultures remaining today suggest a maximum population density of one person per square mile at this level of culture. So although the earth was not crowded ten thousand years ago, the population may have been within a factor of four of its limit.

In most hunting and gathering cultures, men hunted and women gathered. Modern studies of primitive peoples suggest that woman's labors provided most of the food except in the far north, where people had to be almost totally carnivorous. The hunt yielded a little high quality protein and a lot of prestige. As the women gathered fruits and seeds, they sometimes scattered some of them in the hope of producing more of the favored foods. When this was successful, agriculture began.

Agriculture was first practiced between nine and eleven thousand years ago in the "fertile crescent" of the Middle East, the area bordering what is now Iraq and Iran. The transition from hunting-gathering to agriculture represented a transition from one energy plateau to another. It was an enormous step. The taming of the plant allowed man to appropriate an increased portion of the biosphere's energy for himself and to concentrate himself in towns and cities where people could devote themselves to pursuits other than finding food.

About 7000 B.C., man began burning vast areas of grassland and forest in order to plant crops. This had various effects, depending on the nature of the soil and climate. Burning did not hurt the rich volcanic slopes of Costa Rica, which have remained fertile for thousands of years. Since the beginning of agriculture, however, some areas have been rendered useless because man tried to take more energy out of the system than he put into it.

When man turned from hunting to farming, he tapped the reserves of soil whose fertility had accrued through unmolested generations of plant life and death and the integrated activity of animals and micro-organisms. Man burned, planted, and harvested; soon the investment of the years was used up and he had to move on. By the time of Christ there were between 200 and 300 million people in the world, and environmental problems were already critical in many places. The per capita use of power remained low: about 100 watts for food and another 100 for fire and animals. But the number of men was increasing. That made all the difference.

Hunters and Gatherers

During the half million years before the invention of agriculture, man discovered many uses of fire, invented the bow, further refined stone tools, invented or improved clothing, devised primitive means of land and water transportation, and domesticated the dog. All these inventions had one thing in common: by increasing the fraction of solar energy available to man, they tipped the ecologic balance in favor of an increased human population and forced corresponding adjustments in all other populations.

Fire kept man warm. It cooked his food, protected him from predators, and drove game toward hunters waiting in ambush. It cleared underbrush from the forest to make hunting easier, and it burned the brush from grasslands to maintain the grasslands and improve the game. At first, man took advantage of natural fires for these purposes. Later, he learned to start his own fire from zealously guarded coals or a slow-burning log. Using fire by no means implied knowing how to make it. The art of making fire was mastered relatively late—around 6000 B.C.— and even then, not by all cultures.

Between 35,000 B.C. and 7000 B.C., man expanded over the face of the globe. It was not an exploratory spirit so much as the quest of game that led him through Siberia, over the land bridge across the Bering Strait, into North America, and then eastward across the continent and southward to the tip of South America. During this time, he tamed his second source of energy: the wolf.

From the beginning, the association between wolf and man had advantages and disadvantages for both. In the northern hemisphere, wolves were the dominant carnivores preying on herds of large mammals. After man invented the bow he found himself in direct competition with wolves for game. Wolves sometimes stole all or part of the kill, or even killed man himself. They often drew too near the fire for man's comfort. As for man, he sometimes killed wolves, but he sometimes fed them, too, and adopted orphaned pups. Somewhere in prehistory, man and wolf declared an uneasy truce. Wolf became dog.

Man and wolf-dog became hunting partners. Wolf-dog extended man's senses and man enhanced wolf-dog's efficiency in the kill. Man induced wolf-dog to pull sleds of stone, skin, or wood. Now, with fire and dog, man could survive in the northern lands wherever there was game.

After the bond between man and dog became very strong, dog protected man's flocks of sheep and goats from attack by wild wolves. This was a remarkable achievement, considering that today, after the selective breeding of thousands of generations of herd dogs, the instinct to pursue and kill still lurks beneath the surface. It is widely believed that once a dog has tasted blood he is of no more use for herding.

The basis for the early domestication of the wolf may not have been entirely utilitarian. Men and wolves are social animals, with many similarities in their social relationships. This potential for mutual satisfaction of mutual needs made the relationship between them uniquely rewarding. But friendship aside, both the hunter of the cold regions and the herder farther south owed an irredeemable debt to the source of energy that was the dog.

Just as wolves were tamed many times, so was fire. How many times did man gain fire only to lose it again? Fire mattered most to those living where it was cold. If we read the record correctly, man used fire to warm his bones for many thousands of years before it occurred to him that there was any other use for it. With tools to serve as fang and claw and with clothes and fire to take the place of fur, he strengthened his grip on existence. Man cherished fire as he cherished life. Many anthropologists believe that small bands of hunters, pursuing game in the snowy north, frequently lost their fire and died. Accidents like this may have contributed to the disappearance of Neanderthal Man.

Half a million years ago there were several varieties of erect, tool-using primates who were men or almost men. Probably some of them could speak. For more than a million years, most of them had lived where the climate was warm and friendly. This was the time of the Pleistocene, when the mild earth grew inhospitable and great walls of ice crept imperceptibly over most of Europe and North America, only to retreat and then advance again. Between the glaciers, man began to extend his range northward, following herds of game which followed the edge of the melting glacier. Many species of mammals met extinction during the Pleistocene epoch. Of the several types of man entering the Ice Age, only one, *Homo sapiens,* survived. With help from nature, he annihilated or assimilated all the rest.

Man had no physical advantage over other animals. His simple tools merely gave him an equal chance, for he was slow-footed, weak, and without claws or fangs. Most men feared the fire that lightning brought and ran from it, with the other animals. But now and then in the cold regions, a man would pause to look at a burning log and wonder dimly. The man would watch the log uncertainly, curiously, and then warm his hands before moving on. Perhaps fire need not be wild and threatening, perhaps he could use it. Half a million years ago, near what is now Peking, *Homo erectus Pekinensis* rolled a glowing log to the mouth of his cave.

According to Greek legend Zeus did not intend that man have fire, but Prometheus stole it from heaven and gave it to him. The sequel is not clear. According to Hesiod (ca. 700 B.C.), Zeus threw a tantrum and ordered the creation of Pandora, who came to earth and released her great jarful of evils so that war, violence, greed, and all their accompanying plagues spread over the land. Thus, the gift of Prometheus became man's everlasting curse. Aeschylus, however, exalts Prometheus as the bringer not only of fire but through it survival, along with all the arts and sciences, and everything human and good. We need not take one side or the other. It is both ways.

REFERENCES

1. Mumford, L. *Technics and Civilization.* (New York: Harcourt, Brace, and Company, 1934), p. 184;
2. Ibid, p. 71.
3. Ibid, p. 59.
4. McLuhan, T. *Touch the Earth. A Self-Portrait of Indian Existence.* (New York: Outerbridge & Dienstfrey, 1971), p. 51.

SUGGESTED READING

Coon, C. *The Story of Man.* New York: Alfred A. Knopf, 1955.

Harrison, G. *The Conquest of Energy.* New York: William Morrow & Company, Inc. 1968.

Landsberg, H., and Schurr, S. *Energy in the United States: Sources, Uses, and Policy Issues.* New York: Random House, 1963.

Mumford, L. *Technics and Civilization.* New York: Harcourt, Brace, and Company, 1934.

Payen, J. *History of Energy,* trans. by J. White. London: Leisure Arts Ltd., 1966.

Starr, C. "Energy and Power." *Scientific American* 224, 3 (1971): 36–49.

Taylor, G. *The Transportation Revolution 1815–1860.* New York: Holt, Rinehart and Winston, Inc., 1951.

CHAPTER 5

Limits

All our drive and optimism are bound up with continuous growth; "growth addiction" is the unwritten and unconfessed religion of our times. In industry and also for nations, growth has become synonymous with hope. Undoubtedly, quantitative growth will have to go on for many more years, but unless we prepare for a turning-point well before the end of the century, it may by then be too late. . . . The insane quantitative growth must stop; but innovation must not stop—it must take an entirely new direction.

Dennis Gabor

You can't win. You can't break even. You can't get out of the game. Thus paraphrased, the message of the three hallowed laws of thermodynamics is profoundly clear. You can never get more out of a system than you put into it. In fact, you can't even get as much. And although according to this theory all systems are running down, nothing will ever come to a complete stop.

The cycles of the earth operate only because there is a continuous supply of energy from the sun. This energy may flow through many physical, chemical, and biological systems, but in the end it is always dissipated as heat. In every process of energy conversion, some energy loses its capacity to do work. Only the conversion of energy to heat is completely efficient, and even here we distinguish between useful (concentrated) and waste (diffuse) heat.

Energy is required to build all complex structures, from mountain ranges to living organisms. Energy is also required to maintain complexity. Spontaneously, order shakes itself into disorder. The mountain range lifted up through vast expenditures of the energy of the earth is slowly eroded flat. Organisms die, and their complex molecules return to simpler form. When Humpty Dumpty converted his potential energy of position first into kinetic energy of falling and then into the heat of impact and the mechanical energy of scrambling, he was pursuing the inevitable course that all things take. Furthermore, although in theory it is possible to restore Humpty to his original condition through appropriate inputs of energy, in practice there is no way to unscramble a scrambled egg.

EFFICIENCY

We want to get as much return as possible for our efforts. In the case of energy, we want to derive the maximum useful work from the energy we use. The degree to which we achieve this goal measures our efficiency, which can be defined as:

$$\text{Efficiency} = \frac{\text{useful work (or energy) output}}{\text{energy input}}$$

Each process has a maximum theoretical efficiency, which puts an upper limit on our expectations, and an actual efficiency, lower than the theoretical, which we realize with our imperfect systems. The maximum value of the equation is 1 (or 100 percent), because the output can never exceed the input.

Thermodynamics and the Efficiency of a Heat Engine

The study of thermodynamics was born from the discovery of the equivalence between heat and work. Heat can be converted to mechanical energy by allowing it to flow from something warm to something cooler (never the reverse) through a mechanism that diverts part of it on the way. This is the principle of a heat engine, of which the steam engine is a familiar example. The equivalence of heat and other forms of energy is shown by a conversion factor called the mechanical equivalent of heat: 1 kilocalorie equals 427 kilogram meters, or 0.12 kilowatt-hours.

Heat is distributed unevenly over the earth. Could we take advantage of this inequity on a large scale to convert heat into useful work? Could we, for example, extract heat from the oceans? Here is where the laws of thermodynamics frustrate us. Theoretically, we could couple the ocean's warm surface waters with the colder regions below, obtaining work in the process. But the amount of work which heat can do is determined by the initial and final temperatures of the system. The temperatures involved are relatively low and the temperature differences, small. Although a very large quantity of heat is stored in the oceans, the heat is of low intensity (as measured by the water's temperature).

The practical problem of deriving work from heat is defined by the equation for the maximum efficiency of an ideal heat engine: $E = (T_1 - T_2)/T_1$, where T_1 and T_2 are the initial and final temperatures expressed in degrees Kelvin. The equation shows that the greatest efficiency is obtained with a large temperature differential and that for a given temperature difference, the lower the temperatures the higher the efficiency will be. If T_2 were 0° K, the heat engine would be perfectly efficient. The problem is that T_2 can never be 0°, even in theory.

Actual efficiencies are always lower than theoretical ones. In practice, it does not pay to run a heat engine unless the initial temperature is quite high and the differential large.

You will hear much about efforts to increase the efficiency of our various energy conversion processes. These efforts are motivated by two considerations. First, we strive for efficiency as a conservation measure, to make the most of dwindling energy resources. As the following sections will show, however, improvements in the efficiency of energy conversion cannot in the long term solve the world's energy problem. The second reason for improving efficiency, which may be even more compelling than the first, is that wasted energy is the source of much pollution. When we consider what happens to wasted energy, increased efficiency becomes a mandatory goal. When only a small fraction of the energy we use is converted to useful work, the remainder does not disappear. It is still very much with us, and returns to haunt us in many ways which we are only beginning to appreciate and understand. Since we have little control over this energy, we must try to channel as much as possible into processes that are understood and controllable. With this in mind, we will look at past gains in the efficiency of energy conversion and at the prospects for the future.

The Concept of Efficiency

To some degree, each of us is aware of the efficiency of an energy conversion process. For fuel burned in an automobile or power plant, this awareness corresponds to knowledge of the physical calculation of efficiency. But for many processes, our knowledge is less precise. If we build a fire to keep warm, how do we gauge its efficiency? By whether it warms us, our feelings say. But then we would have to consider how many people were kept warm and at what temperature and distance from the fire. The actual calculation of physical efficiency for a campfire warming four people at a distance of four feet would give a value of at most a few percent; but it is unlikely that this number, even if known, would govern our actions in building or feeding the fire. How difficult it was to find fuel and the smokiness of the fire would be more important.

The calculation of efficiency depends on the point of view. For example, if we want to know about the process of transporting the automobile over some fixed distance, we must include in our calculation the nature of the terrain and the mass, including the load, of the automobile. If we want to ask the larger social question of the automobile's efficiency as a means of transporting people, then we must include the number of people in our calculation and obtain figures in terms of passenger miles per gallon of gasoline.

These larger considerations, which are often crucially important in questions of energy supply and demand, depend, however, on the basic efficiency of the energy conversion process—from fuel to work or from one kind of energy to another. Thus, in what follows we shall first examine the problem of the efficiency of energy converters. To the extent that we obtain gains in efficiency, our fuel requirements are eased and the waste heat which may constitute an environmental hazard is diminished. We will return later to some comments on the larger considerations.

Past Gains

The Industrial Revolution ushered in a period in which the overall efficiency of fuel use (whether food or coal) actually declined. The thumping, chugging steam engines of early industrial plants were enormously wasteful machines. James Watt belied his Scottish ancestry in producing a steam engine which wasted more than 95 percent of the energy of its fuel. Even domestic animals were more efficient in their use of fuel than these early steam engines. Efficiency, of course, was not a prime consideration then. Sheer power and independence from the vagaries of falling water, wind, and tiring animals were far more important. Similarly, the great age of railroads was driven by steam engines with efficiencies of 10 percent or less. The advent of the internal combustion engine represented a real gain, for even the early ones had efficiencies near 20 percent. Early electrical plants were even less efficient than early steam engines. In 1900 the average efficiency of conversion of fuel to electricity was less than 5 percent.

Through the development of new processes or improvements in old ones, there have been large gains in efficiency since 1900. The efficiency of electrical conversion now averages about 33 percent, and for the newest plants it is over 40 percent. The change from steam locomotives to diesel power in trains increased efficiency almost sixfold. In terms of actual fuel use, some of these gains seem quite dramatic. For example, in 1900 it took about 7 pounds of coal to generate a kilowatt-hour of electricity, while in 1960 it took less than a pound. We have also made gains in space heating. From the fireplaces of earlier times to the central oil and gas furnaces of today, we have had about a fourfold increase in the efficiency of fuel use (figure 5-1). Efficiency, however, was

Figure 5-1. Changes in the efficiency of home heating, 1880–1970.

not the sole consideration in adopting these changed methods. Cleanliness, convenience, and a host of other factors played large roles. Even now, efficiency of fuel use does not govern the choice, for the introduction of electric heat, however convenient, represents an efficiency of fuel use only half that of a modern oil or gas furnace.

A similar situation holds for lighting. The incandescent bulb, which shows no sign of disappearing from use, is an extraordinarily wasteful device: only 5 percent of the electricity is converted into visible light. (Even so, it is about five times more efficient than the carbon filament lamps of 1900.) More efficient forms of lighting are known: fluorescent lights, with an efficiency of about 20 percent; high intensity lamps, reaching efficiencies as high as 35 percent; and various vapor lamps with efficiencies exceeding 30 percent. Clearly, if the cost of energy is not the prime consideration, the choice of lighting, heating, or other conversion processes will not be governed by considerations of efficiency.

Table 5–1 presents the efficiencies of some energy converters in common use. Not all processes show steady improvement in technical efficiency. The internal combustion engine of 40 years ago was only slightly less efficient than that in common use today. In the case of automobiles, the increase in horsepower and size without a corresponding increase in the number of passengers has meant that the overall efficiency of automobile transportation has actually declined.

Perhaps the most dramatic gain in industrial processes has come through the introduction of the electric motor. Electric motors can operate at efficiencies ranging between 70 and 90 percent or more, while the old central steam prime mover had an efficiency of 10 percent or less. Since we must allow for the inefficiency of the electrical conversion process, the overall efficiency of electric motors drops to between 25 and 35 percent (the efficiency of generating electricity multiplied by the efficiency of the motor itself). In industrial processes, however, the electric motor's range of sizes and its ability to be turned on and off instantly provide for an efficiency of design which partially offsets the inefficiency of the electric conversion process.

Effect of Efficiency on Energy Demand
Past gains in the efficiency of energy conversion are of far more than historical interest. If efficiency had remained constant at 1910 levels, the expansion of energy consumption would have been far greater than what we have experienced. Estimates of future demand are often made by projecting past experience. But this implies that improvements in the processes of energy conversion will continue at the same rate as in the past. We would like to know, therefore, to what extent past gains in efficiency have held down the increase in demand for energy. We would also like to know the prospects for continued gains in the future.

But there is another reason for our interest in efficiency: the burden of pollution placed on the environment by the conversion of energy. The relationship is not simple except in the case of thermal pollution. In this case, all of the fuel consumed eventually winds up as waste heat, which may be a local or global environmental problem. The more efficiently we employ energy to do work, the smaller the thermal burden on the environment will be. Pollution by chemicals also results from energy conversion. The more fuel we consume, the more chemical

Table 5-1. Technical Efficiency of Energy Conversion

Device	Efficiency of Electrical Conversion (percent)	Efficiency of Primary Fuel Use (percent)
Space heating		
gas furnace	–	75–85
oil furnace	–	60–75
coal furnace	–	55–70
electric resistance heater	95	30–38
Water heating		
gas water heater	–	60–70
oil water heater	–	50–55
electric water heater	90–92	29–37
Cooking		
gas stove	–	60–70
electric stove	75	24–30
Home appliances		
gas clothes dryer	–	45–50
electric clothes dryer	57	18–23
gas refrigerator	–	30
electric refrigerator	50	16–20
gas air conditioner	–	30
electric air conditioner	50	16–20
small motor appliances	50–70	16–28
Lighting		
high intensity lamp	33	11–13
fluorescent lamp	23–28	7–11
incandescent lamp	4	1.3–1.6
mantle lamp (gas or kerosene)	–	0.5
Transportation		
diesel engine	–	38
gas turbine	–	36
automobile engine	–	23–25
Wankel rotary engine	–	18
steam locomotive	–	8
Miscellaneous		
large electric motor	90–95	29–38
large steam boiler	–	88
storage battery (wet)	–	70–75
fuel cell	–	60
steam turbine	–	45
gas laser	38–40	12–16
steam power plant	–	32–40
nuclear power plant	–	32–33
solar cell	–	10

pollutants will be released for any given level of pollution control. Since pollution control can never be perfect, one way to minimize chemical pollutants is to consume less fuel.

It is difficult to estimate the overall gains in efficiency for the United States or the world because the estimate depends on different effects in different sectors of energy use. Our estimate of an upper limit for efficiency gains is approximately a factor of 5 in the period since 1900. Another estimate is a factor of 4.[1] One way to arrive at such an estimate is to compare the total horsepower in prime movers in the United States with the increase in the gross national product. Figure 5-2 shows the ratio of horsepower in prime movers (excluding private automobiles, which may be considered as consumer items) at constant dollars for the period 1880 to 1970. It appears that efficiency declined somewhat in the period before 1920. During this time, relatively inefficient methods were replacing older, more efficient methods for reasons that had little to do with efficiency. The graph indicates that the prime gains in efficiency occurred between 1930 and the present. The amount of gain appears to be about a factor of 2, but this conclu-

Figure 5-2. Historical changes in Gross National Product dollars generated per horsepower of installed prime mover capacity. Private automobiles have been excluded from the prime movers because they are consumer end products and not part of the productive machinery of society.

   The curve shows the decline in productive efficiency until the 1920s and the improvement since then. While the reasons for these changes are complex, we cannot expect continuous improvement in the future.

sion is too simple because the efficiency of use of prime movers depends on factors other than the efficiency of energy conversion. The degree to which the prime movers are fully utilized, for example, would influence the apparent efficiency. Overall, improvements in efficiency have probably been more than a factor of 2 and less than a factor of 5 in the past fifty years.

Without improvements in efficiency, growth of the demand for energy in these years would certainly have been larger. It is not clear how much larger the demand for energy would have been, since improvements in efficiency may provide incentive for growth by reducing the cost of some activities. (Thus, it would be a mistake to conclude that we would presently be using from 2 to 5 times as much energy in the absence of these improvements.) If future gains in efficiency do not continue as in the past, however, we should expect demand for energy to expand at a faster rate than a simple projection of the experience of the past 50 years would indicate.

Prospects for the Future

It does not take an elaborate engineering argument to show that the improvements in efficiency of the past 70 years cannot be continued indefinitely. The present efficiency of energy utilization for the entire economy has been estimated to be about 50 percent.[2] This estimate is on the conservative side because it does not take account of losses in extracting, refining, transport, and distribution of fuel. Since we cannot get more energy out of an energy conversion process than we put in, a doubling of efficiency would carry us to the magical 100 percent level which occurs occasionally in textbooks but never in real engineering or industrial processes. The question, then, is what can we expect to achieve if improvement by a factor of 2 is an unreachable upper limit.

Futuristic dramas and science fiction take energy conversion problems rather lightly, and our spectacular achievements of the past should make anyone careful in pronouncing anything impossible. Nevertheless, the limitations that we must live with for the next fifty or one hundred years already seem to be known. The theoretical efficiency of heat engines is $E = (T_1 - T_2)/T_1$. In order to approach 100 percent efficiency with such an engine, it would be necessary to operate at initial temperatures near $1500°$ K ($2650°$ F) and low temperatures near $4°$ K ($-452.5°$ F). These temperatures correspond with those of molten rock at the upper end and liquid nitrogen at the lower. Such an engine, if it could be built, might have an efficiency above 99 percent, but it would not be of much use because more energy would be required to maintain the operating temperatures than could be obtained from running it.

Operating a heat engine between the freezing and boiling points of water yields efficiencies of only 35 to 40 percent. Theoretical efficiencies of about 60 percent might be attainable with a lower temperature of 311° K (100° F) and an upper temperature of 811° K (1000° F). This is about the largest temperature range used in present-day electric power plants which, however, do not achieve 60 percent efficiencies because engineering problems of the real world eat into the theoretical maximum very rapidly. Since it is impossible to maintain a constant high temperature, the efficiency promptly drops below 55 percent. In the overall operation of the power plant, the efficiency of conversion from chemical fuel to heat (about 85 to 95 percent) must be included. And finally, the generators themselves—inherently highly efficient devices—are not 100 percent efficient. With current technology, efficiencies in electric power plants thus have a practical limit of 45 to 50 percent. The best operating plants do achieve efficiencies of 42 or 43 percent. We cannot go much further.

Thermionic devices and solar cells (see chapters 9 and 10) are occasional favorites of science fiction writers. But these too are heat engines and subject to the same theoretical limitations. Currently their efficiencies range between 10 and 15 percent. We will get no remarkable improvements from this source.

Owing to their use in the space program, fuel cells have received a good deal of attention. The separation of water into hydrogen and oxygen gases by solar energy might be a scheme of some interest for the future (chapter 9). The hydrogen and oxygen can be recombined to generate energy. Such a process might be attractive for transportation, for of presently realizable devices only the fuel cell promises a power source with a weight to horsepower ratio equal or superior to the ratio for the internal combustion engine. The $H_2 - O_2$ fuel cell is also pollution free, the only combustion product being water. Nevertheless, the theoretical maximum efficiency for such a fuel cell is about 80 percent and the best ones now available, which are far too expensive for routine use, achieve an efficiency of only 50 to 55 percent. It seems unlikely that this figure will improve very much. Such things as photosensitive semiconductors and thermoelectric devices may have their special uses, but their efficiencies also have rather stringent limitations.

Efficiency in Transportation: An Illustration

Another way to look at gains in efficiency is to look at the principal uses of energy and inquire what gains might be made in specific areas. In transportation, the efficiency of the internal combustion engine has been remarkably resistant to improvement. Efficiencies of 21 or 22 percent characterized automobiles in the 1920s. Efficiencies today are about 25 percent, and any slight gains in utilization of fuel have been more than offset by the trend toward larger, heavier automobiles with overpowered engines. The hydrogen-oxygen fuel cell might produce a significant gain in engine efficiency, but that must be coupled with the efficiency of generating the fuel in the first place. While it is hard to estimate the efficiency of producing the fuel in the absence of a working scheme, one would expect the efficiency of the process to be less than 50 percent. In this case the overall efficiency of the fuel cell makes it a questionable improvement over the internal combustion engine, although it would represent a gain for pollution control.

We mentioned that the electric motor is very efficient, but as long as the efficiency of generating electricity at a central power plant is only 35 or 40 percent, the overall efficiency of electric automobiles will also be about the same as that of the present internal combustion engine. The switch to electric automobiles might be an attractive alternative, but not on account of their efficiency.

GROWTH

Most of us think that what is familiar is normal and that what is normal must be right. Each one of us grew up and is living in times characterized by the runaway growth of most human institutions. This growth is so much a part of everyday life that we take it for granted, believing that growth must be desirable—even necessary.

However, many scientists, economists, and environmentalists are now expressing concern over the tremendous growth in consumption of resources which has characterized the twentieth century. Growth in consumption is related to both population growth and increasing affluence. All forms of growth are coming under attack, for it is becoming more and more obvious that our planet cannot sustain unlimited growth.

Exponential Growth—What is it?

Because growth is a matter of controversy and concern, it is important to understand some characteristics and results of the various kinds of growth. Growth usually occurs in one of three ways: at a constant rate, or at a rate which changes by a constant amount in each unit of time, or at a rate which changes with time by an amount which depends on the size of the growing thing. If you are given to saving dimes in a coffee can under your bed, three regimens of saving, representing the three modes of growth, would give the following results after one year (table 5–2):

Table 5-2

Rate of Saving	Rate of Growth at End of Year	Total Savings at End of Year
10¢ per month	$ 0.10 per month	$ 1.20
Increase of 10¢ per month	1.20 per month	7.80
Double each month	204.80 per month	409.50

There are examples of each type of growth in everyday life. The first is illustrated by the way the bathtub fills up when you plug the drain and turn on the water. Or you may actually be squirreling away a dime a month under the bed. The second is illustrated by the acceleration of a falling object: the rate of descent increases 9.75 meters (32 feet) per second during each second of the fall, regardless of how fast the object is traveling or how long it has been on its way. The third type of growth is represented by the exponential growth rate that characterizes most living organisms and populations at one time or another, as well as many human institutions. The classic example is the compound interest offered by the savings and loan company.

It is helpful to think of exponential growth in terms of the length of time required to double the amount you started with. Table 5-3 lists the doubling times at various rates of growth.

Table 5-3

Annual Percent Increase	Doubling Time (years)
0.5	140
1.0	70
2.0	35
3.0	24
5.0	14
7.0	10
10.0	7

One of the things that has been growing exponentially is the use of energy, both in the United States and in the world. It has been largely the growth of energy use that has permitted other kinds of growth—growth of food production, steel and aluminum production, transportation, communication, population, pollution, and general environmental degradation. Although some of the undesirable consequences of energy use may be unnecessary, they are realities, and as we look toward the future it seems probable that they will remain realities for some time.

The amount of energy used in the United States has doubled four times since the beginning of this century. It is expected to double twice again before the century's end. The rate of increase in energy use for the world is even greater, and can be expected to remain so, as people of poor nations strive for a decent life.

The results of exponential growth are always shocking. Many examples, some real, some facetious, dramatize what happens when growth proceeds unchecked. *Escherichia coli* is a common bacterium that, under appropriate conditions, reproduces itself by cell division every 20 minutes. Suppose that a student in microbiology inoculates one liter of nutrient medium with one milliliter of a culture of *E. coli* containing about 100 living bacteria. From time to time, he withdraws a sample from the culture, makes a series of dilutions, and plates samples of these dilutions onto solid culture medium. The next day he counts the number of colonies that have grown on the plates, each colony representing the progeny of a single cell in the original culture.

After 3½ hours, the number of bacteria in the original culture increased to around 3000; at 5 hours it was more than 50,000; at 6½ hours it was passing the million mark; at 8 hours, more than 25 million; and at 12 hours there are 100 billion cells! Then something happened. Samples taken during the next 24 hours continued to indicate that there were about 100 billion living cells. Then the number began to fall, slowly at first, then faster and faster, until another day went by and most of the cells were dead.

Then there was the clever lad who elected to receive, not a million dollars, but one cent the first day, two the second, four the third, eight the fourth, and so on every day for a month, until he was reckoning his wealth in millions of dollars. And the pair of grasshoppers that reproduced until their great great great . . . grandchildren formed a mass heavier than the earth. And finally, it has been pointed out that if science grows as it has been growing, in less than a hundred years there will be twice as many scientists as people. In 400 years, high energy physicists will be working on the ultimate experiment. They will have constructed an unprecedentedly powerful particle accelerator which will finally unravel all the mysteries of the universe. Unfortunately, the entire mass of the universe must be converted to energy in order to do the definitive experiment.

Because projections of exponential growth curves always lead to absurdity, we tend not to take them seriously. We are alternately advised, "Don't worry, it won't happen," and "Do worry, it won't happen." The thing to remember is that the projection of the exponential phase of a growth curve is only a mathematical abstraction, not a prediction. Although it is certain that the absurdity will not come to pass, what happens instead should concern us. The bacteria ran out of food and poisoned themselves in their own wastes. Some of the grasshoppers brought the wrath of man and DDT upon themselves; most of the rest starved or were eaten by blackbirds. The physicists had their research grants cut off long before they could design their doomsday machine. Only the little boy escaped disaster. Was it because he was a very intelligent boy, who stopped himself before natural limits stopped him?

There is urgency in the voices of those who warn of the immediacy of our growth-related problems. The reason for this urgency is incomprehensible to those who do not grasp the implications of exponential growth. Human populations and institutions have been growing for hundreds of thousands of years. What, then, does this mean, that we have only a few more years to reverse the trends before nature enforces her own brutal controls? Imagine the germ of a rare disease—so rare that it infects only two-millionths (two ten-thousandths of a percent) of the earth's surface. Suppose that it doubles the area it infects each year and we arbitrarily decide to do something about it when it covers half the earth. After 10 years of exponential growth it has spread over one one thousandth of the earth, 0.1 percent. After 15 years it is spreading faster, but still it covers only 3 percent of the earth. In the nineteenth year we are jolted to our senses: by the end of the year our germ will have reached the halfway point in its conquest, leaving us one year in which to save ourselves. What is so insidious about exponential growth is the shocking rapidity with which natural limits are reached after long periods of apparently modest and harmless increase. If you double your use of something each year, one year before it is all gone it is only half gone. Each year you use as much as you used in all the years before, combined.

There is no longer any doubt that the earth's resources are finite. Most disagreement among experts revolves around assigning numerical values to various limiting factors. But by now it should be clear that the difference between optimistic and pessimistic estimates of any resource becomes insignificant so long as we persist in growing. The predicament is illustrated by some simulation studies done at the Massachusetts Institute of Technology.[3] The question posed to the computer was, what will happen under various patterns of growth in world population, resource use, and pollution? The answer was clear. It makes little difference, in the long run, what assumptions are made. The day of reckoning for industrial society and for the world is hastened or delayed by only trivial amounts as long as we persist in any of the conventional types of growth. We are approaching a number of natural limits simultaneously. Exponential growth will not continue much longer.

Figure 5–3 shows some of the things that can happen to an exponential growth curve when it is deflected from its steep ascent. Figure 5–3, *a* is the typical growth pattern of a bean plant or a man. Size increases slowly at first, then rapidly, and then slowly again until it reaches its maximum and remains constant. Exponential growth characterizes immature organisms and systems; the stable, mature organism or system reaches a steady, no-growth state.

The population of *E. coli*, trapped in the closed system of a culture flask, followed a growth curve like the one in figure 5–3, *b*. This is the kind of curve that has been predicted for a human population that

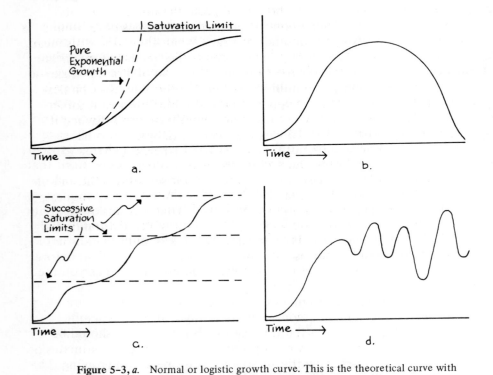

Figure 5–3, *a*. Normal or logistic growth curve. This is the theoretical curve with pure exponential growth shown for comparison. This normal curve is closely approximated in real life by the growth of many plants and animals.

Figure 5–3, *b*. Growth curve typical of a population in a closed system (fruit flies in a bottle or bacteria in a test tube) that exhausts its resources.

Figure 5–3, *c*. Succession of normal curves, each beginning from the plateau of the last. The beginning of a new phase of exponential growth may mark a technological breakthrough. Growth in speed of transportation might follow a curve like this.

Figure 5–3, *d*. Growth curve oscillating around its limit. Typical of populations of rabbits varying in response to populations of predators, or of production of copper in past years.

does not control its increase in numbers or consumption of resources.[3]

Sometimes, as a growth curve approaches its natural limit, it levels off for a while, only to undergo another exponential spurt that is followed by another plateau, then another spurt, and so on. This may be what has happened to human population growth in the past, as innovations in agriculture and technology sequentially removed natural limits. This cannot continue indefinitely.

Finally, a growth curve that is trying to avoid its inevitable ceiling may break into oscillations (figure 5–3, *d*). The production of copper and zinc, metals which are in great demand and short supply, represents this kind of curve over the past century.

What will happen? This issue causes harsh controversy among scientists, economists, and political leaders, because a world without growth threatens many of our cherished institutions, beliefs, and theories. But inevitably we will deal with the problem, either by passive surrender to fate or by constructive action. Since the use of energy is fundamental to human culture, a first step in the control of growth might be the examination of our uses of energy and a voluntary restriction of energy use to the satisfaction of basic needs. Others may gaze into the cloudy crystal ball to foresee factors that might change growth patterns, either by design or by accident, and to foresee conditions that might accompany variously altered growth patterns. One thing is clear: the longer we postpone action to control growth, the fewer are the alternatives open to us. Increases in technical efficiency are almost exhausted, and technological innovation will mean mostly undirected social change if efficiency cannot be increased. The gains deriving from growth need a new balancing against the risks.

REFERENCES

1. Summers, C. "The Conversion of Energy." *Scientific American* 224, 3 (1971): 148–160.
2. Cook, E. "The Flow of Energy in an Industrial Society," *Scientific American* 224, 3 (1971): 134–147.
3. Meadows, D. H.; Meadows, P. L; Randers, J. H.; and Behrens, W. *The Limits to Growth*. New York: Universe Books, 1972).

SUGGESTED READING

Cook, E. "The Flow of Energy in an Industrial Society." *Scientific American* 224, 3 (1971): 134–137.

Forrester, J. W. *World Dynamics.* Cambridge, Mass: Wright-Allen. 1971.

Johnson, W., and J. Hardesty. *Economic Growth vs. the Environment.* Belmont, California: Wadsworth Publishing Company, Inc., 1971.

March, R. *Physics for Poets.* New York: McGraw-Hill Book Company, 1970.

Meadows, D. H.; Meadows, P. L; Randers, J. H; and Behrens, W. *The Limits to Growth.* New York: Universe Books, 1972.

Summers, C. "The Conversion of Energy." *Scientific American* 224, 3 (1971): 148–160.

The No-Growth Society; A collection of essays, *Daedalus* Fall, 1973.

CHAPTER 6

The Energy We Eat

Times are changing, mister, don't you know? Can't make a living on the land unless you've got two, five, ten thousand acres and a tractor. Cropland isn't for little guys like us any more. You don't kick up a howl because you can't make Fords, or because you're not the telephone company. Well, crops are like that now. Nothing to do about it.

John Steinbeck, 1939

Feed men, and then ask them of their virtue.

Fyodor Dostoevsky

The kind of energy that has always been of first importance is food. Throughout most of human history, man has relied on his own labor to provide food. If the energy value of the food obtained had not substantially exceeded the energy expended in obtaining it, our species would not have survived.

Through the development of agriculture, man was able to manipulate the flow of energy in various ecosystems in order to divert an increasingly large fraction of the earth's productivity to his own use. He did this by simplifying the complex natural ecosystem—by decreasing the number of species in the system and by controlling the species that competed with him for the yield. Maintenance of the simplified system required an endless input of energy. At first this was restricted to manpower, as techniques for preparing the soil, planting, weeding, driving off pests, and harvesting were developed. Later, animal power was exploited. Still later, inanimate energy from wind and water was put to work, and finally, energy from the fossil fuels was utilized in food production.

In many parts of the world, agriculture still depends on energy from people, animals, and the sun. If conditions are favorable, such solar agriculture can give very high yields—for example, in wet rice culture, up to 50 calories are returned in harvest for every calorie of human energy investment. Modern agriculture, however, depends on converting fossil fuels into meat and potatoes, and there is an increasingly unfavorable ratio of energy input to food output. It is due to large-scale energy subsidy that agricultural yields have increased manyfold in the United States during this century. In 1900, a single farmer could feed about five people. By 1940 he could feed 10 and in 1960 he could feed 25. Today, the labor of one farmer feeds nearly 50 people, owing to the development of new fungicides, herbicides, rodenticides, insecticides, miticides, nematocides, antibiotics, vaccines, fertilizers, equipment, and specialized varieties of plants and animals. But it is not just one farmer who feeds 50 people. It is one farmer, many tons of coal, many barrels of oil, and an immense food processing and distribution system. In this chapter we will see how the present situation has come about.

ENERGY IN ECOSYSTEMS

Life can be viewed as a ceaseless web of energy conversions which follow well-known principles of energy conservation and transformation. Many ecologists describe an ecosystem in terms of the energy that flows into and out of it and from one trophic level to another (that is, from green plants to herbivores to carnivores or from any of these levels to decomposers). The tropical rain forest is an example of a complex ecosystem characterized by a large mass of living organisms and efficient use of available energy. In the rain forest there are many hundreds of species of plants, each specialized in its structure and function to fill a unique niche, and each accompanied by its cadre of insect predators specialized to deal with it. Armies of microorganisms live in association with roots, soil, and dead matter. Fungus-eating flies, beetles, termites, and other small animals feed on the microorganisms. They in turn are eaten by a variety of amphibians and reptiles. Birds and mammals feed on everything, including each other. Man, the most relentless and least specialized predator of all, is the one creature likely to upset the balance.

A great deal of energy is expended in maintaining the integrity of such a system. In the rain forest, energy flows through an intricate network of feedback loops that regulate all the interrelationships among species. Epidemics are virtually impossible because of the low density of any particular population. If one species increases, others usually increase to counteract it until order is restored. Similarly, should a species decline, its predators also decline or shift their attention to an alternative food source until decreased predation permits recovery of the original population. Even if one species should disappear, the system survives because there are many alternative pathways along which energy and materials can flow. Diversity of species insures that nutrients will be cycled effectively and soil structure preserved.

This complex, stable natural system supports the highest productivity and the greatest mass of living organisms possible under prevailing climatic conditions. Man can glean very little from this system, however, for little remains after respiration, predators, parasites, and decomposers claim their share. The situation in a rain forest is in sharp contrast to that in a field of grass. Energy is stored in a field of grass: it is used primarily for growth, rather than for maintaining the structure of the system. But a field of grass generally lacks stability because it contains relatively few species and few feedback loops which regulate interactions among species. Many ecological niches are empty, inviting other species to invade. Under many conditions, the short-lived, rapidly growing, prolific species in the open field tend eventually to be displaced by a succession of slower growing, longer lived, less prolific species until a system develops which is relatively stable under the prevailing conditions of soil and climate. Left undisturbed, a meadow usually becomes a forest.

The achievement of agriculture is to simplify the system so that, as in a field of grass, the maximum amount of solar energy is channeled into growth. Man supplies the energy for maintenance. He plows and plants. He fights off competitors, predators, and disease. He supplies fertilizer to replace losses from harvesting. He shelters his animals, feeds and vaccinates them, and helps them to breed and to bear and raise their young. Thus, only through a steady input of energy is man able to divert most of the productivity of his fields to his own ends.

It is a difficult struggle to maintain the simplified system however much energy is put into it. Where fields lie barren for part of the year, erosion and deterioration of soil structure claim their toll. Bigger and better pests continually appear. Where irrigation is practiced, water shortages and increasing salinity haunt the farmer. And if a wheat field is abandoned, does a crop of wheat come up the next year? Of course not. This illustrates a major difference between wild plants and the plants that are adapted to modern agricultural methods. Wild plants are hardy, physiologically adaptable, and able to withstand adversity. Man's crops are highly specialized for growth, and consequently they are dependent on man for protection and even their own propagation.

THE PENALTY FOR IMPROVEMENT

The success of modern agriculture depends in part on the development of fast growing, high yielding strains of plants and animals, whose productivity in turn depends on energy-intensive agriculture. For more than ten thousand years man has engaged in selective breeding of domestic plants and animals. One of the most remarkable stories is that of maize, or corn. The first evidence of wild maize is from Mexico, dating from more than 7000 years ago. The plant probably looked similar to any other grass that grows in meadows, and the ear was no larger than your thumbnail. Lurking in the small seed, however, was the potential to become the corn of today, with huge ears of closely packed grain. The yield of modern hybrid corn is more than 90 bushels per acre in the midwestern United States. But corn can no longer survive without man. Even if it weathered a dry season on poor soil, escaping disease and predation, it would perish within a generation or two, for it can no longer shed its seed to propagate itself.

Other domestic plants and animals have also become increasingly dependent on man for their survival. It seems that an organism can be either a generalist or a specialist, but not both. An organism can process just so much energy in its lifetime. If this energy is channeled largely into growth, man must tend to the other needs of the organism. Our improved plants and animals are not truly improved, but are merely specialized. They are specialized in growing wool, fat roots, or giant fruits, in laying eggs or making milk. In diverting their energy into rapid growth, they sacrifice many qualities that allowed their wild forebears to survive. Selective breeding may solve specific problems, but we are fooling ourselves when we expect a plant to resist disease, discourage predators and competitors, withstand unfavorable climatic and nutritional conditions, grow rapidly, reproduce abundantly, and still yield a bountiful harvest that is tasty, nutritious, and beautiful. One manifestation of the penalty for improvement is that, in the plant world, favorite varieties of grapes, roses, and citrus, to name a few, are routinely grafted onto wild rootstocks to increase their vigor.

Another feature of modern crop plants and domestic animals is genetic uniformity. Just as species diversity enhances a natural system's chances for survival, genetic diversity enhances a species' chances. If misfortune befalls a genetic subset of a group, the remaining members can avert disaster for the population as a whole. In addition to being specialized for growth of one sort or another, domestic plants and animals also tend toward genetic uniformity, which implies uniform resistance or susceptibility to adversity. Through modern practices in animal breeding, a dairy bull can spread his genes around the world before some camouflaged weakness makes itself known in his offspring.

Vegetative propagation of plants and other common practices insure dependably uniform crops down to the end. For a popular variety of potato known as the lumper, the end was the Irish potato famine of 1846.

It is contradictory to desire uniformity and diversity at the same time. Modern agriculture values uniformity above all else. The risks are well known, but the benefits seem worth the gamble. As a result, there have been some disastrous epidemics in our country, including southern leaf blight of corn, fungus disease of a popular strain of oats called Victory, and the wildfire spread of a virulent new race of wheat stem rust which attacked a variety of wheat bred for resistance to the old race of wheat stem rust. The problem of plant breeders is that while they make hundreds of experimental crosses, nature tries millions. One mutant fungus spore or one fecund insect can undo years of the work of man.

The high-yielding varieties of grain that are being spread throughout the world as the green revolution represent the most extensive experiment in uniformity of crops yet tried. When things go well with the green revolution they go very well indeed; but the miracle grains are susceptible to widespread disaster and they produce no miracles unless grown under the most favorable conditions. But complex as are the problems of the green revolution, the alternative seems to be starvation for about a billion people.

LAND RESOURCES AND AGRICULTURE

There are three ways in which we can try to feed the growing number of human beings on earth: open up new agricultural and grazing lands, increase the productivity of the lands already in use, and develop new sources of food. The long-term success of any of these depends on the size of the population we are trying to support and on our ability to design self-sustaining systems for which there is a non-depletable source of energy and in which materials are recycled.

We are familiar enough with the surface of our planet to know that no hidden paradise remains to be discovered. The area of the earth's ice-free land surface is about 32 billion acres. Roughly one quarter of this is potentially arable, another quarter is potentially grazable, and half is useless for agriculture, although some of it is forested. Much of the unused potentially arable land is in the tropics, where its potential may be more theoretical than practical. It certainly is not farmable with today's knowledge and techniques and economic restrictions. Practically all the land that can be cultivated under existing social and economic conditions is already under cultivation.

In North America, large amounts of arable land are not being farmed. However, we should not be optimistic about possibilities for expansion, for the best land is already cultivated and what remains has serious deficiencies. Furthermore, buildings and highways are spreading so malignantly over so much of our prime farmland that projections for California, for example, indicate that in less than 50 years half of the state's agricultural land will have been converted into nonagricultural uses. It is doubtful that, in opening new lands, we can run fast enough to stay where we are.

There are sound reasons for not rushing to open up vast new areas for crops or grazing, even if technical and economic obstacles could be overcome. One reason is that agriculture, especially as practiced in industrialized nations, depends on the activities of unmanaged ecosystems for the cycling of wastes and other materials. The capacities of some of these systems are already overtaxed, and further reduction in their size would intensify the problems. Another is that biologists emphasize the importance of maintaining reservoirs of wild plants and animals from which new and valuable domesticates may be developed. In general, the best plan seems to be to increase the productivity of lands already under cultivation, which inevitably requires an energy subsidy. The rest of this chapter analyzes the energy intensive food system in the United States and questions the extent to which it is desirable or even possible to transfer this technology to the developing nations.

ENERGY USE IN AN INDUSTRIAL FOOD SYSTEM

In a modern industrial society, only a tiny fraction of the population is in frequent contact with the soil, and an even smaller fraction of the population raises food on the soil. The proportion of the population engaged in farming halved between 1920 and 1950, and then halved again by 1962. Now it has almost halved again and yet a majority of the remaining farmers hold part-time jobs off the farm.[1] Simultaneously, work animals declined from a peak of more than 22 million in 1920 to very small numbers at present.[2]

In economic terms, the value of food as a portion of the total goods and services of society now amounts to a smaller fraction of the gross national product than it once did. Energy inputs to farming have increased enormously since 1920,[3] and the apparent decrease in farm labor is offset in part by the growth of support industries for the farmer. But with these changes on the farm have come a variety of other changes in the U.S. food system, many of which are now deeply embedded in the fabric of daily life. In the past fifty years, canned, frozen and other processed foods have become principal items in our diet. At present the food processing industry is the fourth largest energy consumer in the Standard Industrial Classification groupings. The use of transportation in the food system has grown apace, and the proliferation of appliances in both numbers and complexity still continues in homes, institutions, and stores. Hardly anyone eats much food as it comes from the fields. Even farmers purchase most of their food from markets in town.

Present energy supply problems make this growth of energy use in the food system worth investigating. It is the purpose of this chapter to do so. But there are larger matters at stake. Georgescu-Roegen notes that "the evidence now before us—of a world which can produce automobiles, television sets, etc., at a greater speed than the increase in population, but is simultaneously menaced by mass starvation—is disturbing."[4] In the search for a solution to the world's food problems, the common attempt to transplant a small piece of a highly industrialized food system to the hungry nations of the world is plausible enough, but so far the outcome is unclear. Perhaps an examination of the energy flow in the U.S. food system as it has been developed can provide some insights that are not available from the usual economic measures.

Measures of Food Systems

Descriptions of agricultural systems are given most often in economic terms. A wealth of statistics is collected in the United States and in most other countries indicating production amounts, shipments, income, labor, expenses and dollar flow in the agricultural sector of the economy. In what follows, we will make use of these statistics, for these values are of considerable use in determining the economic position of farmers in our society. But agricultural statistics are only a tiny fraction of the story.

Energy flow is another measure available to gauge societies and nations. Only after some nations shifted large portions of the population to manufacturing, specialized tasks, and mechanized food production, and shifted the prime sources of energy to fuels that were transportable and usable for a wide variety of activities could energy flow be a measure of a society's activities. Today it is only in one-fifth of the world that these conditions are sufficiently advanced.

What we would like to know is: how does our food supply system compare in terms of energy use to other societies, and to our own past. Perhaps, knowing this, we can estimate the value of energy flow measures as an adjunct to, but different from, economic measures.

Energy in the United States Food System

In the morning, breakfast offers orange juice from Florida by way of the Minute Maid factory, bacon from a midwestern meat packer, cereal from Nebraska and General Mills, eggs from California, milk from not too far away, and coffee from Colombia. All these things are available at the local supermarket (4.7 miles each way in a 300 h.p. automobile), stored in a refrigerator-freezer and cooked on an instant-on gas stove (see appendix D).

The present food system in the United States is complex and the attempt to analyze it in terms of energy use will introduce questions far more perplexing than would the same analysis performed on simpler societies. Such an analysis is worthwhile, however, if only to find out where we stand. We have a food system and most of us get enough to eat from it. If, in addition, one considers the food supply problems, present and future, of societies where a smaller fraction of the people get enough to eat, then our experience with an industrialized food system is even more important. There is simply no gainsaying the fact that most nations are trying to acquire industrialized food systems of their own, whether in whole or in part.

What economics tells us is that food in the United States is expensive by world standards. In 1970 the average annual per capita expenditure for food in the United States was about $600.[3] This is larger than the per capita gross domestic product in more than 30 nations of the world. These 30 nations contain most of the world's people and a vast majority of those who are underfed. It would be convenient to know whether we can put our hands into the workings of our own industrialized food system to extract a piece of it that might mitigate their plight, or whether they must become equally industrialized in order to operate such a food supply system. Even if we consider the diet of a poor resident of India, the annual cost of his food at U.S. prices would be about $200—more than twice his annual income.

The analysis of energy use in the food system begins with an omission. We will neglect that crucial input of energy provided by the sun to the plants upon which the entire food supply depends. Photosynthesis is about 1 percent efficient; thus the maximum solar radiation captured by plants is about 5×10^3 kcal/m² per year. Ultimately we can compare the solar input with the energy subsidy supplied by modern technology.

Seven categories of energy use on the farm were considered. The amounts of energy used are shown in figure 6–1. The values for farm machinery and tractors are for the manufacture of new units only and do not include parts and maintenance for existing units. The amounts shown for direct fuel use and electricity consumption are a bit too high because they include some residential uses of the farmer and his family. On the other hand, some uses in these categories are not reported in the summaries employed to obtain the values for direct fuel and electricity usage. These and similar problems are discussed in the appendix. Note the relatively high energy cost associated with irrigation. In the United

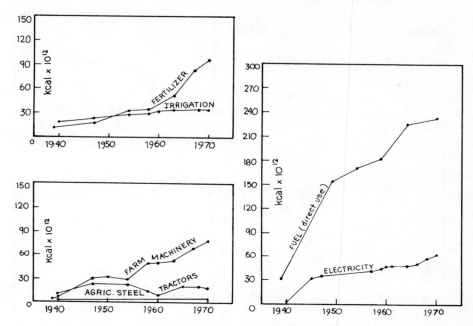

Figure 6-1. Energy use on farms, 1940–1970. Transportation is included in the food processing sector (see Appendix D, table D-1, note 15).

States, less than 5 percent of the cropland is irrigated. In some countries where the green revolution is being attempted, the new high yield varieties require irrigation while native crops did not. If that were the case in the United States, irrigation would be the largest single use of energy on the farm.

Little food makes its way from field and farm directly to the table. The vast complex of processing, packaging, and transport has been grouped together in a second major subdivision of the food system. Figure 6–2 displays the energy use in food processing and packaging. Energy use for transport of food should be charged to the farm in part, but we have not done so because the calculation of the energy values is easiest (and we believe most accurate) if they are taken for the whole system.

After food is processed there is further energy expenditure. Transportation enters again, and some fraction of the energy used for transportation should be assigned here. But there are also the distributors, wholesalers and retailers, whose freezers, refrigerators and very establishments are an integral part of the food system. There are also the restaurants, schools, universities, prisons, and a host of other institutions engaged in the procurement, preparation, storage, and supply of food. We have chosen to examine only 3 categories: the energy used for

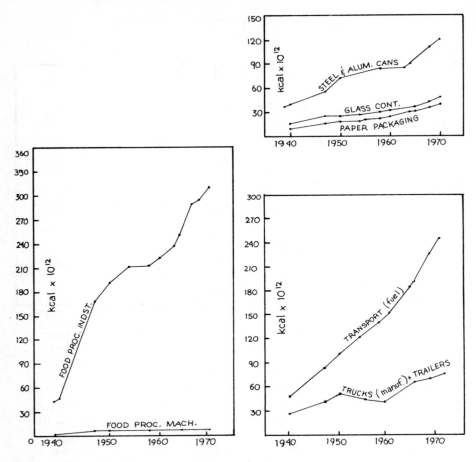

Figure 6-2. Energy use in the food processing sector.

home refrigeration and cooking, for commercial refrigeration and cooking, and that used for the manufacture of the refrigeration equipment. Figure 6-3 shows energy consumption for these categories. There is no attempt to include the energy used in trips to the store or restaurant. Garbage disposal has also been omitted, although it is a persistent and growing feature of our food system. Twelve percent of the nation's trucks are engaged in waste disposal which is largely, though not entirely, related to food. If there is any lingering doubt that these activities—both the ones included and the ones left out—are an essential feature of our present food system, one need only ask what would happen if everyone should attempt to get on without a refrigerator or freezer or stove? Certainly the food system would change.

Figure 6–3. Commercial and home energy use in the food system. These are selected uses only.

We have summarized the numerical values for primary energy use by the U.S. food system, from 1940 to 1970, in table 1 in Appendix D. As for many activities in the past few decades, the story is one of continuing increase. The totals are displayed in figure 6–4 along with the energy value of the food consumed by the public. The food values were obtained by multiplying the annual caloric intake with the population. The difference in caloric intake over this 30-year period is not significant and the curve mostly indicates the population increase in this period.

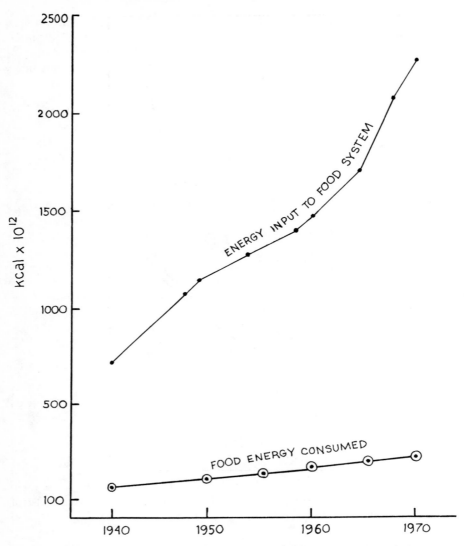

Figure 6–4.   Energy use in the food system, 1940–1970, compared to caloric energy content of food consumed.

PERFORMANCE OF AN INDUSTRIALIZED FOOD SYSTEM

The difficulty with history as a guide for the future or even the present lies not so much in the fact that conditions change—we are at least continually reminded of that fact—but that history is only one experience of the many that might have been. The U.S. food system developed as it did for a variety of reasons, many of them probably not understood. It would do well to examine some of the dimensions of this development before attempting to theorize about how it might have been different, or how parts of this food system can be transplanted elsewhere.

Energy and Food Production

Figure 6–5 displays features of our food system not easily seen from economic data. The curve shown has no theoretical basis, but is suggested by the data as a smoothed recounting of the history of increasing food production. It is, however, similar to growth curves of the most general kind, and it suggests that, to the extent that the increasing energy subsidies to farm production have increased that production, we are near the end of an era. Like the logistic growth curve (see figure 5–3) there is an exponential phase which began in 1920 or earlier and lasted until 1950 or 1955. Since then the increments in production obtained by the growth in energy use have become smaller. It is likely that further increases in food production from increasing energy inputs will be harder and harder to come by. Of course, a major modification in the food system could change things. However, the argument advanced by the technological optimists—that we can always produce more if we

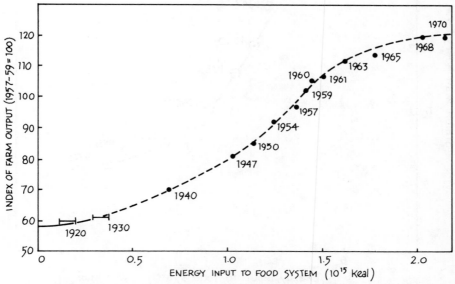

Figure 6–5. Farm output as a function of energy input to the U.S. food system, 1920–1970.

have enough energy and that no other major changes are needed— is not supported by our own history.

Energy and Labor in the Food System

One farmer now feeds 50 people, and the common expectation is that labor inputs to farming will continue to decrease in the future. Behind this expectation is the assumption that continued application of technology—and energy—to farming will substitute for labor. Figure 6–6 is the substitution curve of energy for labor on the farm. It shows the historic decline in farm labor as a function of the energy subsidy to the food system. Again the familiar "S" shaped curve may be seen. Reduction of farm labor by increasing energy inputs cannot go much further.

The food system that has grown during this period has provided a great deal of employment that did not exist 20, 30 or 40 years ago.

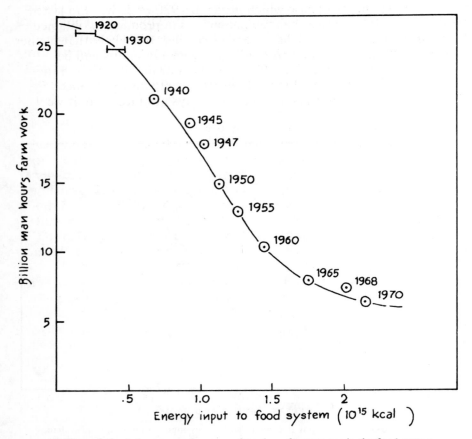

Figure 6–6. Labor use on farms as a function of energy use in the food system.

Perhaps even the idea of a reduction of labor input is a myth when the food system is viewed as a whole, instead of examining the farm worker only. Pimentel and associates cite an estimate of two farm support workers for each person employed on the farm.[3] To this must be added employment in food processing industries, in food wholesale and retail establishments and in the manufacturing enterprises that support the food system. Yesterday's farmer is today's canner, tractor mechanic and fast food carhop. The process of change has been painful to many ordinary people. The rural poor, who could not quite compete in the industrialization of farming, migrated to the cities. Eventually they found other employment, but one must ask if the change was worthwhile. The answer to that question cannot be provided by energy analysis any more than by economic data, because it raises fundamental questions about how individuals would prefer to spend their lives. But if there is a stark choice of long hours as a farmer, or shorter hours on the assembly line of a meat packing plant, it seems clear that the choice would not be universally in favor of the meat packing plant. Thomas Jefferson dreamed of a nation of independent small farmers. It was a good dream, but society did not develop in that way. Nor can we turn back the clock to recover his dream. But in planning our future, we had better look honestly at our collective history, and then each of us look closely at his own dreams.

The Energy Subsidy to the Food System

The data on figure 6–5 can be combined to show the energy subsidy provided to the food system for the recent past. We take as a measure of the food supplied, the caloric content of the food actually consumed. This is not the only measure of the food supplied, as many protein-poor peoples of the world clearly show. Nevertheless the ratio of caloric input to output is a convenient way to compare our present situation with the past. Figure 6–7 shows the history of the U.S. food system in terms of the number of calories of energy supplied to produce one calorie of food for actual consumption. It is interesting and possibly frightening to note that there is no indication that this curve is leveling off. Fragmentary data for 1972 suggest that the increase continued unabated. We appear to be increasing the energy input even more. Note that a graph like figure 6–7 could go to zero. A natural ecosystem has no fuel input at all, and those primitive people who live by hunting and gathering have only the energy of their own work to count as input.

Some Economic Features of the U.S. Food System

The markets for farm commodities in the United States come closer than most to the economist's ideal of a free market. In a free market there are many small sellers, many buyers, and thus no individual

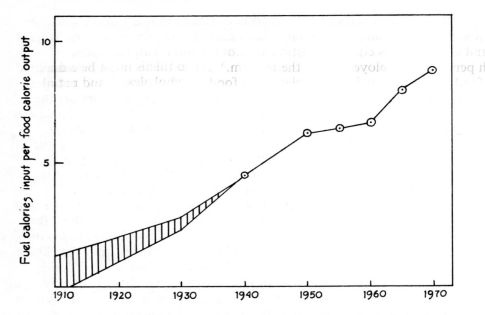

Figure 6-7. Energy subsidy to the food system to obtain one food calorie. The values for period 1910–1937 cannot be fully documented, and thus we present a range of values for that period.

is able to affect the price by his own actions in the marketplace. But a market would satisfy these conditions only in the absence of intervention in its function. Government intervention in the prices of agricultural products (and hence of food) has been a prominent feature of the U.S. food system for at least thirty years. Between 1940 and 1970 total farm income has ranged from $4.5 to $16.5 billion, and that part of the National Income having its origin in agriculture (which includes indirect income from agriculture) has ranged from $14.5 to $22.5 billion. Meanwhile government subsidy programs, primarily farm price supports and soil bank payments, have grown from $1.5 billion in 1940 to $6.2 billion in 1970. In 1972 these subsidy programs had grown to $7.3 billion despite foreign demand for U.S. agricultural products. Viewed in a slightly different way, direct government subsidies have accounted for 30 to 40 percent of farm income and they have accounted for 15 to 30 percent of the National Income attributable to agriculture for the years since 1955. The point is important because it emphasizes once again the striking gap between the economic description of society and the economic models used to account for that society's behavior.

The issue of farm price supports is related to energy in this way: first government intervention in the food system is a feature of almost all highly industrialized countries (and, despite the intervention, farm incomes still tend to lag behind national averages); and secondly, because reduction of the energy subsidy to agriculture (even if we could manage it) might reduce farmer's incomes. One reason for this state of affairs is that quantitative demand for food has definite limits and, without farm price supports, the only way to increase farm income is to increase the unit cost of agricultural products. Consumer boycotts and protests in the early 1970s suggest that there is considerable resistance to this course of action.

Government intervention in the functioning of the market for agricultural products has increased with the use of energy in agriculture and the food supply system and we have nothing but theoretical suppositions to suggest that either event could happen alone.

SOME ENERGY IMPLICATIONS FOR THE WORLD FOOD SUPPLY

The food supply system of the United States is complex and interwoven into a highly industrialized economy. We have tried to analyze this system owing to its implications for future energy use. But the world is also short of food. A few years ago it was widely predicted that the world would experience widespread famine in the 1970s. The adoption of new high-yield varieties of rice, wheat, and other grains has caused some experts to predict that the threat of these expected famines can now be averted—perhaps indefinitely. Yet, despite increases in grain production in some areas, the world still seems to be headed towards famine. The adoption of these new varieties of grain—dubbed hopefully the green revolution—is an attempt to export a part of the energy-intensive food system of the highly industrialized countries to non-industrialized countries. It is an experiment, because the whole food system is not being transplanted to new areas, but only a small part of it. The green revolution requires a great deal of energy. Many of the new grain varieties require irrigation in places where traditional crops did not, and almost all the new crops require extensive fertilization. Both irrigation and fertilization require high inputs of energy.

The agricultural surpluses of the 1950s have largely disappeared. Grain shortages in China and the U.S.S.R. have attracted attention because they have brought foreign trade across ideological barriers. There are other countries that would probably import considerable grain if they could afford it. But only four countries may be expected to have any substantial excess agricultural production: Canada, New Zealand, Australia, and the United States. None of these is in a position to give grain away, because they need the foreign trade to avert ruinous balance of payment deficits. Can we then export energy-intensive agricultural methods instead?

Energy-intensive Agriculture Abroad

It is quite clear that the United States food system cannot be exported intact at present. For example, India has a population of 550×10^6 persons. To feed the people of India at the United States level of about 3,000 kilocalories per day (instead of their present 2,000) would require more energy than India now uses for all purposes. If we wished to feed the entire world with a food system of the U.S. type almost 80 percent of the world's annual energy expenditure would be required.

The recourse most often suggested is to export only methods of increasing crop yield, and to hope for the best. We must repeat that this is an experiment. We know that our food system works (albeit with some difficulties and warnings for the future) but we do not know what will happen if we take a piece of that system and transplant it to a poor country that is lacking the industrial base of supply, transport system, processing industry, appliances for home storage and preparation, and most of all, a level of industrialization permitting higher food costs.

The energy requirements of green revolution agriculture have some important political and social implications. To the extent that the Western, highly industrialized countries must continue research and development for the new strains continually required to respond to new plant diseases and pests that can and do sweep through areas planted with a single variety (consider the recent problem with corn blight in the midwest), the Western countries will possess a hold over the developing countries. Political radicals sometimes dub this state of affairs "technological imperialism," but, whatever the name, the developing countries resent their dependence upon the vagaries of another nation's priorities. In order to avoid this source of friction the improved agriculture must be managed within the developing countries. In many of the developing countries such internal programs have begun. But establishment of anything like the agricultural extension network of the United States will require a significant expenditure of energy. Failure to establish networks of this type has, in some green revolution areas, favored the better-educated farmer against the peasants, who have little access to or knowledge of the new grain varieties. The necessity to fertilize and irrigate also favors the larger, more affluent farms—often with the result of driving more peasants off the land and into the cities, where developing nations face a difficult problem already.

Fertilizers, herbicides, pesticides and in many cases, machinery and irrigation are needed to have any hope of success with the green revolution. Where is the energy for this to come from? Many of the nations with the most serious food problem are also those with scant supplies of fossil fuels. In the industrialized nations, solutions to the energy supply problems are being sought in nuclear energy. This technology-intensive solution, even if successful in advanced countries, poses additional problems for underdeveloped nations. To create the base of industry and technologically sophisticated people within their own country will be beyond many of them. Once again they face the prospect of depending upon the good will and policies of industrialized nations. Since the alternative could be famine, their choices are not pleasant, and their irritation at their benefactors—ourselves among them—could grow to threatening proportions. It would be comfortable to rely on our own good intentions, but our good intentions have often been unresponsive to the needs of others. The matter cannot be glossed over lightly. World peace may depend upon the outcome.

Choices for the Future

Application of energy on our farms is now near 10^3 kcal/m² per year for corn,[3] and this is more or less typical of intensive agriculture in the United States. With this application of energy we have achieved yields of 2×10^3 kcal/m² per year of usable grain—bringing us to almost half of the photosynthetic limit of production. Further applications of energy are likely to yield little or no increase in the level of productivity. In any case research is not likely to improve the efficiency of the photosynthetic process itself. There is a further limitation of improvement of yield. Faith in technology and research has at times blinded us to the basic limitations of the plant and animal material with which we work. We have been able to emphasize desirable features already present in the gene pool, and to suppress others that we find undesirable. At times the cost of increased yield is the loss of desirable characteristics—hardiness, resistance to disease and adverse weather and the like. The further we get from characteristics of the original plant and animal strains, the more care—and energy—is required. Choices must be made in the directions of plant breeding. And the limitations of the plants and animals we use must be kept in mind. We have not been able to alter the photosynthetic process, or to change the gestation period of animals. In order to amplify or change an existing characteristic we will probably have to sacrifice something in the overall performance of the plant or animal. If the change requires more energy, we could end with a solution that is too expensive for people who need it most. These concerns are intensified by the degree to which energy becomes more expensive in the world market.

WHERE NEXT FOR FOOD?

Figure 6–8 shows the energy subsidy ratio to energy output for a number of widely used foods in a variety of times and cultures. For

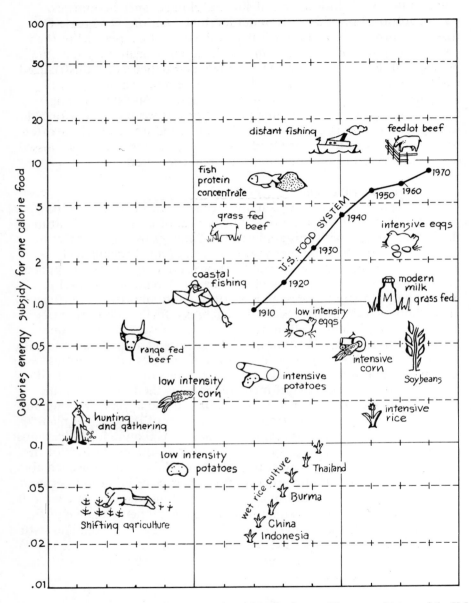

Figure 6–8. Energy subsidies for various food crops. The energy history of the U.S. food system is shown for comparison.

comparison the overall behavior of the United States food system is shown, but the comparison is only approximate because, for most of the specific crops, the energy input ends at the farm. As has been pointed out, it is a long way from the farm to the table in industrialized societies. Several things are immediately apparent, and coincide with expectations. High protein foods, such as milk, eggs, and meat, have a far poorer energy return than do plant foods. Because protein is essential for human diets, and because the amino acid balance necessary for good nutrition is not found in most cereal grains, we cannot abandon meat sources altogether. Figure 6–8 indicates how unlikely it is that increased fishing or production of fish protein concentrate will solve the world's food problems. Even if we leave aside the question of whether the fish are available—a point on which expert opinions differ—it would be hard to imagine, with rising energy prices, that fish protein concentrate will be anything more than a by-product of the fishing industry, for it requires more than twice the energy of production of grass-fed beef or eggs. Distant fishing is still less likely to solve food problems. On the other hand, coastal fishing is relatively low in energy cost. Unfortunately, however, coastal fisheries are threatened with overfishing as well as pollution.

The position of soybeans may be crucial in figure 6–8. Soybeans possess the best amino acid balance and protein content of any widely grown crop. This has long been known to the Japanese, who have made soybeans a staple of their diet, and to beef feedlot operators. Are there other plants, possibly better suited for local climates, which have adequate proportions of amino acids in their proteins? There are about 80,000 edible species of plants, of which only about 50 are actively cultivated on a large scale (and 90 percent of the world's crops come from only 12 species). We may yet be able to find species that can help the world's food supply.

The message of figure 6–8 is simple. In primitive cultures, 5 to 50 calories of food were obtained for each calorie invested. Some highly civilized cultures have done as well and occasionally better. In sharp contrast, industrialized food production requires an input of 5 to 10 calories of fuel to obtain 1 calorie of food. We must pay attention to this difference—especially if energy costs increase. If some of the energy subsidy for food production could be supplied on-site, with renewable sources—primarily sun and wind—we might be able to provide an energy subsidy. Otherwise the choices appear to be less energy-intensive food production or famine for many areas of the world.

Energy Reduction in Agriculture

It is possible to reduce the amount of energy required for agriculture and the food system. A series of thoughtful proposals by

Pimentel and associates deserve wide attention.[3] Many of these proposals mitigate environmental problems, and any reductions in energy
use provide direct reduction of the pollutants due to fuel consumption
as well as more time to solve our energy supply problems. Among the
suggestions made by Pimentel and associates are the following.

First, we should use natural manures. The United States has a
pollution problem from runoff from animal feedlots, and yet we apply
large amounts of manufactured fertilizer to fields. More than one
million kcal per acre could be saved by substituting manure for manufactured fertilizer (and as a side benefit, the condition of the soil would
be improved). Widespread use of natural manure will require decentralization of feedlot operations so that manure is generated closer to the
point of application. Decentralization would increase feedlot costs, but
if energy prices rise, feedlot operations will rapidly become more expensive in any case. Crop rotation is less widely practiced that it was even
twenty years ago. Increased use of crop rotation or interplanting winter
cover crops of legumes (which fix nitrogen as a green manure) saves 1.5
million kcal per acre compared to commercial fertilizer.

Second, weed and pest control could be accomplished at a much
smaller cost in energy. A 10 percent saving of energy in weed control
could be obtained by using the rotary hoe twice in cultivation instead
of using herbicides (again with pollution abatement as a side benefit).
Biologic pest control—that is, the use of sterile males, introduced predators and the like—requires only a tiny fraction of the energy needed for
pesticide manufacture and application. A change to a policy of "treat
when and where necessary" in pesticide application would bring a 35 to
50 percent reduction in pesticide use. Hand application of pesticides
requires more labor than machine or aircraft application, but the
reduction of energy is from 18,000 kcal per acre to 300 kcal per acre.
Changed cosmetic standards, which in no way affect the taste or edibil-
ity of food stuffs, could also bring about a substantial reduction in
pesticide use.

Third, the directions in plant breeding might emphasize hardiness, disease and pest resistance, reduced moisture content (to end the
wasteful use of natural gas in drying crops), reduced water requirements,
and increased protein content—even if it means some reduction in
overall yield. In the longer run, plants not now widely cultivated might
receive some serious attention and breeding efforts.

The direct use of solar energy on farms, a return to wind power
(using the modern windmills now in use in Australia), and the production of methane from manure are all possibilities. These methods
require some engineering to be economically attractive, but it should be
emphasized that these technologies are now better understood than is
the technology of breeder reactors. If energy prices rise, these methods

of energy generation would be attractive alternatives even at present costs of implementation.

Energy Reduction in the U.S. Food System

Beyond the farm, but still far short of the table, many more energy savings could be introduced. The most effective way to reduce the large energy requirements of food processing would be a change in eating habits towards less highly processed foods. The current dissatisfaction with many processed foods from "marshmallow" bread to hydrogenated peanut butter could presage such a change, if it is more than just a fad. Technological changes could reduce energy consumption on an industry by industry basis but the most effective way to encourage the adoption of methods using less energy would be to increase the cost of energy. Such price increases almost certainly await us.

Packaging has long since passed the stage of simply holding a convenient amount of food together and providing it with some minimal protection. Legislative controls may be needed in packaging to end the spiralling competition of manufacturers in amount and expense of packaging. In any case, recycling of metal containers and wider use of returnable bottles could reduce this large energy use.

The trend toward the use of trucks in food transport to the virtual exclusion of trains should be reversed. By simply reducing the direct and indirect subsidies of trucks, we might go a long way toward enabling trains to compete.

Finally, in the home we may have to ask whether the ever larger frostless refrigerators are needed, and whether the host of kitchen appliances really mean less work.

Store delivery routes, even by truck, would require only a fraction of the energy used by private autos for food shopping. Rapid transit, giving some attention to the problems of shoppers with parcels would be even more energy-efficient.

If we insist on a high energy food system, we should consider starting with coal, oil, garbage—or any other source of hydrocarbons—and producing food in factories from bacteria, fungi, and yeasts. These products could be flavored and colored appropriately for cultural tastes. Such a system would be more efficient in use of energy, solve waste problems, and permit much or all of the agricultural land to be returned to its natural state.

Energy, Prices, and Hunger

If energy prices rise—as they have already begun to do—the rise in the price of food in societies with industrialized agriculture can be expected to be even larger than the energy price increases. Slesser, in examining the case for England, suggests that a quadrupling of energy prices in the next forty years would bring about a sixfold increase in food prices.[5] Even small increases in energy costs may make it profitable to increase labor input to food production. Such a reversal of the fifty year trend toward energy-intensive agriculture would present environmental benefits as a bonus.

We have tried to show how analysis of the energy flow in the food system illustrates features of the food system that are not easily deduced from the usual economic analysis. Despite some suggestions for lower intensity food supply and some frankly speculative suggestions, it would be hard to end this chapter on a note of optimism. The world drawdown in grain stocks which began in the mid 1960s continues, and some food shortages are likely throughout the 1970s and early 1980s. Even if population control measures begin to limit world population, the rising tide of hungry people will be with us for some time.

Food is basically a net product of an ecosystem, however simplified. Food starts with a natural material, however modified later. Injections of energy (and even brains) will carry us only so far. If humankind cannot adjust its wants to the world in which it lives, there is little hope of solving the food problem for mankind. In that case the problem will solve mankind.

REFERENCES

1. *Statistical Abstract of the United States,* 1973.
2. *Historical Statistics of the United States* (Washington, D.C., 1960).
3. D. Pimentel et al., "Food Production and the Energy Crisis." *Science* 182 (1973): 443–449.
4. N. Georgescu-Roegen, *The Entropy Law and the Economic Process* (Cambridge, Mass.: Harvard University Press, 1971), 301.
5. M. Slesser, "How Many Can We Feed?," *The Ecologist* 3 (1973): 216–220.

SUGGESTED READING

Hirst, E. *Energy Use for Food.* Oak Ridge National Laboratory report ONRL–NSF–EP–57, 1973.
Kormondy, E. *Concepts of Ecology.* Englewood Cliffs, N.J.: Prentice-Hall, Inc., 1967.
Odum, H.T.: *Environment, Power, and Society.* New York: Wiley-Interscience, 1971.
Slesser, M. "How Many Can We Feed?" *The Ecologist* 3 (1973) 216–220.
Rappaport, R. A. "The Flow of Energy in an Agricultural Society." *Scientific American* 224, 3 (1971): 116–133.

PART II

Energy Resources and Their Use

CHAPTER 7

The Fossil Fuels

The time has come to inquire seriously what will happen when our forests are gone, when the coal, the oil, and the gas are exhausted.

Theodore Roosevelt, 1908

Industrial civilization depends on the continuous availability of work and power supplied by machines, which in turn require a constant supply of energy. Since the invention of the steam engine, most of this energy has been obtained by the burning of fuel. Energy and fuel are so nearly synonymous in our thinking that we are dismayed by the prospect of switching to new types of energy for industrial and domestic use. We cannot take for granted a comfortable future based on nuclear fission, nuclear fusion, or solar energy because we have not yet mastered these technologies; and unless we master them before the fires of our fuel-based culture die out we will never do it.

When the history of man is complete at some unknown date in the unknowable future, the period in which he burned the fossil fuels will be a brief chapter.

After two million years on this planet, man discovered first "sea coales," then oil shale (the "rocks that burn") and petroleum. Then, in an unbridled spree, he dug up the earth wide and deep and, within 1500 years, burned all that he could extract. The place of the fossil fuels in man's cultural history is illustrated in figure 7–1.

The fossil fuels include the petroleum family of hydrocarbons classified as crude oil, natural gas, and tar sands, and also coal, lignite, and a related material known as oil shale. We will look at these individually, considering the changing pattern of relationships among them.

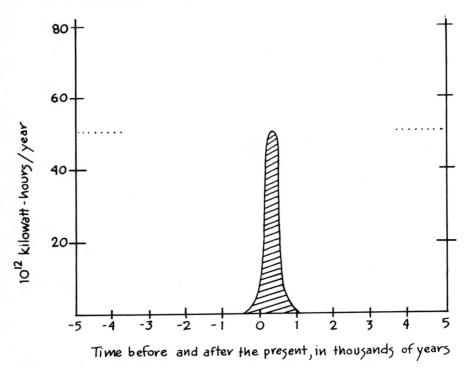

Figure 7-1. The period of exploitation of the fossil fuels, in the time frame of human history. (Redrawn, by permission, from M. K. Hubbert, "Energy Resources" in *Resources and Man,* National Academy of Sciences-National Research Council (San Francisco: W. H. Freeman and Co., 1969), p. 206.)

PETROLEUM—ORIGIN AND NATURE

Half a billion years ago, when the continents were still bleak and lifeless expanses of rock, the oceans already teemed with life. Plants were simple, although some of them reached great size, for their watery home did not evoke the range of chemical and structural adaptations that future land plants would devise. Representatives of all major groups of animals except the vertebrates were present; but even then, there was something that would eventually become a fish. Marine life, then as now, was most abundant in shallow seas and coastal waters, where light could penetrate to support photosynthesis and thus provide food for non-photosynthetic creatures.

Half a billion years ago, anaerobic microorganisms inhabited the stagnant ooze that collected in hollows on the sea floor. These organisms were probably evolution's refugees from a pre-photosynthetic past, when free oxygen was absent from the earth. They needed oxygen to maintain their metabolic fires and they got it by extracting it from organic molecules. Plants and animals lived and died in oxygenated waters and their corpses settled into the bottom mud, where anaerobic decomposers fed on them. A residue of hydrocarbon molecules (compounds of hydrogen and carbon) was left behind. The process was slow and energetically inefficient, but time is plentiful in earth history. Continuing accumulation of sediments increased the temperature and pressure in layers below, causing further molecular rearrangements to give a medley of straight-chain, branched-chain, and ring-shaped molecules. Thus time, microbial action, heat, and pressure changed cast-off parts of organic molecules to petroleum—one of the most complex natural mixtures to be found on earth.

Although the oldest known petroleum was formed at least half a billion years ago, most of the commercially valuable deposits are less than half that old. Early stages of petroleum formation are still in progress in the Black Sea and the Gulf of Mexico, where studies of bottom sediments show that the first recognizable stages of conversion of organic sediments into oil require 3000 to 9000 years.

The sediments where petroleum is formed contain a high proportion of sea water, in which droplets of petroleum are dispersed. With time, these sediments are buried under further layers of mud and organic matter. As the rocks become consolidated, the liquid migrates outward and upward in response to movements of the earth or variations in pressure from above. Eventually, the petroleum separates from the water, either rising higher by virtue of its lower density, or being held back because of its greater viscosity. Thus petroleum leaves the rocks in which it was formed and moves through porous formations until its further progress is blocked by a roof of impervious rock. There it collects in "oil pools," which are not pools at all but rocks whose pores are filled with oil instead of groundwater (figure 7–2).

Constituents of petroleum range from tarry and waxy compounds with molecular weights of 300 or more and boiling points well above 500° C to methane with a molecular weight of 16. They also include variable amounts of molecules containing oxygen, nitrogen, and sulfur.

The lighter molecules like methane are gases under usual conditions of temperature and pressure. If more gas is present than the liquid petroleum can hold in solution, it bubbles to the top and forms a gas cap over the oil pool (figure 7–2). The gas, oil, and underlying groundwater are often under high pressure. This pressure is one cause of oil well gushers or blowouts, which were romanticized in the past by Hollywood but which today spell tragedy. In a properly controlled well, the natural pressure aids in the removal of oil or gas. Today, drilling and

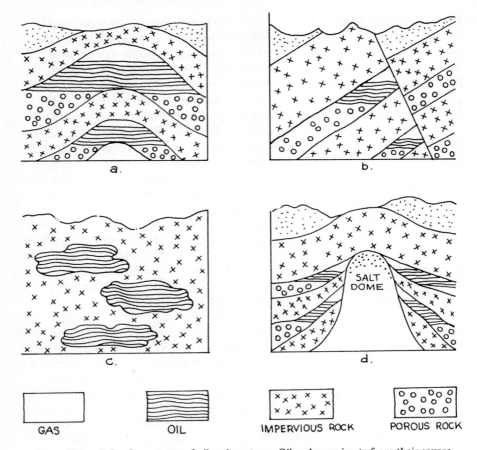

GAS   OIL   IMPERVIOUS ROCK   POROUS ROCK

Figure 7-2. Some types of oil and gas traps. Oil and gas migrate from their source into porous or fissured reservoir rocks, where they rise until the structure provides a trap to impede further progress. Here they form "oil pools" and "gas caps."
a, Oil and gas collected in alternating layers of porous and impermeable rock.
b, Oil and gas trapped where tilted reservoir rocks are cut off by a fault.
c, Oil pools in lenticular bands of porous rock which pass into impervious rock.
d, Oil and gas trapped at the boundary of a salt dome. Other buried structures can also form this type of trap.

production of an oil field are carefully planned to take advantage of the reservoir pressure.

Wherever a crack in the impermeable cover of an oil or gas reservoir provides a passage for escape, oil or gas will escape. Furthermore, if, through erosion or another process, covering rocks are stripped away, the pressurized petroleum may force its own passageway through the roof of rock. Natural seeps of oil and gas and surface deposits of asphalt (the tarry residue left behind after volatile constituents evaporate) have been known since prehistoric times. Along the coast of the Caspian Sea, blazing jets of escaping natural gas were worshipped by ancient fire worshippers. Perhaps the fiery furnace into which King Nebuchadnezzar was wont to toss people was a burning seepage of natural gas, for the "Eternal Fires" of Mesopotamia were a curiosity in biblical times as they are today. The Egyptians used material from natural petroleum seeps for the preparation of mummies; the Greeks used it for weapons. More than 5000 years ago, the Sumerians drove their chariots over roads paved with asphalt. In the Middle East and on the Pacific coast of America, ancient peoples used asphalt to caulk their boats. And although the 21-meter (69-foot) hole dug by Colonel Edwin Drake in 1859 is heralded as the first oil well, the Burmese had been collecting oil from surface exudations and shallow hand-dug wells for centuries. So although widespread use of petroleum as a fuel dates back little more than 100 years, petroleum products have been important in human culture since antiquity. Our recent habit of burning this resource is considered by some people as squandering a precious material that has many more vital uses.

Oil Production: History and Projections for the Future

As layers of rock formed while the continents rose from the seas only to be submerged, rise, and be submerged again, and as areas of the solid earth cracked, buckled, and slid across one another, potential oil and gas traps became arranged in stacks (figure 7–2). Eventually oil migrated to these traps, each pool constrained beneath its impenetrable roof of caprock. The story of oil production is largely the story of success in tapping deeper pools by drilling to greater and greater depths, from that first well of 21 meters (69 feet) to modern wells that pierce the earth to a depth of 8 kilometers (5 miles) or more.

While basic drilling technology has changed relatively little, discovery of oil and gas fields has become an increasingly complicated venture, requiring the skills of geologists and geophysicists as well as engineers. The first oil fields were discovered by chance or by digging in the vicinity of natural seeps. The modern oil industry began in 1848, when drillers searching for water struck oil instead. Then Drake decided to drill for oil on purpose. After much difficulty in mustering and maintaining support for his project, he finally achieved his goal. Soon, "wildcatters" were sinking wells at sites chosen merely on a hunch. A few of these paid off fabulously, but most yielded nothing. As early as 1855, however, geologists were pointing out the tendency of oil pools to occur in certain types of geological structures. The rational search for oil then became the search for potential oil traps. Today, teams of earth scientists employ geologic, seismic, magnetic, gravitational, and electrical techniques to dog oil into its last hideouts: the bottom of the sea, the hostile desert, and the forbidding subpolar regions.

The quest for oil was originally sparked by a growing scarcity of whale oil and other illuminants. It was the kerosene fraction that was in demand, although there was a small market for lubricating oils and oil for medicinal purposes. The infant petroleum industry mounted a sustained effort to find and create new markets for other refinery products. The story of petroleum in nineteenth century America is a story of vast overproduction, profligate waste, falling prices, and a frantic struggle to stimulate new uses for a product that could hardly be given away. With the advent of electric lighting, the situation for petroleum would have been grim indeed had it not been for three circumstances: the demonstration that oil could fire a boiler as well as coal, the shift of oil production to California, Texas, and Oklahoma, where coal was scarce and expensive, and the rise of the automobile.

By 1910, fuel oil was the number one refinery product and the production of kerosene was falling rapidly. By the end of World War I, fuel oil had made heavy inroads into the coal market in manufacturing, shipping, and railroads. Then came a rapid expansion of oil for domestic use and for the generation of electricity. During World War I, the demand for gasoline began to increase even more rapidly than the demand for fuel oil, as Americans began their love affair with the internal combustion engine. In the late 1920s, gasoline gained first place among refinery products and has been there ever since. Figure 7–3 shows the changing proportions of major petroleum products used since 1880.

Production of crude oil in the United States and in the world is growing exponentially. Although we know that exponential growth cannot continue indefinitely, planners tend to confuse the projection of a growth curve with a prediction, and the prediction becomes a self-fulfilling prophecy. Predictions of the demand for oil for 1980 and 2000 are running headlong into predictions of chronic shortages.

Oil Reserves

There is confusion about the magnitude of our oil reserves, stemming from misunderstanding of the word reserves. Proved reserves of oil (or of any depletable resource) are the amounts proved by exploration to exist and known to be recoverable by methods that are technically and economically feasible. For economic reasons, the rate of oil exploration is geared to the rate of production. So when we are told that our proved reserves will last for 20 years at current rates of consumption, this does not mean that we will run out of oil in 20 years. Because the word reserves has been interpreted in this way, however, we have become complacent because new discoveries always come along to shove the day of reckoning well into the future. The ceiling we face is not the current value of proved reserves but the total (unknown but finite) amount of recoverable oil that exists.

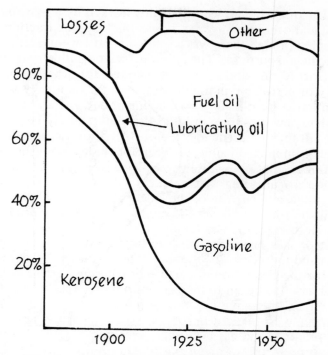

Figure 7-3. Changing proportions of major petroleum products. (Adapted from H. Landsberg and S. Schurr, *Energy in the United States: Sources, Uses, and Policy Issues* (New York: Random House, 1963), p. 40.)

While others are squabbling about numbers and the significance of new discoveries and technologies, let us take an analytical look at trends in the oil industry. In the 48 contiguous states of the United States, we may already have reached the peak of oil production. Although the untapped resources of Alaska might postpone the peak for the country as a whole, the main effect of Alaskan oil will probably be to retard the rate of decline of production. The world's peak production may be expected at some time around the turn of the century. The industry must come to terms with these facts, because in every aspect it has been geared to an annual increase in production of at least 5 percent. The situation for an industry which must count on phasing itself out at that rate is entirely different.

In the face of many unknowns, including the absolute amount of oil, future political and economic conditions, and unforeseen breakthroughs in technology, M. King Hubbert describes the situation for oil in the following way.[1] The amount of an exhaustible resource that is ultimately produced cannot exceed the amount initially present, and every drop that is withdrawn decreases the amount that remains. With the

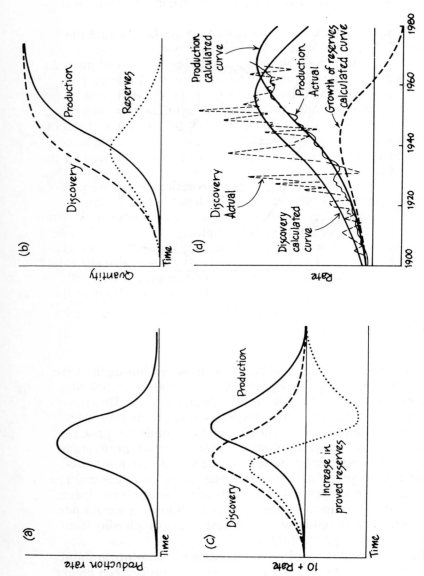

Figure 7–4. Relationships between discovery, production, and reserves of a depletable resource.

a, Theoretical production rate as a function of time.

b, Cumulative quantities discovered, produced, and identified as reserves.

c, The relationship between rates of production, discovery, and addition to reserves as a function of time.

d, Actual discovery and production rates plotted against the theoretical curves.

(Redrawn, by permission, from M. K. Hubbert, "Energy Resources," in *Resources and Man,* National Academy of Sciences-National Research Council (San Francisco: W. H. Freeman and Co., 1969), pp. 168, 172, 173, 178.)

inevitable peaks and valleys smoothed out, the production of an exhaustible resource is described by the curve in figure 7–4, *a*. This is a normal
growth curve, in which each increment of growth is determined partly
by the current rate of growth and partly by the ultimate size that will
be reached.

The cumulative amount of production always lags behind the
cumulative amount of discovery, which is a fancy way of saying you
have to find the oil before you can pump it out. The amount of proved
reserves follows a course determined by the relationship between production and discovery. Cumulative discovery and production tend
toward the same maximum value (assuming that all the discovered oil
is produced), and reserves fall to zero (figure 7–4, *b*). The rates of discovery and production first increase, then decrease, until they reach zero,
as shown in figure 7–4, *c*. This figure also shows the path followed by the
change of proved reserves.

The curves in figures 7–4, *a, b, c* are theoretical, but if we plot
actual data on graphs like these, the correspondence between theory
and experience is striking (figure 7–4, *d*). One more example will illustrate
the ephemeral nature of our oil binge. The typical growth rate of crude
oil production in the continental United States exclusive of Alaska has
been 5.86 percent per year. Using the best current estimates of the total
amount of oil available and assuming that the rate of production will
follow the normal type of curve shown in figure 7–4, *a*, we discover that
80 percent of America's oil will be produced during the 65-year period
between 1934 and 1999.[1]

Future Changes
The future will see increased emphasis on more complete recovery of oil from oil fields. In the past, with the pump alone, as much as
three-quarters of the oil has been left in the ground. With fluid injection, solvent injection, and fracturing techniques, the amount of recoverable oil has reached 40 percent. Some improvement in this figure is
probable. The future will also see increased production of oil offshore,
from the continental shelves. However, such developments will not
change the overall picture. Hubbert's critics say he does not allow for
the unpredictability of the future. But the production of oil and other
fuels appears to be following a typical growth curve despite the considerable social and technological changes that have already occurred. We
could alter the course of production intentionally, but we don't seem
to be planning to do it. As for errors in estimates of recoverable oil, we
found in chapter 5 that within a wide range, the numerical value of a
limit is insignificant if growth persists. If we could double our efficiency of extracting oil (unlikely) and if estimates of oil resources prove
too low by a factor of ten (very unlikely), the peak of production would

be delayed by little more than half a century. Despite impressive advances in the theory and technology of petroleum exploration, success, as measured in terms of discoveries per foot of exploratory drilling, has fallen in the last 35 years from more than 250 barrels per foot to 35. Crude oil supplies are running out.

Natural Gas and Natural Gas Liquids: History and Projections

Natural gas was a nuisance to the early oil men. They usually allowed it to escape into the atmosphere or burned it on the spot. Only a tiny fraction was salvaged for use as fuel in the immediate vicinity of the oil field.

The problem with putting natural gas to work was twofold. First, there was no known use for it that another fuel could not serve as well. Second, there was no way of delivering it from the gas field to the consumer. The oil industry would be half a century old before its offspring gas could make its own way.

In the late 1920s, development of high-pressure pipe, improved welding techniques, and power equipment for laying pipe made possible the transport of gas at reasonable cost. Meanwhile, because gas and oil often occur together, the gas industry found itself in the strange position of seeing the amount of its product increase automatically as oil production increased, while its market possibilities dwindled correspondingly. As a result, the price of gas remained very low despite relatively high transportation costs, and it is still artificially low today.

Gradually, the advantages of gas as a fuel became apparent. It was a clean fuel, just as the commercials said. It required no storage bins or tanks, but could be piped in as needed, like water. It was burned in simple, inexpensive, almost maintenance-free furnaces. With the growing demand for gas as fuel, its only other major use, for the production of carbon black, declined sharply. Today, natural gas is the most sought-after member of the petroleum family for home and industrial heating and electric power generation. The gas that cooks a roast in New York may have come virtually nonstop through pipelines from Texas. Only parts of New England, lacking the lure of a large market, are beyond the range of gas.

The natural gas of commerce is methane (CH_4), first member of the paraffin series of hydrocarbons whose general formula is C_nH_{2n+2}. As byproducts of the production of natural gas, other paraffins are extracted. Collectively, these are known as natural gas liquids. A fraction of this mixture, composed primarily of propane (C_3H_8) and butane (C_4H_{10}), is marketed as bottled gas or liquefied petroleum gas for cooking and heating. The remaining heavier fraction is often added to the gasoline fraction of crude oil, which it resembles in composition.

Hubbert has also applied his methods of analysis to the production of natural gas and natural gas liquids.[1] Again, rather than looking

at the statistics of production, we will consider the more fundamental
question of how far along its path from birth to death the exploitation
of this resource has progressed. Figure 7–5 summarizes the story for gas.
Although the numbers are different, production of natural gas liquids
follows the same course. As in the case of oil, we see that 80 percent of
America's resources will be used up in 65 years, the period between
1950 and 2015. Less than a human lifetime. The peak of production
may be expected somewhere around 1980; the peak of discovery has
already passed. New discoveries are not keeping pace with the growing
demand. In the past decade, what was a 20-year reserve has plummeted
to an uncomfortable 12-year reserve, excluding the resources of Alaska.

Worldwide, the use of natural gas has been hampered by the
same transport problems that plagued the United States half a century
ago. The wasteful flaring of gas at its source has continued until today,
although three recent trends promise to end the waste: an increase in
electrical power-generating facilities and gas-consuming industries near
sites of gas production, the building of pipelines, and the construction
of special tankers for transport of gas in liquid form at low temperatures.

Figure 7-5. Cycle of natural gas production in the United States. (Redrawn, by
permission, from M. K. Hubbert, "Energy Resources" in *Resources and Man,* National
Academy of Sciences-National Research Council (San Francisco: W. H. Freeman and
Co., 1969), p. 190.)

Tar Sands: Nature and Outlook

Tar sands are reservoirs of a heavy type of petroleum, still a liquid, but too viscous to be extracted by conventional pumping. The geological history and chemical nature of this material are similar to those of crude oil. It can be processed with minor modifications in current refining equipment and techniques, but its physical properties create stubborn problems in its recovery from the earth. For this reason, known deposits have only recently been exploited, and so far on a tentative basis. For this reason too, there has been little effort to conduct a world survey of tar sand resources. They represent an enormous potential supply of energy, however. The tar sands of western Canada, which are the best known deposits of their kind, may hold almost twice as much oil as was originally contained in the conventional crude oil deposits of the continental United States.

With present technology, the oil-bearing rock must be mined much as coal is mined. The people who live in the province of Alberta may object to having more than 40,000 square kilometers (16,000 square miles) of their land dug up, chewed, and spit back. They may object even more to having it done to run the motor boats and air conditioners of their neighbors to the south. The mining has begun. Since 1967, oil from the Athabasca tar sands has been trickling into the United States. So far the amounts are negligible. Total production is about 50,000 barrels per day, only 0.3 percent of the 14.7 million barrels consumed daily in the United States. But the industry plans to push ahead until a maximum production rate is reached in the 1990s.

Development of methods for extracting hydrocarbons from tar sands while leaving the rock in place is almost certain. One promising method is to inject steam into the rock and drive out the hydrocarbons in a steam emulsion. However, about 17 percent of the fuel obtained in this way is needed to produce the steam used in producing the fuel. Another method is underground burning, with air injected at one well to support combustion and drive hydrocarbon vapors toward another well, the producing well. This technology will probably improve, if there is incentive. North America needs oil now, and to that end, a quarter of a million tons of Alberta's soil and rock are dug up each day to produce a paltry 50,000 barrels of oil.

COAL AND OIL SHALE

Origin

Between 440 and 400 million years ago, plants began tentatively to invade the land. They were simple at first. Very few of their direct descendants survive today. But they were successful pioneers, modifying land and atmosphere and preparing the way for the lush growth to come.

There was a period of mountain building when the seas shrank and continents became dry. The first amphibians ventured ashore. Then the seas came back, spreading over much of the continents and creating vast areas of warm, swampy lowlands. It was about 345 million years ago, the beginning of the great fern forests, the time of the first seed plants, and the start of the greatest period of coal formation the world has known (figure 7–6).

Psilopsida, Lycopsida, Sphenopsida. These are strange names of strange plants of that time. They have either become extinct or been so greatly diminished in size and number that you may never have noticed them. There is the whisk fern, not a fern at all but one of three remaining species of Psilopsida and the only one in North America. And the little club mosses (not real mosses) that represent what once was a large and diverse group, the Lycopsida. Of the Sphenopsida, only horsetails, *Equisetum,* remain to remind us of giant plants that once grew 15 meters (50 feet) tall in bamboo-like groves. Evolution has been kinder to the ferns, although the ferns of today are only a faded memory of the past. Enormous cycads, first plants to produce seeds, once flourished—then vanished, leaving their chapter in the earth's diary of rock.

In the warm, humid climate of the coal swamps and forests, plant growth far exceeded losses to predation and decay. Plant material falling into stagnant swamps underwent partial decay probably resembling the process of humification that goes on today. During humifica-

Figure 7–6. Reconstruction of a prehistoric coal forest. (Photograph of a diarama, courtesy of Field Museum of Natural History, Chicago, Ill.)

tion, gases, chiefly carbon dioxide and methane, are driven off and water is removed from organic molecules, leaving a residue that is enriched in carbon. This dark brown, jelly-like humus soaks into less destructible fragments of woody tissue, often preserving details of cellular structure with great clarity. Humified material and other plant remains collect to form peat. The deposits continue to be gradually enriched in carbon, as more methane, (in this context known as marsh gas) is driven off. Burning methane, its pale ghostly flames flickering over a bog, is known as the "will-o'-the-wisp."

Peat forms in swampy lowlands and water-logged uplands, in cool humid regions where temperature inhibits decay and tropical swamps where plant growth outdistances decay. Shallow lakes in glaciated areas, flood plains, and deltas are often converted to peat bogs in the normal course of ecological succession. Study of borings made through the delta of the Ganges River reveals a sequence of layers of peat, sand, and clay, indicating repeated uplifting and subsidence of the land. These conditions are thought to resemble the climates and geographic conditions under which the great coal seams of the past were formed (figure 7–7).

The pressure of accumulating sediments and the accompanying increase in temperature drive off more and more water and gases from the peat. When almost nothing but carbon remains, about 100 centimeters of peat has been compacted into less than 10 centimeters of coal. Fossilized spores, pollen, and other plant structures remain to reveal the essential nature of coal. Unlike petroleum, coal gave away the secret of its origin many years ago.

The type of plant residue (predominantly trees or predominantly algae, for example) determines the type of coal, while the stage of chemical alteration determines its rank. The rank of a coal is correlated with the maximum depth of sediment under which it was buried. A high rank anthracite may once have been buried under 5½ kilometers (3½ miles) of sediments.

Coal of lowest rank, most like peat, is called lignite. It is often of relatively recent origin, less than 150 million years of age. Next comes bituminous coal from 300 million years ago. Then anthracite, coal of the highest rank, hard and brittle, burning with a hot and smokeless flame.

Special types of coal contain less carbon than normal coals of corresponding rank but are richer in hydrogen. Some of them, when ground and heated to around 500° C (900° F), yield a mixture of hydrocarbons resembling petroleum. These are the oil shales, toward which an oil-hungry world is casting greedy glances. Oil shale, a finely textured sedimentary rock (not necessarily a shale), also differs from normal coal in containing a very large amount of inorganic matter. The

Figure 7-7. Coal seam minable by strip mining methods. (Courtesy of Eugene Cameron)

organic portion is derived primarily from pollen, spores, and algae, unlike that of normal coals which originate from leafy and woody plant material. Although oil shale usually accumulates at the bottom of shallow lakes, some of it is of marine origin. The oldest known oil shales are 600 million years old.

History and Outlook for the Future

English monks of the ninth century gathered "sea coales" from rocky shores to burn for cooking and comfort. Within a few centuries, coal mines were scattered over Europe, for fuel wood had grown scarce. Oil shale, too, was first burned in Europe during the Middle Ages. In the nineteenth century, small oil shale refineries produced candle wax, kerosene, lubricants, and gas, using techniques that later would be applied to the refining of petroleum.

In America, feverish expansion had caused such depletion of fuel wood that by 1850, shortages of wood gave impetus to the coal and oil shale industries. Drake's oil well put an abrupt end to exploitation of oil shale, but the use of coal continued to grow. Coal rapidly became the primary fuel for industry and transportation, while wood continued to supply domestic needs. Then, in the first part of this century, coal took over the domestic scene as well. Since World War I, the use of coal has increased with our growing production of electricity. The iron and steel industry continues to require large amounts of coking coal.

The 1920s saw the beginning of the switch from coal to fuel oil for residential heating and industrial use. The rise of the automobile and the conversion of railroads to diesel engines after World War II switched the transportation market from coal to oil. An expanding network of high pressure gas transmission lines enabled gas to steal what remained of coal's residential and commercial markets and to make inroads on the oil market itself. At present, except for its role in the iron and steel industry, the use of coal is almost completely tied to the electrical utilities. The situation is tense, for air and water quality standards and shortages of low-sulfur coal have caused power companies to seek oil, gas, or nuclear fuel for their new installations. Figure 7–8 shows the changing pattern of coal use between 1920 and 1970. The overall trend in fuels from wood to coal to oil to gas to, perhaps, nuclear is shown in figure 7–9.

To the business mind, environmental and mine safety legislation has cramped the coal industry unbearably. Low-sulfur coal is mined primarily in the southern Appalachian bituminous fields and the northern Rocky Mountain sub-bituminous and lignite fields. With the major use of eastern coal having been until now for manufacture of metallurgical coke, most of this coal is already owned by or contracted to steel producers at prices about twice as high as utility coal brings. New mines are needed, but environmental concerns interfere, while coal men warn that construction of a new mine requires between two and five years plus a large initial investment, an assurance of at least a 20-year supply of recoverable coal, and usually a long term purchase agreement.

The longer term outlook for coal is brighter than the immediate stalemate implies, if we can decrease the occupational and environmental hazards of mining. Coal's possibilities as a raw material seem limited mainly by man's ingenuity. Long after the last oil and gas wells have been sealed shut, liquefaction and gasification of coal may provide the petroleum products to which we are now accustomed. Coal will be the raw material for an ever more diverse petrochemical industry, and through microbiological and industrial processes it may even be converted to food. In view of these possibilities it seems very strange that the major portion of federal funds for energy research (86 percent in fiscal year 1970) is devoted to nuclear fission and fusion, while coal scrambles with a host of other contenders for its share of the rest.

Figure 7-8. Trends in the use of coal, 1920–1970.

Synthetic Fuels From Coal

Pollution from our present uses of coal may never be controllable. Liquid and gaseous fuels are more versatile than coal, which is why
they were able to steal its market. For these reasons, conversion of coal
to other fuels looms importantly ahead (Appendix E). It is thought that
the conversion process will cause only minor pollution, and the resulting
fuels will be clean. However, production of synthetic fuels from coal
will increase destruction of land surfaces through mining and hasten the
depletion of coal resources—facts which are often overlooked in projections of coal supply and use.

During the nineteenth century, "coal gas" or "town gas," a
byproduct of the coking industry, was widely used in Europe and
America for cooking and heating. The gas was a mixture of carbon
monoxide, carbon dioxide, hydrogen, methane, and minor constituents.
The production and use of town gas, however, has little relationship to
modern processes for making synthetic fuels.

During World War I, Germany made aviation gasoline by hydrogenation of coal. Today, South Africa produces most of her gasoline
and some other petroleum products from coal. The South African plant
liquefies about 2000 tons of coal per day, consuming an additional

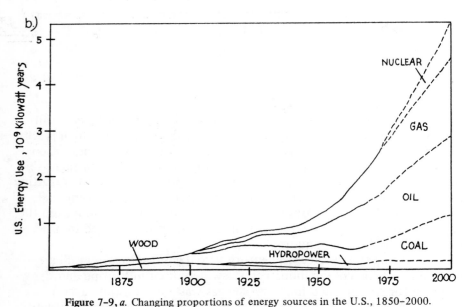

Figure 7-9, *a*. Changing proportions of energy sources in the U.S., 1850–2000. (Adapted from H. Landsberg and S. Schurr, *Energy in the United States: Sources, Uses, and Policy Issues* (New York: Random House, 1963), p. 30.)

Figure 7-9, *b*. Changing energy sources and growth in energy use in the U.S., 1850–2000. (Adapted from C. Starr, "Energy and Power," *Scientific American* 224, 3 (1971): 39.)

2400 tons to run the process. The main products are 3660 barrels of gasoline and 370 barrels of diesel fuel. Synthetic gasoline is too expensive to compete with the natural product in the United States, but improved technology and the uncertain future of petroleum imports and production could change the picture. At the moment, several schemes for liquefaction of coal are at or near the pilot plant stage in this country, but are stymied for lack of funds.

Rising prices for natural gas and improved gasification techniques could make gas derived from coal competitive in price with natural gas before the end of the 1970s. Several processes for conversion of coal to gas are under consideration or have already reached the pilot plant stage. The resulting gas may be almost pure methane, suitable for transmission through pipelines, or it may be a mixture of compounds having less potential energy but well suited for the generation of electricity at the site of production.

The net chemistry of coal-to-gas conversion is a reaction of carbon (coal) with hydrogen to form methane. The usual commercial source of hydrogen is natural gas. It would be absurd to produce hydrogen from natural gas for reacting with coal to produce a substitute for natural gas. But where will the hydrogen come from? For many laboratory and pilot experiments, it has in fact come from natural gas. But there is a more abundant source at hand: water. When finely ground, hot coal reacts with steam, and a mixture containing carbon monoxide, carbon dioxide, methane, hydrogen, and unreacted water results. The proportions of the various gases depend on the temperature and pressue under which the reaction is carried out. This mixture is then cleaned and perhaps further converted to methane, depending on whether it is to be transported by pipeline or burned on site. However it is accomplished, gasification of coal requires energy. In one process, about two-thirds of the coal is gasified while the remaining third becomes char, which is burned to generate steam for further gasification.

With technology as it was in 1971, the cost of synthetic methane would have been about twice the cost of natural gas.[2] An equivalent amount of energy in the form of synthetic oil would have cost about three-quarters as much as synthetic gas, or 30 percent more than natural crude oil. The estimates for synthetic gas are probably more realistic than those for oil, partly because the technology is further along and partly because estimates for synthetic oil are spurred by a competitive desire to have the number come out favorably. In any case, the numbers given are very rough. Unforeseen improvements in technology can be nullified by unforeseen problems; and relative costs are subject to extreme fluctuation as a result of political action here and abroad—changes in oil import policies or pollution standards, for example.

As for oil shale, there are still knotty problems, only some of them technical. There are a host of pre-existing mineral claims on prime oil shale lands in America, some of them more than 50 years old. Legal questions may occupy the courts for so long that they may constitute the main hope of conservationists who want to delay large-scale production of oil shale. If we tried to exploit everything at once in these rocks, which also contain valuable sodium and aluminum minerals, the major portion of oil from the shale could be consumed on the spot to provide energy for the other mining operations—hardly a solution to the nation's energy problems.

So far, technical problems and abundant cheap petroleum have thwarted growth of an oil shale industry in America, but the planning has gone on even though actual mining has not. When our petroleum resources are near exhaustion or when foreign oil becomes unavailable or too expensive, large-scale production of oil shale will probably begin. Already, large industries operate in the U.S.S.R. and mainland China, and there are plans for development in Brazil. A prototype leasing and development program in the Green River Formation of Colorado, Utah, and Wyoming is imminent. It is only a prototype program, but if government and industry did not have intentions of pursuing it further, it would not be undertaken.

Coal and Oil Shale Reserves

We can gauge coal resources with more certainty than petroleum, which often lies well-hidden or deep within the earth. The proof of an oil deposit is in a producing oil well. Even exploratory drilling can give, at best, only a rough indication of how much petroleum may eventually be recovered. Coal, in contrast, is usually found close to the surface. The stratified deposits are continuous over large areas and frequently are visible as outcrops at the surface, thus facilitating accurate surface mapping with the help of only a few widely spaced drill holes. Taking minable coal to be 50 percent of the coal in seams a minimum of 30 centimeters (12 inches) thick, extending to a depth of 1200 meters (4000 feet) or in some cases 2000 meters, (6000 feet), a recent United States Geological Survey study[3] estimates the total original minable coal of the United States to be almost 1½ trillion metric tons, and that of the world to be 7.6 trillion metric tons. (A metric ton is 1000 kilograms, or 2200 pounds.) About half of these amounts has been established by exploration and mapping; the other half is inferred on geological evidence but has not actually been determined. In the first thousand years of coal mining, less than 10 percent of this supply has been removed from the ground. However, if present rates of increase in production continue, it will take only about 340 years to use the next 80 percent of the world's coal—the consequences, again, of exponential growth.

By all estimates, the amount of oil held in oil shale is immense. The practical potential, however, varies according to whether you are talking to an oil man, a geologist, a politician, or a conservationist. High grade, accessible oil shales in the United States, those that are at least 3 meters (10 feet) thick and contain 25 or more gallons of oil per ton of shale, might provide 80 billion barrels of oil. This is four times as much as is in Alaska's crude oil deposits, but it is only a 15-year supply at current rates of consumption in the United States. Less accessible or lower grade shales containing between 10 and 20 gallons of oil per ton could provide about 2 trillion barrels of oil, enough to keep us going for a couple of centuries at the current rate. These shales are marginally or submarginally producible under present conditions. Suspected deposits and possible extensions of known deposits might yield an additional 33 or 34 trillion barrels. By far the largest part of the oil, some 140 trillion barrels, is in "organic-rich shales," a euphemism for shales whose exploitation as fuel may forever remain economically, energetically, and environmentally impractical. Perhaps the best use of shale oil will be in the petrochemical industry, where the quantities required are insignificant compared to quantities burned as fuel, the market can bear a much higher cost for raw materials, and there is at least a theoretical opportunity for recycling. Thus shale oil may be our future source of dyes, drugs, synthetic rubber and fibers, fertilizers, paint, detergents—even food.

FUEL SHORTAGES

Our current fossil fuel shortages and those in store for the near future are often said to be caused by economic conditions and by our new-found concern for the environment rather than by actual lack of fuel. This does not make them less real. In fact, economic and environmental problems are related to the fact that our highest grade fuel supplies have been exhausted. As exploration becomes more difficult and less rewarding, as the cost of producing fuel from poorer and more deeply buried deposits increases, and as the demand for clean fuel grows, it is possible to imagine a time when, no matter how much fuel remains in the earth, it will cost more than the market will pay to produce it and more energy will be consumed in its production than can be derived by burning it. At present, 7 percent of our annual energy production (20 percent of the energy consumed by industry) is used in the extraction and refining of petroleum. Processes for gasification of coal and *in situ* extraction of hydrocarbons from tar sands require even larger amounts of energy than are currently involved in the production of petroleum.

Although we are using fossil fuels at a rate more than one hundred thousand times as fast as they can be replaced, substantial amounts remain for half a dozen human generations or so. The problem, then, is not a shortage of fuel but the problems of producing and using it. Development of a national energy policy is receiving concerted attention in the government because of the serious political, economic, and environmental problems caused by our growing rate of energy consumption.

Until World War II, the United States was a net exporter of energy, including petroleum. Since 1947–48 we have depended increasingly on foreign oil, despite efforts of the government and oil industry to restrict imports and keep the country self-sufficient in petroleum production. Now we import almost 30 percent of the petroleum we use, most of it from South and Central America, Mexico, and Canada. Although we are the largest exporter of coal in the world, the energy value of our coal exports is only about one-fourth that of our petroleum imports. Predictions for the future indicate that we will rely more heavily on foreign oil, with perhaps as much as 40 percent of it imported by 1980 or 60 percent by 1985.

Japan and western Europe are in a worse predicament than the United States, as they are industrialized areas almost totally dependent on oil imported from developing nations—although recent oil and gas discoveries in the North Sea promise to ease things for Europe.

The developing nations realized that they were being taken, for their most valuable resource, which they needed to build a better future, was being sucked away, at bargain prices, into the overdeveloped countries. The Organization of Petroleum Exporting Countries (OPEC) was formed during the 1960s to combat the economic power of the international oil companies. Since then the OPEC countries have raised the price of oil sharply. When the industrialized countries were shopping for the cheapest foreign oil concessions they called it free enterprise; when the OPEC countries demanded higher prices, some called it conspiracy.

Meanwhile, in the Congress of the United States and among leaders of finance and the energy industries, the question of foreign oil is still debated. Some claim that national security demands that we be self-sufficient, or at least able on a moment's notice to become self-sufficient, in petroleum production. Dependence on foreign oil that can be withheld suddenly on political grounds or made more expensive could cause a paralyzing energy shortage, as events in the Middle East during the last part of 1973 demonstrated. This reasoning lay behind the establishment of our controversial oil import quotas. Others claim that we are pushing the domestic production of a resource we really want to conserve, and at prices which cost the American consumer billions of dollars annually above what foreign oil would cost. We should get as much foreign oil as we can while we can, they say. And then there are those who ask quietly if it is right to demand an end to oil production in the Santa Barbara Channel and let production of gasoline for Santa Barbara's automobiles pollute the coast of Venezuela instead.

ENVIRONMENTAL PROBLEMS

Environmental degradation accompanies every stage of discovery, production, and use of fossil fuels. Some of the results of our addiction to energy are obvious: oil-smeared beaches, the wasteland of southern Appalachia, belching smokestacks, and traffic jams. Other problems are more insidious.

Discovery
Damage to the environment from exploratory activities is generally transient and negligible. Exploration in subpolar regions is an exception. The arctic already shows scars which justify alarm over the impact of future activity. Life clings precariously in the far north. Soil and even climate are easily disturbed. A few hundred species of plants (compared to thousands in the tropics), a few dozen species of higher animals, some insects, soil invertebrates, and microorganisms have adapted to the short growing seasons, low temperature, and lack of moisture. Where the ground is permanently frozen, a condition known as permafrost, the cover of vegetation provides shade and insulation which maintain the frozen state. If vegetation is disturbed, thawing occurs. Upper ground thaw kills plants and permits still more thawing. With permafrost and groundcover destroyed, erosion can be rapid and severe. Recovery could take centuries.

Prospecting in the north requires the transport of equipment and people. We have learned through our mistakes how to build roads that hold environmental disruption to a minimum, but this requires care and we are not always careful. The mere presence of people places a severe strain on the arctic environment. As one ecologist said, "You can't just bury your garbage."

Production

Coal
For more than 5000 years, man has tunneled into the earth to gain buried treasure. About 1000 years ago the mining of coal began. The pick and shovel of the coal miner, his hand drill and mule cart, were

the same as those of any other subterranean digger. There were problems with pollution of streams and groundwater and with the ugliness of the mines themselves; with long-burning underground fires and subsidence of the surface; and with sickness, injury, and death among miners. But these seemed a small price to pay for the energy that would perfect the world.

The true cost of underground mining is revealing itself today. When rock that has lain buried and undisturbed through geologic ages is broken up and exposed to air and water, chemical changes occur. Sulfide from the ubiquitous iron pyrites (fool's gold) is oxidized to sulfate and sulfuric acid. Entering the groundwater, the sulfuric acid causes "acid mine drainage." Many materials that are relatively insoluble in less acid water dissolve under the conditions of the mines. These include iron, magnesium, manganese, copper, zinc, and calcium. When the drainage from mines pollutes water supplies most aquatic plants are killed, the water can no longer support fish life, the water becomes unacceptable for recreational uses, and costs of treatment for municipal water supplies are increased.

In some densely populated areas of Pennsylvania, the land is sinking into a maze of forgotten tunnels, some of them mined out and abandoned a century ago. Expensive as subsidence control projects are, post-subsidence repair can cost up to 10 times as much. There are some sixty thousand abandoned coal mines in the United States. They can be filled, and foundations of the buildings standing upon them strengthened, but acid water problems remain. The mines can be sealed off at a cost of up to $20,000 per mine, and the water can be treated—at considerable cost and with variable success. The basic problem remains. The scale of mining forces the earth to come to a new balance, and the balance is not to our liking.

About 50 years ago, strip mining began. Powerful earth-moving machinery easily and economically scraped away surface layers of soil and rock, permitting recovery of 90 percent or more of the underlying coal. But by the 1950s the penalties for stripping became apparent, and Appalachia became the battle cry for social and environmental reformers.

Material stripped from the surface and piled to one side or pushed down a mountain invites erosion by wind and water. Sediment washed from strip-mined slopes often clogs stream channels, destroying fish habitats and subjecting adjacent land to flooding. It covers highways and settles on farmland, killing crops. Costs of water treatment for municipal and industrial supplies increase. Reclamation, especially in mountainous or agricultural areas, becomes a myth perpetrated by the public relations experts at the coal companies. In arid regions, reclamation is frankly admitted to be impossible. As in underground mining, water supplies become contaminated with acid and high concentrations of dissolved salts.

Strip mining for coal has occurred in about half of the states in the United States. It provides almost half of the coal on the United States market today. It has not yet touched Alaska, where vast coal seams lie shallowly buried. The largest earth-moving machine can chew up more than 3,000,000 cubic meters (4,000,000 cubic yards) of soil and rock in a month. It is feasible to remove surface material to a depth of 65 meters (200 feet) in order to get at a coal seam. Some 6250 square kilometers (2500 square miles) of land in the United States have already fallen to the bulldozer and power shovel, and projections indicate that by 1980 this number could reach nearly 11,000 square kilometers (4300 square miles)—the equivalent of four-fifths of the area of Connecticut. It is a mere 6 percent of the total area thought to overlie coal recoverable by stripping.

The cumulative environmental debt of coal probably exceeds $4 billion in the United States.[4] This debt will grow before it shrinks. Necessary as figures like this are, it seems absurd to give people money for the misery they have suffered and say the debt is canceled.

Tar Sands and Oil Shale

Insofar as they must be mined, the exploitation of these resources presents the same problems as the mining of coal. In addition, for oil shale, there is the problem of disposing of spent shale after processing; for the volume of waste material is greater than the volume of material originally mined. The president of Atlantic Richfield suggested filling in some of the surplus canyons and valleys in uninhabited areas of the west, but there is little applause for that idea. The first extensive production of oil shale will occur in 42,500 square kilometers (17,000 square miles) of the Rocky Mountains' Green River Formation, a dry semiwilderness region where, as in the arctic, the environmental impact of people will probably be worse than the impact of actual production. A prototype program calls for employment of 18,000 workers, accompanied by their families, automobiles, sewage systems, power plants, and so on.

Rich oil shales in northwestern Alaska promise up to five times as much oil as the Prudhoe Bay oil field just to the east. Production of this shale would pose problems of gargantuan scale and would bring environmental ruin.

Petroleum and Natural Gas

"See the Oil Wells in the Sea," beckoned an advertisement for the Southern Pacific Railroad's Los Angeles-Santa Barbara run when the first offshore wells were sunk off Summerland in the 1890s. Several famous gushers of the past have attracted attention from tourists, while more recently the Santa Barbara oil spill lured sightseers (figure 7–10). Most people, however, do not like to see oil wells.

When all goes well, drilling for oil is not particularly disruptive. The leakage from normal operations is negligible compared to the total efflux of oil into the environment. Routine offshore production accounts for only 4 or 5 percent of the oil that pollutes the sea. But there are accidents. Offshore blowouts are always potentially disastrous because coastal ecosystems are especially sensitive to oil and because it is difficult to control, contain, and clean up a spill at sea. Yet all the offshore accidents, spectacular and unsung combined, contribute less than 5 percent of the petroleum that we dump into the sea.

Onshore spills are easier to deal with. The arctic, again, presents special problems, for the effects of oil pollution are most severe at high latitudes and in cold weather. Spilled oil is eventually degraded by chemical weathering and the action of microorganisms. The rates of these processes are influenced by the temperature, the general rule being that the rate of a chemical reaction is roughly cut in half for each 8 or 10 degree (Celsius) drop in temperature. In addition, microbial activity in the arctic is limited by lack of nutrients, so oil spilled in the arctic will stick around for a long time.

Perhaps the worse consequence of oil production is that it spawns storage, refining, and transport facilities, which are the real villains of oil pollution. It is not the sight of a few offshore platforms that alarms residents along the Atlantic seaboard. It is the anticipation of surrendering the coast from Florida to Maine to ceaseless tanker traffic and belching refineries.

Processing

In the past, little was done to treat coal except for crushing and sorting by size and perhaps cleaning. Today about half of the coal produced in the United States is cleaned, a process which pollutes water, adds three-quarters of a billion kilograms of particulate matter to the atmosphere, and creates 90 billion kilograms of solid waste each year.

Petroleum, on the other hand, has always been treated extensively in order to derive a variety of end products. Our comments on refining of petroleum apply equally to oil shale and tar sands.

There is nothing subtle about the pollution from a petroleum refinery. You can see and smell it. Each year the petroleum refineries of the world spew more than 12 billion kilograms of carbon monoxide, about 3.5 billion kilograms of sulfur oxides, and almost 11 billion kilograms of gaseous hydrocarbons into the air, as well as about a billion kilograms of particulate matter. On a weight basis, they are the largest industrial polluter, although almost half of the material is carbon

Figure 7-10, *a*. Santa Barbara oil spill, 1969. This picture was taken about three weeks after the initial blowout. The two largest leaks are marked by the bubbling gas escaping along with the oil.

Figure 7-10, *b*. A closer view of platform A in the Santa Barbara Channel shows the leaking area at the corner of the platform. The dark area at top of picture is covered by little or no oil, in contrast to the thick accumulations (lighter area) occupying most of the picture. Photo credit: Marine Studies Center, University of Wisconsin monoxide, least troublesome of the major air pollutants. Water pollution is also a problem. Refinery effluents contain ammonia, phenols, naphthalene, cresols, sulfides, and other noxious chemicals.

Many refineries are located along the seacoast, where crude oil arrives by tanker and refined products depart. Through normal operation and accidents, these facilities contribute about 15 percent of the oil with which we pollute the sea. An estimated 1500 oil spills each year are attributed to land-based facilities, many of which are refineries. About 83 percent of these accidents pollute the sea and another 8 percent foul inland lakes and rivers.

Transportation and Storage

Transportation and storage of coal create no special problems except aesthetic ones. Increasing numbers of "unit" trains consisting entirely of coal cars shuttle back and forth between mine and power plant or steel mill. A few pioneering coal pipelines are in operation. Coal deteriorates on storage and there is a possibility of spontaneous fires and water pollution; however, proper management prevents these problems.

Petroleum and natural gas are moved chiefly by pipeline and tanker. About 70 percent of our domestic crude oil and gas flow under high pressure through 323,000 kilometers (200 thousand miles) of pipelines. Accidents are frequent. The federal government has only recently begun to collect data in this area and the earliest information is incomplete. Data from 1970 suggest that the accident rate may be well over 1000 per year. Pipeline leaks account for about a quarter of all offshore spills.

Most leaks are small, but there are a few dramatic ones, like the break in Lima, Ohio, in 1969, which poured 700,000 gallons of crude oil into the Ottawa River. The danger of an oil pipeline spill is mainly to wildlife, while a gasline leak raises the spectre of fire, explosion, injury, and death in populous areas. It is possible to reduce but never to eliminate damage from these accidents through proper surveillance and safety devices, including automatic monitoring and closely-spaced shutoff valves. But with perhaps 252,000 gallons of oil in each kilometer of pipe, even with safety locks every 15 kilometers (10 miles), 4 million gallons of oil could escape during a pipeline leak.

Since the discovery of oil in Prudhoe Bay, a word association test would probably produce one response with regularity: "pipeline— Alaskan." The difficulties and dangers of such a pipeline are legion. Underground pipe carrying hot oil could melt the permafrost, with consequences ranging from minor to severe. Insulating the pipe would raise the temperature of the oil, not reduce melting; and if the oil were not hot, it would not flow. Muddy slush in the thawed area could flow

down the slightest slope, damaging the pipeline as well as the local
environment.

Permafrost is not the only problem. Animal ecologists fear that
herds of migratory game will be disturbed if their paths cross that of
man. There are extensive fault zones and areas of seismic activity. The
act of laying a pipeline could cause more disturbance to the environment than the presence of the pipeline itself—a somewhat specious
argument used by the oil industry, since you can't have a pipeline if
you don't first construct it. Original plans for the Alaskan pipeline
called for the state to take over the service roads after the pipeline was
completed—a public road into the backland!

Overland, oil moves through pipelines, but much oil must cross
the water. In 1967, the wreck of the tanker *Torrey Canyon* off the
coast of England shook the world. The next year it was *Ocean Eagle,*
near San Juan, Puerto Rico. Accidents like this are now so common that
they are no longer big news. More than half of the world's annual production of petroleum, about 300 billion gallons, is shipped in a growing
fleet of about 4000 tankers. It crisscrosses the seas, touching every
major island and coastline. Through spillage or leakage, an estimated
0.1 percent of this transport—more than a quarter of a billion gallons—
is lost each year to the marine environment. This equals the annual
marine production of petroleum-like materials from natural processes
like submarine oil seeps and decay of organic matter.

With the number and size of tankers growing year by year, we
can expect nothing but more accidents and more pollution. Capacity of
the world's tanker fleet doubled during the 1960s and will probably
double again during the 1970s. The once-supertanker *Torrey Canyon,*
at 120,000 tons, is dwarfed by the 800,000 ton ships now on the drawing boards. These super supertankers pose problems in addition to
pollution. Only four ports in the United States can handle the
60-foot draft of a 200,000 ton tanker. Colossal dredging projects will
be necessary to deepen and maintain shipping channels to accommodate the mammoth new tankers that are thrusting themselves into the
seaports of the world.

Oil tankers are notorious polluters in their routine operation.
"Normal" tanker activity accounts for one-quarter of man's discharge
of oil to the oceans, five times as much as is contributed by major spills
or offshore production. It involves both the disposal of oil from boiler
and engine rooms (a problem common to all shipping) and disposal of
wastes from the cargo. The problem of cargo wastes is being decreased
by improvements in the design and operation of tankers and by efforts
to reprocess waste oil. However, the immense world fleet will not be
retired overnight to be replaced by cleaner ships, nor will the political,
economic, and institutional difficulties of salvage be worked out easily.

In many tankers, seawater ballast is taken into the same tanks that carry oil. When the ballast is drained, there is always a residue of oil, or worse yet, an oil-water emulsion. Who is responsible for disposing of this waste? The owner of the tanker? The owner of the cargo that created it? The owner of the receiving terminal? The owner of the next cargo, for whose load the waste must be discharged? Waste oil is usually claimed by nobody and often dumped into the sea.

Recent development of refrigerated tankers for transport of natural gas has greatly expanded the market for this fuel and has not yet posed any serious problems.

Storage facilities for petroleum and natural gas are subject to damage from earthquakes, sometimes leading to fires like those that raged in Seward, Alaska, after the earthquake of 1964. Transfer of petroleum to and from storage tanks is an additional source of spillage and pollution.

Biological Effects of Oil Pollution at Sea

The effects of spilled oil would be less noticeable and less severe if the oil were distributed uniformly over the seas, but it is not. It is concentrated in coastal regions which also receive a disproportionate share of man's other wastes and which constitute a particularly intricate, valuable, and vulnerable system of living organisms and physical processes. The largest part of marine biological resources occurs in coastal areas. Moreover, tanker traffic is concentrated in particular lanes, so that, for example, about one-quarter of the world's production of oil passes through the English Channel.

Oil can kill in three ways. It can coat an organism or its respiratory surfaces, causing death by suffocation. It can kill through one of its deadly constituents, largely water soluble compounds of low molecular weight like phenol, that are acutely toxic to many plants and animals. The third route to death is subtle and insidious, difficult to detect and often impossible to prove. It may lead, paradoxically, to local death of a species while sparing the individual. It is the effect of chronic pollution: impaired physiology, genetic aberrations, cancer, decreased fertility or sterility, reduced growth, increased susceptibility to disease and other stresses, or disruption of chemical communication leading to abnormal feeding, defensive, reproductive, and migratory behavior.

Chronic oil pollution may also lead to depletion of oxygen in the water through an excessive increase in the biochemical oxygen demand. The biochemical oxygen demand is a measure of the oxygen needed to oxidize all the organic matter present. Oxygen is depleted by the respiration of a large population of bacteria feeding on petroleum and of the protozoa that feed on the bacteria. Thus both direct and indirect effects of oil cause changes in the number and kind of species in polluted water.

Although many aquatic plants are relatively immune to oil, the widespread use of petroleum products for weed control in irrigation ditches and elsewhere testifies to their potential powers. The first effect of oil is to kill many plants that are rooted in bottom sediments, but when revegetation takes place, growth is likely to be more luxuriant than before because animal predators have been destroyed and because the decomposing petroleum is excellent fertilizer. Accumulation of petroleum sludge alters the properties of bottom sediments and plays havoc with growth and reproduction of bottom-dwelling organisms.

There are few records of the effect of oil on aquatic mammals. The experience in Santa Barbara suggests that it is minimal for seals, sea lions, whales, and dolphins. Fuel oil is known to destroy the waterproof qualities of muskrat fur.

Waterfowl suffer acutely from oil pollution. A single oil spill can kill 30,000 birds. Many experts believe that a far greater toll than this is exacted slowly but inexorably far out at sea, where the passing of the victims goes unnoted. Oil sticks to a bird and he can't remove it. It destroys his buoyancy so he must struggle to stay afloat. It also destroys his natural insulation, exposing him to cold air and water. It mats his feathers so he can't fly. In preening, he swallows toxic oil. As a result of all this, he has trouble finding food. Suffering from exhaustion, exposure, sickness, and starvation, he has a slim chance for survival.

Use and Disposal

Many kinds of processes lead to pollution of one sort or another, but there is only one major cause of air pollution: burning. About 80 percent of all air pollutants are generated by the burning (and steps that lead to burning) of fossil fuels, and most of the rest comes from the burning of something else. Table 7–1 shows the sources of major air pollutants.

Fossil fuels contain many elements besides the carbon and hydrogen that characterize pure hydrocarbons. The worst offender is sulfur, the oxides of which, when released to the atmosphere, injure both physical structures and living things. The magnitude of the sulfur problem can be illustrated by imagining we could remove all the sulfur from the coal and oil burned in a year in the United States. We would have a mountain of sulfur greater than the annual United States production of this element.

Coal

Coal is dirty. Both pollution and evolution are documented by the darkening of certain moths in industrial regions of Great Britain.

Table 7-1. Sources of Air Pollution in the United States (1968)

Source	Carbon Monoxide 100×10^6 tons	Sulfur Oxides 33×10^6 tons	Hydrocarbons 32×10^6 tons	Nitrogen Oxides 21×10^6 tons	Particulates 28×10^6 tons
Fuel burning for transportation	63.8%	2.4%	51.9%	39.3%	4.3%
Fuel burning in power plants, home furnaces, and other stationary sources	1.9	73.5	2.2	48.5	31.4
Industrial processes other than fuel burning, including petroleum refining	9.6	22.0	14.4	1.0	26.5
Solid waste disposal	7.8	0.3	5.0	2.9	3.9
Forest fires, coal waste fires, agricultural burning, gasoline marketing, etc.	16.9	1.8	26.5	8.3	33.9

Reprinted, by permission, from J. Holdren and P. Herrera, *Energy* (San Francisco: Sierra Club. 1971), p. 145.

Initially, these moths were pale animals that avoided predators by sitting on pale objects. The occasional dark mutant was quickly spied by a hungry bird. In the cities, however, there was nothing pale to sit on. Dark mutants multiplied unmolested, while wild types had little chance for survival.

In one hour's operation a typical coal-fired electric power plant producing one million kilowatts of power also produces, from 300,000 kilograms (340 tons) of coal: 850,000 kilograms (940 tons) of carbon dioxide, 12,000 kilograms (13 tons) of carbon monoxide, 15,000 kilograms (17 tons) of sulfur oxides, 3,400 kilograms (3.4 tons) of nitrogen oxides, and 31,000 kilograms (34 tons) of ash.

Most of the particulate matter (ash) that tries to escape up the stack can be trapped by various devices. The most effective of these are very expensive, and their operation consumes as much as 5 percent of the electricity produced. The 1 percent or more of particulates that evade the best efforts at capture blow about creating dirt, causing or exacerbating respiratory problems, reducing the amount of sunlight that reaches the earth, and acting as nuclei for local fog. Increasing the height of the stack and decreasing the size of the particles merely disperses the particles higher, wider, and more permanently.

Only the inorganic form of sulfur (mostly pyrites) can be removed before burning. The rest, about half of it, is bound in organic compounds. Although theoretically sulfur oxides can be removed from stack gases, no existing method is satisfactory. For this reason, many standards for air quality specify a maximum permissible sulfur content of fuel before burning, rather than a maximum level of sulfur emission.

Nitrogen oxides persist in the atmosphere for only a few weeks. They are rapidly dispersed by winds, washed down by rain, or incorporated into living matter. Before this happens, however, they participate in a series of photochemical reactions that lead to smog. They also cause cumulative respiratory damage which takes the form of emphysema or greater susceptibility to other respiratory problems. It has been suggested that eutrophication of lakes near urban areas is hastened by nitrogen oxides precipitated with rain.

Advanced technology promises to reduce most of these pollutants, but this is still in the future. Experiments are slow because of their large scale and great cost. Even with the new technology, it will be many years before existing coal plants of traditional design can be phased out.

Petroleum
Many power plants burn residual fuel oil, the dregs of the refining process. These plants produce about the same levels of sulfur and nitrogen oxides and carbon monoxide as coal-fired plants.

The major portion of carbon monoxide is produced by the inefficient internal combustion engine, making it more of a hazard than the same amounts would be if spewed high into the air from a smokestack. The half-life of carbon monoxide in the atmosphere ranges between one month and five years, which means that high local concentrations can build up unless dispersion mechanisms are efficient. Theoretically, air movement should be more than adequate to ventilate the most crowded city streets, but cleansing winds cannot reach small pockets of pollution and the deep chasms among city buildings. The efficiency of gasoline combustion decreases with start-stop driving so that an idling engine produces about 2½ times the pollutants of one operating at cruising speed. Thus, both driving conditions and the number of cars in cities lead to enormous rates of carbon monoxide emission. Improvement brought about by emission controls is offset by increased numbers of vehicles and less than optimal functioning of pollution control devices.

The city dweller breathes air containing, on a year-long average, about 8 parts per million of carbon monoxide, with the level sometimes reaching 50 parts per million. Only 1 part in a million produces detectable physiological effects. Carbon monoxide competes vigorously with oxygen for binding sites on red blood cells and clings tenaciously once it has found a site. Thus it accumulates in the blood during prolonged exposure. It is not like the pollutants that burn your eyes or make you cough. It makes you just a little less alert, so that perhaps you don't stop quite soon enough to avoid that other car. And of course every molecule of carbon monoxide represents wasted energy, the energy to be derived from burning carbon monoxide to carbon dioxide.

Hydrocarbons enter the atmosphere largely through evaporation, but also through incomplete combustion. At least 2½ percent of our annual production of gasoline, more than a billion kilograms, is lost by evaporation during transfer from refinery to truck to holding tank to car and during standing in reservoirs and carburetors.[5] The loss may be as high as 15 percent of the gasoline marketed.[6]

Hydrocarbons in the atmosphere undergo a series of chemical reactions which result in smog. Some hydrocarbons are potent carcinogens. Rain brings many of the molecules back to the ground, where they are metabolized by soil bacteria and do no further harm. Others enter rivers or lakes or the sea, where they join industrial hydrocarbon wastes and used crankcase oil in adding to the burden of hydrocarbons in the hydrosphere. All of them represent energy which has eluded us, only to return to cause us sorrow.

A home furnace in good condition is a relatively efficient device, but it is not pollution-free. Space heating with oil and gas produces annually 1 billion kilograms (1 million tons) of nitrogen oxides, 1 billion kilograms (1 million tons) of hydrocarbons, 1 billion kilograms (1 million tons) of particulate matter, 2 billion kilograms (2 million tons) of carbon monoxide, and 3 billion kilograms (3 million tons) of sulfur oxides.

REFERENCES

1. M. K. Hubbert, "Energy Resources," in *Resources and Man,* National Academy of Sciences-National Research Council (San Francisco: W. H. Freeman and Company, 1969), pp. 170–184.
2. H. Hottel and J. Howard, *New Energy Technology* (Cambridge, Mass. MIT Press, 1971).
3. P. Averitt, "Coal Resources of the United States," *U.S. Geol. Survey Bull.* (1967): 1275.
4. G. Garvey, *Energy, Ecology, Economy* (New York: W. W. Norton & Co., Inc. (1972), p. 88.
5. E. Goldberg, "The Chemical Invasion of the Oceans by Man," in *Global Effects of Environmental Pollution,* ed. Singer.
6. G. Garvey, *Energy, Ecology, Economy* (New York: W. W. Norton & Company, Inc., 1972), p. 122.

SUGGESTED READING

Francis, W. *Coal, Its Formation and Composition,* 2d ed. London: Edward Arnold Ltd., 1961.

Hottel, H., and Howard, J. *New Energy Technology—Some Facts and Assessments.* Cambridge, Mass.: The MIT Press, 1971.

Hubbert, M. K. "Energy Resources." In *Resources and Man,* National Academy of Sciences-National Research Council. San Francisco: W. H. Freeman and Company, 1969.

La Brecque, M. "Polar Deserts: Vulnerable Frontier." *The Sciences* 12, 4 (1972): 6–9, 26–28.

Lachenbruch, A. "Some Estimates of the Thermal Effects of a Heated Pipeline in Permafrost." In *Man and His Physical Environment,* edited by G. McKenzie and R. Utgard, pp. 74–76. Minneapolis: Burgess Publishing Company, 1972.

Macrae, J. *An Introduction to the Study of Fuel.* New York: Elsevier Publishing Company, 1966.

Poland, J., and Davis, G. "Land Subsidence Due to Withdrawal of Fluids." In *Man and His Physical Environment,* edited by G. McKenzie and R. Utgard, pp. 77–90. Minneapolis: Burgess Publishing Company, 1972.

Stacks, J. *Stripping.* San Francisco: Sierra Club, 1972.

Steinhart, C., and Steinhart, J. *Blowout: A Case Study of the Santa Bar-

bara Oil Spill. Belmont, Calif.: Duxbury Press, A Division of the Wadsworth Publishing Company, 1972.

U.S., Coast Guard, Battelle Memorial Institute. *Oil Spillage Study Literature: Search and Critical Evaluation for Selection of Promising Techniques to Control and Prevent Damage.* Report to Department of Transportation. Washington, D.C., 1967.

U.S., Congress, House, Hearings before the Committee on Interior and Insular Affairs. *Fuel and Energy Resources.* 92nd Cong., 2nd sess., 1972. Parts I and II. Serial No. 92–42.

U.S., Congress, Senate, Hearing before the Committee on Interior and Insular Affairs. *Advanced Power Cycles.* 92nd Cong., 2nd sess., 1972. Serial No. 92–21.

Vandale, A. "Subsidence—A Real or Imaginary Problem?" In *Man and His Physical Environment,* edited by G. McKenzie and R. Utgard, pp. 91–94. Minneapolis: Burgess Publishing Co., 1972.

CHAPTER 8

Nuclear Energy

The problem of transmutation and the liberation of atomic energy to carry on the labour of the world is no longer surrounded with mystery and ignorance, but is daily being reduced to a form capable of exact quantitative reasoning. It may be that it will remain forever unsolved. But we are advancing along the only road likely to bring success at a rate which makes it probable that one day will see its achievement. Should that day ever arrive, let no one be blind to the magnitude of the issues at stake, or suppose that such an acquisition of the physical resources of humanity can be safely entrusted to those who in the past have converted the blessings already conferred by science into a curse.

Frederick Soddy, 1920

"And just at that instant there rose as if from the bowels of the earth a light not of this world, the light of many suns in one, . . . a great green supersun climbing in a fraction of a second to a height of more than eight thousand feet, rising ever higher until it touched the clouds. . . . Up it went, changing colors . . . from deep purple to orange, expanding, growing bigger, . . . an elemental force freed from its bonds after being chained for billions of years. . . . Then out of the great silence came a mighty thunder. . . —the first cry of a newborn world."[1]

Thus does science writer William L. Laurence describe the explosion of the first atomic bomb in the New Mexican desert on July 16, 1945—"first fire ever made on earth that did not have its origin in the sun."[1] Many discoveries, combinations of serendipity and calculated experiment, mark the amazing trail to man's use of nuclear energy. The Atomic Age has many birthdays and many parents.

127

THE ATOM

History

In the nineteenth century, as Queen Victoria aged, much of the Western world seemed to age with her. The spirit of revolution and romanticism with which the century had begun gave way to the manners and moralities of Thackeray and Trollope novels. The spirit of those times has come, in our day, to be considered the epitome of the ordered and repressed life. It was the Victorian age.

In the rarefied world of physics, giants like LaPlace and Maxwell were finishing the work begun two centuries before by Isaac Newton. By the 1880s it was commonly heard that physics was nearly finished. The best men of the times were busy refining measurements and explaining details. The universe was at last understood as a vast machine whose minutiae needed only to be worked out, to describe both the past and the future with a mechanical simplicity. Even the violent notions of Karl Marx caught the spirit of the times.

The crack in this wall came from an unexpected quarter. In 1895, an undistinguished middle-aged physics professor named Wilhelm Roentgen was experimenting with a cathode ray (electron) tube, when he noticed that something emitted from the tube caused fluorescence of a platinum-containing screen that lay nearby. The mysterious something was called X rays. Its discovery precipitated a flurry of experimental activity, until within weeks, surgeons were viewing X ray images of their patients' bones while Victorian ladies blushed.

Meanwhile, in Paris, Henri Becquerel was investigating the relationship between X rays and fluorescence. He was searching for a fluorescent material that would give off X rays when exposed to ordinary sunlight. With a large collection of fluorescent substances at his disposal, he chose a salt of uranium for his studies. After exposing the uranium sample to sunlight he placed it against a photographic plate wrapped in heavy black paper. When he developed the plate, he found that it had been blackened—surely by X rays, since whatever it was had penetrated the thick paper. An overcast sky prevented the impatient Becquerel from repeating his experiment, so he put an unexposed photographic plate, carefully wrapped, in a drawer and laid the uranium on top of it. Days later, he developed the plate to see whether there had been any residual activity in the uranium. The plate was even blacker than the first had been! Further experiments revealed that the radiation from uranium was totally unaffected by light or by any other conditions that Becquerel could devise. Becquerel had discovered radioactivity.

It soon became evident that the uranium-bearing ore, pitchblende, contained more radioactivity than could be accounted for by uranium itself. In solving this mystery, Marie and Pierre Curie discovered two more radioactive elements, which they named polonium and radium.

Meanwhile, basic notions of the atom itself were being revised. In 1897, J. J. Thomson discovered electrons and correctly deduced that they arose from molecules of gas that became ionized, or positively charged. The negative electron must then be a constituent of the atom— which was not a billiard ball after all, but something with a structure. Physicists around the world began to construct hypothetical models of that structure and to test the models experimentally. Radioactivity was to be their key to the puzzle.

Rutherford showed that one type of emission from radioactive material, called alpha radiation for want of a better name, was identical with atoms of helium stripped of their two electrons. He next used alpha rays to probe atomic structure. By analyzing the deflection of the relatively heavy, positively charged alpha rays when they passed through thin gold foil, he concluded that the positive charge and most of the mass of the atom are concentrated in a space no more than 10^{-12} centimeters in diameter, one ten-thousandth of the diameter of the whole atom. The atom was mostly empty space.

Rutherford continued to shoot alpha rays at various things, in search of experimental data on nuclear structure. His most sensational discovery was that the emission of radiation is accompanied by a profound chemical change, the transformation of one element into another. Alchemy had died hard. Atomic theory had struggled for centuries to assert itself. Now the immutable atom was not immutable after all, but could be changed at the whim of man. Visions of splitting the nucleus titillated the brains of physicists, while the young Houtermans boldly suggested that the reverse process, nuclear fusion, powered the stars. The sober reflections of Frederick Soddy, Rutherford's assistant, are expressed in the quotation at the beginning of this chapter.

In 1932, upon Chadwick's discovery of the neutron, physicists had yet another weapon for their seige of the nucleus. With neutron bullets, Irene Curie, daughter of Marie, and her husband Frederic Joliot created new radioactive elements from stable ones. In Rome, Fermi began a systematic study of the elements, bombarding each in turn with neutrons and characterizing the products. By the time he reached uranium, its 92 protons and 146 neutrons constituting the largest nucleus in nature, a pattern had emerged. The products of a nuclear reaction were neighbors of the parent element, often having one or two more protons than the original nucleus. When he reached uranium, Fermi was hoping to create brand new elements—previously unknown transuranium elements.

He calculated that such transuranium elements would emit strong radiation of a particular range. To detect it, he used a thin strip of aluminum foil to filter out shorter range radiation. This filter prevented him from realizing that something very strange was happening. When an array of elements appeared as a result of bombarding uranium with neutrons, Fermi confidently announced that his goal of creating elements beyond uranium had been reached.

In Germany, Ida and Walter Noddack had been searching for natural transuranium elements for years. As accomplished chemists, they showed that Fermi's chemical analyses failed to substantiate his conclusions. Ida Noddack suggested that, instead, Fermi had broken the uranium nucleus into a number of large fragments. Her peers ignored her because it seemed kinder than ridiculing her. Every self-respecting physicist knew that only particles of enormous energies not yet even approached by man could split the atom.

But peculiar things continued to happen. In Zurich one day, investigators forgot to place the aluminum filter in front of their apparatus and they saw wild oscillations on the screen. Concluding that the instrument was at fault, they replaced it, and this time they remembered to put the filter where it belonged. This event was repeated, with variations, in Cambridge, Paris, and Berlin. Through the cloud of their preconceptions, scientists were unable to understand what they saw. Irene Curie correctly identified lanthanum among the products of her experiment, but then retracted her report for technical—and mistaken— reasons. Meticulous chemical detective work by Hahn, Strassman and Meitner identified new radioactive forms of barium, cerium, and lanthanum in the products of nuclear reactions, but their physicist instincts shouted "impossible!" They couched their report in doubts and apologies (all the while fearful that Irene Curie would discover her error and beat them into print), explaining that their conclusions could be deriving from an unlikely combination of mistakes.

But Strassman was a respected chemist and his data were above reproach. When the results became known, investigators in several laboratories hastened to repeat their own experiments. This time, they omitted the filter so that all radiation would be detected. And now, with open minds, they could comprehend what they saw. They saw intense electrical pulses, unlike anything other experiments had ever shown, representing tremendous energies that could come only from the splitting of the atom.

By the late 1930s, the aims of Hitler had become clear. In the minds of some who knew the secret of atomic energy lurked a fear that Hitler might create an atomic bomb. Impossible, said none other than Neils Bohr. Energy cannot be released like that. Atomic energy is only a laboratory tool. He was seconded by Einstein and Rutherford, among others. But then Hahn, Strassman, and Meitner showed that one lazy neutron could split uranium. And on March 3, 1939, Leo Szilard and Walter Zinn showed that in the events following absorption of a neutron by a uranium nucleus, additional neutrons—more than one—are discharged. Those neutrons could enter and split other uranium nuclei, in a so-called chain reaction. Although many obstacles remained, scientists could no longer delude themselves. A uranium bomb was possible.

The rest of the story is well documented and well known. Sequestered in secret cities not shown on any map, in an historic race with imagined counterparts in Nazi Germany, American scientists built the first atomic bombs. To their chagrin it turned out that Hitler was not trying to build bombs at all, having been persuaded that the war would be over before the project could be completed. Germany's aborted efforts in applied atomic physics were aimed at obtaining an additional energy resource, a "uranium machine," to supplement inadequate supplies of conventional fuels and power. But America had the bomb, and, perhaps to avoid being charged with a 2 billion dollar boondoggle, the military seemed determined to use it. On August 6, 1945, America dropped an atomic bomb on Hiroshima.

Since then we have had more and bigger bombs, and the Cold War, and the nuclear arms race, and fallout, until the subject of nuclear energy has become so fraught with emotion that it is difficult to confront the facts rationally. Amidst it all there have been rosy fantasies of a utopia which only abundant energy from the peaceful atom can bring. We are getting things into better perspective now. People no longer dive into fallout shelters when the factory whistles blow, but the peaceful atom is turning out to be less peaceful than we had hoped. In the following sections we will consider what nuclear energy is, how we can use it, and what the penalties for its use may be.

The Nature of Nuclear Energy and Atomic Fuel

The energy of chemical reactions is derived from rearrangements of the outer electrons of atoms. Most of an atom's energy, however, is concentrated in its nucleus—between 1 and 10 million times as much as resides in the outer electrons. At the same time, most nuclei are very stable, remaining unaffected by the levels of disturbance familiar in the world of chemistry. That is why the nucleus was so long in yielding to man's probes.

Essentially all of the atom's mass is in its nucleus, which is composed of protons and neutrons, collectively called nucleons. The number of nucleons is indicated by a superscript to the left of the symbol for an element, as in ^{235}U. The number of protons in the nucleus establishes the chemical identity of the element (uranium has 92), but the number of neutrons in an element may vary. Thus we have ^{233}U, ^{234}U, and so on. The different nuclear species of an element are called isotopes.

The source of nuclear energy is explained by the equivalence of mass and energy, expressed in that most famous of equations, $E = mc^2$. The energy of a system equals its mass times the square of the velocity of light. The mass of a single proton is 1.673×10^{-24} grams, and that of a single neutron is 1.675×10^{-24} grams. The mass of a nucleus, however, is always less than the sum of the masses of its nucleons. The amount by which it is less defines the mass defect of the nucleus and represents the amount of mass that was converted to energy when the nucleus was formed. Dividing the mass defect of a nucleus by the number of nucleons gives the mass defect per nucleon, which varies from element to element, reflecting the stability of the nucleus. Because the mass defect per nucleon is not the same for all nuclear species, it is theoretically possible to obtain energy from the fusion or fission of nuclei. High stability is associated with low energy levels (large mass defects).

Figure 8–1 shows how the mass defect per nucleon varies with the mass number, or number of nucleons per nucleus. Not all points lie on the curve because, for reasons explained by quantum mechanics,

Figure 8–1. Relative stability of atomic nuclei, as defined by the relationship between mass number and mass defect per nucleon. This graph illustrates the theoretical possibilities of deriving energy from fission or fusion of atomic nuclei. A large mass defect is associated with a low energy state which, in turn, implies a stable structure. The exceptional stability of the helium nucleus is striking. All nuclei with even numbers of protons, neutrons, or both, tend to be more stable than nuclei containing odd numbers of these particles.

some nuclear configurations are more stable than others. The helium nucleus with mass number 4, for example, is an extraordinarily stable structure—so stable that alpha particles (identical with helium nuclei) are often emitted intact during nuclear reactions. With the peaks and valleys smoothed out to make the overall trend more apparent, the curve is seen to rise steeply at first, illustrating the vast energies that are released when small nuclei fuse. It reaches a plateau in the region of medium-sized nuclei, then falls off again—but not nearly so sharply as it rose—for the heavy nuclei. The mass defect for a uranium nucleus is 7.5 million electron volts per nucleon, while that for its fission products is about 8.4 million electron volts per nucleon. Thus energy, about 0.9 million electron volts (3.8×10^{-14} calories) per nucleon, is released whenever a uranium atom undergoes fission. This is a small amount of energy, but a nucleon is a small thing. There are 6×10^{23} of them in a gram of matter. The energy released by fission of one gram of uranium is about the same as the energy released by burning two and a half tons of coal.

Radioactive decay also releases energy, as nuclei tend toward more stable configuration at lower energy levels. Radioactivity is the source of the heat generated in the crust and upper mantle of the earth.

In theory, any time that the end products of a nuclear reaction have a greater mass defect per nucleon than the reactants had, energy is released. In practice, however, very few nuclear reactions yield net energy because, even under the most favorable conditions, more energy must be supplied to accelerate projectile particles than is derived from successful collisions. The notable exception is uranium. One isotope of uranium (^{235}U) is a nuclear fuel because its nuclei are fissionable by impact with slow neutrons (neutrons traveling perhaps a mile per second) and—what is most important—each fission yields an average of 2.5 additional neutrons, making a self-sustaining reaction possible.

Less than 1 percent of natural uranium is ^{235}U. Essentially all the rest is ^{238}U, which is not readily fissionable. On absorption of a neutron, however, it undergoes changes leading to the formation of an isotope of the manmade element plutonium (^{239}Pu). Plutonium is fissionable, reacting with slow neutrons such as ^{235}U does. America's second atomic bomb was a plutonium bomb. Similarly, an isotope of thorium (^{232}Th) can be converted to fissionable ^{233}U by absorption of a neutron. This process is called breeding, and ^{238}U and ^{232}Th are fertile.

Until recently, scientists confidently asserted that no nuclear chain reaction can occur in nature because concentrations of fissionable material are too low. Now they have found an unprecedentedly low ratio of ^{235}U to ^{238}U in an African uranium mine. The most likely explanation seems to be that almost 2 billion years ago an unlikely combination of conditions did permit a reaction which consumed most of the ^{235}U isotope. The presence of water and the absence of neutron-absorbing elements could have had this effect, as we will see in the next section.

THE PEACEFUL ATOM

How a Nuclear Reactor Works

At first, nature seemed to conspire against any use of fission. The only fissionable fuel, ^{235}U, was hopelessly diluted, 140 atoms to 1, by ^{238}U. There was no way, then, to separate one isotope from the other. A fissionable fuel could be produced from ^{238}U, but only neutrons from concentrated ^{235}U could do the job. No wonder that, even with knowledge of uranium fission, no German bomb project got off the ground.

Some scientists suspected that only under certain conditions could ^{238}U trap neutrons and extinguish the nuclear reaction. They found that slow neutrons could split ^{235}U nuclei but were not absorbed by ^{238}U. Enrico Fermi, the man who had split the atom without knowing it, supervised construction of the first atomic pile, or nuclear reactor, a project begun at Columbia University and culminated on December 2, 1942, in the squash court beneath the stands of the University of Chicago's Stagg Field. It was fashioned of a carefully calculated arrangement of graphite and uranium oxide bricks, interspersed with rods of cadmium and boron. Graphite was the moderator, slowing neutrons to speeds that would ensure their capture by ^{235}U and not ^{238}U. The cadmium and boron rods, avid neutron scavengers, could be inserted or withdrawn to control the rate of the reaction. Fermi turned on the world's first reactor at 3:25 in the afternoon. At 3:53 he turned it off, proving that a nuclear chain reaction could be started, maintained at a desired rate, and stopped at will. Today's reactors surpass Fermi's pile in both scale and sophistication of design, but their fundamental principles are the same.

Most of a nuclear power plant is basically the same as a fossil fuel plant. Only the primary source of energy differs. In both types of plant, heat from the energy source is usually used to produce steam, which turns a turbine, which drives a generator to set up a current of electricity. We will focus here on the initial step of the process, production of heat in the nuclear reactor.

Every reactor has a fuel supply, a means of controlling the rate of fission, and a means of transferring heat from the reactor to wherever it will be used. There are many variations in reactor design, but the most significant feature of a reactor is whether it is a net consumer or a net producer of fuel. Because two and one-half neutrons are produced in every fission of ^{235}U, while only one is needed to maintain the reaction, and because neutrons can convert ^{238}U and ^{232}Th to fissionable fuel, it becomes possible for a reactor to produce up to one and one-half times as much fuel as it uses. By the ratio of fuel produced to fuel consumed, a reactor is classified as a burner, a converter, or a breeder. The fuel cycles of burners and breeders are illustrated in Box 8–1.

BOX 8–1 FUEL CYCLES IN BURNER AND BREEDER REACTORS

The nucleus of uranium-235 can be split by the capture of a neutron: $^{235}U + n \rightarrow$ *fission products + n + heat. In a burner reactor, this becomes a cycle:*
$^{235}U \rightarrow$ *fission products + n + heat* $\rightarrow$ $\rightarrow$ *electricity.*

Non-fissionable ^{238}U *can be converted to fissionable* ^{239}Pu *by capture of a neutron:* $^{238}_{92}U + n \rightarrow ^{239}_{92}U \rightarrow ^{239}_{93}Np + electron$ $\rightarrow ^{239}_{94}Pu + electron.$ *Similarly:* $^{232}_{90}Th + n \rightarrow ^{233}_{90}Th \rightarrow ^{233}_{91}Pa + electron$ $\rightarrow ^{233}_{92}U + electron.$

In a breeder reactor, part of the neutrons released in fission cause additional fissions, and part of them convert fertile isotopes to fissionable fuel. The cycle in a plutonium reactor would operate as shown below. There need be only enough ^{235}U *to start the reaction. After the plutonium cycle is started, the bottom loop can operate alone.*

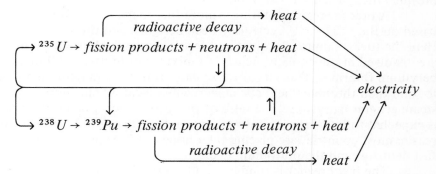

Figure 8–2. Plutonium cycle in a breeder reactor.

Most of today's reactors are burners, able to release only 1 or 2 percent of the energy potentially available from uranium. The fuel for a burner is uranium dioxide which has been enriched to contain about 3 percent ^{235}U. (The two isotopes of uranium can now be separated on the basis of the 1 percent difference in their weights.) The uranium is sealed into metal tubes which—when they are functioning properly—prevent the escape of radioactive fission products from the fuel rods. Ordinary water acts as both moderator and coolant. As in Fermi's reactor, movable rods of boron or cadmium regulate the rate of fission. Additional boron, as boric acid, may be dissolved in the moderator. Steam generated from the cooling water in the reactor may be used directly to drive a turbine, or heat from the coolant may be transferred through a heat exchanger to a separate system for steam production (figure 8–3).

Reactors which create significant amounts of fuel, but not as much as they consume, are called converters. Their more favorable conversion rate is accomplished by modification of the fuel rods, which are blanketed in layers of fertile material. Conversion of ^{232}Th to ^{233}U proceeds readily using the slow neutrons produced in a conventional water-cooled, water-moderated reactor. Although present conversion rates are low, converters with ratios in the vicinity of 1 can probably be built to operate on the ^{232}Th–^{233}U cycle.

The United States has given most attention to a converter that uses helium as a coolant, graphite as a moderator, and highly enriched uranium dicarbide fuel containing 90 percent ^{235}U, with thorium dicarbide as the fertile material for breeding. Gas turbines replace the usual steam turbines, eliminating the steam cycle. These and possibly other types of converters will be used increasingly in the near future as a compromise between the present generation of wasteful burners and the breeders that we cannot yet build.

A breeder reactor produces more fuel than it uses. Breeders based on the ^{232}Th–^{233}U cycle have been designed and show promise. Here the fuel (uranium fluoride) and fertile material (thorium fluoride) are dissolved in the coolant, which is a mixture of molten lithium and beryllium fluorides. This mixture circulates through a graphite moderator and then through a heat exchanger, where heat is transferred to a steam generating system. The ratio of fuel production to consumption is expected to be relatively low, perhaps only 1.06 or 1.07, and for this reason most countries are placing their hopes on breeders that utilize fast neutrons and the plutonium cycle.

The fast breeder is fundamentally very different from reactors using slow neutrons. The moderator has been eliminated. In order to maintain the reaction, fissionable material must be packed in concentrated form in a small space. The fuel is surrounded by fertile material,

(a.) Boiling Water

(b.) Gas Cooled

(c.) Pressurized Water

Figure 8–3. Schematic diagrams of three types of burner reactors.

a, In a boiling water reactor, water is used to remove heat from the nuclear fuel, boils and converts to steam. This occurs when the water is in contact with the reactor. The steam then travels directly to the turbine generator.

b, Reactors of this type use either helium gas or carbon dioxide gas to remove the heat produced by the nuclear fuel. The gas carries the heat from the reactor to a steam generator in which heat converts water into steam. The gas returns to the reactor to pick up more heat and the steam goes on to spin the turbine.

c, This reactor differs from the boiling water type in that steam is not permitted to form in the water used to cool the reactor. The heat produced by the fuel in the reactor is carried by the cooling water to a steam generator. There the heat passes from the reactor cooling water to a second water system in which steam forms.

which is ^{238}U left over from the production of fuel elements It is not possible to use water for a coolant because of its simultaneous role as moderator and because it is unable to transport heat fast enough from the reactor's intensely reactive core. Coolant for a fast breeder must have a high capacity for heat transfer and little or no tendency to interact with neutrons. The leading candidates for coolants are helium under pressure and liquid sodium. Although technical and economic obstacles prevent construction of a large fast breeder reactor, several small ones are already operating in the United States and Europe and several larger ones are scheduled for completion in Europe in the mid-1970s.

Nuclear Fuel Supply

It is customary to speak of nuclear fuel reserves in terms of the price per pound of the uranium oxide U_3O_8. Known and estimated total supplies of uranium in various price ranges are shown in table 8–1. This table also presents estimates of uranium requirements between now and the year 2000, based on projections of a nuclear power industry depending on burner reactors. It is clear that reserves of inexpensive uranium will be exhausted by the end of the century if we continue to rely on reactors that consume more fuel than they produce. Even if conversion ratios are improved, so long as they are less than 1, the initial

Table 8–1. Estimated Reserves of Uranium in the U.S. as a Function of Price

Price per Pound of U_3O_8	Tons of Known or Suspected Uranium (as U_3O_8) at This Price
less than $8	594,000
$8 to $10	346,000
$10 to $15	510,000
$15 to $30	790,000
$30 to $50	7,760,000
$50 to $100	15,000,000

These estimates are likely to be low, as estimates of total reserves often are. Uranium prospecting was vigorous in the past, but it has slowed down in recent years because the growth of the nuclear power industry has not been hampered by shortages or predicted shortages of fuel. Cumulative consumption of U_3O_8 may reach 1,600,000 tons by the year 2000. According to the table above, the price of uranium will have risen from less than $8 per pound to about $18 per pound by that time. This increase, while it seems large, would have a negligible effect on the cost of electricity.

From Atomic Energy Commission. 1970. Potential Nuclear Power Growth Patterns, as quoted in H. Hottel and J. Howard, 1971. New Energy Technology. Cambridge, Mass.: MIT Press. P. 34.

supply of ^{235}U and all the fuel it breeds will be depleted in a relatively
short time, leaving a useless residue of fertile material that cannot be
bred because there is nothing to breed it with. For this reason the fast
breeder program in the United States has been speeded up almost to the
proportions of a crash project.

But economic statistics are misleading. The price of fuel for a
nuclear power plant is a relatively small cost, in contrast to overall costs
for nuclear energy and fuel costs for fossil plants. If the cost of uranium
were multiplied by 70, the cost of electricity from a nuclear plant
would barely double. Another look at table 8–1 will indicate that
neither the amount nor the cost of fuel will limit us, for there is plenty
of uranium. However, social and environmental penalties for mining it
may preclude its use. For this reason, some experts believe that, unless
fast breeders become a reality before high grade ores are depleted of
^{235}U, the history of nuclear energy will be very brief; whereas if fast
breeder technology is perfected in time, there will be enough uranium
and thorium ore to last for thousands of years.[2]

The Promise of Nuclear Energy

The first full-scale commercial nuclear power plant began operating in the U.S.S.R. in 1954. The first nuclear plant in the United
States was placed in service in Shippingport, Pennsylvania, in 1957. It
was followed by others in Illinois (1960), Massachusetts (1961), New
York (1962), and California (1963). This was a period of acknowledged
experiment and testing. The plants were relatively small, each producing
as much electricity as a small fossil fuel plant. The largest of the five had
a capacity of 265 megawatts. But orders for nuclear power plants began
to pour in, and by the end of 1970, nineteen operating plants represented 2 percent of America's electric utility capacity, while fifty-three
additional plants were under construction and thirty-four were being
planned. By mid-1971 there were twenty-five plants in operation, forty-
eight under construction, and sixty-three on order. The Federal Power
Commission estimates that the percentage of the total electric generating capacity contributed by nuclear plants will grow from 2 percent
in 1970 to 24 percent in 1980 and 41 percent in 1990.[3] The first
large-scale commercial breeders are expected to begin operation in the
mid-1980s. Meanwhile, the size of individual nuclear units will increase
from approximately 1000 megawatts in the early 1970s to between
3000 and 3500 megawatts, with several of these units comprising a
nuclear power facility.

General environmental concern and local action to block construction, coupled with unexpected cost increases and technical problems, have recently slowed the growth of nuclear power. In the future,

these factors will probably be offset by increasing shortages of fossil fuels and rigid air quality standards. Nuclear energy today is heavily subsidized by fossil fuels at all stages from the mining of uranium to the actual generation of electricity. (Because nuclear plants must operate at lower temperatures than fossil plants for reasons of safety, some nuclear plants use a conventional fossil fuel plant as a final step to boost the temperature of the steam.) Without fossil fuels, we would not have nuclear power either.

Nuclear power plants have certain advantages over fossil fuel plants. Outstanding among these is their lack of kinds of air pollution associated with burning conventional fuels. Nuclear fuel is less bulky than coal by several orders of magnitude, and thus unsightly storage problems and endless processions of coal cars to and from the power plant are eliminated. Because the amount of fuel required is small and partial refueling is done only once or twice a year, transportation costs are small, making the cost of a nuclear plant practically independent of its location. Thus nuclear energy may be a good choice for areas far from a source of fossil fuel. Nuclear plants are quiet. They are less ugly than fossil fuel plants (figure 8–4). Enthusiasts boast that although there have been accidents, the impact has never been felt beyond the confines of the power plant. But skeptics warn that next time the public may not be so lucky.

Optimists describe deserts bursting into bloom, watered by fresh water from the sea, and abundant food and comfortable lives for all— these miracles to be mediated by cheap, abundant nuclear energy. But there are serious fallacies behind these rosy pictures. Because electricity from nuclear power plants is very expensive on a small scale, it is not an alternative for developing countries with small needs for power. Proposed nuclear agro-industrial complexes would provide some relief, but not much. Plans call for large-scale desalination of seawater (for irrigation of surrounding intensively farmed areas) to be coupled with production of fertilizer and other industries. The food produced at such an establishment would feed about 3 million people. But 23 such plants would be required each year, at a cost of $41 billion, just to keep pace with population growth.[4] It looks as if scale, time, and cost are working against us. In addition, major technological successes, including modern agriculture, tend to be major causes of environmental problems.

Other Uses of Nuclear Energy

There are uses for the fissionable atom besides generating electricity. All of them involve some mix of the problems already discussed. Our preoccupation with nuclear weapons continues. The first nuclear-powered submarines have won many advocates for a nuclear navy, with its practical and strategical advantages. The AEC seems eager to apply

Figure 8–4, *a.* The external appearance of this nuclear power plant on the shore of Lake Michigan is like that of any other business establishment.
Figure 8–4, *b.* A clue to its internal complexity may be found in its control room.
Photo credit: Marine Studies Center, University of Wisconsin.

its expertise to a variety of peaceful pursuits as well. These include nuclear blasts to assist mining operations, to enlarge existing harbors or create new ones, and to facilitate the production of natural gas from impermeable formations. Considerable effort has been invested in attempts to increase gas production. The hazard of radioactivity remains, although it has been reduced, and possible seismic effects must always be considered. In 1971, the Chairman of the Federal Power Commission told a Congressional committee that an analysis by his staff indicated it would be 20 years before gas produced from such "stimulated" reservoirs would approximate 10 percent of the gas consumed in 1969. This level of production would be brought about by 4000 nuclear explosions of 100 kilotons each in 1000 wells, during the next 20 years.

At the other end of the scale, there are a number of experimental dogs whose hearts beat at the command of plutonium-powered pacemakers. The variety of potential nuclear-powered gadgets is limited only by the scope of man's imagination.

Nevertheless, nuclear energy is failing by a wide margin to fulfill the predictions of the 1950s, when the chairman of the Atomic Energy Commission thought it not unlikely that "our children will enjoy in their homes electrical power too cheap to meter, will know of great periodic regional famines in the world only as matters of history . . . and will experience a life span far longer than ours."

IS THERE A PEACEFUL ATOM?

The Atomic Energy Commission (AEC) was established after World War II as a civilian agency that would search out, promote, and supervise peaceful uses of the atom. After a quarter of a century, about 7000 full-time employees and many more workers under grants and contracts still pursue the original mission, at a cost of around $2 billion a year to the American taxpayer. Many portentous questions remain unanswered. Yet we are embarking on a course that will make us dependent on nuclear energy by the end of the century.

The problems related to the use of nuclear energy fall into three classes. Most important of these, imprinted in our minds by the victims of Hiroshima and Nagasaki and by worldwide fallout from testing of nuclear weapons, is radiation. There are also the social and ecological consequences of mining large amounts of low grade uranium and thorium ore, and the biological and climatic effects of producing enormous amounts of waste heat. On a second look, the revolution to be brought about by nuclear energy appears to be merely an extension of well-known patterns and problems.

Radiation

Radiation released during transformations of radioactive nuclei may be particulate, electromagnetic, or both. The particles of most significance are positive and negative electrons (beta rays), alpha particles, and neutrons. The electromagnetic radiation consists of gamma rays.

There are more than a thousand different radioactive isotopes, many of them manmade. With each isotope is associated a characteristic time called the half-life, a statistical property giving the time required for half the nuclei to decay. (This exponential decay is the opposite of exponential growth, discussed in chapter 5.) After one half-life has elapsed, half of the original nuclei remain; after two half-lives, one quarter; after three half-lives, one eighth; and so on. The half-life varies tremendously from isotope to isotope. Half of the nuclei of polonium-212 decay in less than a millionth of a second, while the half-life of thorium-232 is 10 billion years.

Measurement of Radiation

Radioactivity and radiation are measured in special units. A curie (so named in honor of Marie and Pierre Curie) is the quantity of a radioactive isotope equivalent in activity to one gram of radium, in which there are 3.7×10^{10} nuclear disintegrations per second. Smaller units are the millicurie (10^{-3} curie) and the microcurie (10^{-6} curie). The longer the half-life of an isotope, the larger is the total number of radioactive nuclei in a curie. A curie of polonium-212 would consist of 3.7×10^{10} atoms (about as many atoms as there are in a billionth of a milliliter of the air around you), and its decay would be complete in a few dozen microseconds. In contrast, a curie of thorium-232 would contain billions of billions of billions of atoms (2×10^{28}), and its activity would be virtually undiminished after millennia. Even so, a curie of thonium-232 would make up a cube less than one meter on a side.

We often want to measure radiation rather than the amount of a radioisotope. The radiation that concerns us is ionizing radiation, that is, radiation which imparts energy to the matter it strikes, creating positive and negative charges or ions. Units which measure radiation are simply units representing the amount of energy that radiation imparts to matter. The roentgen is a unit of exposure to X rays or gamma rays, equivalent to the amount of radiation that imparts 87.8 ergs of energy to one gram of dry air.

The dosage actually absorbed is expressed in rads. Rads measure the energy imparted to matter by both particulate and electromagnetic rays. One rad corresponds to 100 ergs per gram of matter. Air, water, and most biological materials absorb roughly equivalent amounts of radiation. When exposed to 1 roentgen they absorb about 0.9 rad. An exception is bone, which, with its high content of calcium and consequently higher average atomic weight, sometimes responds differently to exposure to radiation.

The biological effects of radiation depend on its properties. For this reason the rem (roentgen equivalent man) was defined to be the unit of human biological dose of ionizing radiation. A rem is a rad multiplied by a factor which depends on the type and energy of the radiation. This factor is usually 1, making a rem equal to a rad, except in the case of very energetic alpha rays, when it may be assigned a value of 10 or 20.

Biological Effects of Radiation

Particles emitted from radioactive nuclei usually carry more than a million times the energy of the same particles at rest (in normal thermal motion). Charged particles lose this energy bit by bit in collisions with atoms. Most of the collisions are with electrons, which are usually driven away from the influence of the nuclei which controlled them, leaving behind positively charged ions and broken chemical bonds. The ions have different chemical properties from the atoms or molecules that gave rise to them. If enough ionizations occur, the function of an entire cell can be disrupted. This is how radiation damages living things.

An average charged particle ionizes on the order of 10^5 atoms before coming to rest. The heavier the particle, the shorter is its disruptive path. Thus an alpha particle travels only one-tenth as far as a proton, which, in turn, travels only one-sixtieth as far as an electron. Since an alpha particle, a proton, and an electron will ionize the same number of atoms if they have the same initial energy, the trail of an alpha particle, while shortest, must be the most devastated. For this reason alpha particles are exceedingly dangerous when they arise from a source within the body—in the bones or lungs, for example—but virtually harmless if created only a few centimeters outside the body.

Although they bear no charge, gamma rays also interact with orbital electrons. They transfer such large amounts of energy in each collision that electrons escape with enough energy to cause further ionizations, creating secondary tracks.

Neutrons usually interact with nuclei. A collision between a neutron and a nucleus may knock the nucleus away from one of its electrons with enough force to form an ion. When a neutron is captured by a nucleus, emission of particles, gamma rays, or both follows. These emissions cause further ionizations, a phenomenon that is exploited in fast neutron therapy of malignant tumors.

Exposure of the whole body to a concentrated dose of more

than 600 rads brings death in a few weeks, from irreparable damage to bone marrow, lymph nodes, and spleen. A dose this size causes an average of more than a million ionizations in each cell of the body.[5] With an acute dose of 100 to 600 rads, the same types of changes occur although the chances of recovery are increased as the dose becomes lower. Doses of 100 rads or more would be experienced only in nuclear war, in a major nuclear accident, or in radiation therapy.

The causal relationship between radiation and cancer and leukemia is well documented although incompletely understood. Cancers have been produced in adults by single or extended doses of 100 rads. Doses to the fetus of only 5 rads have been implicated in the development of cancer. There was an increased incidence of leukemia among early radiologists and among survivors of Hiroshima and Nagasaki. Workers painting radium dials in the years before World War II moistened and shaped their brushes on their tongues. The radioactive material they ingested in this way collected in their bones, where it caused a high incidence of cancer. Deposits of radioactive iodine in the thyroid can cause cancer of this organ. Inhalation of radon and its radioactive "daughters" (successive stages in the disintegration of uranium) has led to a high rate of lung cancer among uranium miners (Box 8–2).

Chronic exposure to radiation also results in a shortening of the lifespan which cannot be attributed to any particular cause of death. It has been compared to the aging process, and is probably due to cumulative minor damage to cells in all parts of the body.

If radiation causes ionizations in the hereditary material (DNA) of a sperm or an egg cell, a change or mutation can occur in the genetic information passed on by parent to offspring. Mutations are likely to cause abnormality or death of organisms developing from affected cells. The defects are inheritable and may be passed on to future generations. Not all genetic damage is as dramatic as a stillbirth, abortion, or gross defect. Many mutations are subtle and at present impossible to detect. They may predispose an organism to certain diseases, or render it generally less fit than one not carrying the mutation.

Some of the radiation to which we are exposed is natural, arising from cosmic rays, solar radiation, and radioactive elements in the earth. It varies between 80 and 150 millirads per person per year. It varies both with the latitude and the altitude at which a person lives and with the composition of the rocks beneath him and the house around him. Because man has lived in this level of radiation for about 2 million years, many people consider it safe and conclude that additional amounts of radiation of the same order of magnitude are also safe—or at least, insignificant. However, it is reasonable to assume (even though we cannot measure it) that some fraction of the cancers, genetic defects, and dis-

BOX 8-2   DECAY OF ^{238}U

Radium-226 is the sixth member of the radioactive disintegration series that begins with uranium-238. The preceding members do not contribute significantly to the radiation hazards from mines and mining, but radium gives rise to the gas radon which pervades the atmosphere of the mine and, with its decay daughters, is the source of potentially harmful radiation. Radon itself is inhaled but, being a gas, is exhaled again. The daughters, however, remain in the lungs, where they emit energetic alpha rays. Radium is dangerous if it enters water supplies or food chains, and it is selectively deposited in bone, where it emits destructive alpha rays. The radioactive decay series beginning with ^{238}U is given below.

Element	Radiation	Half-life
Uranium-238	alpha	4.5×10^{10} years
Thorium-234	beta	24 days
Proactinium-234	beta	1.1 minutes
Uranium-234	alpha	2.4×10^{5} years
Thorium-230	alpha	8.0×10^{4} years
Radium-226	alpha	1.6×10^{3} years
Radon-222	alpha	3.8 days
Polonium-218	alpha or beta	3.0 minutes
Lead-214	beta	27 minutes
or Astatine-218	alpha	2 seconds
Bismuth-214	beta or alpha	20 minutes
Polonium-214	alpha	1.5×10^{-4} seconds
or Thallium-210	beta	1.3 minutes
Lead-210	beta	22 years
Bismuth-210	beta or alpha	5.0 days
Polonium-210	alpha	140 days
or Thallium-206	beta	4.2 minutes
Lead-206	stable	stable

eases of aging from which man has always suffered is caused by the natural radiation around and in him, and that any increase in exposure will bring about a corresponding increase in radiation-induced disabilities.

Exposure to radiation in medical diagnosis and therapy adds, on the average, 65 millirads per year per person. Although exposure from a single diagnostic X ray has been reduced through improved equipment and technique, overall medical exposure is increasing because of increased reliance on radiological methods.

People do not become disturbed about natural background radiation or medical exposure. The first is unavoidable and the second is a matter of personal choice, in which the benefits are usually clearly seen to outweigh the hazards. But when people are told they will be exposed to manmade radiation without being given a chance to say no, they become alarmed and angry. Two different curves describe the acceptable balance between benefit and risk, depending on whether the activity is voluntary or involuntary.[6] In general, when the decision is his own, a person is willing to accept between 1000 and 10,000 times the risk that he will tolerate if the choice is made for him. Thus a skydiver may rage at the thought of having fluoride added to his drinking water.

Much of the controversy about radiation standards for the general population and for workers who receive occupational exposure centers around the existence or nonexistence of a threshold dose below which no damage occurs. The problem is to establish dose-response curves which describe the relationship between the dose and its effect. Several types of curves are illustrated in figure 8–5. For a few effects, such as the development of cataracts, a fairly definite threshold has been established. Certain types of damage occur only when the radiation has more than some minimum amount of energy. Factors like nutritional status and oxygen concentration influence the extent of damage. The body has mechanisms, which we are only beginning to understand, by which it repairs radiation damage. An acute dose overwhelms the capacity for repair, and this may explain why a given dose becomes less harmful as it is spread out over time. It also helps to explain why cells that are growing, dividing, or metabolizing rapidly are more sensitive than inactive cells, and why a fetus is more sensitive than an adult. The active, growing, dividing cell does not have time to repair itself before the damage is expressed.

A linear relationship between dose and response has been established experimentally for doses exceeding 20 or 25 rads. Extrapolation of this curve to low or attenuated doses is risky, for the reasons mentioned above. But chronic, low level exposure concerns us most, and for this, data become scarce and inconclusive. Many radiologists believe that for cancer induction there may be a practical threshold if not an abso-

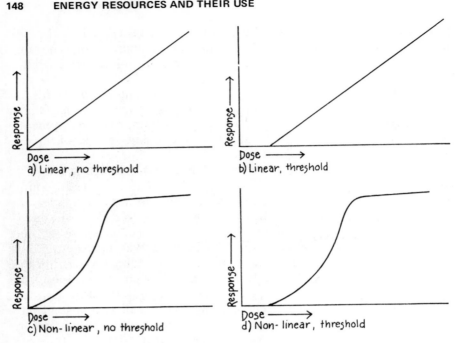

Figure 8–5. Types of theoretical dose-response curves.
a, Response is directly proportional to dose and the slightest dose elicits a small response.
b, Response is directly proportional to dose, but a certain minimum dose is required before a response is evoked.
c, A sigmoid dose-response curve, typical of many curves in biology. There is no threshold, although for low doses the response is very slight.
d, Similar to the curve in *c,* but there is no response until some minimum dosage is reached.

lute one. A latent period occurs between the time of exposure and the development of a cancer. This latent period increases as the dose rate and the dose decrease. When it becomes longer than a normal lifespan, you will die of something else before your cancer develops.

For genetic effects, no such practical threshold can exist. Although statistics for people are lacking, experiments with lower animals suggest that there is no threshold for genetic effects, although the effects do depend on the dose rate.

Standards

Taking into account all that is known about the effects of radiation on man, the Federal Radiation Council and the National Council on Radiation Protection propose radiation standards to the Environmental Protection Agency and the AEC, which are empowered

to establish and enforce them. The AEC sets industrial standards govern-
ing occupational doses, doses to the general public, and maximum
emission levels for various types of facilities. The Environmental Protection Agency is responsible for environmental quality standards. In
practice, the real work of regulation is carried out by the AEC, as it has
always been.

Standards for doses of manmade radiation have been revised
repeatedly since the first occupational limits were established in England
more than 50 years ago. In the United States they are currently set at an
average of 0.17 rem per person per year for the general population, with
a maximum of 0.5 rem per year for an individual. Radiation workers
are limited to 5 rem per year. Medical exposure is excepted from these
limits. Although the permissible doses of manmade radiation approximate those from natural sources, there is widespread concern that the
standards are not strict enough. But every activity bears some risk. If
3000 extra cancer deaths each year seem unthinkable, remember that
many people die whenever London or New York has a good smog.
While this is no excuse for killing people with radiation, it may put
things into better perspective. A cost-benefit analysis might show the
annual per capita medical cost for nuclear energy to be many times less
than the cost of preventing this expense.

Regulating the release of manmade radioactivity could reach
great levels of complexity. It is not enough to monitor the release of
each individual radioisotope. Each one should be followed through all
the physical, chemical, and biological pathways by which it is concentrated or dispersed. Because each nuclear facility is a unique case, each
facility, in the extreme, would require its own standards, in order to
insure a uniform and acceptable level of risk. This would make regulation the problem rather than the solution.

It is misleading to compare the total exposure to manmade
radiation with the exposure to natural radiation because the radioisotopes involved are not the same. Some radioisotopes released by man
do not occur in nature at all. The dangerous iodine-131 is one of these.
Plutonium-239 is another. It is not as if we walk around in some level of
generalized radiation which is suddenly raised by a factor of two or so.
We are exposing ourselves to brand new hazards. A few examples should
illustrate the problems faced by makers of standards. Radioactive
krypton, a chemically inert gas, is considered practically harmless, and
has been intentionally vented to the atmosphere. Similar amounts of
iodine-131, zeroing in on thyroid glands, would be intolerable. The rate
at which radioisotopes are released is only one factor related to their
ultimate concentration in the environment. For gaseous emissions,
prevailing wind and precipitation patterns must be considered. For
isotopes in liquid effluents, the characteristics of the body of water

receiving them are important. Radioactivity from one nuclear power plant using the cooling capacity of a swiftly flowing river might have no significant effect on the environment. But what about the second plant on the same river? Or the tenth?

The situation with lakes is even more complex. Lakes are fed by some rivers and drained by others. Each lake has its characteristic flushing time, which is the time required for a complete renewal of its water. Despite the wailing over Lake Erie, this lake could be restored, not necessarily to its former condition, but to a satisfactory condition, within a short time, because its flushing time is about three years. Lake Michigan, on the other hand, has a flushing time of many decades—perhaps as much as a century; and the flushing time for Lake Superior is 500 to 1000 years. While radioisotopes discharged into Lake Erie are soon washed out again, those discharged into Lake Michigan or Lake Superior can accumulate to dangerous levels.

If mixing of the water is incomplete, radioisotopes may collect in certain regions of the lake. Concentration of radioisotopes in the food chain is a matter of major concern. Research into these areas is clearly indicated.

Meanwhile, simple standards have been set following recommendations of national and international advisory bodies. The standards accept the most conservative interpretation of available data and incorporate an additional safety factor. Necessary measurements can be made, so that the standards can be enforced. This is important. As we should have learned from Prohibition and attempts to legislate sexual activities, an unenforced or unenforceable law can be worse than none at all.

Until now, standards have been set with only man's safety in mind. What of the effects of radiation on other species? When we think of protecting man, we mean protecting individual men, not *Homo sapiens* in general. With other species, however, the concern is for survival of populations, the fate of an individual mattering very little. In many species, individuals are damaged but populations adapt and survive. The implications of this adaptability are profound. Chronic exposure to radioactivity will probably increase the mutation rate in most or all organisms, leading to increased variation and increased possibilities for adaptation. Think of the consequences for organisms like bacteria, insects, and rats, creatures with short life cycles which are already adapting faster than we can devise ways to control them.

Sources of Radiation from Nuclear Power

It is easy to focus on the power plant and forget the other steps in the total nuclear energy cycle. The problems begin in the uranium mines, where miners in the past have been exposed to dangerous levels of radon and its daughters. During the last fifteen years the plight of uranium miners has received considerable attention, with the result that the radiation hazard has been greatly reduced. Miners now contracting lung cancer were exposed to levels of radiation up to 20 times the maximum permitted today. Unfortunately, it will be at least another decade before we have enough data to show whether today's standards are adequate.

Another problem is the radioactive residue left from treating uranium ores. A typical mill must dispose of about 10 curies of radium each day. There is no satisfactory way to deal with the millions of tons of radium-rich wastes which lie exposed and vulnerable to erosion by wind and water. Part of this material was once used as landfill and homes were built on it. But that no longer seems like a very good idea.

Processing uranium fuel involves a number of steps. These are primarily chemical and metallurgical processes with which we have had a great deal of experience. The hazards are negligible. After being milled into "yellowcake," ore is refined into "orange oxide," then hydrogenated and converted to "green salt." The green salt is converted to uranium hexafluoride for enrichment at one of the three gaseous diffusion plants located at Oak Ridge, Paducah, and Portsmouth. The enrichment step, in which ^{235}U is concentrated severalfold, requires an enormous amount of energy, which is derived from burning high sulfur coal. The gaseous diffusion plants use more than 45 billion kilowatt hours of electricity annually, more than is generated in the power plants for which they provide nuclear fuel. (Not all of the enriched uranium is destined for the generation of electricity, but much of it is.)

The greatest dangers in the entire uranium fuel cycle arise during reprocessing of used fuel elements, owing to the variety of concentrated radioactive materials that must be handled without the built-in protective mechanisms that exist in the power plant itself. Unspent uranium and newly created plutonium are separated for use in new fuel elements; radioactive fission products and byproducts are separated for disposal or storage. Standards for chemical reprocessing plants are more lenient than those for power plants, an admission that the radioactivity cannot be adequately contained. The advent of a successful fast breeder will increase the problem because of the quantities of plutonium that must be processed. Plutonium is the deadliest element known. One millionth of a gram injected into the bloodstream of a dog can cause bone cancer.

Transportation of nuclear fuels and radioactive wastes poses another potential hazard, in the event of accident or sabotage. So far the record has been good. But as traffic in radioactive materials increases, accidents are bound to occur. If plutonium becomes a major energy source worldwide, let us hope for more political stability and individual sanity than exist today. There is little comfort in knowing that nuclear weapons so far have kept an uneasy peace among nations possessing them, when anyone with a chunk of plutonium can build a bomb.

Although the probability of a major accident in a nuclear power plant is very very small, it can never be zero. The consequences of such an accident can be as great as you care to imagine. How small is very small? One accident in a thousand years of a reactor's operation? With 100 reactors, then, there would be a major accident every ten years. With 1000 reactors, there would be a disaster each year. We do not yet have enough experience to know how small a very small probability is. Placing the reactor underground wherever geology permits offers an additional measure of real security as well as a psychological advantage.

Nuclear power plants continuously produce gaseous, liquid, and solid radioactive wastes. A typical 800 megawatt plant produces the same number and kinds of nuclear fissions in 10 years' operation as were produced in all the aboveground testing of nuclear weapons. More than 3 million curies of strontium-90, for example, are formed each year in such a plant. In addition to the mass of radioactive fission products which is very nearly equal to the mass of fuel consumed, the materials of the reactor itself and the coolant are made radioactive by neutron bombardment. Although the idea of this much radioactivity is frightening, most reactors release substantially less radioactivity to the environment than the regulations allow. There is no immediate cause for alarm. The problem, again, is growth. Safely within the limits now, we will approach the danger point rapidly as exponential growth of nuclear power continues.

By committing ourselves to the use of nuclear fission we are also committing ourselves and our descendants to the permanent custodianship of staggering amounts of radioactive wastes. Already, hundreds of millions of curies are awaiting development of a satisfactory disposal scheme. The plan is to concentrate the wastes as much as possible, solidify them in an insoluble form, and bury them in special containers deep within geologically stable structures safe from large earth movements, invasion of groundwater, and incursions by man. Certain salt beds meet the criteria for burial sites, as do some water-free granite structures near the oceans. No one has a plan for what to do if, despite all precautions, something goes wrong at the graveyard, although the wastes can theoretically be retrieved. None other than the Director of the Oak Ridge National Laboratory has compared the social commitment to nuclear energy with the social commitment made thousands of years ago to agriculture. It is a turning point. There can be no going back.

Mining

By the time it reaches the power plant, the concentrated energy in uranium fuel gives uranium a tremendous advantage over coal, many tons of which must be burned each day. Much of this advantage is negated in the mines, however, where a ton of earth must be dug up to get a pound of uranium oxide. And very soon these relatively rich deposits will be gone.

More than half the uranium ore in this country is amenable to mining with open pit methods, which resemble the strip mining of coal. To the usual environmental problems is added radioactivity. In addition, the volume of waste remaining after uranium has been removed is at least as great as the amount of material that was dug up. The earth has been grossly disturbed. Reclamation is at best difficult and at worst impossible.

Waste Heat

The inexorable laws of the universe decree that all the energy we use will ultimately be degraded to useless heat. The production of electricity in the present generation of nuclear power plants is a relatively inefficient process because for reasons of safety the nuclear plant must operate at a lower temperature than the fossil fuel plant. The efficiency of the steam cycle depends on the initial and final temperatures of the system, with the greatest efficiency resulting from the largest temperature differential (see chapter 5). Future generations of nuclear reactors will probably overcome this problem, making nuclear power plants no less efficient than fossil plants. But any steam plant discharges large amounts of heat to the environment, whether to the atmosphere or to cooling water. When you put heat somewhere, something happens. Most of the things that happen are considered undesirable by most people, although some waste heat could be used to our advantage. The effects and possible uses of waste heat will be considered in chapter 10.

NUCLEAR FUSION

Scientists have been observing fusions of light nuclei in the laboratory for several decades. Their studies have given insights into the nature of matter, but because of the tremendous amount of energy required to induce fusion and the infrequency of the fusions themselves, they have failed to advance us significantly toward the goal of gaining useful energy from the fusion process. Since about 1950, several nations have pursued research programs aimed specifically at making fusion an energy source for man.

Although many fusion reactions occur in the stars, earthlings are limited to those involving the two heavy isotopes of hydrogen, deuterium (^{2}H) and tritium (^{3}H). Tritium is so rare in nature that it must be made artificially if we are to obtain useful quantities of it. The best way to make it is by bombarding the lithium isotope of mass 6 with neutrons. The reactions of interest are summarized in Box 8–3.

Technology for separation of deuterium from sea water is well developed. It poses no foreseeable environmental problems even if conducted on a large scale. If we were to remove only 1 percent of the deuterium from the sea, we would have fuel equivalent in energy value to half a million times the earth's initial stock of fossil fuels.

The situation with lithium is quite different. The isotope of interest, ^{6}Li, comprises only 7 percent of natural lithium. Known and inferred reserves of lithium are small because this metal, unlike most, does not tend to concentrate in ores, but occurs diffusely throughout the oceans and the earth's crust. Geologists believe that the minable lithium deposits of the world would yield only about as much energy as the world's initial supply of fossil fuels. This may or may not be a cause for pessimism. If we actually develop a fusion reactor based on deuterium and tritium fuel, the major problems of fusion will have been solved. Use of the deuterium-deuterium reaction would be only one technical step away. The question of recovering lithium from seawater is controversial. Some forecasters look to the sea as a source of most of our future minerals, but others point out that mining the sea will probably be incompatible with farming it, which we also propose to do.

Controlled nuclear fusion looks like a nearly ideal source of energy (although coal did, too, a couple of centuries ago, as did nuclear fission in the 1950s). There appear to be no problems in obtaining cheap and abundant fuel if deuterium is used. The fusion plant itself would provide both heat and electricity with high efficiency (perhaps 80 or 90 percent) and few unwanted side effects. The main end product would be helium, for which there are many uses. The amount of radioactive waste would be several orders of magnitude smaller than for equivalent fission plants. The only radioactive material formed in large amounts would be tritium, for which improved methods of handling are needed.

It is difficult to talk about the safety of a fusion reactor since no one is sure what one will be like. However, while there is always the possibility of fission reactions getting out of hand, no such chance exists with fusion. It is hard enough to get sustained fusion started in the first place. Anything that went wrong would quickly quench the reaction.

BOX 8-3   NUCLEAR FUSION REACTIONS OF POTENTIAL
USE IN A FUSION REACTOR

$^2H + {}^2H \rightarrow {}^3He + n + 3.2$ Mev   or
$^2H + {}^2H \rightarrow {}^3H + {}^1H + 4.0$ Mev

These two reactions are about equally probable. When the second occurs it is followed by: $^2H + {}^3H \rightarrow {}^4He + n + 17.6$ Mev. *The overall reaction is* $5\,{}^2H \rightarrow {}^4He + {}^3He + {}^1H + 2n + 24.8$ Mev.

The scheme under most active consideration calls for production of tritium from lithium: $^6Li + n \rightarrow {}^4He + {}^3H = 4.8$ Mev. *The tritium reacts with deuterium:* $^2H + {}^3H \rightarrow {}^4He + n + 17.6$ Mev. *The neutron can react with another lithium nucleus, so that this process is analogous to the breeding of fissionable fuel. The net reaction in the system based on lithium and deuterium is* $^6Li + {}^2H \rightarrow 2\,{}^4He + 22.4$ Mev.

Energy is released when the lithium nucleus is split by a neutron, in apparent contradiction to the general rule that energy is released by fission of heavy nuclei or fusion of light ones. Reference to figure 8–1 shows, however, that the mass defect of the product nuclei is greater than the mass defect of the reactant, due to the extraordinary stability of the helium-4 nucleus.

Although fusion reactors could be the permanent solution to world energy problems, the economic and technical problems may be insurmountable. Why is it such an immense step from an uncontrolled fusion reaction (an H-bomb) to a controlled one, when the step from fission bomb to reactor is so easy? Fission can occur any time that a fissionable nucleus captures a neutron. You need only to make sure that the right number of neutrons is available to an appropriate number of fissionable nuclei. Fusion, on the other hand, occurs only in the stars or under simulated stellar conditions. While nuclear fusion is the source of the heat of the stars, only the heat of the stars allows fusion to proceed. Fusion requires that two nuclei come together with enough energy to overcome the repulsive forces that normally exist between particles of like charge, enabling the very powerful intranuclear forces which act only at exceedingly short range to come into play.

At temperatures of tens of millions of degrees, atoms as we know them cannot exist. Instead, matter is a plasma of free nuclei and free electrons. Even in this state, fusions are relatively infrequent until temperatures of some 100 million degrees are reached. At 100 million degrees, the reaction between deuterium and tritium sustains itself at a rate sufficient to yield useful energy. Even higher temperatures are required for the deuterium-deuterium reaction to be of interest, and for this reason scientists are concentrating on the deuterium-tritium reaction even though its usefulness will be limited by availability of lithium.

Three conditions must be achieved simultaneously in a fusion reactor: a temperature of at least 100 million degrees, a plasma dense enough to insure frequent collisions of nuclei (by most standards, this would be a fairly good vacuum), and a confinement time long enough for the process to yield net energy. What container do you use for a plasma heated to 100 million degrees? No material container would do the job. On a small scale, for a short time, and at great cost in energy, plasmas have been confined within strategic arrangements of intense magnetic fields, called magnetic bottles. No type of magnetic bottle has yet met all the requirements. Some leak too much. Some require so much energy for their creation and maintenance that it is doubtful whether they would ever yield net energy.

Even with an adequate confinement system, the structural materials of the reactor would be subjected to neutron bombardment several times as intense as that inflicted on today's fission reactors. Since one of the major problems with fission is maintaining the structural integrity of the reactor under the onslaught of high energy neutrons, some engineers predict that the useful life of a fusion reactor may be impractically short. To combat this difficulty, some proposed reactor designs rely heavily on unusual materials. One preliminary design, for example, calls for large quantities of the rare metal niobium. Total quantities of this resource appear prohibitively small. Whether the leaking neutrons damage the reactor or not, they will make it radioactive. These radioactive materials constitute a disposal problem. How serious this problem could become depends on both the ultimate design of fusion reactors and their useful lifetime.

Another means of releasing energy from fusion has met with limited success in the laboratory. When tiny pellets of frozen deuterium-tritium fuel are subjected to an intense laser pulse for a tenth of a billionth (10^{-10}) of a second, they explode like miniature hydrogen bombs. There is no need for a fancy magnetic bottle; no need, in fact, for a plasma. The problems are ones of scale. The fact that scientists can explode a few fusion grenades in the laboratory is no guarantee that a safe, economical—or even functional—1000 megawatt power plant can be built on the same principles.

REFERENCES

1. W. Laurence, *Men and Atoms—The Discovery, the Uses and the Future of Atomic Energy* (New York: Simon and Schuster, 1962).

2. M. K. Hubbert, "Energy Resources" in *Resources and Man,* National Academy of Sciences-National Research Council (San Francisco: W. H. Freeman and Company, 1969), pp. 219–228.
3. U.S., Federal Power Commission, *The 1970 National Power Survey* (Washington, D.C.: 1971).
4. P. Ehrlich and A. Ehrlich, *Population, Resources, Environment* (San Francisco: W. H. Freeman and Company, 1970), pp. 95–96.
5. J. Harte, R. Socolow, and J. Ginocchio, "Radiation," in *Patient Earth,* ed. J. Harte and R. Socolow (New York: Holt, Rinehart, and Winston, Inc., 1971), pp. 299–320.
6. C. Starr, "Social Benefit Versus Technological Risk," *Science* 165 (1969): 1232–1238.

SUGGESTED READING

Benedict, M. "Electric Power from Nuclear Fission." *Science and Public Affairs* 27, 7 (1971): 8–16.
Eipper, A. "Nuclear Power on Cayuga Lake." In *Patient Earth,* edited by J. Harte and R. Socolow, pp. 112–134. New York: Holt, Rinehart and Winston, Inc., 1971.
Foreman, H., ed. *Nuclear Power and the Public.* Garden City, N.Y.: Anchor Books, Doubleday & Company, Inc., 1972.
Geesaman, D. "Plutonium and the Energy Decision." *Science and Public Affairs* 27, 7 (1971): 33–36.
Gofman, J. "Nuclear Power and Ecocide: An Adversary View of New Technology." *Science and Public Affairs,* 27 (1971): 28–32.
Harte, J., Socolor, R. and Ginocchio, J. "Radiation." In *Patient Earth,* edited by J. Harte and R. Socolow, pp. 295–320. New York: Holt, Rinehart and Winston, Inc., 1971.
Holdren, J., and Herrera, P. *Energy.* San Francisco: Sierra Club, 1971.
Jungk, R. *Brighter Than a Thousand Suns—A Personal History of the Atomic Scientists.* Translated by James Cleugh. New York: Harcourt, Brace and World, Inc., 1958.
Laurence, W. *Men and Atoms—The Discovery, the Uses and the Future of Atomic Energy.* New York: Simon and Schuster, 1962.
Lederberg, J. "Squaring an Infinite Circle: Radiobiology and the Value of Life." *Science and Public Affairs* 27, 7 (1971): 43–45.
Lilienthal, D. *Change, Hope, and the Bomb.* Princeton, N.J.: Princeton University Press, 1963.
Lindrop, P., and Rotblat, J. "Radiation Pollution of the Environment." *Science and Public Affairs* 27, 7 (1971): 17–24.
March, R. "E = mc^2 and All That." In *Physics for Poets,* pp. 149–159. New York: McGraw Hill Book Company, 1970.
March, R. "Rutherford Picks Apart the Atom." In *Physics for Poets,* pp. 173–187. New York: McGraw Hill Book Company, 1970.

Parsegian, V. "New Goals for Atomic Energy." *Science and Public Affairs* 27, 8 (1971): 2–7.

Post, R. "Fusion Power: The Uncertain Certainty." *Science and Public Affairs* 27, 8 (1971): 42–48.

Rogers, F. "Underground Nuclear Power Plants." *Science and Public Affairs* 27, 8 (1971): 38–41.

Seaborg, G. "On Misunderstanding the Atom." *Science and Public Affairs* 27, 7 (1971): 46–53.

Tamplin, A. "Issues in the Radiation Controversy." *Science and Public Affairs* 27, 7 (1971): 25–27.

U.S., Congress, Hearings Before the Joint Committee on Atomic Energy. *AEC Authorizing Legislation Fiscal Year 1972.* 92d Cong., 1st Sess., 1971. Parts 1 and 2.

U.S., Congress, Hearings Before teh Subcommittee on Research, Development and Radiation of the Joint Committee on Atomic Energy. *Radiation Exposure of Uranium Miners.* 90th Cong., 1st sess., 1967. Parts 1 and 2.

CHAPTER 9

Other Energy Sources

It is the sun that shares our works.
The moon shares nothing. It is a sea.

When shall I say of the sun,
It is a sea; it shares nothing;

The sun no longer shares our works
And the earth is alive with creeping men,

Mechanical beetles never quite warm?

Wallace Stevens

Actual and predicted shortages of fossil fuels, doubts about full-scale commitment to nuclear fission, and the uncertainty of fusion have led to an inventory of all energy sources. For the long term, there are but three major sources of energy: nuclear fission (as accomplished in the breeder reactor), nuclear fusion, and the sun. The promise of these technologies is in the future, however, and promises are not always kept. Meanwhile, there are other sources of energy that can buy time or be of local importance—or even of general importance, should other technologies fall short of their goals.

It is illusory to hope that exploitation of energy can be without environmental effect, because by definition transfers and transformations of energy make things happen. However, the sources of energy discussed in this chapter have some significant advantages over fossil fuels and nuclear energy. Some of them represent the energy of continuing natural processes that cannot be depleted. For the most part they do not spew poisons into the air and water. There is no problem of radioactivity. And they require no mining, with its tremendous cost to people and the earth.

WOOD

Consumption of wood reached its peak in the United States around 1870, when it yielded about 8.4×10^{11} kilowatt-hours of energy. But the relative importance of wood was already declining. In 1850, wood furnished 90 percent of the energy derived from all fuel and water power. Twenty years later it was only 73 percent. Today, we still burn about a quarter as much fuel wood as we did a century ago, but it supplies a miniscule fraction of the energy we use.

Those who glorify a simple way of life epitomized by cutting a supply of fuel wood for the winter may be solving their personal problems, but they are not solving the problems of the nation or of the world. In the future, wood will serve as only a most minor source of energy. Like fossil fuels, it may have such value as a raw material that it will become too precious to burn at all.

NON-COMMERCIAL FUELS AND GARBAGE

Whenever man has abandoned nomadic ways, he has been confronted with problems of waste disposal. One solution has been to burn human and agricultural wastes as fuel. This practice is widespread in poor countries and is still found in parts of the United States. It is not an unmitigated good. Air pollution was not invented during the Industrial Revolution in Britain.

Improved treatment of wastes is increasing their value as fuel at the same time that other technologies are beginning to compete for them. Bagasse, a fibrous by-product of the sugar cane industry and an important non-commercial fuel in some areas, is now in demand for the manufacture of paper. Other agricultural wastes which once were burned are being converted to fertilizer, feed, and food supplements. If we begin to make use of the tons of animal wastes that now pollute the air and water, we may have to decide whether they sould be returned to the earth as fertilizer or converted to methane by anaerobic digestion. It has been calculated that conversion to methane of all animal wastes generated in the United States by a process under study would supply methane at a rate equal to about half our current rate of natural gas consumption.[1]

In Europe, where supplies of fuel have long been limited, a large percentage of municipal solid waste is burned to generate electricity and provide heat. Government agencies in the Unites States, along with universities and electric utilities, are beginning to examine new processes for converting solid waste to fuel. The most promising of these would convert the garbage to pipeline quality gas or liquid fuel. Two processes, both at the pilot plant stage, yield low-sulfur fuels with 50 to 75 percent of the energy value of the original material. One enthusiast estimates that the efficient conversion of garbage to power could furnish up to 6 percent of the energy needs of the United States at the same time that it solved a multi-billion dollar disposal problem.[1] Of course there are difficulties. One of them is poisonous combustion gases from plastics, which might pose a pollution problem. And the more garbage we recycle, the less there will be to burn.

Competing uses for garbage are not yet a problem—today, the problem is that nobody wants it. But whatever its other merits or demerits may be, human garbage is renewable; and one way or another, we will come to use it.

WIND POWER

Early man caught the wind in sails and moved himself over the water. He caught it on propellers and turned machines to do his work. The Dutch have a saying that God made other countries, but the Dutch [and the windmill] made Holland. Western Europe's conquest of the globe and much of her early industry were powered by the wind. By the end of the nineteenth century, several hundred thousand windmills dotted rural and not-so-rural landscapes all over the world (figure 9–1, a). At least 30,000 of them were in Denmark, northern Germany, the Netherlands, and England. In the United States, they meant life itself in dry areas west of the Mississippi River.[2]

Now sailboats are all but extinct, except as pleasure craft. Many of the windmills have vanished; most of the rest stand idle. Even Holland, finding herself sitting on a bubble of natural gas, has turned her back on wind power. The number of windmill manufacturers in the United States dropped from more than 20 in the 1920s to 2 in 1972, reflecting the march of electricity into rural areas. Now the wind is dismissed as being insufficient to contribute significantly to the world's energy needs.

But a renewed interest in wind power among many nations belies that attitude, as do the thousands of windmills manufactured in Australia, western Europe, and the U.S.S.R. for distribution around the world. As a truly renewable, non-depletable, and non-polluting energy source, the wind deserves respectful consideration (figure 9–1, b).

The energy of the wind originates in the sun. The amount of

Figure 9-1, *a.* A beautiful old sail windmill in use on Myconos island off Greece.
Photo credit: Harriet Irwin

b, A Jopp windmill in use in Minnesota. This is a 3 kilowatt, 110 volt d.c., direct
drive unit. Many units similar to this were built and used in the 1930s, 1940s, and
1950s.
Photo credit: Don Marier

wind power available for windmills has been estimated to be about
2×10^{10} kilowatts, roughly 300 times the amount of useful tidal
power, 6 times the world's installed electric power, and 50 percent
more than the total potential hydropower.[3]

The power, in kilowatts, in a current of air one square meter in
cross section varies with the cube of the velocity expressed in meters
per second: power = 6.13×10^{-4} v^3. Only 59 percent of this power is
theoretically recoverable. A windmill works because some of the wind
passes by. The efficiencies of modern windmills range between 50 and
80 percent. For an efficiency of 70 percent, the power available from
each square meter swept by the propeller would be 2.55×10^{-4} v^3. If
the wind's speed were 10 meters per second (a very brisk wind), the
power would be only one quarter of a kilowatt. The annual energy output for windmills varies between 100 kilowatt-hours in relatively calm

areas and 500 kilowatt-hours in windy areas, for each square meter swept. The efficiency varies with the wind's velocity, but not linearly. Below a minimum speed, no useful power is generated; and when the speed surpasses a maximum value there is no corresponding increase in power. Since wind power depends on the cube of wind velocity, doubling the velocity produces an eight-fold increase in power. One would think that a mill designed to function at normal wind velocities would be torn apart in a gale. But modern design insures that this will not happen, just as modern materials enable windmills to function reliably in climates as unfriendly as that of Antarctica.

The technology of windmills is well developed, as is the aerodynamic theory on which it is based. Over the centuries, almost every conceivable design has been tested. Each culture has developed models and materials characteristically its own, from the bamboo-and-sail structures of China to the picturesque Dutch mill to the spider-like wind pump that stands as a monument to the past on countless American farms. Modern materials such as plastics reinforced with glass have improved the performance of windmills and facilitated their manufacture. Extensive wind data are now available for many areas to assist in selecting sites.

The largest mills, ranging in capacity from 100 to 1000 kilowatts, are used for producing electricity. A number of them are hooked into Denmark's electric power grid and they function competitively with other types of power plants. Japan, another nation with a chronic fuel problem, is testing some large windmills.

Smaller mills with an output of 5 to 20 kilowatts are used to pump water or produce electricity in many isolated rural communities. This power is ample for refrigeration and illumination and the operation of radios. Small wind pumps, supplying less than 5 kilowatts, are usually used only for pumping water.

The disadvantages of wind power—its intermittent and unreliable nature, geographical limitations, and inability to supply large amounts of power for heavy industry—are well known. The only way to be sure of having power is to have a backup source ready for when the wind fails; and if this is so, why use the wind at all? For periods less than half an hour or an hour, large fluctuations in velocity make little difference. Over periods longer than a few weeks, wind velocities are monotonously predictable. It is for intermediate periods that an unexpected calm can be disruptive. But all power plants have periodic outages, planned and unplanned. The technology for storing energy in batteries, fuel cells, and pumped storage facilities promises to remove one of the last obstacles to the effective use of wind power (figure 9–2).

Although the seasonal nature of the wind is a disadvantage in some places, in others it is in phase with power needs. In Denmark, for

Figure 9-2. Wind as Power Source. To harness wind effectively one must be able to store the energy captured when the wind blows and release it more or less continuously. One scheme would be to use the electricity gneerated by the wind to decompose water electrolytically. The stored hydrogen and oxygen could then be fed at a constant rate into a fuel cell, which would produce direct current. This would be converted into alternating current and fed into a power line. Off-peak power generated elsewhere could also be used to run the electrolysis cell whenever the wind was deficient. From C.N. Summers, "The Conversion of Energy," *Scientific American* (September 1971) p. 158.

example, where many homes are heated electrically, the wind blows fastest and most steadily during the coldest months when peak demands for electricity occur.

Many countries with great need for energy have excellent potential for wind power. Conditions are favorable along the northwestern and southwestern coasts of Africa and probably along the entire western coast, as well as in Madagascar. There are potential sites along the Red Sea. In the interior of the continent things are less promising, but there are some good sites. In Asia, winds are light and variable during spring and fall, more powerful during winter and summer. Pakistan, India, Israel, and coastal Arabia have many good sites that can supply domestic power the year around with other uses perhaps confined to certain months. Australia has good potential along most of its coast. North America could develop wind power along the Atlantic and Pacific coasts and in the plains states east of the Rocky Mountains. In South America there are excellent sites along much of the west coast and in southern Argentina.

Because windmills require no fuel and are relatively maintenance free, their operating costs are low. Their useful life varies—it may be as short as 15 years, but frequently is much longer. There is no pollution and no damage to the environment. A minimum of land is required for small installations. Most people find that a windmill has functional beauty. Certainly no other power-producing device except the old fashioned waterwheel is a favorite theme of artists and photographers.

Initial cost is a problem if a great many units are required. Windmills cannot compete economically with a 1000 megawatt nuclear power plant. On the other hand, very few rural communities could use a 1000 megawatt nuclear power plant, so the question of scale has two faces. A 1 megawatt nuclear power plant could not compete economically with a windmill.

There are advantages to small, local facilities for generating electricity in spite of the trend in the United States toward gargantuan centralized installations. Wasteful, expensive, and environmentally destructive long-distance transmission of electricity becomes unnecessary, and the impact of a power failure is on the same small scale as the power plant itself.

For the industrialized world, wind power can ease the joint problems of fuel shortages and pollution. In a prototype solar-wind house in Arizona heat is provided by the sun and there are plans for air conditioning. The house is electrified by the wind, which stores energy in batteries. Life is not primitive in this house. Luxuries like food blenders are easily accommodated.

For great areas of the undeveloped world, the wind can supply an increment of energy that will greatly enhance the elusive "quality of life." Industrialization was painful for the Western world. It threatens to be even more painful for many ancient cultures if old ways are suddenly destroyed without adequate preparation for new. Perhaps countries only now beginning to industrialize can prevent some of the misery suffered by the West by adapting native handicrafts to local small scale manufacture of modern products. In many cases, wind power can be adequate for this.

TIDAL POWER

Derived from the energy of the earth-moon-sun system, tidal energy has a future as long as that of the system itself. Tidal energy is expended at a rate of about 3×10^9 kilowatts. Most of this expenditure is in the oceans, especially in shallow seas, bays, and the mouths of rivers where fresh and salt water mix. In these areas the difference in sea level between high and low tide ranges from less than 1 meter to more than 10. To harness the energy of ocean tides requires only the damming of a partially enclosed basin and the installation of facilities for generating electricity.

Tidal electric power is a special kind of hydroelectric power, depending on the alternate filling and emptying of a dammed basin rather than on the one-directional flow of water. The amount of energy available at a site depends on the range of the tide and the area of the enclosed basin, and can be calculated if these values are known. The maximum rate of energy flow at the most promising sites in North America, South America, and Europe is 6.4×10^7 kilowatts.[4] If we assume that 20 percent of this (a liberal allowance) can be converted to electricity, the potential for tidal electricity is about 13×10^6 kilowatts—less than 2 percent of the world's installed electric capacity. But if you happen to live near one of the tidal sites, the tides could give you all of your electricity without poison and forever.

Exploitation of tidal energy has barely begun, although small tidal mills date back to the eleventh century. An eleventh century mill at Dover, England, reportedly caused disaster to ships because of its disturbance of the sea. The world's first and only major tidal electric plant began operating in France in 1966 at the mouth of the Rance River, where the tidal range averages 8.4 meters. Proposed modifications will increase the original 240 megawatt capacity to 320 megawatts, using a creditable 24 percent of the available energy. A smaller, experimental plant has been designed in Russia.

The greatest tidal ranges in the world, exceeding 15 meters, occur in the Bay of Fundy off the eastern coast of Canada. The Canadian government, after investigating the feasibility of developing tidal power in the bay, concluded that although the potential energy production would be great (more than 13 million megawatt hours annually, at three sites), development is not economically feasible now. The United States reached a similar conclusion on the proposed project in Passamaquoddy Bay along the border between Maine and New Brunswick.

Conservation groups oppose tidal projects on the grounds that they will destroy natural scenery and modify coastal environments. These charges are true. But when the environmental costs of a tidal plant are compared with the costs of the alternatives, a tidal plant might prove to be the best choice.

HYDROELECTRIC POWER

The kinetic energy of falling water is derived from solar energy. The kinetic energy of the earth's water is the energy of all the drops of rain that fall and flow to the sea. Like the energy of winds and tides, it is constantly released whether we use it or not, and its lifetime is that of the earth as we know it.

More than 2000 years ago, man began to build waterwheels whose energy was coupled with many kinds of machines. Until the development of the steam engine, water power furnished most of the energy for industry. But hydropower had to be used where it was produced, while the noisy, dirty steam engine had the advantage of mobility. When large-scale generation and transmission of electricity became possible at the beginning of the twentieth century, the old waterwheel gave birth to the hydroelectric plant. Since then, the increase in hydroelectric power has followed a typical growth curve, about two-thirds of the present capacity having been added since World War II.

To produce hydroelectric power, a dam must be built on a river, with turbines and generators at its base. The water behind the dam stores energy that would otherwise have been dissipated as the water descended over the river bed. When tunnels through the dam are opened, water pours through with great force, spinning turbines which drive generators to produce electricity.

In many ways, hydropower is the best source of electricity we now have. It requires no mining, processing, transportation, or burning of fuel. The only waste produced is frictional heat from the turbines and generators, which would have been lost anyway if the water had fallen freely. Stresses on the structural materials of the plant are minimal because no phase of power production involves high temperatures, radioactivity, or corrosive chemicals. In addition, hydroelectric plants are usually part of larger developments involving navigation, recreation, fish and wildlife management, water quality control, water supply, flood control, or irrigation. These features combine to make hydroelectricity very cheap, unless it must be transmitted over long distances. Another advantage is that a hydroelectric plant can be started and brought to full capacity quickly. Thus hydropower is being used increasingly to supply electricity at times of peak demand.

When a lake is created where there was once a river, things cannot be the same as they were before. But even though a hydroelectric plant inevitably changes the environment, it does not poison it. The change may actually please many people, for it provides fishing and recreational activities where once a remote river was enjoyed by only a few.

There are problems—some with partial solutions, some with none. The reservoirs occupy large areas of land which is often prime agricultural land, and its exchange for an increment of electricity may be a bad bargain. It is also difficult to evaluate the exchange of unspoiled scenery for a recreational development. Only a few people derive satisfaction from knowing the wilderness is there, whether or not they ever see it. But when a wild river is developed it is gone forever, and we already have a lot of lakes. Technology cannot choose between producing food and producing electricity, or between fly casting for brook trout and spinning for bass. These questions must be decided by society.

Although there is no thermal pollution in the usual sense, the temperature of the water downstream from the dam can be affected. Water in a shallow reservoir becomes warmer than the river and increases the temperature downstream when it is released. Water at the bottom of a deep reservoir may be very cold. This water lowers the temperature downstream. The cold water may also be depleted in oxygen through the metabolism of microorganisms and failure to mix with surface waters. The problem of cold, oxygen-poor water can be corrected by aerating the water and releasing it from several levels to insure the proper temperature. The problem of warm water remains intractable.

When hydroelectric plants are operated intermittently, the flow of the river is grossly disturbed. Many indigenous species cannot survive the fluctuating flow. A second reservoir downstream can regulate the rate of flow, but this requires a lot of extra space and destroys an additional section of the river.

Dams may destroy the spawning grounds of migratory fish or prevent the fish from reaching them. The effectiveness of facilities for permitting safe passage of fish is limited. The cumulative impact of a series of dams on the Columbia River has greatly reduced game fish runs.

Leakage from the reservoir may cause the water table to rise, bringing with it dissolved salts and impairing the fertility of the soil. If the reservoir is shallow, a high rate of evaporation may lead to increased salinity. Sometimes these undesirable side effects can be prevented or at least minimized if they are foreseen.

At the end of 1970, 53,000 megawatts of hydroelectricity had been developed in the United States and an estimated maximum of 94,000 megawatts remained, not counting Alaska's potential of about 30,000 megawatts. But these statistics are misleading. In reality, hydro-electric power may have gone about as far as it can go in the United States. Development of a hydroelectric site is expensive and is seldom undertaken except in conjunction with other programs To many people, as they contemplate the loss of America's few remaining wild river gorges, the best program is to leave them alone. The best sites are already in use. Most of the remaining ones are in the Pacific Northwest and Alaska, but even here good sites are limited. Economic and other factors will preclude developing many of them. Legislation may prevent use of others (for example, the Wild and Scenic Rivers Act, Public Law 90–542). Plans for Alaska are viewed with particular concern because of the vulnerability of the arctic and sub-arctic environment and because development threatens some of North America's few remaining major wildlife habitats.

Hydroelectric plants supplied about 15 percent of the electricity used in the United States in the early 1970s. Although the amount of hydroelectricity will continue to grow slowly for several decades, due partly to increases in capacity of existing plants, the percentage it con-tributes will probably decrease to around 7 percent by the end of the century. Importing hydroelectricity from Canada, which has an enor-mous undeveloped potential, cannot be a long-term arrangement because in ten years Canada's own growth will require what is available as sur-plus today.

The situation for the world is more promising. About one-tenth of the world's potential hydropower has been developed. Even more sig-nificantly, the global capacity for hydropower is almost four times as great as the total installed electric power capacity.[4] The greatest poten-tial is in Africa and South America, the two continents which are de-ficient in coal.

Hydropower cannot be a long-term solution to the world's energy problems, although it can contribute substantially to the develop-ment of nations that have the greatest need for energy. The problem is silt. All rivers carry silt, tiny soil particles that are swept along with flowing water but which settle out in calm water. Thus a river's burden of silt will be dumped into the reservoir at the hydroelectric plant, a process called siltation, and the reservoir will gradually fill up. When the storage capacity of the reservoir is destroyed, the energy of the waterfall at the dam site will remain—smaller in amount, and subject to fluctua-tions in the river's flow. A small reservoir, fed by a river heavily laden with particulate matter, may fill up in 50 years. Other reservoirs may have a useful life of several centuries. The average is probably about a century. The dams must be maintained long after their usefulness has passed, for the accumulated silt cannot be permitted to wash suddenly downstream.

GEOTHERMAL ENERGY

The fossil fuels, winds, water power, the food we eat, and the tides are gifts to the earth from the sun and the moon. But the earth has its own energy, for mountain building and earthquakes, thermal processes and mechanical deformations. These processes have gone on at an apparently undiminished rate throughout geological time, driven by a reservoir of energy within the earth itself.

During the last century, men discovered that heat flows continuously from the interior of the earth to the surface, from which it is radiated into space. Volcanoes and hot springs gave further evidence for the earth's heat. If the earth is losing heat, the reasoning went, then the earth is cooling off—a theory compatible with the fiery birth of the planet from its parent sun. But that theory of the earth's origin is no longer in favor and there is little evidence that the earth is growing cooler despite its loss of heat. The heat generated by decay of radioactive elements in the crust and mantle is now considered sufficient to account for most or all of the heat flow and most of the geothermal processes that occur. The earth also has gravitational and rotational energy; there are phase changes from liquid to solid and changes in crystal structure brought about by the increase of temperature and pressure with depth, all of which involve changes in energy; and there are little-understood electromagnetic phenomena in the core of the earth. But the energy which directly affects man and the face of the earth is the energy of the radioactive atom. If we use the heat of the earth, we are indirectly using nuclear energy.

The average heat flow from the surface of the earth is about 1.3×10^{-6} calories per second per square centimeter, or about 40 calories per year. This energy would melt a sheet of ice half a centimeter thick in a year's time, a job that could be accomplished by the sun in a few hours. Heat generated in the earth is lost so slowly because rocks are very poor conductors of heat; thus, the surface of a rock exposed to sunlight becomes hot while the underside remains cool.

The total amount of heat stored in the outer 100 kilometers of the earth at temperatures above surface temperatures is about 2×10^{28} calories, or 2.3×10^{22} kilowatt-hours—roughly 150 times the solar energy that strikes the outer atmosphere in one year. Most of this heat is stored in the normal geothermal gradient, but local concentrations occur. Geothermal heat is concentrated along global systems of oceanic

ridges and continental rifts, and their associated zones of earthquake
activity, volcanoes, and other geothermal processes. It escapes to the
surface in geysers, hot springs, and volcanic eruptions. One belt of geothermal activity, the "ring of fire," stretches from South America
through Central America and across western North America to Alaska.
To the west and south it passes through the Aleutians, Japan, Taiwan,
the Philippines, and New Zealand. Another follows the great mountain
ranges that span Asia from northern India and Tibet to the Middle East
and pass into Greece and Italy. These areas are characterized by vast
reservoirs of underground steam and hot water which derive their heat
from the friction of sliding rocks or from passage of groundwater
through recently (during the last 10 million years or so) erupted volcanic rocks.

Hydrothermal energy, the energy of heated water, can be distinguished from geothermal energy, the energy of hot or molten rock,
although both are commonly referred to as geothermal. Strictly speak-
ing, it is hydrothermal energy that can now be exploited economically.
Because the two technologies will probably merge in the future, we will
refer to the earth's heat as geothermal energy whether it is manifested
in hot rocks or hot water.

Hot springs have been used for centuries, for their real and
imagined health benefits and as a source of various chemicals. The first
production of geothermal electricity was in 1904, from a dry steam
field in Larderello, Italy. The first electric power plant to exploit a hot
water reservoir was built in Wairakei, New Zealand, in 1946. Other
power plants using hot water for energy are in Japan, Mexico, and the
U.S.S.R. The extensive Geysers project in California, begun in 1955,
uses steam. In Iceland, geothermal energy has been used since 1925,
mostly for space heating and water heating. Many other countries have
geothermal research programs in progress.

Exploration for buried fields of steam or hot water and their
development involve techniques similar to those used in the production
of petroleum. It is no accident that oil companies have pioneered in the
development of geothermal energy. Under ideal conditions, a reservoir
of steam need only be drilled into so the steam can be brought to the
surface, passed through insulated pipes to a power plant, and run
through a low pressure steam turbine. Using hot water is a little more
complicated. The pressure on the water can be reduced so that part of
it becomes steam. Steam and water are then separated in a centrifuge-
like device and the steam drives a turbine. Or the hot water may be used
to evaporate a second liquid with a low boiling point, like butane or
freon, which then drives the turbine. No fuel is needed. No oxides of
sulfur or nitrogen and no radioactive wastes are produced. Geothermal
electricity can be very cheap.

But it is not quite that simple. Geothermal steam is at a lower temperature and pressure than the steam ordinarily used to generate electricity, making geothermal plants inherently inefficient. A geothermal plant releases from two to three times as much waste heat as a plant burning fossil fuel, and about 75 percent more than a nuclear plant of equivalent capacity. If ten 1000 megawatt geothermal plants were installed in California's Imperial Valley (not an impossibility), the waste heat added to the area of 2500 square kilometers (1000 square miles) would equal 5 percent of the total summer heat from the sun. Although this could have an effect on the local weather, severe environmental consequences are anticipated only in the immediate vicinity of the power plants.[5] There are potential uses for the waste heat, or even for the entire output of geothermal energy if it is not used for electricity. These include space heating, water heating, process heat for industry, and desalination of seawater.

Geothermal Pollution

Although the usual air pollutants are not a problem, noxious gases are often a by-product of geothermal wells. These include hydrogen sulfide, methane, and ammonia. The amount of sulfur released at The Geysers is roughly the same as the amount that would be released by an equivalent plant burning low sulfur oil. Elsewhere in California the amount of hydrogen sulfide released from plants on hot water fields could exceed the production of sulfur in plants burning high sulfur fuels.

Surplus water from a geothermal steam plant is likely to contain chemicals like boron, arsenic, and ammonia, making it imperative to protect local streams and groundwater from contamination. Again, problems related to hot water fields are likely to be much worse. The hot water may be concentrated brine, with almost ten times the concentration of salts found in seawater.

One means of disposing of the brine solves two problems at once. Wherever large quantitites of fluid are removed from the ground, it is possible that the land surface will sink, with potentially disastrous consequences. For disposal and prevention of subsidence, waste brine is pumped back into the ground through wells which must be carefully located and constructed to prevent contamination of water supplies. In the Imperial Valley, where effects of subsidence would be serious, it will be necessary to import seawater for reinjection to supplement the waste brine. Plans for some areas consider desalting the waste water for agricultural use and recovering useful chemicals from the residue. This would not be feasible if subsidence were a problem. Waste water can be pumped back into the ground or spread on the surface, but not both.

Some people fear that withdrawal and reinjection of fluids will

trigger earthquakes. It is impossible to say what the seismic effects will
be, but many geophysicists believe that the probability of a major earthquake would be diminished. Withdrawal of hot fluids would warm the
fault zones, allowing stresses to be relieved gradually by a creeping
motion of the rocks rather than suddenly in a "stick-slip" earthquake.

As in any drilling operation that involves fluids under pressure,
there is always the danger of a blowout. One of the early wells in Mexico
blew out, spouting steam and salt water for days before it was controlled. A blowout similar to the oil well blowout in the Santa Barbara
Channel occurred at The Geysers in 1957. Attempts to cap the well
caused steam to flow through fissures in the ground. The situation was
still not under control in 1972. A large-scale release of salt water into
the environment could be disastrous, especially in an agricultural area.
Regulation and supervision of geothermal developments must be at
least as rigorous as they are for petroleum.

Finally, since the machinery for producing geothermal steam is
just as ugly as the machinery for producing petroleum, geothermal
developments must be counted an esthetic minus. They may even
destroy the famous geysers of the world. We do not know what effect
tampering with a field of steam or hot water may have on nearby
geysers, but we do know that geysers have captured the awe and imagination of men through the ages. Their sacrifice to man's energy addiction cannot be made lightly.

Geothermal Potential

The world's total installed geothermal electric capacity is
around 1000 megawatts, the output of a single large nuclear or fossil
power plant. Past predictions that the potential for geothermal energy
was negligible have been at least partly self-fulfilling. But recent studies
indicate that the potential for the western United States alone may be
from 10^5 to 10^7 megawatts. Additional potential exists in Alaska,
Hawaii, the Gulf Coast, the Appalachians, and the Ozarks. Possibilities
in Russia may exceed the most optimistic estimates for the United
States. Like water power, geothermal energy must be used where it is
found. Fortunately, there is promising geothermal potential in a number of energy-poor countries (for example, Japan) which now depend
heavily on imported fossil fuels.

It is usually said that geothermal energy is a depletable resource,
and rapidly depletable at that, the lifetime of any development being
perhaps 50 years. The experience of Italy suggests, however, that 50
years is a minimum figure—that with careful management the lifetime
of a geothermal field may be centuries. One focus of current research is
to determine the lifetime of these fields and their rate of natural replen-
ishment. At The Geysers, productivity of an individual well begins at

from 7 to 15 megawatts and declines exponentially to between 1 and 3 megawatts, so that new wells must be added regularly. We do not know the life expectancy at the lower level of productivity.

If we learn to use the heat stored in rocks, the supply cannot be exhausted in the lifetime of our species. Geothermal enthusiasts envision drilling 30 to 50 kilometers (20 or 30 miles) through the earth's crust into the mantle and bringing heat to the surface, making geothermal energy available anywhere. Long before we accomplish that, they say, we will circulate water through hot rocks and will no longer have to depend on the specialized conditions that produce natural reservoirs of steam and hot water. However, attempts to do this have met with results so unpromising that the efforts were abandoned. One reason for the failure is the poor thermal conductivity of rock. The difficulty might be circumvented through creation of "hot cavities" by underground nuclear explosions, making it possible to circulate water through the fractured rock to extract the heat. One disadvantage of this method is that the water would become radioactive. The geothermal industry is young, however, and we can only guess at the benefits and penalties its future holds.

SOLAR ENERGY

The earliest myths and legends show man's awareness of his debt to the sun. Solar energy has been used for centuries for drying food, fuel, and other materials and for obtaining salt from brine. Through trial and error and time, native architectures have evolved both to take advantage of the sun and to give refuge from it.

With technological sophistication have come sophisticated schemes for using the sun. The goals are tantalizing because solar energy is widely available, immense in quantity, non-polluting, and free for the taking. But so far the harnessing of solar energy has not been one of technology's outstanding success stories. This is due partly to the dilute and intermittent nature of the energy, but partly also to deeply rooted cultural preferences and the inertia of established industrial and economic patterns.

It is interesting to compare the technological problems delaying the use of solar energy with those related to nuclear fusion. For solar energy, all necessary knowledge and techniques exist and need only to be brought together from their diverse sources. We can calculate with fair accuracy how much a particular application of solar energy would cost under present conditions, and be certain that this cost will decrease, as cost always does, when the components are mass-produced in the future. We can use solar energy now, in many ways, whether or not we choose to do it. Not so, for fusion. We cannot estimate the cost of building a fusion reactor because we have only the foggiest notion of what we are trying to build. There is no guarantee that we will be able to design a safe—or even functional—fusion reactor.

Amount of Solar Energy Available

The total amount of solar energy striking earth's atmosphere in a year is about 35,000 times the energy used annually by man. Its average intensity measured on a plane perpendicular to its path is 1.36 kilowatts per square meter, at the outer limits of the atmosphere. This number is known as the solar constant. Energy is received at this maximum rate only when the sun is directly overhead, because only then does the hypothetical perpendicular plane correspond to the "surface" of the atmosphere. At other times, the rate depends on the angle at which radiation strikes, which in turn varies with latitude, time of day, and season of the year. At any time, about half the earth is receiving no direct radiation at all.

Not all the radiation striking the atmosphere continues directly to earth. Some is reflected back into space or absorbed; some is reflected back and forth a number of times before reaching the earth as diffuse radiation rather than beam radiation coming on a direct line from the sun. As a result, the maximum intensity of solar radiation at the earth's surface is about 1.2 kilowatts per square meter, and this is encountered only on clear days at low latitudes around noontime. The total energy received under these ideal conditions is from 6 to 8 kilowatt-hours per square meter per day.

In addition to predictable variations in insolation related to the days and seasons, unpredictable variations occur due to weather and atmospheric conditions. On a clear day up to 90 percent of the incoming radiation is of the beam type, while on an overcast day it may be 100 percent diffuse. Air pollution is a significant factor. It has reduced the amount of sunlight reaching Washington, D.C., by 20 percent during the last 50 years. Plans to collect solar energy in the southwest may be threatened by the daily smog that rolls in from California.

When all losses are accounted for, the amount of solar energy intercepted by the United States is 600 times the amount of energy it uses. If we could use this solar energy with an overall efficiency of 25 percent (optimistic, but not impossible), it would provide 150 times the energy we used in 1970.

Use of Solar Energy

The two drawbacks to the use of solar energy are that it is dilute and must therefore be collected over large areas, and it is not only intermittent but capricious and must therefore be stored so that it is available when needed. Solutions to these problems depend on the uses for which the energy is intended. In general, the seriousness of the collection problem increases with the scale of the project.

Small-scale Uses

Perhaps the oldest use of solar energy is for drying foods. The material is simply spread out in the sunshine without regard for dirt, insects, and decay. Simple improvements on this ancient practice protect the food from most of the dirt, insects, and decay. More elaborate schemes incorporate a solar collector which supplies hot air to a drying unit. It is possible to construct simple, inexpensive, and easy-to-use solar driers that yield a high quality product and, if widely used, would permit improved utilization of food in developing nations.

Akin to solar drying is solar evaporation for the production of salts, another ancient practice which is used widely today where evaporation exceeds rainfall. Evaporation ponds are used in many industrial processes. They are simple and effective, although they can do much harm to migratory waterfowl that succumb to the temptation to stop for a while and rest.

The most widespread and successful modern use of solar energy is for domestic water heating. Areas between 45° N latitude and 45° S latitude having more than 2000 hours of sunshine per year are potential candidates for solar water heating. This solar belt houses most of the world's people. Canada, northern Europe, and northern parts of the U.S.S.R. are the main areas lying outside of it.

A solar water heater for family use consists of a collecting surface with an area ranging from 1 to 3 square meters, an insulated storage tank, and pipes for circulating water. It requires minimal maintenance and supplies hot water at temperatures up to 93° C (200° F). At the end of 1960, about 350,000 solar water heaters were in use in Japan; this number had more than doubled by 1970. Their popularity had already reached a peak in 1960 and was declining in the United States, although some 25,000 were still operating in Florida. Recently, the United States has seen a revived interest in solar water heating, especially for swimming pools. Australia has a thriving solar water heater industry. A large number of units are installed in Israel. Other countries have been slow to adopt solar water heating either because there has been little demand for domestic hot water or because other forms of energy have been abundant. In the United States, the natural gas and electric power industries would probably have opposed development of the competitive industry.

Solar distillation is similar to solar evaporation, except that the product is water instead of salt. The two processes can often be combined. Solar radiation is admitted to a covered brine basin. As water evaporates, the vapor condenses on the covers and flows into collection troughs leading to a storage tank. This method was first used in Chile in 1872, to provide drinking water for animals working in the nitrate mines. Today, solar distillation supplies water for isolated areas in Australia and small communities along the Mediterranean and the Caribbean. The process is almost ready for extensive commercial application. Large distillation projects, however, encounter the same problems of economy and scale that plague all large-scale users of solar energy. For the present, solar distillation is an attractive method for providing fresh water for families and small groups, but it could not supply the large amount of water needed, for example, in irrigation.

Use of solar energy for cooling and refrigeration is especially appealing because the most energy is available when and where the need is greatest. Refrigeration is vitally important in poor countries, where food spoilage compounds the problem of food shortage. Although this technology is in its infancy, only lack of effort holds it back. Introduction of refrigeration into developing countries may meet resistance because the complexity of the machines makes them useless to their intended users and because there is a well-founded reluctance to eat food that is more than a day old. Nevertheless, the benefits from solar refrigeration would be immense.

Solar air conditioning is a possibility for both hot and temperate climates, but its development, too, is in the early stages. Developing countries would benefit from air conditioning of offices, factories, and hospitals, but it would be a mistake to discard traditional architecture in favor of ill-adapted modern buildings that need air conditioning. In temperate climates, systems for solar air conditioning could be combined with systems for space heating.

Solar air conditioning systems work either on the principles of radiative cooling or of refrigeration. If coupled with solar heating (either of space or water), radiative cooling is simple, effective, and economical where the atmosphere is dry and clear. For heating, rooftop collectors absorb radiation during the daylight hours, transferring it to a heat storage system from which heat is available as required. At night, the collector can act as a radiator, radiating heat which has been removed from the interior of the building during the day and stored in a second heat storage system. Where meteorologic conditions are not favorable for radiative cooling, solar energy can be used to operate a heat pump, transferring heat against a temperature gradient. A solar air conditioner of this type works very much like a gas refrigerator. The technology is rather expensive, but future improvements and needs can be expected to render solar refrigeration more practically and economically attractive.

Several types of solar ovens and cookers have been on the market for decades. This use of solar energy seems simple and rewarding, but it is an example of a good idea that ran afoul of the idiosyncracies of its supposed beneficiaries. Despite extensive field trials in India, Mexico, and Morocco, the cookers have not gained social acceptance. Better ways to store energy, to permit indoor or evening cooking, might solve this problem.

Between 20 and 30 percent of the energy used in the world is for space heating. If solar energy could contribute a substantial fraction of this, it would represent a huge saving in fuel. Space heating with solar energy is feasible in climates as cold as that of Boston. Figure 9–3 shows one arrangement for solar heating and cooling. So far, however, neither government nor industry has promoted the idea. The coal and oil industries have a corner on most innovations in energy technology, from production of synthetic fuels to exploitation of geothermal energy, but solar energy is outside their area of expertise and they are not interested in it. Building contractors are concerned with mass produced housing at the lowest cost. They cannot be expected to experiment with expensive new systems that require fundamental changes in materials and design. The public has not been educated to appreciate the ultimate savings in a home with a high initial cost but low maintenance costs, such as a "solar house" would be.

A number of solar houses have been built and operated with varying degrees of success (figure 9–4). Collectors on the roof transfer heat into a stream of water or air. The heat is carried to a water tank or gravel bin for storage, from which it is circulated to the living area as needed. The houses are constructed with careful attention to reflective or absorptive properties of building materials, location of windows, insulation, and so on, to minimize the amount of heating required. This is sound building practice no matter what the source of heat, but it is often neglected. Economically, solar energy is already less expensive than electricity for space heating in most parts of the country. Rising prices for gas and oil would make solar heating the cheapest method almost everywhere.

A solar heating system would be grossly overdesigned for normal operation if it could supply heat for an extended sunless period during the coldest months. Therefore, solar houses have supplementary heating systems which provide from 20 to 70 percent of the heat. This gives a saving in fuel or electricity of from 30 to 80 percent. The most satisfactory design for the Boston area supplies about half the heat from the solar system.

Large-scale Uses

Solar energy is ideal for small, decentralized applications. But industrialized society also needs large amounts of concentrated energy.

(a.)

Solar collector on roof

SOLAR RADIATION

Auxiliary heater used only when solar is depleted

Winter Operation

Summer Operation

Automatic valve

Hot water

Cool Water

Hot Water

To house hot water system

Hot water storage tank

Hot water coil

Pump

From cold water supply

Pump

Hot water
Warm air (winter)

Cool air (summer)

Air heating unit

House rooms

Air returns

Blower

Cool water return

Hot water

Absorbtion air cooling unit

Warm water return

(b.)

Two glass Cover plates

A

B

Black metal sheet to which ½" to 1" tubing is bonded

C

Insulation (2" to 4" thick)

Roof Surface

Sheet metal trough or pan

Notes:
Ends of tubes mani- folded together
1 to 3 glass covers depending on conditions

Dimensions
Thickness (A direction)
   3" to 6"

Length (B direction)
   4' to 20'

Width (C direction)
   10' to 50'
Slope dependent on location and winter- summer load comparison

Figure 9–3, *a.* Solar home heating, cooling and hot water. Schematic diagram of one alternative.
Figure 9–3, *b.* Solar collector for home heating and cooling system. Diagram of one alternative. From [12].

Solar energy is one of the only three candidates that can fill this need in the long term.

On a large scale, solar energy can be collected either on the surface of the earth or on satellites orbiting the earth. The use of satellites may be an extraordinarily complicated and expensive way to circumvent the inconvenience of cloudy weather and the cycle of days and nights. According to one proposed scheme, a solar power station with a panel of solar cells would be constructed in space from a space shuttle (see Box 9–1). The orbiting station would receive sunlight continuously and convert it to electricity with an efficiency of about 15 percent. This electricity would be converted to microwaves (electromagnetic radiation at frequencies between conventional radiowaves and the far infrared) with an efficiency of 85 percent. In this form it would be transmitted to the earth, penetrating the atmosphere, clear or cloudy, with essentially no loss. An earth-based receiving station would reconvert the microwaves to electricity with an efficiency of perhaps 70 percent. To collect enough energy to supply the power needs of New York City, the orbiting panel of solar cells would have to be 62 square kilometers (25 square miles) in area. The receiver on earth would occupy 90 square kilometers (36 square miles), in order to keep the radiation at a biologically safe level. If the projected electric power production for the year 2000 were to be supplied by space stations of this type, we would need 250 of them.[6]

Most proposals for solar electricity involve covering large areas of desert with collectors of solar energy. These collectors are of two main types. Flat plate collectors are basically blackened surfaces which absorb radiation, both beam and diffuse, and convert it to heat. The heat is transferred to a stream of air, water, or other fluid and carried to where it will be used or stored. Except for a few experimental solar furnaces, all of today's practical solar energy systems use this type of collector.

The technology of flat plate collectors is advanced, but it is uncertain how much mass production will be able to reduce their cost. The maximum obtainable temperatures are rather low, leading to inefficiency and a high level of thermal pollution. The maximum yield of

---

Figure 9–4. Three houses with solar heating. Note the varied architectural treatment of the solar collectors.

a, Solar heated house near Odiello in southern France.

b, The Löf house in Colorado. This house has been operating successfully since 1959. Solar panels may be seen on roof.

c, MIT solar house IV. This experimental house was built as a part of the Solar Energy Research Program at MIT.

Photo credit: Solar Energy Laboratory, University of Wisconsin.

BOX 9–1 SOLAR CELLS

The name solar cell is imprecisely applied to a variety of energy converting devices. It is occasionally applied to any device that produces electricity from solar heat; but most often it refers to one that produces an electric current when light falls on it. The proper name for such a solar cell is a photovoltaic cell, and it is based on a phenomenon known as the photoelectric effect. Many metals and some non-metals exhibit this effect. When light strikes atoms of such a substance, energy is imparted to the outer, most loosely bound electrons. If the energy is sufficient to drive the electrons away from the atoms, and if a suitable collector is connected in a circuit with the electron-emitting substance, an electric current will flow. Devices like that pictured in figure 9–5, a have long been used in a variety of ways (for example, as photo cells in door openers and light meters). Their requirement for a vacuum tube makes them unpromising for large-scale energy conversion.

Semiconductors (primarily silicon crystals) may exhibit photoelectric effects when formed in a p–n junction unit with a metal or another semiconductor (figure 9–5, b). These cells are used as solar converters on many satellites and are sometimes proposed for large-scale conversion of solar energy. Silicon cells are unpromising because it is difficult and expensive to grow large single crystals. Innovations in thin film solar cells using cadmium sulfide should reduce the cost greatly, but fundamental problems remain.

The root of the problems is explained by an equation of Einstein's describing the energy balance in photoelectric conversion: $hc/\lambda = W + \frac{1}{2}m_e v^2$, where h is Planck's constant, c is the velocity of light, and λ is the wavelength of radiation. W is the energy required to eject an electron from the substance, m_e is the mass of the electron, and v is its velocity in a vacuum. W, the photoelectric work function, has a characteristic value for each

---

electricity from a power plant using flat plate collectors would be about 30 megawatts per square kilometer of collector surface.[7] Since the collectors must be spaced in such a way that they do not shade each other, the total area occupied would be not 1, but 2 or 3 square kilometers—between 75 and 100 square kilometers for a 1000 megawatt plant. Seasonal fluctuations in energy can be minimized and overall efficiency

Figure 9-5. Functional diagrams of two types of photovoltaic cells. The semiconductor type is often called a solar cell.

substance. When W is large, the amount of energy in $\frac{1}{2}m_e v^2$ is correspondingly small.

Materials exhibiting the photoelectric effect do not respond to the entire solar spectrum but only to certain wavelengths which are determined by the geometry and dimensions of the crystal lattice. Thus the amount of energy obtainable from a solar cell depends on both the photoelectric work function and the proportion of solar energy that can elicit the photoelectric effect. Because known materials respond to only a narrow range of wavelengths, the efficiency of solar cells has remained discouragingly low—about 12 to 14 percent. Despite the wonders of science and technology, we are limited by the raw materials of the real world. It seems unlikely, for many reasons, that we will be able to produce any material having an efficiency of conversion above 20 percent. With present materials and economic conditions, large-scale conversion of solar energy by means of solar cells costs between 2 and 100 times as much as the less glamorous methods.

of the collectors increased by tilting the collectors toward the equator at an angle equal to the latitude.

The alternative to simple flat absorbing surfaces is a system of lenses or mirrors which focus solar energy on a receiver smaller than the collector, permitting very high temperatures to be realized and reducing the area from which energy is lost by radiation. Ratios of intensity of radiation on the receiver to intensity on the collector can range from 2 or 3 up to more than 10,000. To obtain any but the lowest of these, the collectors must track the sun across the sky. The special mountings and controls for tracking add to the cost and complexity of the system, but without them the use of focusing collectors is not justified.

Only the beam component of radiation can be focused. The inability to use diffuse radiation accentuates the differences in energy available in clear as compared to cloudy weather and in different seasons of the year. In Texas the loss varies from about 10 percent in summer to as much as 42 percent in winter.[7]

Scientists have proposed a variety of designs for solar power plants using focusing systems. One of these would focus energy on a boiler with square aluminum reflectors, 3 to 5 meters on a side.[8] The reflectors would be individually mounted with automatic controls for tracking the sun. If the total projected energy requirements of the United States for the year 2000 were to be met by this—or any similar—system, between 1 and 2 percent of the country would be covered by collecting devices. (By comparison, an area larger than this has already been turned over to the automobile, in the form of parking lots and roads; a tally of the land occupied by fossil fuel and nuclear plants must include land ravaged by the mines that feed them; and 1.25 million square kilometers (half a million square miles) are devoted to the inefficient energy industry called agriculture.) About 15 square kilometers (5.75 square miles) of collector surface could provide energy for a 1000 megawatt power plant, assuming 30 percent efficiency of conversion. Allowing for spacing of the collectors, about 40 square kilometers (16 square miles) of land would be involved, or a square 6.4 kilometers (4 miles) on a side.

Another proposal takes advantage of mass produced plastic Fresnel lenses. These lenses have the optical properties of spherical lenses, but they are telescoped in a way resembling a collapsible drinking cut, at great savings in size, weight, and materials.[9] A third system favors exploiting recent and, hopefully, future advances in the technology of selective surfaces. The selective surface might be a material that absorbs radiation at wavelengths shorter than about 1 micron in the infrared but is transparent to longer wavelengths. This would allow absorption of most of the solar spectrum while minimizing losses from radiation. Selective absorption could also be based on optical interference between layers of material, regardless of the intrinsic optical properties of the materials themselves.[10]

After solar energy is collected, it must be converted to a useful form, and here the problem of storage for sunless periods arises. One solution, suggested with increasing frequency, is to use the energy for producing hydrogen. In many ways, hydrogen is an ideal fuel. It can be produced from water, and on burning it yields only water as a combustion product. With minor modification of existing storage facilities, pipelines, and burners, it could be stored, distributed, and used as natural gas is now. Since large solar plants will be located in desert areas far from population centers where energy is needed, a fuel that can be moved efficiently and relatively cheaply by pipeline has an advantage over electricity which is transmitted inefficiently and at great cost.

Hydrogen could be produced by thermal dissociation of water or by electrolysis. At high temperatures, water dissociates into hydrogen and oxygen. If one of these products is continuously removed so that water cannot be reformed, the reaction will continue rather than coming to equilibrium. If a practical way can be found to remove the small percentage of hydrogen formed (two atoms, or one molecule, for every 999 molecules of water vapor at 1500° C), we could expect a yield of about a third of a pound of hydrogen per day from each square meter of collector area. Oxygen would be a valuable byproduct.[9]

If solar energy were first converted to electricity through a conventional steam cycle or some advanced process, the electricity could be used to decompose water by electrolysis. Here the products, hydrogen and oxygen, are easily recovered, because they form at opposite electrical poles. Although the electrolytic production of hydrogen from solar energy and water is an attractive prospect, the amount of electricity required is very large. One estimate is that if we were to produce an amount of hydrogen equivalent in energy value only to the natural gas consumed in the United States, we would have to quadruple our electrical generating capacity.[11]

Like other forms of energy, solar energy is not entirely free. The process of converting it to useful form has a price, part of which is the large amount of space and materials required for conversion. But when we look at the seashores, hillsides, waterways, and agricultural land that are being sacrificed to the production of energy, devoting a piece of the desert to this purpose does not seem an unreasonable alternative.

The desert is fragile in the same sense that the arctic environment is fragile. Its ecology could easily be upset. The greatest threat to the desert environment is probably not a few solar power plants in themselves, but the influx of people that would accompany the production and availability of power.

Other possible consequences of using solar energy relate to upsetting the heat balance of the earth. Thermal pollution of local water resources could be severe if water-cooled steam electric generating systems were used. Trapping large amounts of solar energy in the desert and transporting it elsewhere for use would alter the distribution of solar energy on earth. By blackening the desert with solar collectors or collecting radiation in space, we are causing the earth to absorb some energy that otherwise would have been reflected. But the desert itself will not heat up because we are taking the energy away; and the areas that use it are already heating themselves with the inevitable waste heat from other sources of energy. If there is a threat to global climate and heat balance, it will not be from the use of solar energy, but from the intemperate use of energy in any and all forms.

CONCLUSION: A LESSON FROM ECOLOGY

The United States is planning to construct great clusters of nuclear power plants, each unit of which will be large by today's standards. They will supply power to areas covering many states, as we grow toward an all-electric economy. Perhaps, before committing ourselves to this course, we should remember the lesson from ecology that teaches us that diversity is the key to survival. A diversity of species lends stability to the environment, genetic diversity enhances the adaptability of a species, and physiological diversity increases the chances of an individual for survival. Yet we behave as if the human species and its cultures were exempt from this rule. We have already experienced what a power failure can do to New York, but we are asking for these crises on an even larger scale. A better plan might be to exploit as wide a variety of energy sources as possible, each according to its best use. Regional energy plans should suit local needs and the availability of resources.

If something goes wrong with your solar heating system, you can go to your neighbor's house to keep warm. If something goes wrong with the central power plant 500 miles away, there is nowhere to go.

REFERENCES

1. J. Solomon, "The Social Redemption of Pure Garbage," *The Sciences* July–August (1972): 13–15.
2. J. Reynolds, *Windmills and Watermills*, (London: Hugh Evelyn Limited. 1970).
3. United Nations. Proceedings of the United Nations Conference on New Sources of Energy, *Wind Power*, (New York, 1964), vol. 7.
4. M. K. Hubbert, "Energy Resources," in *Resources and Man*, National Academy of Sciences-National Research Council. (San Francisco: W. H. Freeman and Company, 1969), pp. 157–242.
5. M. Goldsmith, *Geothermal Resources in California, Potentials and Problems*. Environmental Quality Laboratory Report No. 5, (Pasadena: California Institute of Technology, 1971), pp. 32–33.

6. C. Summers, "The Conversion of Energy." *Scientific American* 224, 3 (1971): 158–159.

TJ 23   7. H. Hottell and J. Howard, *New Energy Technology: Some Facts and*
H 67   ——*Assessments,* (Cambridge, Mass.: The MIT Press, 1971), pp. 331–345.

8. A. Hildebrandt, G. Hass, W. Jenkins, and J. Colaco. "Large-Scale Concentration and Conversion of Solar Energy," *Eos: Transactions, American Geophysical Union* 53 (1972), pp. 684–692.

9. N. Ford and J. Kane. "Solar Power," *Science and Public Affairs* 27, 8 (1971), pp. 27–31.

10. A. Meinel and M. Meinel. "Is It Time for a New Look at Solar Energy?" *Science and Public Affairs* 27, 8 (1971), pp. 32–37.

11. D. Gregory, "The Hydrogen Economy." *Scientific American* 228, 1 (1973): pp. 13–21.

12. NSF/NASA Solar Energy Panel. *Solar Energy as a National Resource.* Report No. NSF/RA/N–73–001, 1972.

SUGGESTED READING

Arp, V.; Bullwinkel, G.; Cunningham, W.; and Romer, H. *Report of the Electrical Power Task Force.* San Francisco: Sierra Club, 1972.

Brinkworth, B. *Solar Energy for Man.* New York: John Wiley and Sons, 1972.

Ford, N., and Kane, J. "Solar Power." *Science and Public Affairs* 27, 8 (1971): 27–31.

Goldsmith, M. *Geothermal Resources in California, Potentials and Problems.* Environmental Quality Laboratory Report No. 5. Pasadena, Calif: Institute of Technology, 1971.

Hildebrandt, A.; Hass, G.; Jenkins, W.; and Colaco, J. "Large-Scale Concentration and Conversion of Solar Energy." *Eos: Transactions of the American Geophysical Union.* (1972): 684–692.

Hubbert, M. K. "Energy Resources." In *Resources and Man,* National Academy of Sciences-National Research Council, pp. 157–241. San Francisco: W. H. Freeman and Company, 1969.

Meinel, A., and Meinel, M. "Is It Time for a New Look at Solar Energy?" *Science and Public Affairs* 27, 8 (1971): 32–37.

National Academy of Sciences: *Solar Energy in Developing Countries: Perspectives and Prospects.* A Report of an Ad Hoc Advisory Panel of the Board on Science and Technology for International Development, Office of the Foreign Secretary.

Rex, R. 1971. "Geothermal Energy–The Neglected Energy Option." *Science and Public Affairs* 27, 8 (1971): 52–56.

Reynolds, J. *Windmills and Watermills.* London: Hugh Evelyn Ltd., 1970.

Solomon, J. "The Social Redemption of Pure Garbage." *The Sciences* July–August (1972): 13–15.

United Nations, Proceedings of the United Nations Conference on New Sources of Energy. *Geothermal Energy.* Vol. 2 and 3. New York, 1964.

United Nations, Proceedings of the United Nations Conference on New Sources of Energy. *Solar Energy.* Vol. 4, 5, and 6. New York, 1964.

United Nations, Proceedings of the United Nations Conference on New Sources of Energy. *Wind Power.* Vol. 7. New York, 1964.

U.S., Federal Power Commission. *The 1970 National Power Survey.* Part I, ch. 7, pp. 1–30.

U.S., NSF/NASA, Solar Energy Panel. *Solar Energy as a National Resource.* Report No. NSF/RANN–73–001, 1972.

U.S. Geological Survey. "Briefs on Geothermal Energy." In *Man and His Physical Environment,* edited by G. McKenzie and R. Utgard, pp. 232–234. Minneapolis: Burgess Publishing Company, 1972.

White, D. "Resources of Geothermal Energy and Their Utilization." In *Man and His Physical Environment,* edited by G. McKenzie and R. Utgard, pp. 235–239. Minneapolis: Burgess Publishing Company, 1972.

CHAPTER 10

Electricity

Poison is in everything and no thing is without poison. The dosage makes it either a poison or a remedy.

Paracelsus

Although the elementary particles of which matter is composed bear electric charge, electricity must be derived from another form of energy. Electricity, then, cannot be considered a primary source of energy, but merely a convenient and versatile form of it. Since it is produced from one of the primary energy sources, it creates new markets for all of them at the same time that it takes their traditional markets away. For example, the current trend is toward electric space heating and electric furnaces for the production of steel. Only the internal combustion engine seems to be holding its own against electricity.

In 1970, 23 percent of the energy used by the United States was used for the generation of electricity. There are interesting problems and implications hidden behind this uninteresting statistic. Since World War I the use of electricity has been doubling at 8 or 10-year intervals, with a similar rate projected for the future, while energy use in general has a doubling time about twice as long. If this trend continues, we will have an all-electric economy by the year 2040. All the technological, environmental, political, and economic problems of all the energy industries are involved in the electric power industry. And the generation, distribution, and use of electricity pose their own unique set of problems and promises.

The increase in generating capacity in the United States has been matched by an increase in the maximum size of generating units and by the trend toward using multiple units in a central power station. In 1920, the maximum generating capacity of a single unit was 50 megawatts. By 1930, it was 200 megawatts. In 1960, the giants had a capacity of about 400 megawatts and by 1970 some 1300 megawatt units were on order. Plans for 1990 assume that individual units of 2000 megawatt capacity will be available.

SELECTION OF SITES FOR POWER PLANTS

Electric utilities once had free rein in selecting sites for power plants. Today, almost every proposal for a new site meets bitter opposition from someone, and construction of new plants is delayed for many months, pending court decisions. Meanwhile, the electric power industry insists it will have to build about 500 new plants during the next 20 years, and this tabulation does not include "small" plants with generating capacity below 500 megawatts.

A proposed site becomes a battleground, most of the attempts to come to a mutual understanding being thinly veiled attempts of each side to convince the other. On the one side are those who would block any expansion of electric power partly on ecologic, partly on emotional grounds. On the other side, the fatalistic attitude has been summarized as follows:

1. There is no current policy or sentiment for modifying the economic growth of the country.
2. There is no experience whatever in maintaining or developing growth of an industrialized economy with restricted amounts of electricity.
3. . . . there is more evidence that general limitation of electrical supply might either curtail the growth of the economy or impede some major objectives of environmental improvement.[1]

There are fallacies in both of the extreme positions, as there always are in extreme positions. Because we cannot change our habits immediately, or stop all growth, we will continue to need increasing amounts of electricity for the next few decades. However, consideration of the results of uncontrolled growth suggests that it may be suicidal not to begin immediately to do something about the situation described in the quotation above, rather than accept it as inevitable.

The United States will continue to need new power plants. We will discuss some of the requirements that must be satisfied and dilemmas that must be resolved in selecting sites for them.

Good highway access is necessary for construction and maintenance. Access by rail or water is also desirable for delivery of equipment and, in some cases, fuel. If adequate roads and railroads do not exist, their cost must be reckoned in the total cost of the plant. Possible seismic activity in the area must be considered, as must meteorologic hazards like tornadoes, hurricanes, ice storms, and sand storms. Design standards for a plant must reflect the probability of these natural phenomena.

An adequate and dependable supply of cooling water is extremely important, and is the source of much of the conflict over sites. Increasingly, the electric power industry is competing with other industry for sites, and all are meeting opposition from those who have other plans for our limited water resources.

New power plants will require large amounts of land, for the power house itself, equipment for controlling air pollution, fuel storage, rail, barge, and truck terminals, and transmission access and switchyards. Table 10–1 shows the requirements for 3000 megawatt fossil-fueled and nuclear plants. If a cooling pond is incorporated into the cooling system, an additional area of 10 to 50 square kilometers would be needed.

There is a geographic pattern in the type of plant that will predominate. The Northeast and Midwest are leaning heavily on nuclear

Table 10–1. Land Requirements for a 3000 Megawatt Power Plant

Type of Fuel	Number of Hectares*	Comments
Coal	365 to 485	Includes about 16 hectares for coal storage and 120–160 hectares for ash disposal.
Oil	60 to 140	Includes onsite fuel storage.
Gas	40 to 80	Assumes pipeline delivery, with only modest onsite fuel storage.
Nuclear	80 to 160	Includes recommended "exclusion zone," in which the reactor licensee has authority to determine all activities. Surrounding the 80 to 160 hectare site should be a zone of low population density whose inhabitants can be protected or evacuated in an emergency. These restrictions will probably be relaxed as experience with reactors increases.

*There are 100 hectares in 1 square kilometer.

From: *Considerations Affecting Steam Power Plant Site Selection,* a Report Sponsored by the Energy Policy Staff, Office of Science and Technology. 1968.

power. Almost all the new plants in the South Central Region will be fossil fueled. Major hydroelectric additions will be in the Northwest, with large amounts of pumped storage anticipated in the Northeast and Southeast. The Northwest, however, which traditionally has depended on hydropower, will soon be forced to shift toward thermal power for lack of hydro sites. This pattern reflects the need to guarantee an adequate fuel supply for the life of the plant, as well as other practical and economic realities.

The most fundamental question in siting a power plant is whether to locate it near or far from the population centers it will serve. A corollary of this, for fossil fuel plants, is the question of whether to transport the fuel to the power plant or build the power plant where the fuel is produced. Neither question has an easy or obvious answer.

For those who raise the point that the people who use the electricity should pay the environmental price for it, there is the counterpoint that some areas, such as Los Angeles, may not be able to afford the environmental price—and one cannot simply say, then let them do without. The argument for locating major power plants at great distances from population centers contends that there the environment is better able to assimilate the various kinds of pollution resulting from generation of electricity, and, by serving a number of load centers, one power plant can take advantage of economies of scale. Against this argument is the increased economic and environmental cost of transmission, the fact that many of the potential uses of waste heat cannot be realized, and the reluctance of many people to destroy any remaining wilderness.

WASTE HEAT

Perhaps the most publicized problem created by the growth of the electric power industry is the problem of waste heat. When we say that the efficiency of a power plant is 33 percent, we are saying that for every kilowatt-hour of electricity it generates, two kilowatt-hours of energy are wasted in the form of heat. Chapter 5 explained why the production of waste heat is inevitable and why we will have to live with large amounts of it so long as we generate electricity by means of a steam cycle.

Only recently has heat come to be considered a pollutant. The electric utilities boast that they were concerned with minimizing waste heat long before the environmentalists had ever heard of it. The reason for their concern was economic. They wanted to get as much electricity as possible from each pound of fuel. The amount of heat released at a particular place was usually small compared to the total energy flow in the area and the total amount of energy used by man was negligible compared to global energy flow. Both situations are changing rapidly.

No matter where or how the waste heat is disposed of, it eventually ends up in the atmosphere, from which it is radiated into space. The possible long-range effects of discharging large amounts of heat into the atmosphere will be discussed in chapter 12. For now, we will consider only the effects of waste heat on water resources and what can be done to alleviate thermal pollution.

Power plants using steam cycles discharge waste heat when steam condenses to water in the condenser. This step is necessary because the efficiency of generating electricity depends on a sharp drop in pressure from one side of the turbine to the other. Waste heat is conventionally transferred to cooling water which, after passing through the system once (hence the name once-through cooling) is discharged to the source some 6° to 14° C (10° to 25° F) warmer than when it began. The only conceivable alternative to water for cooling on this scale is air, which absorbs only about 0.025 percent as much heat as an equal volume of water. From the standpoint of engineering, there is no alternative to water as a coolant. Figure 10–1 shows the thermal discharge from a power plant.

Each day, about 10 percent of the flowing fresh water in the United States is used by industry for cooling. About 80 percent of this, one-third of the water used for all purposes, is used in the generation of electricity. By 1980, the electric power industry will require 17 percent of the nation's flowing fresh water for cooling. A 1000 megawatt nuclear power plant operating with an efficiency of 32 percent will raise the temperature of 50 million gallons of water per hour by 8.3° C (15° F). This is about 50 percent more heat than a fossil fuel plant of equivalent generating capacity would discharge, partly because a nuclear plant is less efficient and partly because about a fifth of the heat from a fossil plant escapes up the stack.

It is important to distinguish between heat and temperature. We have seen, for example, that water is an ideal coolant because it can absorb more heat than most substances for each degree its temperature is raised. Within limits, a power plant can discharge its waste heat to a small amount of water, raising its temperature considerably, or to a large amount with a smaller temperature increase. This is shown in table 10–2. In any case, the total amount of heat released is the same. Because the rate of cooling increases with an increasing temperature of the surface water and the area required for cooling the heated water to a given temperature decreases (figure 10–2), it may be better to discharge a minimum amount of quite warm water rather than a larger amount of cooler water. It may be better to admit that there will be some unwanted side effects of the waste heat and to keep them localized so

Figure 10-1. A plume of warm water discharged from a nuclear power plant on Lake Michigan. This infrared image shows the warm water as a light area in the cool lake. The thermal plume shifts in extent and location in response to winds and currents. The dark circular feature well out in the plume is the water intake. Photo credit: Marine Studies Center, University of Wisconsin.

Table 10-2. Relationship Between Flow of Cooling Water and Temperature Rise

Temperature Rise (°C)	Flow of Cooling Water (cubic meters per second)
2.8	365
6.7	150
10.0	100
15.0	67

These figures are for a typical 2400 megawatt, two-unit nuclear power plant. To limit the temperature increase to 2.8°C (5° F) would create insuperable design problems, while increases above 17° C (30°F) lead to decreased efficiency of the generating system. In practice, the temperature rise is usually between 5.5° and 14° C (10° and 25° F).

Data from M. Eisenbud and G. Gleason, eds. 1969. *Electric Power and Thermal Discharges.* New York: Gordon and Breach. P. 232.

Figure 10–2. Relationship between initial temperature of discharged cooling water and area required for rejecting equal amounts of excess heat. Cooling takes place at the surface, through evaporation, radiation, and conduction. If cooling water from a typical 2000 megawatt power plant is discharged at 37.8°C (100°F), 1100 hectares (about 2700 acres) are required to cool it to 30°C (85°F). If the water is discharged at 41.7°C (107°F), only 800 hectares (about 2000 acres) are required to dissipate the same amount of heat. Over most of this area, surface water from the hotter discharge is at a lower temperature. (Adapted from M. Eisenbud and G. Gleason, eds., *Electric Power and Thermal Discharges* (New York: Gordon and Breach, 1969), p. 340.)

there is hope of controlling them or limiting their spread.[2] However, factors other than the rate of cooling and the area required must be considered.

In a natural lake, about one-quarter of the energy lost to the atmosphere is lost through evaporation and three-quarters is lost by radiation. Waste heat from industrial cooling disproportionately increases loss by evaporation because the vapor pressure of water, which determines the amount of evaporation that can occur, increases with temperature (figure 10–3). The result is that about 40 percent of the industrial heat load is dissipated through evaporation, 30 percent through radiation, and most of the rest by conduction, or the direct transfer of heat from water to air at the interface between them. The exact relationship among the types of heat loss depends on the season of the year and the water temperature.

Biological Effects of Waste Heat

The rate of chemical reactions, including those that occur in living organisms, is approximately doubled for each temperature increase of $10°$ C ($18°$ F). As the rate of metabolic reactions increases, so does the demand for oxygen. (Measurements in the field show, however, that the increase in rate of oxidation may be only 20 or 30 percent per $10°$ C). This increased demand for oxygen is the first effect of thermal pollution. As the water temperature increases, the solubility of gases, including oxygen, decreases until at $30°$ C the water can dissolve only half as much oxygen as it can at $0°$ C. Thus there is less oxygen available to meet the increased demand.

Metabolism is the total of all chemical reactions occurring in a living cell, including both constructive and destructive processes. Although all reactions proceed faster as temperature increases, destructive processes often predominate at high temperatures. At high temperatures, enzymes are inactivated and the balance among chemical reactions in the cell is disrupted. Furthermore, surrounding each cell is a membrane that regulates the exchange of materials between the cell and its environment and on which many chemical reactions take place. The properties of this membrane are altered by high temperatures, sometimes leading to disorganization and death of the cell. These are the direct effects of high temperatures on living cells.

Each type of organism has a characteristic temperature range in which it can survive and, within this range, a much smaller temperature range that favors optimal growth. The temperature range is determined not only by the direct effects of temperature on the organism but by the nature of the plant and animal communities which thrive in that range. The presence or absence of food, parasites, competitors, or predators may determine the ability of an organism to survive at a particular temperature. Thus, some types of game fish vanish from warm water not because they themselves cannot live there, but because the organisms on which they feed cannot survive.

The optimum temperature for an organism is usually close to the maximum temperature at which it can survive. Some people argue that the sun is the largest contributor to thermal pollution, both in an absolute sense and in the extent of natural temperature fluctuations, which may exceed $28°$ C ($50°$ F). With this reasoning they conclude

Figure 10-3. Relationship between vapor pressure of water and water temperature. The vapor pressure of a substance is the pressure exerted by its vapor when in equilibrium with the substance, whether solid or liquid. For pure substances it depends only on the temperature. The vapor pressure of water increases in a nonlinear fashion as the temperature increases, leading to increased amounts of evaporation.

that additional inputs of waste heat are harmless. On the contrary, the upper end of the natural temperature range may be so close to the lethal temperature for many organisms that an additional increment of waste heat may be an unbearable stress. The effects of waste heat vary with the season of the year and with shorter term weather conditions. Waste heat is more likely to be beneficial in cold climates and harmful in hot ones. In addition, as any aquarium enthusiast knows, rapid fluctuations in temperature, such as occur when cooling water is intermittently discharged, can be more harmful than a constant temperature above or below the optimum.

Temperature influences the behavior of organisms, from the tiniest planktonic creatures to the great game fish. The following situations are conjectural, because we have been unable to find evidence that they have actually occurred as a result of thermal pollution from power plants. However, they could occur. There is a daily vertical migration of tiny, surface-feeding animals (zooplankters), in response to diurnal cycles of temperature and light. The effects of various strategies for disposing of waste heat on this behavior are unknown, but they could be significant. Migratory behavior of some species of fish is triggered by temperature. If animals are caused to migrate by exposure to a discharge of warmed water, several kinds of potential trouble await them at their destination. They may find conditions unfavorable for spawning. Temperatures may be too low for development of eggs and survival or growth of the young. Or, the appropriate food may not be available.

In general, plant and animal species of value to people thrive at lower temperatures than nuisance species. An outstanding example of this is the bluegreen algae. Diatoms, basic elements of many food webs, flourish at temperatures between 15° and 29° C (59° and 77° F). Green algae, also important in food webs, thrive in warmer waters at 29° to 35° C (77° to 95° F). Bluegreen algae can grow within and beyond this entire temperature range. At lower temperatures they usually cannot compete successfully with diatoms and green algae, but as temperatures increase so do the bluegreens. Bluegreen algae are not part of the food webs of most animals we wish to encourage. They flourish in the absence of predators, at the expense of green algae and diatoms and, indirectly, of the animals that prey on them. When the bluegreens die, their decomposition by microorganisms further depletes the oxygen supply that has already been diminished by increased temperature. Numerous population studies have shown that if two species are competing for the same environmental niche, one tends eventually to displace the other. This is what happens in the contest between the bluegreen algae and the greens and diatoms. Once the bluegreens have become established in a region of warm water, they have the opportunity to colonize waters relatively unaffected by thermal discharges. What begins as a rather small shift in the balance among species can have far-reaching effects. This replacement of one group of species by another, followed by deterioration of the habitat, often resembles acceleration of the natural aging, or eutrophication, of an aquatic ecosystem. The rate of change is further accelerated by addition of nitrates, phosphates, and organic carbon from agricultural runoff and sewage.

Not all effects of waste heat are undesirable. Up to a certain point, an increase in temperature can result in more rapid development of eggs and faster growth of fish of all ages. There have been plans to use waste heat in nurseries for fish and shellfish. Some waters which are too warm for trout and too cold for bass and catfish might be transformed into excellent fishing grounds by thermal discharges from a power plant. There are many reported cases of improved fishing in the vicinity of such discharges (in contrast to the lack of reports of environmental disasters). If the power plant operates intermittently, however, or is shut down for repairs or as in the case of a nuclear plant for refueling, the fish that depend on the heat it provides may suffer. We must learn many things about the effects of heat on aquatic life and we must know many things about the proposed site for a power plant before we can predict the effects of its thermal discharge. Current concern is well founded because, while the environment has so far been able to assimilate our waste heat, continued exponential growth will rapidly exceed its capacity to do so.

Strategies for Disposing of Waste Heat

The easiest, cheapest, and most efficient way to dispose of waste heat is by the once-through cooling method, by which about 80 percent of all waste heat was discharged in 1970. Warmed cooling water may be returned to the surface, where it will stay because it is lighter than the colder water below, and where it will quickly give up its excess heat to the atmosphere. The warm water can also be returned to a deeper region where the heat will be diluted very rapidly; but because it is dilute and because cooling takes place only from the surface, the heat will be retained for a long time. Many lakes become thermally stratified during spring and summer, with layers of water at different densities and temperatures. Withdrawing water from colder layers and returning it to the surface could upset the thermal stability of these lakes, leading to unpredictable ecologic effects.

All schemes for preventing the effects of waste heat on natural bodies of water involve ways of getting the heat into the atmosphere without heating the natural body of water first. All of them require compromises in cost, efficiency, and environmental effects. Systems for treating the cooling water are discussed below and comparative energy requirements for operating them are shown in table 10–3. The best plan would be to divert as much of the waste heat as possible for useful purposes.

Cooling towers discharge waste heat directly to the atmosphere. In a wet cooling tower, this is accomplished through evaporation, which raises questions of local fog, increased precipitation, and depletion of the source of cooling water. A decision to use such a tower must take all these potential problems into account, as must the design of the tower itself. Where topographic and meteorologic conditions are favorable, fogging is negligible, although the plume of water vapor from the tower may be visible for miles. As for excessive water loss, it is important to remember that much of the cooling from a body of water also

Table 10–3. Power Requirements for Cooling Systems
(percentage of output of 800 megawatt plant)

Cooling System / Type of Fuel	Fossil	Nuclear
Once-through: discharge to lake, river, ocean, or cooling pond	0.4	0.6
Wet cooling tower		
Natural draft	0.9	1.3
Mechanical draft	1.0	1.7
Dry cooling tower		
Natural draft*	0.9	1.5
Mechanical draft	3.0	4.8

*Construction of natural draft dry cooling towers is prohibitively expensive.

Based on data in M. Eisenbud and G. Gleason, eds. 1969. *Electric Power and Thermal Discharges.* New York: Gordon and Breach. P. 372.

takes place through evaporation. The evaporative loss of water from direct discharge is about 1 percent, while that from a wet cooling tower is about 1.5 percent. Because they depend on evaporation, wet towers are less effective when the relative humidity is high.

In a wet cooling tower, water from the cooling coils of the condenser trickles through loose packing at the base of the tower, where it is met by a rising current of air. In many locations, the tower can operate on the principles of a chimney, with a natural draft of air being drawn through. These towers are enormous structures that dominate the landscape (figure 10–4). Where natural draft towers are not feasible, fans can create a forced, or mechanical, draft. Wet cooling towers approximately double the capital cost of the cooling system over the once-through, direct discharge method. Because they are expensive and are likely to create environmental problems of their own, they should not be used unless their use can be justified.

Like wet cooling towers, dry cooling towers may be either natural or forced draft. Dry cooling towers avoid problems of fog, mist, unsightly vapor plumes, and evaporative water loss. They depend on the transfer of heat to air by convection, as the cooling water passes through a heat exchanger in a closed system and never contacts the air directly. For this reason, the effectiveness of a dry tower is independent of humidity. However, its effectiveness decreases as air temperature increases. Because dry towers decrease the efficiency of the power plant and increase the capital costs of the cooling system by up to a factor of five or more, the use of dry cooling towers is usually not justified. In the United States, there are no dry cooling systems at major power

Figure 10-4. Wet cooling tower. Photo: Tennessee Valley Authority.

plants although there are a few small ones; there are a number of relatively large ones operating in Europe, however.

In addition to the chemicals used in the condenser, all cooling towers must use chemicals (for example, chlorine and sulfuric acid) to prevent biological growth, deposition of salts, and corrosion in the system. Discharge of these harmful materials to natural waters must be controlled.

A cooling pond is a manmade lake in which waste heat is dissipated in the same way as in a natural lake. The advantages of cooling ponds are that they are less expensive than towers and they prevent spreading deterioration of natural bodies of water. Their main disadvantage is the amount of land they require, although they can provide opportunities for fishing and recreation if they are properly managed.

Another means of dissipating waste heat is spray canals in which water from the condenser is sprayed from banks of spraying units into a canal that carries it back to the source. Heat is lost primarily through evaporation. Spray canals require only 5 or 10 percent of the surface area required by a pond, and they are less expensive than cooling towers.

So far we have assumed that the cooling water will be used once and returned to its source, with or without prior cooling. All the systems described can also be designed to recycle the cooling water through the cooling system, replacing water lost through evaporation and exchanging an additional fraction to prevent accumulation of salts. These systems may be the best choice for sites where water supply is a problem. A recycling system using dry cooling towers would essentially free the generation of electricity from restrictions of water supply, and would greatly simplify plant siting. Unless there are improvements in current technology, however, such a system would increase the complexity and cost of generating electricity and decrease the efficiency. At least one manufacturer of turbines in the United States is considering new designs less affected by the higher backpressures imposed on the turbine by dry cooling towers. If these and other modifications are successful, the economics of non-evaporative cooling will improve and these techniques may become the solution to cooling problems for the future.

It is clear that there is no ideal solution to the problem of waste heat. Each solution is a compromise, and bears its own economic and ecologic price tag. Sometimes the situation is clearly a trade-off between the economy and the environment, but more often, one set of problems is merely exchanged for another. The best solution may be a combination cooling system, in which once-through cooling is used at times when the extra heat burden can be assimilated without damage to the aquatic ecosystems, with auxiliary use of cooling towers, spray canals, or cooling ponds under certain conditions or in certain seasons of the year.

There are many ways in which we could use energy more efficiently than we do. One of these is to use waste heat from power plants for some of the many jobs for which moderate temperatures are adequate. Already, there are plans for combination power plant-water desalination projects. Power plants could become multipurpose energy sources for urban areas, their waste heat providing energy for space heating in winter and air conditioning in summer. Combination power plant-sewage treatment plants may be feasible, although substantial research in this area is lacking. Addition of waste heat could increase the rate of microbial reactions in sewage treatment. Raising the temperature of the sewage from the usual 21° C (70° F) to 38° C (100° F) would, in theory, double the capacity of the treatment plant, but this has not been verified by experiment. If treated sewage were passed through a filter of coal, more than 95 percent of the remaining organic material would be removed. This combination of coal and sludge could then be burned as fuel for the power plant, the sludge being a cleaner fuel than the coal.

Waste heat could be used to de-fog and de-ice airports or other critical areas. It could warm greenhouses. It could be used in fish hatcheries and shellfish farms. All of these developments could come to pass, but at present, they are in the realm of technological forecasting. If they are realized, it will only be as a result of integrated, long-range planning. They will be competing with the tendency to locate power plants far from population centers where, out of sight, they supposedly will also be out of mind, and where their side effects may or not affect the people they serve.

TRANSMISSION OF ELECTRICITY

In the early days of electric power systems, transmission of power from the generator to the point of use was wasteful and very expensive, and power plants were always located in the vicinity of major load centers (except for some hydroelectric plants, which were spared fuel costs and could afford higher transmission costs). Transmission is still expensive, and is consumptive of space and materials; but with development of high voltage transmission, its cost relative to the cost of transporting fuel has declined steadily, permitting more flexibility in power plant siting. In 1910, after high voltage transmission was introduced into the United States, the maximum line voltage was 110 kilovolts (110,000 volts). By 1920 it had climbed to 200 kilovolts, it was about 350 in 1940, it was past 400 in 1960, and by 1970 an 1100 kilovolt facility was being tested. Now we talk about extra-high voltage, and, for the future, ultra-high voltage.

Electric power is the product of electric current (the rate of flow of electric charge) and electromotive force (voltage, roughly analogous to pressure). From this relationship it is evident that, as voltage increases, more energy is transmitted. Increased capacity, however, is not the only advantage of high voltages. Some energy is always lost during transmission. Most of this loss is due to resistance of the wire, which in turn, is related to the current and the cross sectional area of the wire. In the transmission of any given amount of energy, the higher the voltage is, the lower the current and consequently the lower the resistance loss will be. Alternatively, in transmitting a given amount of energy at some predetermined rate of loss, the higher the voltage is, the smaller the wire can be. Thus the three related gains from high voltage transmission are increased capacity, decreased resistance loss, and decreased size of transmission lines. At high voltages, however, other kinds of energy loss occur. One of these is a leakage of energy called a corona discharge, which occurs because the air around the transmission lines becomes ionized.

Figure 10–5 shows the elements of a power system involved in

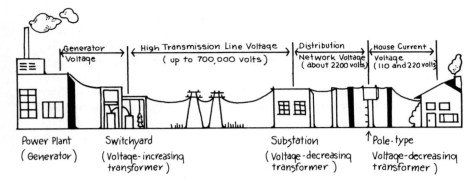

Figure 10-5. Functional diagram of the transmission and distribution system for electric power.

transmitting electricity. Economical voltages for transmission are much higher than those at which the systems that generate and use electricity can operate. In the switchyard of a power plant, a voltage transformer increases the voltage of the power from the generator to the transmission line value. The power is then distributed to various substations near load centers, where another transformer decreases the voltage before it enters the distribution network. Voltage is reduced again in the familiar transformers mounted on utility poles, from which electricity reaches the consumer at a very nearly constant voltage of 110 or 220.

Transmission systems require a great deal of space. Lines connecting a typical 3000 megawatt plant into a transmission system at 500 kilovolts require a right-of-way of 25 to 40 hectares for each kilometer of lines. Thus the advantages of high voltage transmission are obvious.

For esthetic reasons, there is increasing pressure to lay transmission lines underground. At present, however, the cost and technical problems of placing high voltage lines underground are insuperable. Underground lines in the lower-voltage distribution network are feasible, but they cost from 9 to 16 times as much as overhead lines in suburban areas, and up to 40 times as much in rural areas.

The power grid connecting load centers and generating centers has become bewilderingly complex, to assure reliable service and ability to meet peak or unexpected demands and emergencies. The interconnection of power systems was stimulated by the shocking blackout in the northeast in 1965. Already, a 500-kilovolt loop spans a major section of the eastern seaboard from north to south, and strengthening of east-west connections is underway. Major load centers in Michigan, Indiana, and Ohio are connected, forming part of a loop around Lake Erie to connect centers in Canada and the United States. Construction of lines connecting the Pacific northwest with the Pacific southwest is in progress.

Interconnections between utilities in the Great Plains and the Rocky Mountain areas are more difficult because the load centers are smaller and farther apart, but there are plans for development on a modest scale. As the transmission system grows in size and complexity, the location of a power plant will become independent from the location of the need for power.

Whether this grid is necessary can be debated. The cost in dollars will be about $8 billion, in the period from 1967 through 1975. The environmental cost has not been measured, nor has the net value to society. It is as sobering as it is comforting to think of this stupendous web crisscrossing the country from Atlantic to Pacific and from Canada to Mexico, able to carry power from anywhere to anywhere in seconds. Although it serves us, we are at its mercy.

It could be argued that commitment to a great web of unsightly, sputtering, humming, and crackling overhead transmission lines is premature because of potential improvements in underground transmission. Low temperature transmission holds the most interest. When some materials are cooled to very low temperatures their resistance to the passage of electricity decreases until it suddenly vanishes and they become superconductors. At first this phenomenon was merely a laboratory curiosity, but it soon became a laboratory tool. Work is now underway to develop underground transmission of electricity based on the principles of superconductivity. Table 10–4 compares some properties of several proposed low temperature systems. The hydrogen-cooled system is of most interest, because of the large gain in capacity per degree of cooling. A superconducting transmission line sounds very attractive, but the problems of cooling thousands of miles of underground cable to 4 degrees above absolute zero may be knottier than even conservative technologists expect.

In fact, the practicality of any low temperature system is still open to question because no commercial system has been designed yet. Economic estimates are unreliable because, as in the case of fusion reactors, no one is certain what is being estimated. The cost in both

Table 10.4. Operating Temperatures and Relative Load Capacities of Low Temperature and Superconducting Transmission Systems

Coolant	Operating Temperature °K	Operating Temperature °C	Relative Conductivity of Metal Transmission Line
Oil (reference)	293	20	1
Liquid nitrogen	77	–196	8
Liquid hydrogen	20	–252	500
Liquid helium	4	–269	superconductor

dollars and energy of refrigerating the transmission lines may be so great that the system is rendered useless.

Advanced Systems to Improve Efficiency and Meet Peak Demands

The supply of electricity must respond almost instantaneously to variations in demand. There are daily, weekly, and seasonal cycles of demand, which vary with the major uses of electricity and the climate. A persistent problem in the electric power industry has been to find ways of meeting peak demands and of using the generating capacity when demand is low. Systems operate most efficiently and economically at full load, and for this reason, despite current shortages of electricity and fuel, the power companies still encourage off-peak use of power.

East-west connection of power systems will permit exchange of power between time zones, as the time of peak demand marches daily across the country. Traditionally, additional generators have been brought into service when extra power is needed. A hydroelectric plant is ideal for this purpose because it can be started and stopped quickly. The flexibility of hydropower spurred development of pumped storage systems. Here, surplus power generated during off-peak hours is used to pump water from a low reservoir to a higher one. When demand is high, the water is allowed to flow back to the lower level, and its kinetic energy is converted to electricity as in any hydroelectric plant. But because of the laws of thermodynamics, more energy is expended in pumping the water to the higher level than is recovered when it falls. Therefore pumped storage is not a source of energy, but merely a technique for balancing temporal variations in supply and demand.

Gas turbines and diesel engines are also widely used to meet peak demands or to supply power in emergencies. Both can be started and brought to full capacity within a few minutes. Both have negligible requirements for water, which renders their siting independent of water supply. The units are prefabricated and can be put into operation in a few months—a major advantage in these days of power shortages and delays in construction of major new facilities.

A gas turbine, as the name suggests, is driven by hot combustion gases rather than by steam or water. Most gas turbines burn clean fuel—natural gas or the lighter petroleum fractions. They are noisy and inefficient, but their advantages outweigh these disadvantages for the purposes they usually serve.

Diesel engines are widely used in transportation, in mining and the petroleum industry, for generating electricity in isolated areas, and for supplying power in emergencies. They are designed to burn either natural gas or various petroleum fractions, and are more efficient than either gas turbines or small steam turbines. Their economy, versatility, and mobility make then desirable additions to utility systems even though their capacity is limited to about 6 megawatts. Total installed diesel capacity in the electric industry is expected to double between 1970 and 1980, from 4000 to 8000 megawatts, and to triple between 1970 and 1990.

The efficiency of steam electric plants is limited by the temperature range within which they operate. Because the lower temperature is set by the temperature of the environmental heat sink, efforts to increase the temperature range must be directed toward increasing the upper temperature. Much higher temperatures can be achieved in burning fossil fuels than can be used in a steam system, where the materials cannot tolerate more drastic conditions than those already imposed on them. The practical limit is about 570° C (1050° F) and 248 kilograms pressure per square centimeter (3500 pounds per square inch).

In the past there was some effort to find an alternative vapor to steam, which could take advantage of the high temperatures at a lower pressure. Some plants were designed to work on a mercury vapor-liquid mercury cycle, but they were not satisfactory. There is presently no other candidate for an alternative vapor.

There are other ways, however, to take advantage of the temperatures that combustion of fossil fuels can provide. When used in conjunction with a steam cycle, they are called topping cycles (and the steam cycle, appropriately, is the bottoming cycle). Waste heat from the topping cycle heats steam for the steam cycle, thus increasing the temperature range in which the combined system operates and raising its efficiency. Optimistic estimates say the efficiency of some combined cycles could reach 70 percent, but since these advanced systems have yet to be put into operation, there are still many unknowns.

Most promising for the near future is a topping unit that uses hot combustion gases directly to drive a gas turbine, with the somewhat cooled gases then rejecting their heat to a conventional steam generating system. Some gas turbines already operate in this way to provide extra power for peak demands, although most of them operate without the steam cycle. This system, and gas turbines in general, must burn clean fuel in order to hold air pollution and maintenance costs to tolerable levels. Current research emphasizes a gas turbine topping cycle in conjunction with gasification of coal for onsite production of electricity.

The field of magnetohydrodynamics (MHD) holds promise for greater efficiency in energy conversion, although difficult problems with materials and design block the road between theory and application. MHD is based on the fact that an ionized gas, passing through a magnetic field, generates a current of electricity. In an MHD generator, a stream of hot gas takes the place of the cumbersome steam turbo-generator, allowing temperatures up to 2800° C (5000° F) in an efficient, one stage conversion process.

Plans call for fossil fuels to be burned in pre-heated air in a high-temperature combustion chamber. The combustion gases will become highly ionized, and the electron density will be further increased by seeding the gas with a readily ionized salt like potassium sulfate. Ionized gas and seed will then be released at high velocity through an MHD channel, across an intense magnetic field. As they pass through the channel they will induce a direct current voltage between electrodes in the channel walls. The MHD cycle can be used either alone or as a topping unit for a gas turbine or steam cycle. At somewhat lower temperatures, liquid potassium, cesium, or sodium could replace the hot gas as the ionized fluid in the MHD channel. This alkali metal system might use heat from a fission reactor instead or from the combustion process.

One problem common to both gas turbine and MHD cycles is that, at the high combustion temperatures involved, much larger amounts of nitrogen oxides are formed than are formed in the conventional fossil fuel plants of today. At present there is no satisfactory way to decrease their formation or remove them from stack gases.

Two other methods of generating electricity convert heat directly to an electrical current, bypassing the intermediate conversion to mechanical energy. One of these is called thermionic generation and is based on the thermionic effect—the phenomenon of electron emission, or the boiling off of electrons when a metal is heated beyond a certain point. The process requires temperatures above 1400° C (2500° F), and at such temperatures the functional life of the components is short. Although thermionic generation has useful applications in space technology, large-scale commercial applications seem unlikely. A similar situation holds for thermoelectric generation, which is based on the voltage difference produced between them when two different conductors are joined and heated. Thermoelectric generation powered by the sun or another heat source has potential applications in communication and other specialized areas, but like thermionic generation it is very inefficient and has little to recommend it for large-scale power generation.

HOW MUCH ENERGY DOES IT REALLY TAKE TO OPERATE AN ALL-ELECTRIC HOME?

When we say that a power plant generates electricity with an efficiency of 40 percent we are looking at only a small segment of the chain of events that begins in the coal or uranium mine or the oilfield and ends when you switch on an electric light in your home. For each 100 kilowatt-hours of energy in the form of fuel in the ground, about 35 are lost during extraction or otherwise rendered irrecoverable. Perhaps 2 more kilowatt-hours are lost during processing and transportation. Thirty-nine are wasted in the conversion to electricity. Two are lost in the transmission of electricity to the consumer. The final conversion may be very efficient or very inefficient, but we will assume an average efficiency of about 75 percent, which means that 6 more kilowatt hours are lost. Thus only 16 of the 100 kilowatt-hours of potential energy contained in the original fuel are actually converted to useful work—an overall efficiency of 16 percent (figure 10–6).

100 kilowatt-hours potential energy in ground

35 kilowatt-hours lost or irrecoverable after extraction

2 kilowatt-hours lost in processing and transport

39 kilowatt-hours lost in conversion to electricity

2 kilowatt-hours lost in transmitting electricity

6 kilowatt-hours lost in final conversion

16 kilowatt-hours of useful energy

Figure 10–6. Energy losses in production and use of electricity. Starting from fuel in the ground, the fate of the energy to final use is traced.

But even now the story is not complete. At each step of the way a great deal of energy is required to maintain the energy system. The refining of petroleum uses 10 percent of all energy used by industry. The fabrication of uranium fuel rods requires large amounts of energy. Gas pipelines use about 4 percent of the energy used by the transportation sector of the economy. Rail and marine transport of fuel also requires energy. Up to 10 percent of the output of a power plant can be consumed onsite in devices for pollution control. Beyond that, there is a substantial investment of energy in all the equipment that brings energy to us in the final form of electricity. Perhaps, after all, we should not feel so superior in our efficiency to a green plant.

REFERENCES

1. F. Warren, in *Electric Power and Thermal Discharges,* ed. M. Eisenbud and G. Gleason (New York: Gordon and Breach, Inc., 1969), p. 24.
2. G. Garvey, *Energy, Ecology, Economy* (New York: W. W. Norton & Company, Inc., 1972), pp. 157–173.

SUGGESTED READING

Eisenbud, M., and Gleason, G., eds. *Electric Power and Thermal Discharges.* New York: Gordon and Breach, 1969.

Sierra Club. Papers presented at the Conference on the Electric Power Industry, 1972, Johnson College, Burlington, Vermont.

U. S., Cong., Senate, Hearing before the Committee on Interior and Insular Affairs. *Advanced Power Cycles.* 92nd Cong., 2nd sess., 8 February 1972. Serial No. 92–21.

U.S., Federal Power Commission. *The 1970 Federal Power Survey.* Washington, D.C., 1971.

U.S., Office of Science and Technology, Executive Office of the President. *Considerations Affecting Steam Power Plant Selection.* Washington, D.C., 1968.

PART III

Prospects for the Future

CHAPTER 11

Where Does the Energy Go?

In what we call progress, 90 per cent of our efforts go into finding a cure for the harms linked to the advantages brought about by the remaining 10 per cent.

Claude Levi–Strauss

When passing Gary, Indiana or Pittsburgh, Pennsylvania, it is easy enough to identify the miles of factories with energy use. But it is not always so obvious just where the energy goes, or what it is used for.

Americans should learn something about their patterns of energy consumption. Only with such knowledge can we make intelligent choices about changing. For in the final analysis, we have only two options in energy use: we must either find ways to supply ever increasing amounts of energy, or curb our demands.

One way to meet the energy crisis is to slow the growth in consumption. There are some clear benefits to be gained from slowing down. It would give us more time to supply the energy that is needed and would also conserve our supply of fuels for needs still further in the future. And for each gallon of fuel not consumed, there is less pollution to control.

For many people, the growth in energy use is an abstract statistic, unrelated to their own lives. Most people have very little idea of the amount of energy they use. A questionnaire on energy consumption was prepared by a group of students at the University of Wisconsin and administered to more than one thousand people. The students could not even find a unit or a measure of energy that people knew well enough to answer a question. Watts and calories sounded familiar to many people, but they could not relate these units to their own domestic energy use. Kilowatt-hours were even less useful, while joules and ergs brought only perplexed stares. Finally settling on the 100-watt light bulb as a unit, the students found that most of those questioned could not guess their own use within a factor of one hundred.

So again we ask: where does it all go?

CONVENTIONAL SECTORAL BREAKDOWN

Conventional sectoral breakdowns of energy use have been dictated in part by the way in which statistics are collected, in part by the needs of government economists, and partly by historical accident. Figure 11–1 presents one of the most common sectoral divisions of energy use. While there are a number of difficulties in this kind of partitioning, figure 11–1 clearly indicates that the division of energy consumption among these sectors has been remarkably stable for the last 25 years. During this period energy use has doubled (table 11–1), yet the only trend observable is gradual enlargement of use in the sector labeled "other."

Figure 11–2 displays the flow of energy through an industrial society from fuel to its ultimate fate. From this flow diagram it is clear that the conventional sectors discuss a slice across figure 11–2. Even then, the energy lost in generation of electricity is ignored. But, for the present, we must make do with the categories for which we have data, and we will examine these categories in more detail.

The Industrial Sector

The industrial sector is the most homogeneous; more than 70 percent of the elements included in this sector would correspond with our usual idea of manufacturing industries. Among the six industries which account for two-thirds of the energy used by this sector are the food processing and the petroleum industries. The food processing industry accounts for more than 5 percent of all industrial energy use (chapter 6). In 1968, the petroleum industry and related fuel producers accounted for about 11 percent of industrial use. However, only one-third of the fuels produced are consumed by industry. If the energy costs of the petroleum industry were assigned to the ultimate fuel users we might better understand the savings to be gained by measures to reduce energy consumption. In figure 11–3 we have a breakdown of energy consumption in the industrial sector. A more detailed look at the six leading industrial energy consumers will be useful.

Table 11-1. Energy Use (in 10^{15} kcal) by Sectors

	1929	1939	1947	1955	1960	1970
Household and Commercial	1.78	1.82	2.65	2.73	3.24	3.98
Transportation	1.65	1.46	2.06	2.04	2.32	4.11
Industry	2.35	1.96	3.14	3.96	4.02	5.22
Other	0.52	0.56	0.94	1.37	1.85	2.97
Total	6.30	5.80	8.79	10.10	11.43	16.28

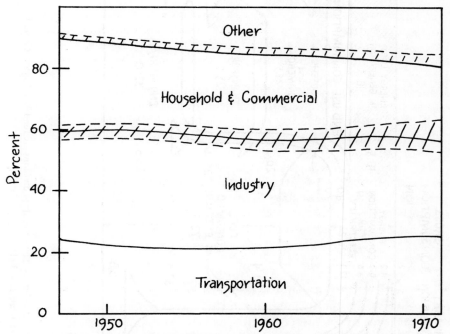

Figure 11-1. A traditional sectoral division of energy use, 1947–1971. (The shaded area represents energy consumed for generation of electricity). Source: (1), (7), and Statistical Abstract of the U.S. (Washington, D.C. annual).

Primary Metals Industries

Two-thirds of the energy consumed in production of primary metals goes to the basic iron and steel industry. During the 1960s energy use was reduced by about 10 percent per unit of output, primarily because of the more efficient use of blast furnaces.

Statistical data suggest an even larger decline in energy consumption. Use of electricity increased by about 20 percent in response to

Figure 11–2. Energy flow in the United States. The percentage divisions are for 1970. Source: Cook, E. "The Flow of Energy in an Industrial Society." *Scientific American* 224, 3 (1971).

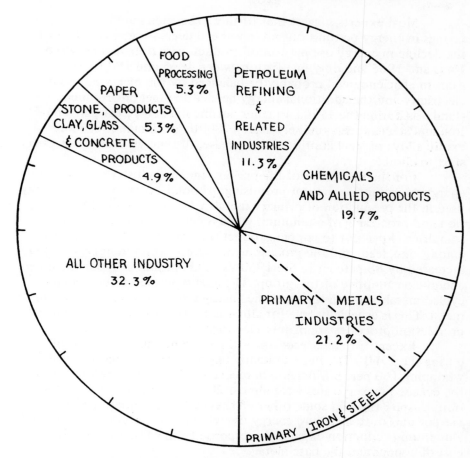

Figure 11-3. Division of energy use in the industrial sector, 1970. Source: U.S., Office of Science and Technology, Executive Office of the President, *Patterns of Energy Consumption in the United States* (Washington, D.C., 1972).

several factors, including the need to meet air and water quality standards. If purchased electric power is charged to the steel industry in terms of fuel consumed, the decline in energy use per unit output is near 10 percent. Electric energy accounted for about 10 percent of the energy used for iron and steel production in 1969.

The use of natural gas in the iron and steel industry doubled during the 1960s. The price increases associated with the shortages of domestic natural gas mean that this trend cannot continue. Use of natural gas in the steel industry will probably decline (or at most remain stable) for the remainder of this century. This change, together with the need to meet environmental standards, will increase the use of electricity in steel production.

Most experts suggest that further efficiencies are possible, but savings in energy per unit output have been decreasing (four-fifths of the decline in energy use per ton of product were obtained between 1960 and 1965 and only one-fifth between 1965 and 1970). Further gains in efficiency will probably be balanced by the increased use of electricity and the additional energy needed to meet environmental standards during the 1970s. Further decline in energy cost per ton of iron and steel appears unlikely after 1980. If the demand for more exotic alloys of steel continues to increase, the energy cost of steel may start to climb.

For the remainder of the primary metals industry, the trends in energy consumption are not promising. About 12 percent of the energy used in the production of primary metals was consumed in the production and processing of aluminum, while 8 percent went to ferrous foundries, 4 percent to copper production, and the rest was scattered among zinc, lead, and the processing of metals. Aluminum production increased by 88 percent in the 1960s, and aluminum is by far the most energy-consumptive of this group. The energy needed to process recycled metals is much less than the energy required to produce virgin metal. This is especially true for aluminum and copper, as the primary production processes are mainly electrical.

Except for zinc, recovery of the principal metals improved during the 1960s. The most dramatic improvement in recovery was a whopping 160 percent increase in recovered aluminum. By the end of the decade recovery rates were almost 20 percent of primary production. Despite this and some other efficiency-based reductions in energy use per unit output, future energy use will almost certainly increase as aluminum production expands in response to shortages and the high cost of copper and the base metals.

In this industry a growing proportion of energy is used for rolling, drawing, casting, and forging of metals. This trend appears to be part of a long-range development in technology, and will continue. Thus, gains in efficiency in foundries are likely to be canceled by the need for more and more complicated (and energy-consumptive) processing.

New air and water quality standards mean higher energy consumption per unit output. It will take another decade of experience to learn how much energy will be needed to meet these standards.

Chemicals and Allied Products

The second largest industrial user is the chemical industry. In this area uses for energy are as diverse as the estimated ten thousand industrial chemicals manufactured. Even the industry is not very well defined. There are some giant chemical producers (names like DuPont,

Dow, Union Carbide, and Olin come to mind), and the largest 20 companies account for three-fourths of production in most categories. Nevertheless, 43 percent of the 500 largest corporations manufacture chemicals, often as byproducts of their primary product. The trend from coal to oil and natural gas as the primary raw materials of chemical production in the past 35 years has been followed by entry of the oil industry into production of chemicals.

Fuel use in the chemical industry differs notably from that in other industries, for about half the fuel consumed is used as raw material rather than for production of energy. This use has been growing rapidly. Use of oil and natural gas as the basis of chemical production is less sensitive to higher prices than are energy uses, and thus it will probably continue to expand, even at the expense of energy uses. Increased production of coal, or of gasified coal, may supply some of this expansion.

Two-thirds of the energy used in the chemical sector goes to the production of eleven products: chlorine-caustic soda, synthetic soda ash, acetylene, oxygen, carbon black, ammonia, manufactured aluminum oxide, phosphorus, methyl alcohol, sulfur, and ethylene and related products (including propylene, butadiene, and aromatics). Most of these products are supplied to other industries as materials for manufacture of final products. In most cases we must look to the final products to determine whether savings are possible. Some means of producing these eleven products are energy intensive and others are not (table 11–7, p. 242). Often there are several choices available for the manufacture of chemicals. These choices may differ in energy requirements per unit output by a factor of ten or more. Which is chosen depends upon several factors, but prominent among these is the absolute price of energy and the relative price of energy and labor. The future of energy use in the chemical industry depends also on the degree to which substitution of manufactured for natural materials continues. For example, many products of the chemical industry have replaced textiles, wood, hides, rubber, and mined chemicals. Production of chemical foods is possible, although insignificant at present.

Petroleum Refining

Petroleum refining and associated industries are the third largest industrial consumer. However, it might be desirable to apportion these energy costs among the fuel users. It takes about 200,000 kilocalories per barrel to process crude oil into the more than one thousand finished petroleum products on the market today. This amounts to about 11 percent of the energy content of the oil. The proportion of energy used per barrel of crude oil has changed little in the past ten or fifteen years, and no great changes in this energy consumption are expected in the near future. Newer refineries succeed in obtaining a more profitable. (and, at times, more useful) mix of products, but do not achieve any significant decrease in energy consumption per unit output.

Food Processing
The food processing industry was discussed in connection with the agriculture-food supply system. Although food processing has reduced its percentage share of total industrial energy use, its absolute increase for the past decade has exceeded increases in output. Processed food accounts for an ever larger portion of our diets, although the return to natural foods could reverse this trend. Decreasing the energy consumed in food processing will be difficult, because the four largest energy consumers in this area (meat, dairy products, grains and sugar) are not much affected by the change in lifestyles (with the possible exception of some reduction in meat consumption).

Paper
In one of the periodic efforts of the government to avoid being buried in its own accumulation of paper, an official of the Department of the Army was asked to provide final approval for destruction of unused records more than 20 years old. He replied with an approving endorsement, and, almost as an afterthought, penciled at the bottom of his memo, "be sure to make a Xerox copy of anything you are going to destroy." The story, while probably apocryphal, suggests what any adult American knows: that consumption of paper has increased enormously as our society has grown more complex. Use of forms, reports, packaging, and packaging within the packaging seems to expand each year. Energy use in the paper and paper products industry has grown by about 20 percent in the past twenty years. This expansion in energy use has been outstripped by the increase in production, and energy use per unit output dimished by about 15 percent during the 1960s. This decline is due partly to changes in the major types of paper products (for example, kraft paper, used for packaging material, requires less energy to make than other types), and partly to technological improvements in the manufacturing process. As these improvements spread through the industry, some further reduction in energy per pound of paper may be possible, but improvements will be harder to come by in the future. Pulp yields, for example, increased from 96 to 98 percent between 1958 and 1967. The next improvement will be much more difficult, and we will never reach 100 percent recovery.

Stone, Clay, Glass
Many of the raw materials for stone, clay, glass and concrete products are mined or they are obtained from the byproducts and waste of other industries (slag and sludge, for example). Most of the

energy consumption is for mechanical crushing, grinding and blending and for heat to obtain chemical changes at high temperatures. In 1967, cement production consumed 43 percent of the energy in this group, glass production consumed 16 percent (the largest end use is glass containers), concrete products consumed 15 percent and structural clay products 14 percent.

Thus, cement, concrete products, and structural clay products together account for almost three-fourths of the energy consumed in this industry. They are used primarily in the construction of roads, buildings and the like. A functional look at energy consumption would assign their cost to the construction industry, and the next largest item — glass containers — would be assigned to the food system. Energy costs of these products vary considerably according to the kiln time and temperatures needed. While there have been improvements in kiln design and certain economies of scale are possible, there are few prospects for dramatic energy savings per unit output in this sector. Even recycling offers little help here.[5]

Transportation

In years gone by, the transportation services moved both goods and people by the same methods. Currently, however, those modes of transport which handle most freight carry very few passengers, and vice versa. Figure 11–4 presents a breakdown of energy consumption of the transportation sector. This is the only sector in which the use of electricity is not expanding. Even though electric mass transit is attractive in many ways, this mode of transportation was never used extensively in the United States, and it has declined in recent years. Most transportation is powered by petroleum products, and 53 percent of the total refinery output goes to this sector.

The transport of people is dominated by the private automobile. In 1970, autos accounted for almost 88 percent of all intercity passenger miles, a proportion that has seen little change in the past twenty years although the fuel efficiency has worsened. Air travel, the least efficient mode of passenger travel, accounted for 9 percent of intercity passenger miles in 1970 — up from 4 percent in 1950. Here too, there has been declining efficiency of fuel usage. Air transport has used almost one-third more energy per passenger mile in the past decade. Most of the remaining intercity passenger travel is provided by buses, although as recently as twenty years ago, railroads provided more than 5 percent of all intercity passenger miles. Increased fuel consumption per passenger mile in aircraft and automobiles is not primarily due to technological developments. For aircraft, scheduling has resulted in a drop in percentage load and a corresponding increase in energy cost per passenger mile. The new, larger jets contribute a share to the increase. For autos, the increase is the result of ever larger engines and the growing number of

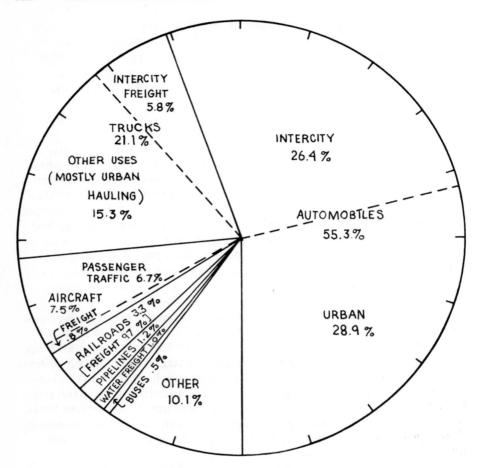

Figure 11–4. Division of energy use in the transportation sector, 1970. ("Other" includes general aviation, non-bus mass transit, recreational and passenger boating, recreational vehicles, and other uses.) Source: E. Hurst, *Energy Consumption for Transportation in the United States* (Oak Ridge National Laboratory Report, ONRL–NSF–EP–15.)

energy-consuming options, from air conditioners to devices for pollution control.

Table 11–2 summarizes the modal split and the efficiencies of intercity passenger transport in 1970. This choice of modes was not made with energy use, or even minimum cost in dollars, in mind. Energy consumption per passenger mile has been rising steadily for twenty years or more. It seems doubtful that this trend can continue.

Over half of the total fuel energy for transportation is consumed in urban areas; since we expend this energy in less than 2 percent of the

Table 11–2. Intercity Passenger Transport, 1970

Mode	Passenger Miles $\times\ 10^9$	Percentage of Total Passenger Miles	Energy Consumed (kcal $\times\ 10^{12}$)	Efficiency (kcal/ Passenger Mile)
Automobiles	1020	88.1	940	920
Airplanes	104	9.0	306	2940
Buses	25	2.2	7.6	308
Railroads	8	0.7	1.9	240

Sources: *Statistical Abstracts of the United States*; Interstate Commerce Commission, Federal Aviation Administration, and Department of Transportation gross data.

land area, and the remaining half in the other 98 percent of the nation's area, our urban air pollution problems should not surprise us. The auto dominates intracity transport, with 94 percent of the total passenger miles. Well over half of all auto trips are in urban areas and for less than five miles. Table 11–3 summarizes the data for urban passenger transport in 1970. Although there are no data available for walking and bicycling, anecdotal evidence suggests that both have been declining for many years. The recent rise in bicycle sales may reverse the trend for bike travel, but this increase only began in the 1970s.

There has been a dramatic decline in mass transit: from 31 percent of urban passenger miles in 1950, mass transit dropped to 13 percent in1960, and is still falling. It is surprising that the efficiency has not also declined precipitously. Note that the efficiencies given in table 11–3 are from experiential data. They differ from those in other estimates. (See Box 11–1 for a discussion of such estimates.) Before concluding that we need only walk or ride bicycles to solve our energy

Table 11–3. Intracity Passenger Transport, 1970

Mode	Passenger Miles $\times\ 10^9$	Percentage of Total Passenger Miles	Energy Consumed (kcal $\times\ 10^{12}$)	Efficiency (kcal/ Passenger Mile)
Automobile	739	94	1130	1530
Mass Transit (almost all bus)	49.5	6	14.8	300
Walking	–*	–	–	75
Bicycle	–	–	–	45

* = no data
Sources: *Statistical Abstracts of the United States*; Department of Transportation, Interstate Commerce Commission, and Federal Aviation Administration gross data.

problem, we should recall the discussion of energy in the food system (chapter 6). The energy required for walking and bicycling is derived from our food system, and at the present energy cost of a kilocalorie of food, it is more efficient, in terms of energy conservation, to take the bus.

To a considerable extent, the nature of a freight shipment determines the mode of transport. It is foolish to consider shipping iron ore by airplane, and it is quite impossible to ship strawberries by pipeline. To a large extent, then, the present modal mix of freight shipments is determined by what we have to ship. There have been changes in the proportions of freight carried by various modes in recent years. In part these shifts are due to changes in industrial activity and in part they represent real choices in competing modes — usually for reasons of economy or convenience. The most notable of these shifts has been the expansion in freight transport by truck at the expense of rail freight transport. For their specialized uses, pipelines have also cut into rail freight owing to the lower cost per unit shipped. The railroads' share of freight transport has dropped from more than 60 percent of the total in 1940 to 40 percent in 1970. The shift to trucks is further explained by the superhighways which have been built at public expense. These provide an indirect subsidy to trucks as a mode of transport. Table 11–4 presents the modal division of freight transport in 1970, together with the associated energy costs.

Present trends suggest a continuing shift from rail to truck if, and there are two big ifs, the construction of high speed roads continues and the price of energy does not rise too dramatically. Air freight, which has expanded its volume by a factor of 10 in the last 20 years and doubled twice in the past ten years, must slow its rate of growth. Should the same growth continue for another 20 years, air freight would carry 2 or 3 percent of the total freight and consume

Table 11–4. Freight Transport, 1970

Mode	Volume (Ton-Miles $\times 10^9$)	Percentage of Total	Energy Consumed (kcal $\times 10^{12}$)	Efficiency (kcal/ Ton-Mile)
Railroads	768	40	131	170
Trucks	412	21.4	370	900
Pipelines	431	22.4	49	114
Water carriers	307	16	42	136
Airways	3.4	0.2	34	10,000

Sources: *Statistical Abstracts of the United States*; Interstate Commerce Commission, Department of Transportation, and Federal Aviation Administration gross data.

almost half of the freight transportation energy. This is unlikely to say the least. Efficiencies of pipelines, water carriers, and railroads have been improving and could be improved further. Trucks seem not to be improving their efficiency much (fig. 11–5).

Residential

"You've come a long way, baby" begins one particularly obnoxious cigarette advertisement. In the American home, the changes in lifestyle in the last two generations are staggering. One evidence of the change is the large number of appliances to be found in most homes. There is a tendency to confuse this increase in number of appliances with increased energy use, but such is not the case. The bulk of residential energy use still goes for space heating and for storage and preparation of food. Meanwhile, our favorite candidates for foolish energy use, the electric comb and the electric knife, consume less than one-ten thousandth of residential energy.

Figure 11–6 shows the distribution of residential energy consumption in 1968. Heating is the big consumer. Although heating declined as a percentage of total residential energy consumption in the last decade, the average energy expenditure for heating per household rose by almost 20 percent. Any examination of future prospects for energy use must look closely at trends in home heating. The fastest growth in residential energy use is for electric heating. Between 1960 and 1968 energy used for this purpose increased by a factor of 5, but even in 1968 only 5.6 percent of all residences were heated electrically, and they used less than 7 percent of all energy used for residential space heating. Because of the low efficiency of fuel use in electric heat (see chapter 5), growth in the use of electric heat could increase domestic energy requirements enormously. About one-third of the increase in per household heating between 1960 and 1968 is due to the growing use of electric heat. The remainder is not easy to account for. The most likely explanation is that the general increase in affluence, including larger housing space, has caused the increase. Between 1960 and 1968 the annual consumption for electric heat per household increased from 11,908 kilowatt-hours to 14,153 kilowatt-hours — an increase of about 20 percent. We would like to stress this point because many believe that increases in residential energy consumption are primarily due to the number and size of large appliances used.

The second largest residential use is water heating. In 1960, 75 percent of all residences had water heaters, but by 1968, 94 percent had them. In addition, the energy consumption per unit rose by a little over 5 percent. In this case the increased consumption is probably due to the growing number of dishwashers and automatic washing machines.

BOX 11-1   ESTIMATES OF ENERGY USE PER UNIT ACTIVITY

Estimates of energy consumption per unit activity (per ton-mile of transport services, per kilocalorie of food produced, per ton of product manufactured, and so on) are very useful when one wishes to consider alternatives for use of energy resources, or simply to understand the quantitative effect of energy conservation measures. Unfortunately, estimates of these quantities vary widely. Some of the variation is no doubt due to careless work, but there are real difficulties in making estimates of this kind and these account for most of the differences.

For example, consider the efficiencies of truck transportation of freight in kcal per ton-mile. An estimate could be derived from the efficiency of fuel use in a truck of a certain average size and the load capacity of such a truck. This neglects the effect of speed, traffic conditions, the truck's mechanical condition, and fuel mileage. Another estimate could be made by testing a truck under specified experimental conditions of load and traffic. Yet another method would be to use gross experiential data, that is, to divide the total fuel used in truck transport by the number of ton-miles of freight carried. This last method would be the best if statistics of exactly the sort wanted were always available, but they seldom are. It has the advantage of including, as a matter of course, the average load factor, traffic conditions and associated energy using activities that should be charged to trucking, but it has the disadvantage of including truck uses that seem very far from freight transport. For example, more than 10 percent of all trucks are engaged in garbage disposal. Should such uses be included in truck freight transport? Is efficiency the same as for freight transport?

All three methods of estimation — theoretical, experimental and experiental — have their place, and all have serious deficiencies. Figure 11-5 shows a group of estimates of truck efficiencies from four different sources. One can observe a trend of improving efficiency until 1960. But note that there is a difference of about a factor of two in the estimates. This degree of difference is not uncommon. It often depends on what is included as well as how the estimate was made. Since we are more concerned with comparative values than absolute figures for energy use, this discrepancy is usually not important as long as the same numbers are used throughout.

Figure 11-5. Estimates of the energy cost of truck transport, 1940–1970. Sources: *a,* S.H. Schurr and B.C. Netschert, *Energy in the American Economy, 1850–1975* (Baltimore: Johns Hopkins Press, 1960). *b,* data from *Statistical Abstracts of the United States. c,* R. Rice, *Technology Review* (1973). *d,* E. Hurst, *Energy Intensiveness of Passenger and Freight Transport: 1950–1970* (Oak Ridge National Laboratory Report, ONRL–NSF*EP–44, April, 1973).

   In general, in this book, we have chosen to avoid extreme values and to choose somewhat conservative values. Much more detailed work remains to be done on this subject. A more detailed discussion of difficulties of this kind is to be found in a study by Schurr and Netschert.[1]

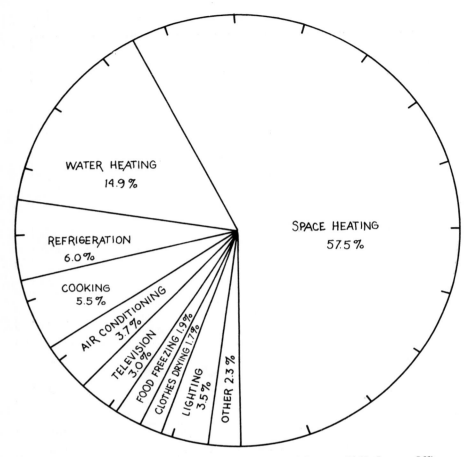

Figure 11–6. Division of energy use in the residential sector, 1968. Source: Office of Science and Technology, Executive Office of the President, *Patterns of Energy Consumption in the United States* (Washington, D.C., 1972).

Refrigeration and cooking consume about equal amounts of energy, and both are chargeable to the way in which we feed ourselves. But there the similarity ends. Energy consumption for ranges declined 3 or 4 percent during the 1960s, despite the addition of such features as self-cleaning ovens, while energy consumption for refrigerators increased more than 50 percent. The increase for refrigerators is a consequence of the growing popularity of frostless units, which require about 50 percent more energy. Since the refrigerator runs continuously, added features are reflected in increased energy costs. The average storage capacity of units has increased in recent years, more than cancelling some improvements in insulation technology. The decline in energy consumption for cooking is almost certainly a reflection of changes in cooking and eating habits, such as the trend toward more pre-cooked and instant foods. Since such pre-cooking and processing is then charged to the food processing industry, the total energy bill probably has not declined.

Other residential uses do not constitute large segments of domestic energy consumption, but of these, air conditioning and clothes drying deserve special mention. Between 1960 and 1968, the average annual growth rate for residential air conditioning was 16 percent, which implies that energy use for air conditioning increased by more than a factor of three in that period. At the same time, the consumption per unit for room-sized units increased by 10 percent. If more than two room-sized air conditioners are wanted, there is an apparent energy economy to be had by using central air conditioning. Often the actual result does not bear out the energy saving, however, because of the tendency to turn on the central unit at the outset of warm weather and allow it to run in response to a thermostat, whether needed or not. Most new homes are designed for central air conditioning. This represents a commitment to use of air conditioning for the life of the house, since a house so designed is difficult to cool by any other method (such as fans or open window ventilation patterns).

The use of clothes dryers is expanding. In 1960, 19 percent of homes had clothes dryers; by 1969, 40 percent had them. For electric units, per unit consumption has risen slightly, while the reverse has happened for gas units. It is difficult to estimate the level of saturation for these appliances. Again a lifestyle change is involved. It is clear to anyone touring a city neighborhood of even very modest means, that the process of outdoor clothes drying has almost disappeared, even in warm sunny weather. Here is a clear example of technology changing our lives, in ways not anticipated by the individual. An item of undeniable convenience in winter (ask any mother with a diaper-laden wash) has become the norm even when not necessary or particularly more convenient. And to restore something lost from the sunlight outside, some dryers will provide imitation sunlight with the process.

The Commercial and "Other" Sector

In the center of any middle-sized American town there is a profligate use of energy that is scarcely matched in any other country. As evening comes, the signs light up and the garish kaleidescopes of blinking colors compete for one's attention. Mercury vapor lamps hanging from steel poles make one's companions look like corpses. A commercial strip, we say, and hurry.through to our homes or jobs.

The commercial and "other" sector includes many activities that are not so obtrusive — health services, motion pictures, wholesale and retail trade, offices, schools, museums, commercial farms, fisheries, hotels, motels, and a host of minor pursuits. The inclusion of agriculture in this sector emphasizes the unsatisfactory nature of the present sectoral divisions. All governmental activities are included in the "other" sector.

In figure 11–7 we attempt a functional division of energy use for the commercial and "other" sector. Data for 1960 were used for this sectoral subdivision because more recent data showing defense consumption were unavailable. More energy is used in defense than in all other government activity. The remainder of government use was scattered

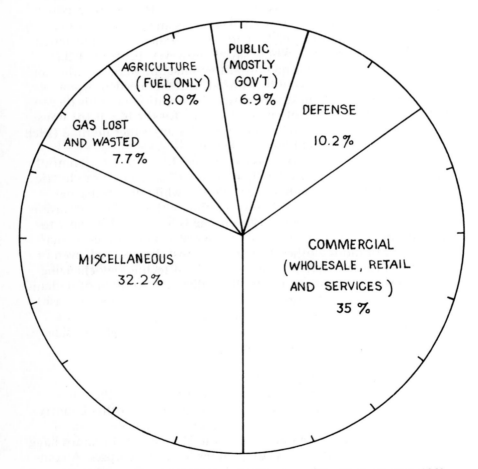

Figure 11–7. Division of energy use in the commercial and "other" sector, 1960. Source: H.H. Landsberg and S.S. Schurr, *Energy in the United States: Sources. Uses, and Policy Issues* (New York: Random House, 1968).

and surprisingly small, in view of the fact that one worker in ten was employed by the government in 1960. The rise in government employment — in 1970, 15 percent of all employed persons worked for the government — suggests that this use is growing, but it is still not especially significant. Government is primarily a service activity and, as such, is a low energy consumer. In any case, the total amounts involved suggest that measures like turning off the lights in government offices are not likely to alleviate energy shortages, although they may be of symbolic value. Space heating, asphalt and road oils, air conditioning, outdoor lighting, and possibly water heating almost certainly account for more than half of the non-defense government usage.

In the commercial sector, end uses divide into categories much like those in the residential grouping. This is not surprising when it is remembered that the sector includes offices, hotels, restaurants, and large apartment buildings. Table 11–5 provides an end use breakdown, and also indicates some trends of change since 1960.

Figure 11–8 compares the growth in commercial space heating with the growth in air conditioning from 1960 to 1968. Although space heating accounts for a smaller percentage of the sectoral total, it has increased by one-third while the population has increased only 11 percent. And this does not even include the total fuel use chargeable to electric heat in commercial establishments (motels for example). The most rapid increases in the commercial sector are in air conditioning (about 90 percent of new commercial space is air conditioned) and in "other," which is probably a reflection of the increasing mechanization of office work, quick food service and the like. The energy consumed by air conditioning doubled between 1960 and 1968, while "other" use tripled. Such growth rates cannot be sustained very long.

Our increasing affluence and resulting change in habits have produced other developments in the commercial sector. Commercial

Table 11–5. End Uses of Energy in the Commercial Sector

	1960	1968
Space heating	54.2%	47.7%
Asphalt and road oils	12.8%	11.2%
Water heating	9.5%	7.5%
Air conditioning	10.0%	12.7%
Refrigeration	9.3%	7.6%
Cooking	1.7%	1.6%
Other	2.5%	11.7%

Source: Office of Science and Technology, Executive Office of the President, *Patterns of Energy Consumption in the United States* (Washington, D.C.: 1972).

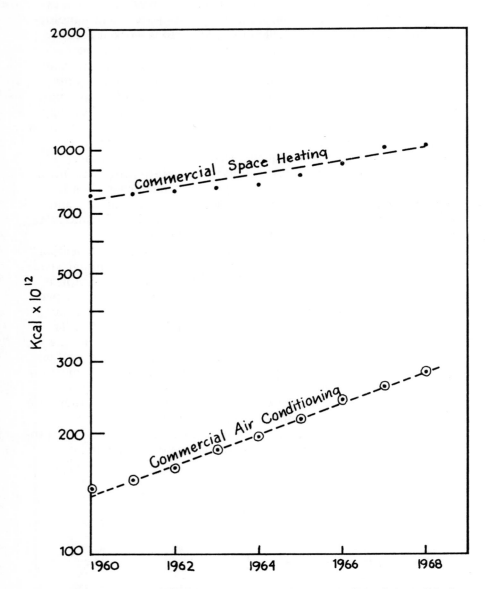

Figure 11-8. Growth in energy use in commercial space heating and air conditioning, 1960–1968. Source: Office of Science and Technology, Executive Office of the President, *Patterns of Energy Consumption in the United States* (Washington, D.C., 1972).

establishments served 17.5 percent of all meals in 1968, compared to 15 percent in 1960. Not only are more people eating out, but more live in universities and other residential institutions. In general, commercial establishments have been more economical of energy than the home. Figure 11–9 illustrates this point — it shows that despite serving an increasing proportion of meals, the commercial establishments increased their consumption of energy for refrigeration and cooking more slowly than did the residential sector.

Two-thirds of the Nation's Energy
There are many ways of classifying energy consumption. Upon leaving the sectoral classification of energy use, we should review the

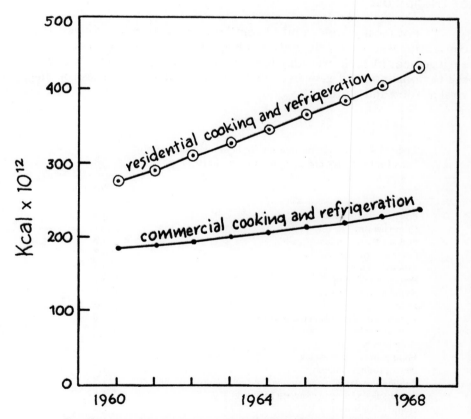

Figure 11–9. Growth in energy use for residential and commercial cooking and refrigeration, 1960–1968. Source: Office of Science and Technology, Executive Office of the President, *Patterns of Energy Consumption in the United States* (Washington, D.C., 1972).

activities which consume the greatest amounts of energy. In table 11–6 we present those activities which accounted for more than one per cent of the energy consumed in 1970. Together, the 17 end uses listed in table 11–6 accounted for two-thirds of all U.S. energy consumption.

Of the seventeen activities listed in table 11–6, five involve direct personal use of energy, six are industries which produce consumer products, two involve commercial transportation, and two are the price of energy production intself. If we look at energy consumption in this way, energy statistics lose their abstract, impersonal quality, and we may be able to relate energy consumption to our everyday life.

TOWARD A FUNCTIONAL CLASSIFICATION OF ENERGY USE

For most people, a bit of translation is required to convert the conventional sectoral categories of energy use into the events and environment of their everyday life. To begin a view of energy use from the personal point of view, we must start with such necessities for survival as food and clothing.

Table 11–6. End Uses Accounting for More than 1 Percent of Total United States Energy Consumption, 1970

Use	Percentage
Private automobiles	13.8
Home heating	10.4
Primary metals industry	6.8
Chemical industry	6.3
Trucks (all uses)	5.3
Petroleum refining	3.9
Residential hot water	2.7
Defense*	2.6
Agriculture (direct fuel use only)	2.0
Natural gas lost and wasted	1.9
Air passenger traffic	1.7
Food processing industry	1.7
Paper products industry	1.7
Public (non-defense government and public institutions)	1.7
Stone, clay, glass and concrete industry	1.6
Home refrigeration	1.1
Home cooking	1.0
TOTAL	66.2

*Note: Defense use is calculated on the basis of 1960 data.

The treatment developed in chapter 6 indicates how the food system might be handled in a new classification. Our breakdown of the food supply system is as complex as any regrouping that might be attempted, since food supply involves elements from all the conventional energy use sectors. There have been striking changes in food consumption patterns and associated energy use in the past generation, and these changes are, in general, understood. For example, the proportion of meat in the average United States diet has inceased by 25 percent since 1950. This is largely a matter of preference and affluence, urged onward by the low price of meat relative to other commodities. The extent of packaging and processing of food is again a matter of preference and convenience. In a subsequent section we will examine the energy savings that might be made in the food system. Here we need ask only if the diet of 1970 made you healthier or happier than the diet of 1960 or 1950.

Clothing production does not consume a large amount of energy. The entire textile industry accounts for only 0.6 percent of energy use, and this industry makes a great many things in addition to clothes. Even if we make generous allowances for the supplying industries, for wholesale retail trade, and for domestic energy use in washing and drying of clothes, we will not find clothing to be an area of high energy consumption. But even here savings would be possible without a substantial change in lifestyle. For example, production of synthetic fibers consumes more than twice the energy needed for production of the natural fibers they replace.

Shelter is a more complex matter. In a functional classification, the housing category would include the energy consumed in construction and in the building materials industry as well as the energy used in operating a home (such as space heating, hot water heating, and lighting).

Employment, and the buying power it brings, is necessary in all present social systems. Unfortunately, it does not lend itself to energy use classification and one must be content with attention to the service or product with which the employment is associated. To that end one can resort to a classification of producer goods industries, consumer goods industries, and service industries. Nowhere among the 17 leading energy users is an activity that would be called a service industry. But a comparison of absolute energy use per job in service industries against that in durable goods industries might shed some valuable light on our societal choices. A society emphasizing service industries would consume less energy. Should we consciously aim for such a society?

Consumer goods are those products which are used directly as they are finished by the industry. They might be further divided into necessities and luxuries. To do so implies a value choice that is more an

individual than a public matter. We might choose to include among
necessities those products used or purchased by more than half the
population. Such a division would yield data that might advance understanding of society's energy use. However arbitrarily the division is
made, the energy invested in the necessities is of more importance to
society than the energy used on luxuries. A rough average of energy
consumption per job could be calculated for these two kinds of industry.

Producer-products industries are very large energy users. From a
functional point of view it would be desirable to apportion these energy
costs among the manufacturers and the consumers. Such a division is
beyond elementary techniques, but well within the methods devised by
Leontieff and others for tracing economic flow. Apportionment of
energy costs among end products would make clear the energy requirements of goods and the energy requirements per job. It seems that basic
statistical data to accomplish this kind of classification are available.

In a functional analysis of energy use, the conventional transportation sector would be divided into two parts. The energy used in
the transportation of goods would be charged to the goods transported.
All that would remain is the transportation of people. This area sub-
divides easily into necessary transport associated with one's employment, and transportation for leisure or recreation. Such a division
would be advantageous because, for most of us, the issues in work-
related transportation are convenience, economy, and speed rather than
preference for a given mode of transport. Transportation for personal or
family business (shopping, medical care, banking, and so on) should be
included under necessary transportation. Transportation for employment and family business account for two-thirds of all automobile use,
and more than 60 percent of these trips are less than 5 miles.[2]

There are some uses of energy that are not easy to relate to
individuals. Public uses such as street lighting, government services,
defense, education, and the like are part of the common effort to make
individual life more pleasant and free from threat. These uses should
retain a category of their own. The energy consumption and losses
associated with the procurement, conversion and transport of energy
supplies could be assigned in proportion to fuel and energy used, but it
might be more informative to maintain a separate category for these. If
we had such a category at present, it would be clear that the AEC's
nuclear energy program has each year consumed more energy than it
has produced.

A final category would be energy use for recreation and leisure.
This category, consisting mostly of services and transportation, is small
but not trivial (one-third of automobile travel would be here — 4.5 per-

cent of all energy use). If the trend toward greater fuel use in recreation continues, this sector could become large.

If we wish to answer the question "Where does it all go?", we will more likely find our answer with a functional classification of energy use than with the present sectoral classification. This question is more than trivial if we believe that we have a right to participate in energy policy choices. This suggested classification would then sub-divide energy consumption as follows:

A Functional Energy Consumption Classification

1. Food system energy
2. Clothing
3. Housing: a. construction; b. operation
4. Consumer goods: a. "necessities" (with a definition according to use) b. luxuries
5. Transportation of people: a. for employment and family business; b. for leisure and recreation
6. Public uses: a. defense; b. other
7. Leisure and recreation
8. Conversion and transportation energy losses

REDUCTION OF ENERGY DEMAND

Can we substantially reduce our consumption of energy? Can we do so without a major change in society? A large amount of energy is employed wastefully in the United States. This waste must stop. The first energy shortages of the 1970s caught most people by surprise. Energy had been considered cheap and infinitely available. Today it is neither. The changeover from waste to frugality will involve a change in habits for millions of Americans. But it is necessary. Energy prices are rising and the limits on the supply of fossil fuels can be seen.

The changes do not require a major reorientation of society, although, with time, they will produce a rather different society. For the present, we would like to know how much could be saved by "tightening the belt."

Residential Savings

Home heating is the largest single source of energy consumption in the residential sector. Anecdotal information suggests that the prac-tice of turning down the heat at night was, until quite recently, less common than 20 years ago; and when it is done, the lowered temper-ature is more likely to be 65 degrees than 55 or 60. Temperature settings lowered only 1 degree bring a 3 to 4 percent reduction in fuel use. Thus, simply by lowering nighttime temperature settings by 5 to 10 degrees and reducing daytime temperatures 3 degrees (all Fahrenheit) we reduce home fuel consumption by 15 percent. Such a reduction represents a savings of slightly more than 2 percent of 1970 energy consumption. [In this discussion we will express potential savings as a percentage of 1970 energy consumption.]

In chapter 5 we noted that the efficiency of conversion of most gas and oil furnaces was 60 to 75 percent. In practice these efficiencies are seldom reached for two reasons: first, the best efficiency figures are obtained only when the heating unit is operated at full load, and second, thin layers of soot and other unattended items of maintenance reduce operating efficiency rapidly. The National Bureau of Standards estimates from field samples that average operating efficiencies range from 35 to 50 percent. To correct the first difficulty would require a change in the philosophy and technology of design. But the second problem is easily remedied by careful attention to maintenance.

Public appeals to make changes of this sort have been notoriously unsuccessful, however. In part at least, there is a good reason. Given the present price of fuel and the costs of furnace service, it is often cheaper to ignore the needed maintenance than to have it done, and it is too much trouble to set the thermostat down (or install one controlled by a clock). The remedy that economics might suggest is to raise the price of fuel so that it will be worthwhile to make these efforts. A 25 percent increase in the price of fuels would allow home heating bills to remain unchanged if the suggested savings measures were instituted — for fuel consumption would be reduced 10 percent by better maintenance of heating units and 15 percent by lowered temperatures. Between 1969 and 1973 price increases for oil have been more than 25 percent, but have been insufficient to stimulate fuel-saving practices.

Better insulation would reduce fuel requirements for home heating. Most houses are not well insulated. Optimum insulation (from a total cost viewpoint) would reduce fuel needs by more than 40 percent. Each fuel price increase would make it more economical to increase insulation efforts still more. A modest fuel price increase would make the optimum insulation package provide fuel savings of 50 percent or slightly more. Changes in insulation affect cooling as well as heating. If one adds some careful control of ventilation to inhibit heat loss, further savings are possible. The National Bureau of Standards estimates that present fuel use could be decreased by more than a factor of 2.

Thus for home heating, fuel savings of 50 percent from better insulation and 25 percent from better furnace maintenance and lower temperatures are possible. These measures should reduce United States fuel consumption by 8.6 percent. These savings measures should also apply to the commercial sector (fig. 11–7). Since space heating of commercial establishments involves about 3.5 percent of United States energy consumption, an additional 1.2 percent of the total could be saved.

   We replace about 2 percent of all buildings annually. In the design of buildings there are many ways to reduce heating and cooling energy requirements. Heat is required only to replace whatever heat is lost to the outside, and heat is lost only through the outside walls (including doors and windows). If a building has more volume for a given area of outside surface, less heat will be lost. Earlier builders knew this simple recipe and low, flat "ranch" houses were never constructed in the northern part of the country for this reason.

   Domestic hot water heating consumes 2.7 percent of all energy, and, since much of it is done electrically, the fuel demand is quite large. In this area a technological change could be of enormous help. The use of solar water heaters on rooftops could provide all the domestic hot water necessary — even in areas as far north as Boston, Detroit, or southern Minnesota. It would probably be desirable to use a supplementary heater for the longest sequences of cloudy days and extremely cold weather (although water may be heated satisfactorily in bright sun no matter what the outside temperature). Use of a supplementary heater would hold down the high capital costs for such units by permitting the use of moderate-sized collector plates and storage tanks. Owing to their low operating costs, such solar units are already economically competitive with gas or electric water heaters even though their initial costs are high. How much the initial cost could be reduced by a mass production effort is unclear, but substantial reductions could be expected. Even if supplementary water heaters were allowed for, more than 2 percent of the nation's fuel consumption could be saved through solar water heating. (See chapter 9 for a more extended discussion of solar energy use.) Solar heating of residences with direct units on the roof is also possible and economically competitive with other methods, especially if fuel prices rise. Unfortunately, many houses would be difficult to refit with solar units.

   Refrigeration and cooking consume more than 2 percent of the nation's fuel. Energy consumption per refrigerator continues to rise. Savings are possible here, both by design modifications and by changes in habits of use (a refrigerator operates most efficiently when fully loaded, as does a freezer). But in the absence of a widespread change in lifestyle, the most effective way to reduce the energy consumption of these and other appliances is a substantial rise in energy prices. Coupled with measures that indicate the amount of energy consumed by an appliance, a price rise could bring major savings in residential energy consumption. Such price rises are not likely to be popular, but they may be preferable to the continuing subsidies to the energy industry which help prevent them.

In both the residential and commercial sectors the fastest growing use of energy is air conditioning. Presently installed units and new
ones offered in the market differ in their energy requirements by a
factor of 2 or more for the same amount of cooling. There is no reason
for this to continue; if enforceable regulations set standards for units,
the expected growth due to this use would be slowed a good deal.

A number of other residential energy savings are possible.
Although we suggest turning off lights, TVs, and stereos when they are
not in use, these measures taken together would not equal the savings
possible in home heating alone. This does not mean that small savings
should not be encouraged. Efforts to produce these smaller savings will
be welcome, and may best serve to encourage everyone to think about
energy as something to be conserved.

The measures suggested above would reduce United States
energy consumption by 12 percent. A sober government report on
energy conservation concludes that less ambitious measures could save
5.3 percent of the expected consumption in 1980. A substantial price
increase for fuel would bring more residential savings, perhaps substantially more.

Commercial Energy Savings

Most of the comments made about household savings apply to
the commercial sector. In addition, this sector has some special features.
Most retail stores are air-conditioned. Many of them, especially suburban
supermarkets, are large single-story buildings with flat, black roofs.
Such a design requires an excessive amount of air conditioning. Small
design changes, or incorporation of such establishments into multi-
story buildings, would reduce total air conditioning loads. The use of
heat pumps for heating and air conditioning, and the use of engine-
driven gas air conditioning units for large commercial establishments
could reduce energy consumption for these uses by 50 percent. Lighted
outdoor advertising, which seems to us about the most profligate use of
energy to be found, must be charged to the commercial sector.
Reliable totals of the energy consumed in lighted advertising signs are
hard to find, but it would be easy to reduce the total expended by
more than half and still maintain lighted identification of the establishment.

Government activities are usually included in this sector. As we
have seen (table 11-6), the large end use here is in the defense program.
Defense strategists pretend that energy shortages do not apply to them.
This state of affairs seems very strange, because, while the energy
shortage is new to most citizens, we have often been short of fuels
during wars. If we maintained a defense posture requiring more men
than we could count on, or more industrial output than might be mar-
shaled, we would think it foolish, yet we do exactly that in the case of

energy. The result is that our position on world issues must take into account our possible need for fuel in an emergency.

Our defense posture must be redesigned. A crude guess is that half of present defense fuel usage could be eliminated without changing the level of defense effort. That would amount to 1.3 percent of our total energy consumption.

Industrial Energy Savings

There are more misconceptions about the behavior of industry and industrialists than about astrology or the inner workings of the Kremlin. As some conservatives would have it, businessmen are long-suffering pillars of society, helping the public and planning for a richer, more satisfying future. In this view, business can be relied upon to act first and foremost in the public interest. Many on the left hold that the board rooms of industry are filled with genuinely malevolent men, bent upon gouging money from the citizenry. This caricature — for it is that — assumes that first place is given to any program that will persecute the public for profit.

The power and political influence of big industry is undeniable, but the forces which motivate application of that power are more impersonal than is generally believed. It may be that such misconceptions arose because no one — liberal politician, conservative industrialist, or even Marxist — cares to contemplate a world where impersonal economic forces, modified by government regulation, produce actions which affect individual lives and jobs. And the corporate giants, if not accountable to individual managers, become mindless institutions, grinding inexorably along, resisting change and striving for advantage. Yet such is approximately the case. Industry responds to threats to survival and seeks whatever operating position yields greatest financial return — in both short and long run.

Industry consumes a large amount of energy for an incredible variety of processes. In many sectors of industry, the amount of energy used for manufacturing and production processes has declined per unit product as a part of the never-ending effort to reduce costs and have a greater return. For example, steel production is the largest industrial consumer of fuel. Through new processes, notably the basic oxygen process, energy consumption in steel production may be reduced 25 percent by the year 2000.[3] Manufacture of aluminum requires more than three times as much energy per ton as manufacture of steel, and titanium requires more than six times as much. Table 11-7 shows the energy requirements for manufacture of a variety of materials. (Such a table should be used with caution, however. A ton of aluminum will make twice as many cans as a ton of steel.) The source material for metals can make a large difference in the energy required for manufacture. Titanium manufactured from high grade titanium-bearing soils

Table 11-7. Energy Cost of Production of Selected Materials

Material	Energy Required (kcal × 10⁶/ton)	Range of Values Cited (kcal × 10⁶/ton)
Metals		
Steel (structural)	17	8– 19
Aluminum	60	46– 62
Copper	18	16– 19
Zinc	13	12– 14
Lead	11	10– 12
Titanium	121	108–177
High-grade steel alloys	51	–
Recycled aluminum	10	9– 12
Recycled copper	1.4	
Chemicals		
Ammonia (NH_3)	27	10– 55
Soda ash (Na_2CO_3)	4	–
Sulfur (from pyrite)	3	–
Inorganic chemicals (average)	2.3	–
Miscellaneous		
Cement	2	–
Glass	6.2	–
Plastics (average)	2.5	–
Paper	6.0	3.8– 7.5
Fired clay products (bricks, terracotta, china)	6.0	3.5– 14
Cotton fabric	10	9– 13.5
Nylon fabric	22	19.5– 27.5

Sources: A. B. Makhijani and A. J. Lichtenberg, *An Assessment of Energy and Materials Utilization in the U.S.A.,* Memorandum no. ERL-M310 (revised) (Berkeley: University of California, 1971).
U.S., Office of Science and Technology, Executive Office of the President, *Patterns of Energy Consumption in the United States,* (Washington, D.C., 1972).
Raw data from *Census of Manufactures,* 1967. R. N. Shreve, *Selected Process Industries* (New York: McGraw-Hill, 1950).

requires almost twice as much energy per ton as titanium manufactured from the mineral rutile, and recycled titanium scrap takes only one-third as much. A change in ore grade of copper from 1 percent copper sulfide (which is only one of several copper ores mined) to 0.3 percent copper sulfide increases the energy required for production by a factor of two.

The situation is even more complex in the chemical industry. One chemical engineering text describes eleven processes in commercial use for the manufacture of ammonia (and this list does not even include the electric arc process used by some countries) and concludes that "the design of an ammonia converter is still more or less of an art."[4] Clearly, to study the savings that might be derived by converting from one industrial process to another would be an incredibly complex job.

One can, however, make some generalizations. In the metals

industries, recycling of scrap always consumes less energy than original manufacture. This applies to most other materials as well (although Hannon[5] has shown that such is not the case for glass). Thus, measures to encourage recycling will be repaid by energy savings, and will also conserve depletable resources.

The most effective means of persuading industry to reduce energy consumption is to increase the price of fuels relative to other goods and services. If the price of energy is increased substantially, processes using less energy will become the most profitable and will come into widespread use. If the cost accountants for a manufacturer find that overall costs can be minimized by adopting a less energy-consumptive process, that process will be adopted. Should prices be increased in this way, there will be additional incentive for recycling as well. Raising fuel prices is not likely to produce unemployment. As fuels become more expensive relative to labor costs, there will be less pressure to substitute energy and machinery for human labor.

How much energy can be saved by increased prices is not clear, but since manufacturing processes frequently differ by a factor of 2 in their energy requirements, we would think it possible to cut energy use in half in thirty years for the same output. A report by the Office of Emergency Preparedness estimates that industrial energy use can be decreased by about 6 percent by 1980, with little more than gentle pressure.

Transportation Energy Savings

The transportation energy figures in tables 11–2, 11–3, and 11–4 suggest remedies in this area: transport people by bus and send freight by train, boat, and pipeline. While this is true as far as it goes, the problem is a little more complicated.

The private automobile is the largest single energy user in our society. In addition, large amounts of energy are used annually to construct highways. The energy cost of a mile of federally aided highway was about twice that of a mile of railroad track in 1970, and this energy cost has doubled since 1960.

Plans for more efficient engines are discussed, but prospects for a large improvement are slight. This is very strange, for we know very well how to cut the energy use of the automobile: reduce its weight and engine size. Small autos with small engines have long been available, but only recently have they become popular. Any serious effort to reduce energy consumption should begin by replacing large autos with small ones. It would take about a decade to replace most of the present stock. The energy saved would amount to about 7 percent of the United States total.

Since the average occupancy is less than 2 persons per auto, small cars would not necessarily cause a change in life style. Increased

Table 11–8. Estimates of Energy Savings Possible* with Existing Social Patterns

Area of Saving	Our Estimate	OEP Report
Residential/commercial	–	5.3
Residential heating	8.6	–
Commercial heating	1.2	–
Residential hot water	2.0	–
Defense	1.3	–
Industry	18	6.0
Small Automobiles	6.9	–
Transportation mode shift	5.0	5.0
Totals	43.0%	16.3%

* = in percent of total use

fuel prices will undoubtedly provide pressure for the manufacture of smaller cars, but the industry will probably resist. Perhaps if all autos with engines larger than 150 horsepower were required to be licensed as trucks, we would have a further incentive to buy small cars.

Other savings in transportation are possible. A shift of freight from truck to rail would help, as would efforts to increase the service and availability of urban mass transit. Improved train service could reduce energy use in intercity passenger transport. Estimates of the effectiveness of these measures vary from about 5 percent to 12 percent of total United States energy use in 1980.

Total Reduction of Consumption

In the foregoing sections we have tried to estimate the amount of energy savings that might be possible without major changes in society. Table 11–8 summarizes our estimates alongside those reported by the Office of Emergency Preparedness. These two estimates differ largely in the conception of what is possible without major social and economic changes. Other estimates from the literature range from very small to more than 50 percent.

Why, then, have these changes not been made? Although energy is cheap, it has never been free. Now that we are conscious of our fuel shortages, and prices are increasing, can we expect these changes to occur naturally? It seems we cannot, for despite urban power shortages in recent years, there has been no substantial checking of the rate of growth in energy consumption.

This chapter cannot end on the note of optimism implied by the estimates of savings possible. Energy use has been doubling every 15 years. If all the suggested energy conservation measures were to be accomplished in the next few years (probably an impossible feat), all we will have done is postpone our problems by a decade or two. We most certainly should conserve, but, unless changes are made in the rate of growth, conservation measures will not be of much help. If we make the effort to save energy, will our society and our government be likely to use the time gained to change society in ways that will slow growth in fuel use? The economist, John Maynard Keynes, was not optimistic:

I think with dread of the readjustments of the habits and instincts of the ordinary man, bred into him for countless generations, which he may be asked to discard within a few decades.

REFERENCES

1. S. H. Schurr and B. C. Netschert, *Energy in the American Economy, 1850–1975* (Baltimore: Johns Hopkins Press, 1960).
2. U.S., Congress, House, Hearings before the Subcommittee on Science, Research, and Development, *Energy Research and Development,* Min. 9–BO, 1972.
3. U.S., Congress, Senate, *Conservation of Energy, A Report to the Senate Committee on Interior and Insular Affairs.* Serial no. 92–18 (Washington, D.C. 1972).
4. R. M. Stephenson, *Introduction to Chemical Process Industries* (New York: Rheinhold, 1966).
5. B. M. Hannon, *System Energy and Recycling: A Study of the Beverage Industry* (Urbana, Ill.: University of Illinois, Center for Advanced Computation, 1971).
6. U.S., Office of Science and Technology, Executive Office of the President, *Patterns of Energy Consumption in the United States* (Washington, D.C.: 1972).
7. H. H. Landsberg and S. H. Schurr, *Energy in the United States: Sources, Uses, and Policy Issues* (New York: Random House, 1968).

SUGGESTED READING

Cook, E. "The Flow of Energy in an Industrial Society." *Scientific American* 224, 3 (1971): 134–147.

Darmstadter, J. *Energy in the World Economy.* Baltimore: Johns Hopkins Press, 1971.

Landsberg, H. H., and Schurr, S. H. *Energy in the United States: Sources, Uses, and Policy Issues.* New York: Random House, 1968.

Schurr, S. H., and Netschert, B. C. *Energy in the American Economy, 1850–1975.* Baltimore: Johns Hopkins Press, 1960.

U.S., Office of Science and Technology, Executive Office of the President. *Patterns of Energy Consumption in the United States.* Washington, D.C., 1972.

CHAPTER 12

Climate Modification and Energy

The play seems out for an almost infinite run,
Don't mind a little thing like the actors fighting.
The only thing I worry about is the sun.
We'll be all right if nothing goes wrong with the lighting.

Robert Frost

Our successes in changing the environment to suit our wants and needs have always been accompanied by unintended, unexpected, and unwanted side effects. Many side effects of the production and use of energy have been discussed in earlier chapters in terms of damage to wilderness and wildlife and hazards to human health and happiness. Man's ability to modify the environment, whether intentionally or inadvertently, goes even further than we have indicated. We can change the climate, and some people have suggested that we have already begun to do so. Certainly we can do it on a local scale, when we build cities or cut down forests. In this chapter we are concerned with the observed and possible effects of energy use on climate.

In order to understand our potential role in changing the climate, we must understand something of the structure, composition, and circulation of the atmosphere. We will reexamine the energy balance of the earth and look briefly at climatic changes in the past — changes that occurred without the intervention of man.

STRUCTURE AND COMPOSITION OF THE ATMOSPHERE

The atmosphere is an unconfined mixture of gases moving cease-lessly above the earth. We divide it into a series of layers, each of which is characterized by certain physical properties and related phenomena (figure 12–1). The boundaries between these layers are neither sharp nor invariable, but rather they represent regions of transition.

The layer nearest the ground, extending upward from about 8 kilometers (5 miles) at the poles to more than 16 kilometers (10 miles) at the equator, is the troposphere, seat of most of the phenomena col-lectively called the weather. There is extensive vertical mixing of air in the troposphere, and temperature decreases fairly uniformly with height. Of the total mass of the atmosphere, about 90 percent is in this layer.

The transition between the troposphere and the stratosphere is marked by a low point in the vertical temperature gradient. The lower part of the stratosphere has an approximately constant temperature. Wind speeds are high and circulation patterns are stable, relative to those of the troposphere. There is very little water vapor, although cirrus clouds sometimes form in the lower region. In the stratosphere is the layer of ozone which protects us from most of the ultraviolet rays of the sun. The ozone reaches its highest concentration between 24 and 29 kilometers (15 and 18 miles) above the earth, where it acts as a heat source for the upper atmosphere by reradiating the energy it absorbs both downward toward earth and upward toward space.

Above the stratosphere the temperature declines sharply with increasing height until it reaches a low point about 80 kilometers (50 miles) above the earth. This region of decreasing temperature is called the mesosphere. Above the mesosphere is the thermosphere. It is char-acterized by rapidly increasing temperatures which may reach $1500°$ K ($2500°$ F) and by bands of ionized gases and free electrons (hence the other name for this region, the ionosphere). Major belts of ionized gas occur at heights of about 100 kilometers (60 miles) and 240 kilometers (150 miles). They are responsible for the auroral displays which occur in the lower thermosphere.

Hourly weather is associated with changes in the lower tropo-sphere, where frictional interaction with the earth is greatest and most of the exchange of matter and energy between the atmosphere and the earth's surface occurs. Daily and weekly changes in weather are related to circulation of both upper and lower troposphere. Still longer-term changes, including those related to the seasons and to events in the sun and variations of solar activity, are associated with changes in the upper atmosphere.

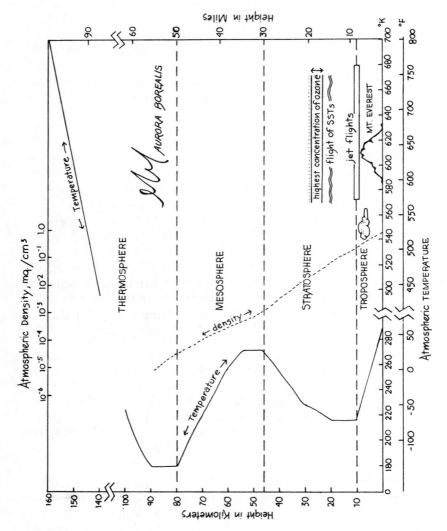

Figure 12-1. Structure of the atmosphere.

To a height of about 80 kilometers (50 miles) the dry atmosphere is a mixture of nitrogen and oxygen with small amounts of other gases, as shown in table 12–1. In addition, the troposphere always contains water vapor in amounts varying from only traces in polar and desert regions to as much as 4 percent in the tropics. The troposphere also contains salts, primarily chlorides and sulfates, whipped into the air by the action of the wind on the sea. Pollen and spores and bacteria, dust from the surface of the earth and dust thrown out by volcanic eruptions, dust, chemicals, and smoke resulting from the activities of man, and hydrocarbons produced by plants are all part of the troposphere and all participate in the phenomena of the weather.

INTERACTIONS OF SOLAR RADIATION WITH THE ATMOSPHERE

The outer atmosphere intercepts solar radiation at an average rate of about 1.7×10^{14} kilowatts. This radiation spans much of the electromagnetic spectrum (figure 12–2) except for a few wavelengths which are absorbed by the atmosphere of the sun. More than 90 percent of the radiation, however, is of wavelengths between 0.4 and 4.0 microns, corresponding to the visible and infrared regions of the spectrum. There have been no documented changes in intensity of radiation in the visible or infrared, but large variations occur in the amount of X ray and ultraviolet radiation received. These changes are related to the rotation of the sun and variations in sunspot activity, and are

Table 12–1. Composition of the Atmosphere

Substance	Percent by Volume
Nitrogen	78.09
Oxygen	20.95
Argon	0.93
Carbon dioxide	0.034
Neon	1.8×10^{-3}
Helium	5.2×10^{-4}
Krypton	1.1×10^{-4}
Hydrogen	5.0×10^{-5}
Xenon	8.0×10^{-6}
Ozone	1.0×10^{-6}

Variable constituents: water, in solid, liquid, and gaseous state, averaging about 0.6 percent; solid particles, including dust, pollen, spores, and salts; carbon monoxide, nitrogen oxides, sulfur oxides, gaseous hydrocarbons, and other organic and inorganic molecules.

Figure 12-2. The electromagnetic spectrum, showing the wavelengths that account for about 90 percent of the energy of solar and terrestial radiation. There is some overlap between regions of the spectrum, as indicated, because phenomena associated with the various regions overlap.

accompanied by changes in the upper atmosphere of the earth. Similarly, there are variations in the sun's output of energy at wavelengths greater than 10^5 microns, but so little energy is involved that this is of mainly theoretical interest.

Solar energy in wavelengths less than 0.2 microns is absorbed and converted to heat by oxygen in the thermosphere. The state of the thermosphere, including its temperature, is governed by the variable energy that is available at these short wavelengths. Longer ultraviolet wavelengths, up to 0.3 microns, penetrate into the mesosphere and stratosphere before they are completely absorbed by ordinary molecular oxygen and ozone. By the time solar radiation reaches the lower stratosphere, about 3 percent of it, the shortest wavelengths, has been absorbed. Most of this has been converted directly to heat, but some has caused ionization of gases or dissociation of molecules (for example, molecular oxygen, O_2, into atomic oxygen, 2O).

About 35 percent of the energy of wavelengths longer than 0.3 microns is reflected from the atmosphere and the surface of the earth and plays no part in the earth's heat balance. The amount of reflected energy is called the albedo (chapter 2). The albedo of clouds ranges from a few percent for light cirrus clouds to more than 80 percent for dense cumulus clouds. On the average, it is about 50 to 60 percent. Since the average cloud cover of the earth is about 50 percent and the albedo of the clouds is 50 percent, we can see that roughly 25 percent of the energy striking the atmosphere is reflected back into space by clouds. Any change in the extent of cloud cover would immediately affect the amount of energy received by the earth. Similarly, a change in the distribution of clouds would affect the distribution of incoming solar energy.

Ten or twenty percent of the incident solar energy is absorbed in the atmosphere, chiefly by water vapor and carbon dioxide. This absorption is specific for certain wavelengths, largely in the infrared (figure 12–3 and table 12–2). Radiation in the visible range of the spectrum passes through the atmosphere freely. Transparency to light with wavelengths ranging from 0.3 to 1.0 microns produces the "optical window" in the atmosphere. There is also a very narrow window in the infrared between 10 and 12 microns and a wide "radio window" that passes radiation between 10^4 microns and 2.5×10^7 microns in wavelength. Radiation that strikes the earth is converted to heat and is either stored, reradiated as long wavelength radiation, transferred back to the atmosphere by conduction or convection, or used to evaporate water and stored as latent heat of vaporization. A very small part of it participates, as light, in photochemical reactions, including the most important photochemical reaction of all — photosynthesis.

The radiative characteristics of a body can be predicted from its temperature. Because the earth is relatively cool, its radiation is largely confined to the less energetic, longer wavelength region of the spectrum between 5 and 100 microns (compared to the sun, which radiates primarily in the visible range). More than 90 percent of the energy radiated by the surface of the earth is of wavelengths that are absorbed by water vapor and carbon dioxide; much of it is absorbed or reflected back to earth by clouds. The transparency of the atmosphere to visible light coupled with its opacity to infrared creates the greenhouse effect, which warms the surface of the earth. The effective radiating surface of the earth is not the actual surface, but a region including the top of the clouds, the top of the troposphere, and the lower part of the stratosphere. Here, energy absorbed from the surface of the earth is radiated both back to the surface and out into space.

CIRCULATION OF THE ATMOSPHERE AND OCEANS

The atmosphere is a great heat engine that runs on solar energy, moving the surplus energy that falls in the equatorial zone to the poles, where there is a deficit. The oceans are another such heat engine running on the same principle and interacting with the atmosphere.

If the earth did not rotate, the circulation would be very simple. It could be simulated by heating a fish tank at one end and cooling it at the other. Warm fluid, either water or air, rises at the heated end (the equator) and moves toward the cool end (the pole), where it is cooled, sinks, and flows back to the heated end again. The movement occurs because a pressure gradient is associated with the temperature gradient. Fluid moves from the cold region of high pressure toward the region of low pressure created by the rising heated fluid.

The earth's rotation makes things a bit more complicated, but the circulation can still be simulated by a simple experiment: heating a

BOX 12-1 ATMOSPHERE ABSORPTION OF SOLAR RADIATION

Fig. 12–3, a. Theoretical curves showing spectral distribution of energy radiated by the sun and the earth. All bodies whose temperatures are above absolute zero radiate energy. The characteristics of this energy depend on the nature of the body and its temperature. The emission spectrum of a "perfect radiator" depends only on temperature: the higher the temperature, the shorter the wavelengths that predominate. (As the heating element of an electric stove heats up, its color changes from black to dull red to fiery red or reddish orange. At still higher temperatures it would become white hot.) Sun and earth emit energy approximately as if they were perfect radiators at temperatures of 6000° K and 245° K, respectively. We believe the temperature of the radiating surface of the sun to be about 6000° K. Note, however, that 245° K (–28° C) is much colder than the surface of the earth. This temperature corresponds to the temperature of the region of the troposphere which is the effective radiating surface of the earth. Radiation from the solid earth is trapped in the atmosphere, eventually reaching this region at the top of the densest clouds, from which it is radiated both outward to space and downward toward the earth again.

b.   The portion of a beam of solar radiation that reaches the top of the troposphere. The shortest wavelengths have been entirely absorbed by molecular oxygen and ozone. The major portion of the beam is transmitted unaffected. Carbon dioxide absorbs a small amount of energy in the infrared, and there is an additional small absorption band due to ozone.

c.   The portion of a beam of solar radiation that reaches the surface of the earth. Absorption in the troposphere is due primarily to water, although carbon dioxide absorption bands are stronger than in the upper atmosphere. Most of the light in the visible range reaches the surface. When the transmission spectrum of the

pan of water at its rim (the equator) and cooling it at the center (the pole), while it is rotating from west to east. On the earth and in the pan, this sets up an east-to-west circulation near the poles (the polar easterly winds), and a west-to-east circulation in the middle region (the westerly winds of middle latitutdes), and an east-to-west circulation near the equator (the trade winds). More rapid rotation and a larger dif-

Figure 12-3. Absorption spectra for H_2O, CO_2, and total atmosphere.

atmosphere is compared with the earth's radiation spectrum, however, the basis for the greenhouse effect becomes apparent. Earth's energy must reach the top of the troposphere before it can be lost to space.

ference in temperature between the rim of the pan and the center modify this general pattern to approximate the flow of the atmosphere even more closely. If the earth were a rotating ball uniformly covered with water, the circulation of its atmosphere might be no more complicated than the circulation of water in a pan.

But continents and oceans are irregularly distributed over the

Table 12-2. Effects of Atmospheric Components on Energy Balance

Substance or Material	Effect
Ozone (O_3)	Absorbs radiation of wavelengths shorter than 0.3 microns and converts it to heat. Reradiates this energy toward earth and into space, warming the stratosphere.
Water vapor	Absorbs radiation strongly in the range of 5 to 8 microns and greater than 18 microns. The average water vapor content of the atmosphere is about 1.3×10^{19} grams, which stores 9×10^{15} kilowatt hours of energy as latent heat. The average annual rainfall is 1.1×10^{17} gallons (4×10^{20} grams). This releases 3×10^{17} kilowatt hours of energy into the atmosphere — 5000 times the world's annual energy use by man.
Clouds	Absorb between 2 and 30 percent of incoming radiation and reflect between 20 and 85 percent, depending on type of cloud and angle of radiation. Absorb long wavelength radiation from earth's surface and reradiate it back toward earth and out to space. Average cloud cover = 50 percent; average albedo of clouds = 50–60 percent.
Carbon dioxide (CO_2)	Absorbs radiation between 0.7 and 18 microns (most strongly between 12 and 16 microns). Reradiates it toward earth and space.
Oxygen (O_2), nitrogen (N_2), and other atmospheric gases	Generally transparent to both solar and terrestrial radiation, although radiation in short wavelengths causes dissociation and ionization of molecules. They scatter radiation in a symmetrical way which depends on the wavelength of radiation and the size of the molecule.
Oxides of nitrogen and sulfur, hydrocarbons, carbon monoxide	Negligible direct effect on heat balance, but some of these undergo photochemical reactions which involve ozone and/or which produce smog.
Particles (smoke, smog, dust, salts, pollen, spores, etc.)	Scatter and absorb solar and terrestrial radiation. Absorption occurs throughout the infrared, and may be most significant in the infrared window (see text). Scattering is asymmetric, depending on the size and shape of particles. Particles increase the albedo of the atmosphere in general, but may decrease the albedo of clouds; act as nuclei for cloud formation and condensation of rain and snow.

face of the earth, and the location of topographic features of land masses further influence patterns of atmospheric circulation. Although the effects of mountains, valleys, lakes, cities, and other features are known, their combined effect is to render details of circulation complex and ever changing, and the dream of the theoretical meteorologist to construct a mathematical model or theory of global circulation continues to elude him.

Ocean currents are established by differences in the temperature and density of water and are modified by the prevailing winds. Some 20 to 25 percent of the energy carried from equatorial regions to the poles is carried by ocean currents. The best defined of the warm currents are the Gulf Stream and the Japanese Current, which moderate the temperatures of lands past which they flow. The cold Labrador Current, in contrast, brings sub-freezing temperatures to the Labrador Peninsula during eight months of the year and the Humboldt Current similarly chills parts of South America. In addition to the heat directly redistributed by the oceans, almost 20 percent of the energy carried poleward is in the form of latent heat in water vapor, most of which evaporated over the oceans. This heat is released to the atmosphere when rain or snow falls.

Thus climates of the earth are determined not only by amounts of energy received from the sun and radiated back from earth, but by the way in which energy is distributed between the equator and the poles — which also determines regimes of precipitation. The distribution of energy, in turn, depends on many interacting variables. To change the climate we do not have to blot out the sun, or warm the earth from the sheer magnitude of our production of heat. We can do, and perhaps are doing, many more subtle things to change the winds, the rains, and the snows.

CLIMATIC CHANGE

Man arrived on earth during an ice age, a period of violent activity on earth — of mountain building, earthquakes, and volcanic eruptions. He has never known the earth as geologists believe it to have been throughout most of geologic time. In "normal" times, the earth is calm and mild. Polar seas are free of ice and polar climates are similar to those of middle latitudes today. There are vast expanses of continental lowlands covered by warm, shallow seas. The awesome mountains which seem so enduring are geologically quite young. The earth has repeatedly thrust up mountains like these, only to wear them down quickly and restore the low relief of the land.

There have been at least four ice ages, and maybe five or six, in the earth's history. All of them may have been associated with volcanic eruptions, violent contortions of the earth's crust, retreat of the seas, and expansion of deserts. Ice ages encompass alternating periods of growth and recession of glaciers, called glacial and interglacial stages. Scientists are not certain whether the period in which we now live is the end of the Pleistocene ice age or merely one of its interglacial stages.

Conceivably, the answer to this question could hinge on the activities of man.

The concept of a stable climate becomes uncertain when we ask, stable over what period? Although names of places bring to mind general notions about their climates — London, Rome, Phoenix — climates everywhere show both cyclical and noncyclical changes. Cycles may be related to sunspots or the rotation of the sun, or to changes in the earth's orbit. Other changes cannot be explained satisfactorily. We may know that the major winds shifted their course without knowing why.

World and local climates have undergone many fluctuations since the last glacier receded 11,000 or 12,000 years ago. These fluctuations are documented by the annual growth rings of trees, the age, depth, and character of annual deposits of silt in lakes, the succession of plant types in deposits of peat, the legends and histories of man, and, within recent times, instrumental measurements. These records show that about 5000 years ago the earth's climate was warm and humid, and it is possible that the Arctic Ocean was free of ice. Then began a period of gradual decrease of temperature and rainfall, but the trend was irregularly punctuated by long droughts. In Europe, where our knowledge is most complete, the main dry periods fell between 2200 and 1900 B.C., 1200 and 1000 B.C., and 700 and 500 B.C. The last drought was intense enough to cause extensive migrations of people away from the driest regions.

Then came a rapid change to a colder and wetter climate. Alpine passes which had been traveled for a dozen centuries were no longer passable. The change was abrupt and for many people catastrophic, but it did not last long. The Christian era was ushered in by conditions much like those of today.

Similar trends seem to have occurred simultaneously in Europe, western Asia, and North America. From about A.D. 180 to 350, it was rainy and rather cold. The fifth and seventh centuries were warm and dry; Alpine passes that had long been closed by ice and which are closed again today were heavily traveled. The ninth century brought heavier rains and cooler temperatures, but warm dry climates returned during the tenth and eleventh centuries. Greenland was settled in 984, but had to be abandoned to the ice about 1410. To this day, its climate is inhospitable to man.

The period from the seventeenth to the mid-nineteenth century was so severe that it has been called the Little Ice Age. During this time remnants of mountain glaciers crept far down into valleys and new glaciers formed. A warming trend began about 1850, melting the glaciers back to their sixteenth century positions. Since 1940, however, average global temperatures have been decreasing. The change is greatest in the polar regions; the tropics have remained about the same.

Many explanations have been invoked to account for these many changes which, except perhaps for the most recent, were unrelated to the activities of man. None of the explanations is completely satisfactory. They include variations in the earth's orbit, disturbances in the crust of the earth, changes in composition of the atmosphere resulting from volcanic activity, changes in cloudiness whose causes can only be guessed at, and, for those who want to push the cause far from home, variations in the radiation from the sun. Whatever the causes, the only unchanging facet of climate is change. It has been a major, if not the major, force in evolution and in the rise and fall of human cultures. If conditions had remained ideal for the dinosaurs, there would probably be no men today to worry about man's influence on climatic change. There is no reason to suppose that our present climate will prevail. The question, then, is what is the natural trend, and how are we influencing it.

Man's Influence on Climate

Homo erectus Pekinensis began to change the climate when he first carried fire to his cave. He changed the climate immediately about himself, the microclimate, from cold and damp to warm and dry. As man spread over much of the earth, as he changed from a hunter to an agriculturalist to an industrialist, his influence on local climate became greater and greater. There is no question about these effects; our bodies can sense them as we move from the central city to the suburbs to outlying rural areas, or from a forest to adjacent farmland. At some point, the cumulative impact of local changes will cause global changes. Here we are on much less firm theoretical and observational ground. We have great difficulty in determining the relative contributions of man and of forces beyond man's control. But the significance of our role behooves us to try.

Man's Influence on Local Climates

In addition to putting excess heat into the atmosphere, man's use of energy can affect climate in a number of ways. Almost any change man makes in the landscape alters the albedo of the surface of the earth. It also tends to change the local balance between evaporation and precipitation, which may affect the distribution of clouds and the albedo of the atmosphere. By adding dust, smoke, carbon dioxide, water vapor, and a variety of chemicals to the atmosphere, man changes its reflective, absorptive, and radiative properties.

Some of the climatic repercussions of man's use of energy are related to the uneven distribution of his inputs into the environment. The rate of world energy use, which is essentially equivalent to world production of heat, is about 7×10^9 kilowatts. This is insignificant compared to the 9×10^{13} kilowatts of solar power that reach the earth's surface, or the latent heat added to the atmosphere at a rate of 4×10^{13} kilowatts through evaporation of water, or the energy of the winds flowing at a rate of about 4×10^{11} kilowatts. Even a local thunderstorm releases energy equivalent to that of many hydrogen bombs. But the sun shines on half the earth at once, the winds blow everywhere, two-thirds of the earth is covered by water and much of the rest is covered by transpiring plants, and thunderstorms release their energy only occasionally at any one spot. Man's use of energy, in contrast, is heavily concentrated in urban and industrialized areas (table 12-3). The results of this concentration, and of man's activities in general, will be considered in the following sections.

Climatic Effects of Cities

About 75 percent of the energy used by man is used in urban industrial areas covering only 0.1 percent of the earth's surface. All the energy used by man eventually finds its way into the atmosphere as heat. Although consideration of table 12-3 should put to rest any fears about heating up the whole earth with our waste heat, it is easily seen that we have heated up our cities. Table 12-4 shows the ways in which cities modify local energy balance and also the climatic effects of these modifications. Waste heat and pollution — the two items related directly to use of energy — have by far the greatest effect on local climate.

Our use of energy produces both sensible heat and latent heat. Sensible heat is conveyed to the atmosphere by direct transfer of heat from molecule to molecule, or by radiation which is absorbed in the atmosphere and converted to heat. It is sensible because we can sense it as an increase in temperature. Latent heat is stored in water vapor, through evaporative cooling processes. It does not affect the temperature until it is released when the water vapor condenses. Sensible heat creates a dome of warm air that hovers low over the city. Released near the

Table 12-3. Comparison of Man-made and Some Natural Flows of Energy

Energy Flow	Rate (watts/square meter)
Average solar radiation at earth's surface	approx. 170
Energy used to evaporate water, average rate	79
Average energy output of urban industrial areas	12
Average net photosynthetic production on land	0.13
Average heat flow from the interior of the earth	0.054
World use of energy (1970), distributed evenly over the continents	0.047
World use of energy (1970), distributed evenly over entire earth	0.013

Table 12-4. Climatic Effects of Urbanization

Urbanization produces many changes that affect energy balance. The albedo of the surface is increased due to the reflectivity of buildings and pavement. In snowy areas, however, there may be a compensating decrease in albedo due to dirty snow and snow removal. Accompanying the change in albedo is a change in heat storage capacity of the surface. Buildings and other obstacles to wind flow create increased atmospheric turbulence near the surface. There is decreased evaporation and transpiration of water and increased runoff of precipitation. Burning of fuel produces air pollution, both gaseous and particulate, and waste heat. These changes are related to the following observed climatic effects:

Typical differences of urban climates from surrounding rural areas

Cloudiness
   5–10% more cloud cover
   100% more winter fog
   30% more summer fog

Precipitation (effect may be more pronounced downwind from urban area, at times)
   5–10% more (total)
   5% more snow

Relative humidity
   2% less (winter)
   8% less (summer)

Radiation striking surface
   15–20% less
   30% less ultraviolet in winter
   5% less ultraviolet in summer

Temperature
   0.5°–1.0° C higher annual mean
   1°–2° C higher winter minimum

Winds
   20–30% lower mean annual wind speed
   10–20% decrease in extreme gusts
   5–20% increase in calms

---

surface, it warms the surface, increasing the temperature gradient in the troposphere and consequently increasing the rate and extent of vertical movement and mixing of air. Latent heat, in contrast, rises higher and travels further, and may show its effect many days later, far from its source.

The dome of warm air is also a dome of polluted air. When the wind blows, a plume of warm, polluted air is carried downwind from the city. On this scale, changes induced locally begin to affect the surrounding countryside. However, incomplete understanding of how regional climatic patterns are determined prevents scientists from estimating the impact of cities on the climate of their surroundings.

At some point, as cities proliferate and expand and merge with one another, their effects will be widely felt. A number of large areas, notably northwestern Germany and southern Belgium, the northeastern United States, and southern California, are putting waste heat into the atmosphere at a rate between 1 and 10 percent of the rate at which they receive energy from the sun. Heat output per unit area is not expected to grow very much, but the size and number of the urban industrial areas will.

Until recently, the amount of waste heat produced was much greater in the winter than in the summer, as a result of space heating. In cities like Moscow and Fairbanks, which have very cold winters, man may approach or surpass the sun's rate of input of energy to the local environment. Further south, however, increasing use of air conditioners has significantly increased the production of heat during warm months. In this sense, the more air conditioners we have, the more we need. Moreover, the trend toward heating the outside in winter may be slowing down, with new emphasis on effective insulation of buildings and increased use of heat pumps which can warm the interior of a building with heat removed from the outside.

Although air pollution is viewed primarily as a health hazard or as contributing to the deterioration of property, we have seen that materials produced during the combustion of fuels can also have effects on climate. The largest concentrations of pollutants remain near their source, but carbon dioxide and particulate matter have increased everywhere. Possible implications of this increase will be discussed in a later section.

Effects of Agriculture on Energy Balance

The unsuspected energy subsidies to agriculture and the myth of one farmer feeding 50 people were discussed in chapter 6. Agriculture, whether modern or primitive, also affects the energy balance of earth. While the magnitude of the effect is smaller per unit area than the effect of urbanization, vastly greater areas are involved.

Conversion of forest or grassland to agricultural land influences the local energy balance in three ways. It changes the albedo of the surface, it changes the relative proportions of sensible and latent heat in the total heat rejected from the surface, and it often increases the amount of dust in the atmosphere. Table 12–5 shows typical effects on albedo and output of sensible and latent heat when forested land or grassland is converted to cropland.

The conversion of temperate forests to agricultural land may have gone about as far as it will go, but large-scale cutting of tropical forests is underway. When tropical forests are cut, moisture can no longer be retained in the soil. Flash floods cause severe erosion. During

Table 12-5. Relationship Between Type of Vegetation and Factors Affecting Heat Balance

Type of Vegetation	Typical Albedo	Transfer of Sensible Heat (watts/sq. meter)	Transfer of Latent Heat (watts/sq. meter)	Ratio of Sensible Heat to Latent Heat	Evapotranspiration (centimeters/month/ sq. meter)
Coniferous forest	0.12	20	40	0.50	4.1
Deciduous forest	0.18	13	39	0.33	4.0
Grassland	0.20	20	30	0.67	3.1
Semi-desert	0.20	67	12	5.6	1.2
Cultivated land, wet	0.20	8	42	0.19	4.3
Cultivated land, dry	0.20	15	35	0.41	3.6
Irrigated oases in Sahara Desert	0.15	-36*	136	-0.26	14.0
Tropical forest	0.18-0.24	—	—	0.1-0.3	—
Tropical forest cleared for cultivation	—	—	—	2.0-6.0**	—

*The negative value for transfer of sensible heat to the atmosphere means that the amount of latent heat of vaporization exceeds the amount of incoming solar energy, and the additional heat required for evaporation is obtained by cooling the air.

**This value is an estimate, or a prediction, of how the ratio might change if extensive areas of the tropical forest of Brazil, Indonesia, or Africa were cut for agriculture.

Source: *Inadvertent Climate Modification: Report of the Study of Man's Impact on Climate* (Cambridge, Mass.: MIT Press, 1971).

dry seasons, clouds of dust may be released into the atmosphere. The ratio of sensible to latent heat increases owing to greatly reduced rates of transpiration. Incoming solar energy is diverted toward warming the surface rather than toward evaporating water. This means that there is more energy immediately available to drive atmospheric motions, the thermal gradient in the lower atmosphere becomes steeper, and vertical air movement increases. Some meteorologists believe that altering the ratio of sensible heat to latent heat over large areas of the tropics may affect the flow of the tropical easterly winds and in this way modify the general circulation of the atmosphere.

About 1.5 percent of the total area of the continents is estimated to be under irrigation. In desert regions, irrigation has a profound effect on the heat balance because of the increased rate of evaporation and excess of evaporation over precipitation (table 12–5). Here the effect is opposite to that of cutting tropical forests. Increased evaporation causes a decrease in the amount of energy immediately available for atmospheric processes. The thermal gradient in the lower atmosphere decreases. Latent heat becomes available days or even weeks later, when the water vapor condenses and precipitates. The energy is released far from where the evaporation took place, and perhaps it is released high in the sky. Evaporation of water is a process that tends to export solar energy to places remote from where it struck the earth. Worldwide, the decrease in transpiration due to the cutting of forests is thought to be of about the same magnitude as the increase of evaporation due to new irrigation, but the two effects cannot compensate for each other because they occur in different parts of the world.

Effects of Artificial Lakes and Reservoirs on Energy Balance

Man changes the area of surface water for many reasons, most of which are related to reclamation of land and to water control. Artificial lakes are frequently formed in conjunction with the generation of electricity, either at a hydroelectric site or as cooling ponds to dissipate waste heat from the condensers in a steam electric plant. The major effect of an artificial lake may be similar to that of irrigation. It leads to increased evaporation without a corresponding increase in precipitation, and increases the latent heat released to the atmosphere (see the discussion of thermal pollution in chapter 10). Man-made lakes and reservoirs are scattered over the earth, however, and are widely separated from each other. Their total area is only about one-tenth the irrigated area of the world. Thus, their climatic effects are expected to remain small and local.

Man's Influence on Global Climate

Determining local climatic effects of human activity is relatively easy. Changes in cloudiness, temperature, rates of evaporation, and other variables can be measured and related to burning of fuel, cutting of forests, and other changes made by man. For comparison, there are data from surrounding areas not directly modified by man (or modified less drastically, or in a different way) and from the affected area before man changed it. The situation for global effects is quite different. The sequence of cause and effect is seldom obvious, and at present it is impossible, in many cases, to determine the relative magnitude of man-made and natural effects. The problem is compounded by our uncertainty about what the natural trend in world climate is.

We do, however, understand the basic dynamics of the atmosphere and we know how individual factors modify the amount, distribution, and flow of energy. We are beginning to understand the many ways in which these factors interact. Climatic studies have frequently been hampered by lack of reliable data, especially long-term records. Data are now accumulating from weather satellites and other sources faster than they can be interpreted. With these data and existing theory, it is possible to formulate hypotheses about climatic change and to test them by computation. When climatic features are represented by mathematical equations arranged for solution by a computer (as, for example, the rate of increase in atmospheric carbon dioxide and the relationship between concentration of carbon dioxide and surface temperature), we have a mathematical simulation or model of the atmosphere. These models, imperfect as they are, are the best means we possess to learn about the tangle of relationships which govern climate and the behavior of the atmosphere. As one meteorologist put it, ". . . we can eventually say what features or combinations of features could have produced the changes. . . . As to what features did produce [them] we shall still have the privilege of arguing." The same may be said for predictions as well as for hindsight.

The best current models, requiring hours of time on the largest computers, are still unable to take all relevant factors into account. They accommodate changes in the water content of the atmosphere, but they cannot say whether this water will result in increased cloudiness, increased precipitation, or both. They do not represent adequately the effects of variable cloud cover and interactions between atmosphere and ocean. Different models may lead to conflicting results and paradoxes — a warming trend predicted by one and a cooling trend by another. Of course these problems did not originate with the use of computers. They reflect the limits to our understanding of natural processes and arise from assumptions we make about the system; they cannot be blamed on the computer or the technique of modeling. It has been suggested, for example, that an ice age could be started by an increase in solar radiation, which would lead to increased evaporation of water, increased cloudiness, increased rain and snow, and decreased temperatures. Most people, however, do not believe that a hotter sun would cause a colder earth.

With this introduction to the problems and promises of climatic models, we will look at some of the observed and predicted changes in variables affecting the climate and their possible outcomes.

Carbon Dioxide

There are about 2.5×10^{18} grams of carbon dioxide in the atmosphere. Each year we release an increasing amount through combustion of fossil fuels. In 1950 it was 6.4×10^{15} grams, by 1965 it had doubled to 12.7×10^{15} grams, and for 1980 we estimate that it will have doubled again to 26.0×10^{15} grams.

The first systematic measurements of carbon dioxide concentration were begun in 1958. They reveal a number of interesting facts. In the northern hemisphere there is an annual oscillation in carbon dioxide concentration which is related to the cycle of photosynthetic productivity. However, the mean annual concentration seems to be growing everywhere at a rate of about 0.2 percent per year. The highest levels are reported from Point Barrow, Alaska, and the lowest from Antarctica. In general, values in the northern hemisphere are higher than those in the southern hemisphere. This might be expected, since most of the fossil fuel is burned in the north. The difference suggests a time lag of about 18 months in the mixing of air between the arctic and the antarctic.

About half of the carbon dioxide added to the atmosphere by man remains there. The remaining half must be taken up by the oceans or the biosphere — there is nowhere else for it to go. As was suggested in the discussion of the carbon cycle in chapter 2, we do not know how much of the excess may be assimilated by plants. In any case, the biosphere is only a temporary sink, because increased photosynthetic production leads to increased breakdown of organic material by herbivores and decomposers, which, in turn, consume oxygen and release dioxide again. Nor do we know how the oceans will behave toward steadily increasing pressures of carbon dioxide. It is generally assumed, for the purpose of designing climatic models, that about half of each increment of carbon dioxide added to the atmosphere will continue to be removed; but most natural processes do not remain so nicely linear.

We assume that this one will remain linear only because we do not know how it is likely to change. In the short term, the assumption is accurate enough.

Simplified models of global climate predict that a doubling of carbon dioxide concentration would increase the average surface temperature by about 2° C, while the stratosphere becomes cooler. The increase in carbon dioxide that is predicted for the year 2000 would cause a warming of about 0.5° C. As temperatures increase absolute humidity will also probably increase, and infrared absorption by the additional water vapor will contribute to the warming effect; this model takes these facts into account. But as usual, the entire picture is not this simple. The temperature increase will probably be greater toward the poles than in the tropics, for as the snow cover recedes the albedo of the surface will decrease and more solar energy will be absorbed. Decreased temperature differential between the equator and the poles has implications for global patterns of atmospheric circulation. It is possible that the Arctic Ocean would become and remain essentially free of ice. If this should happen, patterns of oceanic circulation would also be profoundly changed. On the other hand, if the increased content of water vapor in the atmosphere leads to an increase in cloud cover of only 0.6 percent, the cooling effect of the clouds could negate the warming effect due to carbon dioxide.

We could halt the atmospheric increase of carbon dioxide by turning to sources of energy other than fossil fuels. But no matter what progress is made in the technology of nuclear and solar energy, man will probably be burning large amounts of fuel for at least several centuries to come. By the time we realize that carbon dioxide is causing a problem, it may be too late to do anything about it. Once a trend toward climatic change has started, halting the increase of carbon dioxide is unlikely to stop it because of the way in which the effects of decreasing snow and ice cover and altered patterns of circulation reinforce each other.

Particulate Matter

Estimated amounts and sources of particulate matter injected into the troposphere are shown in table 12–6. The wide range of these estimates demonstrates the need for more systematic observations and a sounder basis for the assumptions that lie behind them. The extreme values in this table indicate that man contributes between 5 and 45 percent of this particulate matter. A value ranging from 17 to 20 percent is generally accepted.

The lifetime of particles in the atmosphere depends on their size

Table 12-6. Estimates of Particles up to 40 Microns in Diameter Added to the Atmosphere Each Year

Natural Sources	Amount (millions of metric tons/year)
Soil and rock debris (includes unknown contributions from man's mining and agricultural activities)	100–500
Forest fires (includes unknown contributions from slash-and-burn agriculture	3–150
Sea salt, from ocean spray	300
Volcanoes	25–150
Particles formed from gaseous emissions:	
Sulfate from hydrogen sulfide	130–200
Ammonium salts from ammonia	80–270
Nitrate from nitrogen oxides	60–430
Hydrocarbons from plant exudations	75–200
Subtotal	773–2200
Man-made sources (primarily combustion of fossil fuels, and almost entirely combustion of *something*)	
Direct emission of particles	10– 90
Particles formed from gaseous emissions:	
Sulfate from sulfur dioxide	130–200
Nitrate from nitrogen oxides	30– 35
Hydrocarbons	15– 90
Subtotal	185–415
Total	958–2615

Source: *Inadvertent Climate Modification: Report of the Study of Man's Impact on Climate* (Cambridge, Mass.: MIT Press, 1971).

and vertical distribution. Particles larger than 20 microns in diameter quickly settle out due to the force of gravity, while gravitational settling of particles less than 0.2 microns in diameter is negligible. It is impossible to say how long an individual particle persists in the atmosphere, because particles are continually merging with one another or reacting chemically with other constituents of the atmosphere. However, the average residence time of matter emitted in particulate form is shown in table 12–7, for various parts of the atmosphere.

Independent of sudden increases in the particulate content of the atmosphere following major volcanic eruptions, there appears to be a global trend toward increase of particles. This conclusion is based largely on measurements of solar radiation reaching the earth's surface and on the assumption that decreases in solar radiation are due to increased scattering and reflection by atmospheric particles. In cities,

Table 12-7. Residence Times of Atmospheric Particles

Region	Mean Residence Time
Lower troposphere	2 days–2 weeks
Upper troposphere	2–4 weeks
Lower stratosphere	6–12 months
Upper stratosphere	to 5 years
Mesosphere	5–10 years or more

there has been a well-documented decrease in solar radiation ranging from 15 to 20 percent during the last 50 years. Evidence suggests that in the northern hemisphere solar radiation has been reduced by about 5 percent even in areas of "clean air." Measurements of electrical conductivity of the atmosphere over the North Atlantic show a consistent decrease in conductivity during this century, which is believed to be caused by a doubling in the number of particles between 0.02 and 0.2 microns in diameter. Because these data were collected in an area undisturbed by human activity, they may represent an overall trend in the northern hemisphere. There are few reliable observations for the southern hemisphere, but the concentration of particulates in the lower atmosphere appears to be smaller there, as should be expected since the major sources of man-made particles are concentrated in the north.

Models of the climatic effects of particles must take into account the particles' horizontal and vertical distribution, their size, and their optical properties. Because such information about particles that occur in real life is entirely inadequate, conclusions about real life based on climatic models are tenuous at best. The most that can be said with confidence is that an increase in particles will increase the albedo of the atmosphere and will probably tend to cool the surface of the earth.

How much and in what way our production of particulate matter will influence the climate remains, then, a vital but unanswered question. It is comforting to note, however, that with a shift to nuclear or solar energy and with stringent pollution controls and attention to agricultural and mining procedures, almost all manmade atmospheric particles could be eliminated. Because the lifetime of particles in the atmosphere is relatively short, the problems of air pollution will not linger to haunt generations of people who may no longer be polluting the air.

Modifications of the Upper Atmosphere

Potential changes in the composition of the upper atmosphere are related to the effects of jets flying in the upper troposphere and lower stratosphere, supersonic transport aircraft (SSTs) flying in the stratosphere, and rockets which travel through all layers of the atmosphere.

By 1990, the number of jet aircraft flights may increase sixfold and more, if SSTs do not begin operation as expected. There is no doubt that condensation of water vapor emitted from these aircraft (causing the infamous "contrails") will increase the cloudiness of the upper troposphere. The effect will be most pronounced in heavily-traveled air corridors and near major jet airports. The primary effect of increased cloudiness will be an increase in the albedo of the atmosphere. However, it is difficult to estimate how large the effect will be, or how it will affect the surface of the earth. It is also possible that ice crystals from the upper troposphere will fall into clouds, seeding them and causing precipitation to occur sooner than it ordinarily would.

Present observations on the effects of jets on high tropospheric clouds are ambiguous. Although there is a significant increase in high cirrus cloudiness in the vicinity of Denver and other major jet ports, it is accompanied by a decrease in cloudiness at slightly lower levels. This leads investigators to believe that either natural forces are at work modifying cloud patterns at both levels, or that perhaps criteria for distinguishing between "upper cloudiness" and "middle cloudiness" have been consciously or unconsciously altered. In any case, the atmospheric effects of current levels of jet traffic seem to be negligible.

Concern about the effect of SSTs centers upon their emission of water vapor, carbon dioxide, and particles. The effects of major volcanic eruptions provide our main experience with modification of the stratosphere. Besides creating glorious sunsets, injection of volcanic dust into the stratosphere causes stratospheric temperature to increase as much as 6° or 7° C. Although we are not certain, we think that increased volcanic activity is associated with decreased surface temperatures, probably because of the particulate matter added to the upper atmosphere. A strict analogy cannot be made between volcanic emissions and the emissions of SSTs, for SSTs will operate within a narrow range of altitude and, primarily, in a few heavily traveled air corridors in the northern hemisphere. Volcanic debris is more widely distributed by latitude and longitude, and through all vertical layers of the atmosphere.

Recognizing that plans for the number and design of SSTs are constantly being revised and that our understanding of processes in the upper atmosphere is very incomplete, recent studies have made some tentative conclusions about possible effects of SSTs. The greenhouse effect of stratospheric water vapor and carbon dioxide is expected to be very small, and insignificant relative to the effect of burning fossil fuel. Because the stratosphere is very dry, it is expected that additional water vapor will cause increased cloudiness only in the coldest regions. The possibility of destroying the ozone layer through increased photo-chemical reactions involving ozone, water vapor, and other gaseous emissions has been carefully studied. Computer models indicate that water vapor has its greatest effect on concentration of ozone at altitudes higher than where most ozone occurs. In conclusion, those who have studied the problem most thoroughly say they do not think strato-spheric flights of SSTs will cause any serious problems, but they are ex-tremely reluctant to try the experiment and find out.

The higher we go in the sky the shakier our theoretical and observational bases for prediction become. Because there is so little matter in the upper regions of the atmosphere, each rocket and each explosion of a nuclear bomb in the atmosphere can cause a significant change in the composition of the mesosphere and thermosphere. We know that we are changing the chemistry and perhaps the circulation of the very high atmosphere, but we do not know the magnitude or the duration of the change, nor what its effects may be.

When we think of modifying the climate, we often think in terms of another ice age, with all living things fleeing in advance of the glaciers. Or we think of melting the arctic ice and flooding all our coastal cities. These may be the most remote results of our activities. Many other changes may come before we freeze or drown. A slight but per-sistent change in temperature or humidity can tip the balance in favor of organisms pathogenic to plants, animals, or man, causing severe epi-demics of diseases and pests that formerly were held in check by climatic conditions. Major epidemics of crops and forest trees in the past have often been associated with just such changes. Or the major winds could shift their course, and fail to bring rain at the usual season; and millions of people who depend on the rains to water their crops could starve. The monsoons have not been visiting certain regions as reliably as they once did, and some meteorologists are building a convincing case against air pollution as the ultimate cause of the shifting monsoons.

Nor are climatic changes necessarily for the worse. If we thought they were, we certainly would not be engaged in research on weather and climate modification. Why, then, do we have an illogical but real fear that the unknown consequences of our actions are more likely to be undesirable than desirable? One can conjure up many explanations from the murky recesses of men's minds. Most simply, however, we are reluctant to undertake any fateful and irreversible course of action.

SUGGESTED READING

—— Inadvertent Climate Modification: Report of the Study of Man's Impact on Climate (SMIC). Cambridge, Mass.: MIT Press, 1971.

—— *Man's Impact on the Global Environment: Assessment and Recommendations for Action.* Cambridge, Mass.: MIT Press, 1970.

Matthews, W., W. Kellogg, and G. Robinson, eds. *Man's Impact on the Climate.* Cambridge, Mass.: MIT Press, 1971.

Matthews, W., F. Smith, and E. Goldberg, eds. *Man's Impact on Terrestrial and Oceanic Ecosystems.* Cambridge, Mass.: MIT Press, 1971.

National Academy of Sciences-National Research Council. *Weather and Climate Modification: Problems and Prospects.* Vol. I and II. Publication No. 1350, NAS–NRC. Washington, D.C., 1966.

U.S., Department of Agriculture. *Climate and Man, Yearbook of Agriculture.* Washington, D.C., 1941.

CHAPTER 13

Policy for Energy or Energy for Policy?

The late twentieth century stands in direct contrast to the expectations of the late eighteenth century. Individuals depend in every way on huge organizations, be they corporations or government agencies. There is concentration of means, of decision making, of power upon the future, of responsibility.

Bertrand de Jouvenel

You boil it in sawdust; you salt it in glue;
*   You condense it with locusts and tape;*
Still keeping one principal object in view,
*   To preserve its symmetrical shape.*

Lewis Carroll

There was a time, not so long ago, when the five foot shelf of Harvard Classics was a common possession of those who aspired to be persons of culture. Nowadays, perhaps reflecting a change in social values, a new five foot shelf adorns the walls of many offices. Its concerns are political and economic, rather than literary and philosophical. The authors are corporate now — the National Industrial Conference Board, the National Academy of Sciences, Shell Oil Company, the Sierra Club, a half-dozen Congressional committees, the National Petroleum Council, American Mining Congress, the National Wildlife Federation, and a host of three and four letter non-words: NASA, NSF, API, USGS, OST, SRI, RAND, and FOE — and the subject is energy policy studies. This new five foot shelf, like its predecessor, goes largely unread, even when arguments are most heated. It serves mainly as a security blanket in the face of problems, and as a last solace that someone is seeking solutions.

There is little consistency among these studies. Some comments about energy policy are meant to show that our problems are not only serious, but insoluble. Other studies are meant to reassure us. Some are the comments of tough-minded experts who thrive on crises, and tell us that our hopes and dreams must be subordinated to this crisis. Some comments come from fuzzy utopians, who see, in energy shortages, a chance — at last — to perfect mankind, and solve the shortages too. Some comments are self-serving, some are altruistic, and a good many are just plain wrong. Appeals are made to free enterprise, social darwinism, self-restraint, more government regulation, less government regulation, and the American way of life. The cause of our present plight is variously given as big business, consumers, government, Republicans, Democrats, environmentalists, economists, scientists, engineers, Arabs, communists, capitalists, and the structure of society itself. The outcome (after a period of travail, of course) is variously predicted as a collapse of society, a new dawn of technological utopia (with energy too cheap to meter), final disruption of the earth's ecosystem, decline in the standard of living to some kind of minimal Malthusian misery, or war.

It's time to back off! It is worth a try to step back, to inquire just where we are headed anyhow, to identify the dimensions of the problem for which a policy is sought. The title of this chapter poses the question from which we may start. There is really only one answer. Society must have a larger policy first — a goal if you prefer. Then, and only then, it is possible to inquire whether this policy is in any way limited by available energy. If it is, we can find ways of supplying the necessary energy, or, if necessary, change the goal to fit the limitations.

ENERGY AND SOCIETY'S GOALS

The issue of "energy policy" has been introduced in this way to show in sharp relief the hidden agendas for society that lurk in the slogans of the various protagonists. Sometimes these slogans are painfully obvious. For example: one of the major oil companies tells us at every turn that "a country that runs on oil cannot afford to run short." The hidden goal here is nothing less than the rigid adherence to the present state of affairs, denying historical differences and future possibilities (and incidentally illustrating an uncommonly low opinion of the public served). Why not "A country that runs on oil had better seek another energy source" or "A country that runs on oil ought to consider walking more."

There are only two inputs to industrialized societies: energy and materials. Many materials can be substituted for one another. We can — and do — substitute aluminum for steel or glass. Similarly, we can substitute one fuel for another when energy is needed. But energy cannot be substituted for materials nor materials for energy. Thus, the supply and control of energy is absolutely essential for any industrialized society. The oil embargo by the Arab nations in 1973 showed with dramatic suddenness how much pressure the control of energy by a few can apply to world politics.

Should the energy resources of the United States come under the control of a few, they could apply enormous pressure towards whatever ends they choose. There appears to be an increasing concentration of control over U.S. energy resources, although there is considerable dispute about the extent to which this implied power has been abused. We will return to this matter later. It is enough here to make clear that *any* goal for society requires energy for its implementation. To find out how much is needed and the conditions under which it can and should be supplied is everybody's business.

Goals for the United States

Below are what we consider to be the minimum societal goals that must be served by any energy policy. Because the purpose here is to find out about energy limitations, if any, and about needed policy and institutional changes, we will exclude matters which do not place demands on energy resources, even though we may feel strongly about society's need to change. These minimum goals are: (1) adequate food, clothing, and shelter for all; (2) opportunity to share in whatever surplus goods and services remain after basic needs have been satisfied; (3) ample employment or other meaningful activity for each person; (4) freedom to practice any lifestyle, subject only to the constraints of the above goals.

Because the United States is but one of many nations that share the resources of this planet, we must set our goals in the larger context of the world community. The constraints placed on our goals by analogous goals for the world would include:

(1) Anticipation of materials and energy needs world-wide such that U.S. actions do not deny to other countries the opportunity to fulfill their own goals.

(2) Active participation in programs to lessen world tensions, to assist poor nations with solution of their problems, and to bring about equitable distribution of the world's resources.

(3) Active participation in programs to diminish the threats to the world ecosystem.

(4) Choice of technologies and policies that offer the opportunity to less developed nations to diminish, rather than increase, their dependence on the industrialized nations.

The ultimate aim of the above goals and constraints is nothing less than a life of dignity, meaning, and satisfaction for each man in a world at peace. Though the importance of this aim to policy makers is easily seen, its translation into actual policy formulations is much more difficult. It is hard to imagine many, liberal or conservative, who would quarrel with the basic objectives. They must, however, state their own basic goals explicitly, and reconcile them with the above constraints, before asking that their policy suggestions be adopted.

WHO CONTROLS ENERGY RESOURCES?

We have suggested that the control of energy resources has been concentrated in the hands of a few. Let us look at the evidence for this comment.

The early days of the oil industry were characterized by free-wheeling competition which was often ruinous to the losers. The final result was the emergence of the large oil corporations. It was against these corporations that the early antitrust actions were undertaken. Competition again became vigorous after the collapse of the stock market in 1929. But during the prolonged depression of the 1930s, the price of oil dropped so low that many small companies went broke. Since then, through merger and purchase, a few corporations have gained control of our oil and gas resources. In 1969, the seven largest companies controlled more than 70 percent of the world petroleum market, and the 25 largest companies controlled almost 85 percent of the world market. Much of the remaining world market is controlled by the nationalized oil companies of other countries.

Industrial groupings of this sort do not respond to the free market mechanisms of classical economics. Each company's share of the market is sufficiently large that its own actions affect the overall price structure as well as its own competitive position. Such oligopolistic or monopolistic industrial groupings are not uncommon in our present society (steel is another example). When such industries have undifferentiated products, as do oil and steel, they inevitably engage in price fixing, whether by actual collusion, by following each other's lead in prices, or through some sort of official or unofficial regulatory mechanism.

Each of the 25 largest companies produces natural gas as well as oil. The price of natural gas is fixed directly by the Federal Power Commission. Until 1971 oil prices were determined by the production control sanctioned by the Interstate Oil Compact Commission. Although the state regulatory bodies which make up the Interstate Compact Commission do not fix prices directly, the effect is the same.

What happens is this: Production quotas are derived from estimates of the major oil companies of what they will market from each state that produces oil. These estimates are combined with estimates of demand that are prepared monthly by the U.S. Bureau of Mines. But estimating demand depends upon knowing the price, because the amount bought, especially by large consumers, varies with the price. The price used in all these estimates is always the same as the present market price or one slightly higher. Now if the demand and supply functions are known — and they are by the professionals who make such estimates — then the assumed price will always turn out to be the actual average price. Thus, the Interstate Compact Commission mechanism, which started out to solve the overproduction problems of the early 1930s, has ended in being a mechanism for price fixing as well as production management. Ended is the correct word, because in the spring of 1972, for the first time since production controls were begun, all wells were put on full production. We could no longer produce as much as was wanted. Notably, when this happened, domestic oil prices were 50¢ a barrel higher than the world market price, showing that the industry had not suffered unduly from the regulatory mechanism.

Most large oil companies are vertically integrated. This means that they control refineries and wholesale and retail outlets as well as production and exploration. In each of the last twenty-five years the largest eight companies controlled between 55 and 60 percent of U.S. refinery capacity. The ten largest oil companies operate or control retail dealerships. Eight of the ten operate in 43 or more states. And make no mistake, retail sales of gas and oil are big business. Service station sales account for 7.5 to 8.0 percent of all retail sales.

In 1972 and 1973 several small independent refineries were operating far below capacity or were forced to close down from the lack of crude oil. Congressional hearings have been punctuated by persistent claims that independent retailers have also been forced to close or reduce business because of supply shortages. The best that can be said of these events is that the major integrated companies must be expected to serve their own franchises first, and the independent refiners and dealers last. At worst these events constitute monopoly activities in restraint of trade. In any case, there is little to be seen of free markets or competition.

Diversification came to the oil industry in the early 1960s. This meant entry into other forms of energy supply, or the acquisition of companies supplying other types of fuel. By 1971, major oil companies owned more than 30 percent of U.S. coal reserves and accounted for 20 percent of production; they owned more than half the uranium reserves and 25 percent of the uranium milling capacity; and they operated or were planning 93 percent of the nuclear fuel reprocessing plants. The continuing pursuit of other energy resources by oil companies may be seen from Table 13–1. All of these companies, remember, produce natural gas as well.

The oil companies – perhaps better called energy companies – are aware that we will turn to uranium-based energy sources in the future. Accordingly, they have moved into this field (table 13–2). Many companies are seeking to enter, or have already entered, several phases of the supply and processing of uranium fuels.

At present, the heavily regulated electric utilities are faced with little interfuel competition to hold prices within reason. It is of no advantage to the energy companies to compete with themselves when they supply all fuels. Table 13–2 shows how little this situation will change if and when nuclear fuels begin to supply a substantial portion of our energy needs. Before Congress the chairman of the board of directors of the Tennessee Valley Authority told of one oil company with coal holdings that said they had no intention of supplying TVA with coal unless the agency would pay a price that would yield the oil company the same return on coal that they expect on oil. The oil companies have always maintained that they were entitled to a higher return than other industries because of the discovery risks oil faces. Whatever the merits of that argument, there is no such risk in coal. Yet this was in 1970, before the fuel shortages that have strengthened the hand of the energy companies.[1] By the winter of 1972–73, cities, school districts, and other public agencies were widely reporting failure to obtain competitive bids for fuel supply – or any bids at all. What

Table 13–1. Production, Planned Production, Leasing, or Other Entry into Other Energy Sources by Largest Petroleum Companies

Energy Source	Number of Companies with Active or Planned Production	Companies with Leases or Other Commitments	Total
Oil Shale	3	14	17
Tar Sands	3	13	16
Coal	7	9	16
Uranium	6	18	24

Source: L. C. Rogers, "Oil-finding Talent Pours into Broad Minerals Drive," *Oil & Gas Journal*, February 24, 1969, p. 37.

Table 13-2. Present or Future Capability of Eight Large Oil Companies in the Nuclear Industry

Company	Exploration or Reserve Holdings	Uranium Mining & Milling	UF₆ Conversion	Fuel Preparation or Fabrication	Fuel Reprocessing	Reactors
Standard Oil	X	X		X	X	
Gulf	X	X		X	X	X
Atlantic Richfield	X		X	X	X	
Continental	X	X				
Getty	X	X		X	X	
Standard of Ohio	X	X				
Kerr-McGee	X	X	X	X	X	
Sun	X	X				

Source: 1

this meant was that the energy companies were prepared to take advantage of fuel shortages to deny bulk purchase economies to large-volume public buyers.

One oil company holds leases on more than three quarters of all the known geothermal prospects for energy supply. Thus, the oil companies are gaining both vertical and horizontal control of energy sources, processing, and marketing. Bruce Netschert, an energy economist for many years, regards the situation this way: "The development of the energy company thus presages fuel markets dominated at both the supply and the consumer levels by firms of immense size and monopoly power. . . . Far from being confronted with by the limitations on market power — indeed, even dissolution and divestiture — that a sound competition preserving antitrust policy might be expected to decree, the energy companies have been able to grow apace, free of the regulation that governs their utility competitors and unimpeded by the strictures of antitrust policy to which many of their less powerful competitors have frequently been subjected."[2]

THE PRIORITIES OF THE ENERGY COMPANIES

Before fuels became scarce the concentration of power in a few large corporations attracted little attention from the public. The aims of the energy companies were mostly realized and the public had a ready supply of relatively cheap energy.

The potential danger posed by the concentrated control of energy can only be compared with the threat posed by a monopoly of material resources. Imagine a situation in which a few large corporations had control over metals, food, timber, synthetic and natural fibers, autos, trucks, trains, bicycles, cement, sand, gravel, chemicals — in short, over all materials and manufactured goods. That is nearly the case, for there is no material that can be substituted for energy. Thus, it is crucial to inquire about the priorities of the energy companies.

In 1972, the American Petroleum Institute (API), primary trade association for the largest energy companies, issued a statement of energy policy which indicates these priorities. It begins with a statement of principles which are purported to be "essential for the protection of long range national interests." The statement calls for: (1) "Maintenance of a substantial domestic energy base," which is said to be vital for national security and for reduction of our balance of trade deficits; (2) "Increased development of domestic energy resources . . . and increased efficiency of utilization"; (3) "Policies . . . to insure continuance of the vital energy flow . . . should be developed by government in consultation with industry." It is asserted at this point that "the market forces of a competitive economy will provide the surest and most economical means to develop and allocate the needed energy supplies;" and (4) balancing the "national goals of protecting the environment and developing secure energy resources required to meet the nation's essential needs at reasonable cost."[3]

Most of these principles are sufficiently general that everyone could accept them, but there are several misleading implications. First, there is no recognition that conventional fuels simply cannot meet long-range U.S. needs. Second, the appeal to a "competitive economy" and "market forces" would suggest that the American Petroleum Institute is unaware that control of energy resources is concentrated and that the usual competitive forces of a free market do not exist in the energy industry. Third, the idea of balancing environmental needs and energy needs could signal a search for a careful course between conflicting goals, but the recommendations following the statement demonstrate an unmistakable thrust toward an energy first, environment second policy. The API is concerned with policy for energy, and not with energy for policy. Perhaps, the real clue is their insistence that when making policy government should consult with industry, and not with labor, citizens' groups or other countries.

The Institute's policy recommendations offer a more specific indication of the energy companies' priorities. These recommendations fall into six categories, and we summarize each category in the following pages.

(1) Recommendations on exploration and development begin with the flat statement that "government should not engage in oil and gas exploration and development," and that research and development should be a private responsibility. It is stated that "federal lands (i.e. public lands) *must* be made more readily available for exploration and development," and that "U.S. jurisdiction over the seabed . . . to the outer edge of the continental shelf should be retained," and "the government *must* give its full support to the competitive overseas efforts of U.S. companies." The juxtaposition of these statements should make clear one set of industry priorities: the government is to help when asked, but otherwise to keep its hands off. Whether the government should engage in exploration is not clear, but if the government does not explore, how are we to know what the nation's supply of fuel resources really is?

Through the most powerful lobby in Washington, the energy companies have been able to exempt themselves from supplying any information on the results of their explorations. The Public Information Act of 1968 (the Moss act) specifically exempts oil company data from being made public, and, in fact, prohibits the government from releasing whatever information it may receive from the energy companies on oil and gas discoveries. Thus the stricture against exploration asks that the government accept only the information which the energy companies choose to supply, and seek nothing more.

The industry demands that public lands be made available for exploration. Public lands belong to everyone, not to an abstraction called the government. Any prudent person ought to know what these lands contain, and what uses might be made of them before selling off mineral exploitation rights. The government, as a representative of the owners, has an obligation to know what it is selling.

The recommendations for "full support" of private overseas efforts, and for the assertion of territorial rights over the continental shelf are direct requests that U.S. foreign policy be made in accordance with the desires of the energy companies. Possibly the energy companies look with envy on the close ties between Japanese industry and the Japanese government. These ties have enabled them to make deals for industrial assistance in exchange for guaranteed oil supplies. But are U.S. oil companies ready to accept the government control that goes with such a policy? Are they ready for employment control and profit control? All too often in the past, full support of U.S. corporations abroad has forced our government to support unpopular foreign governments, in direct contravention of our own national principles. If we have not learned by now the futility of meddling in the internal affairs of other nations, we are doomed to repeat the national trauma of the Vietnam war over and over again.

Freedom of the seas has been the best example of international trust in a distrustful world. Yet even that threatens to slip away from us. First in Malta and more recently in Iceland, Peru, Canada and elsewhere, nations have laid claim to continental shelves and beyond. In the Middle East, such an extension of sovereignty into the Gulf of Aqaba led to war in 1967. Perhaps seabed resources should be used as the basis for new international agreements with the aim of world peace. In any case, the United States, richest nation in the world, should not make policy on the narrow ground of short-term energy needs, and close out our fishing, shipping, and mining interests in the bargain. Do we really want the continental shelves of the rest of the world closed to us in reprisal?

(2) A second set of recommendations relates to taxation and regulation. Four of these recommendations have a single thrust: reduce regulation and increase tax credits and other "incentives."

The energy companies seek an end to regulation of natural gas prices by the Federal Power Commission. They believe, and many outside the industry agree, that natural gas prices have been held to an unrealistically low level. Prices probably should be raised in order to shift some of the largest users away from natural gas as a fuel source. But the energy companies want government regulation of prices to cease altogether. API states that gas "should be allowed to compete freely in the marketplace" — which might be a good idea if there were a free market for natural gas. But can the homeowner with a gas furnace make any choices? Hardly. There is a gas line or there isn't and one can look for alternate sources of supply of natural gas about as successfully as one can seek an alternative telephone company. Much natural gas is distributed by public utilities which also distribute electricity. It would be dangerous and foolish to give up some public check on this activity. The best policy may be to raise the price of natural gas in the interest of preserving supplies for premium uses. But in no case should such a decision be left to private corporations.

The energy industry has enjoyed a favored tax position for many years. Depletions allowances permit oil companies to deduct 22 percent of gross receipts, not to exceed 50 percent of income. Besides this best known of the tax subsidies to the industry, there are other provisions in current tax laws permitting liberal write-off capital expenses, deduction of certain indirect costs as current production costs (even though other industries must count similar expenditures as capital costs), deduction of foreign operating costs even if the operation failed to show a profit, and a variety of capital gains shelters. Large amounts of money are involved in these subsidies. One effect is the encouragement of exploitation, discouragement of draining oil and gas fields, and what has been called the "drain America first" policy. But what concerns us here is the failure of the market and the distortion of energy costs. Table 13–3 shows the taxes actually paid by the five largest oil companies. These are typical values for the oil industry. In 1969, 1970 and 1971 the average corporate income tax paid by the oil industry was 5.8 percent, 10.1 percent and 6.1 percent.[4] This is to be compared to an average of about 42 percent for all industry.

Table 13–3 shows that, in 1971, these oil companies failed to pay their share of taxes in the amount of about 2.6 billion dollars, and thus, each person paid about $12.93 more in taxes than he would have otherwise. For a family of four, this would amount to about 10 percent of their annual costs for fuel and energy. If tax subsidies to the rest of the industry are included, we estimate that each citizen paid an amount in taxes equal to about 20 percent of his energy costs. Without these subsidies, fuel costs would no doubt be higher, taxes on individuals lower, and the consumer would choose how much fuel to buy at higher prices; this situation would come closer to a free market. The API is aware of that, and it makes their appeal to the free market ring hollow.

The reasons given by the energy companies for needing these

Table 13-3. Corporate Income Tax Paid by Five Largest Oil Companies

Company	1971			1962–1971		
	Before Tax Profit (billions)	Percent Tax Paid	Approx. Loss to Treasury (billions)	Before Tax Profit (billions)	Percent Tax Paid	Approx. Loss to Treasury (billions)
Standard Oil (N.J.)	2.74	7.7	0.885	19.65	7.3	6.4
Texaco	1.32	2.3	0.495	8.70	2.6	3.3
Gulf	1.32	2.3	0.500	7.86	4.7	2.8
Mobil	1.15	7.4	0.375	6.39	6.1	2.2
Standard (Calif.)	0.87	1.6	0.330	5.19	2.7	1.9

Source: *Progressive* magazine

public subsidies are that the business is risky, incentives are needed for exploration and development, and incentives are needed to permit accumulation of capital. If the business were risky, one would expect to find large fluctuations in profits, periodic business failures and the rise of new companies as fortune smiled on first one and then another. These conditions do not obtain. From the reports of Council of Economic Advisors to the Congress, it is clear that fluctuations in profits are about the same in the oil business as in other kinds of business or in the average of all businesses. Further, although a few companies have made a successful start in the oil business in the last twenty years, they are very few indeed, and no large companies have gone under. The fact is that the risks are well understood, estimated, and shared. For example, almost all the offshore operations (which are among the most risky) are underwritten by groups of companies so that a single failure means little. Finally, if the business were really as risky as the energy companies sometimes imply, featuring periodic giant profits and punctuated by disastrous losses, they would have advanced the most powerful argument for direct government control or operation, so that this essential supply could be assured.

Profits have been high in the oil industry for years. In refining, for example, profits after taxes have averaged 10.8 percent for the last twenty years. By comparison, the average for all industry for the same twenty years is 5.1 percent after taxes.[5] The energy shortages that began to be felt in 1972 may have caused inconveniences, but have not damaged the profits of the oil companies. Profit increases for the first half of 1973 ranged from a "low" of 37 percent for Standard of Indiana to a staggering 174 percent for Commonwealth Oil.

Walter Heller, former Chairman of the Council of Economic Advisors, sums up the position of most experts outside the oil industry.

> To continue stimulating the overexploitation of oil by tax subsidies in the form of excessive depletion allowances, capital gains shelters, and special deductions becomes ever more anomalous. Here is another case where believers in the market-pricing system ought to live by it. The public is subsidizing these industries at least twice — once by rich tax bounties and once by cost-free or below-cost discharge of waste and heat. . . . The net result is to underprice and overproduce petroleum products and the energy derived from them.[6]

It is certainly true that any collection of energy options for the future will require accumulation of capital, probably large amounts of it. The strange implication in the API statement — and in the statements of the individual oil companies and the electric utilities — is that the industry ought to, or must, finance this sort of expansion from current earnings. This view denies the possibility of investors participating in the growth of industry by purchasing stocks or bonds. It suggests that the energy industry should not — or cannot — compete in the money markets of the nation as even the government must do. As a practical matter, it would further concentrate the control of energy resources and possibly limit the options for the future.

(3) A third set of recommendations from API relate to import policy. They call for import restrictions to prevent free entry of foreign oil and gas. The best clue to the philosophy behind this call is contained in the statement that "the import system should be unencumbered by objectives unrelated to national security." This sounds strangely like the "fortress America" policy that proved so disastrous before World War II. By national security, the API makes clear, they mean a domestic supply of oil. But national security could better be had by reducing world tensions or by reducing dependence on oil.

Several of the recommendations on imports were contradicted by public needs and energy shortages, and import quotas were largely abandoned in April, 1973 — as had been recommended by a presidential task force four years earlier.

(4) Recommendations for synthetic fuels are similar to the recommendations for regulations and taxes. More government (taxpayer) support is recommended in the form of research support and tax subsidies. Every taxpayer should ask himself whether he wants to supply gifts of money and guarantees of profit without the establishment of adequate controls.

(5) Recommendations for environmental protection again demonstrate a parochial point of view. API suggests that "government has the responsibility to establish realistic environmental standards in close consultation with industry." There are many other groups that government should consult as well, but API finds no place for them.

The National Petroleum Council — an oil industry group set up by the Secretary of Interior to advise him — is less shy. They call for the government "to eliminate the serious delays that have been caused by environmental issues."[7] To the extent that these delays are the normal time taken to resolve conflicting goals in the courts, they are part of the price of a pluralistic society.

But there is a clear implication that the proximate cause of our energy problems is the delay caused by opposition to the plans of the energy industry on environmental grounds. Among themselves, oilmen are more candid. Robert Buschman, president of the Texas MidContinent Oil and Gas Association, described at the association's 1972 meeting the "short-sighted environmental policies" as one of the "ill-advised — if not downright foolish — federal policies."[8]

When environmental opposition halts construction of a power plant it is news. When other kinds of delays occur it is not news. An accounting of delayed projects suggests that the industry's attempt to blame delays on environmentalists is simply self-serving. For example, 72 percent of the electric power plants that came into service between 1966 and 1970 experienced delays in construction. Fifty-two percent of these delays were caused by labor problems, 23 percent by equipment failure, 14 percent by late delivery of equipment, 6 percent by slowness in regulatory clearance — including, among other things, environmental opposition —, and 5 percent by weather and design changes. Several plants were delayed for more than one reason. Of the 230 power plants scheduled for completion between 1971 and 1977, 53 were reported as delayed (in 1972). Of these, 30 were being delayed by labor problems, 27 by regulatory matters (including, but not limited to, environmental opposition), and 12 by weather, design changes and other non-environmental matters. (Multiple causes were reported for some delays.)[9] Of course there are cases when environmental considerations and energy industry plans come into direct conflict, but the industry will have to look elsewhere for a villain to take most of the blame.

(6) API's final recommendations suggest coordination of federal energy programs toward a long-range energy policy. This goal is certainly desirable. We indicated earlier in the chapter that a long-range policy is necessary if we are to maintain a supply of energy sufficient to our needs. Government energy policy must have provisions for meeting our needs, developing alternative energy sources, distributing energy among the various sectors, and reducing consumption of energy.

INTERESTED PARTIES IN ENERGY POLICY

Before proceeding to a discussion of energy policy, we should examine the agendas of the groups that have an interest in that policy. Each of these groups has its own priorities and needs. Their interests may be conflicting, and energy policy must be carefully formulated with the aim of reconciling them.

Industry
Industry is one of the largest energy consumers. It is committed, of course, to survival and, almost without exception, to continued expansion. For these ends, a cheap and reliable supply of energy bulks large in fundamental plans. However, the recent energy shortages have demonstrated that the era of cheap energy supplies is over and reliable supplies are in doubt.

The energy shortage threatens continued industrial growth. The desirability of such growth can be questioned, but industrial leaders and many economists (Walter Heller, James Tobin, William Nordhaus, and Robert Lampman, for example) believe that social improvement will end if growth rates are reduced and we eventually arrive at a steady-state economy. The argument goes like this: we have had social gains and improvements in the material standard of living in this period of growth. Since growth has accompanied these changes, the end of growth would mean the end of social improvement. Among the evidence cited is the correlation between increases in the Gross National Product and energy use and the improvement in social conditions. Counterarguments by two economists who have studied the growth issue in great detail, E. J. Mishan and Nicholas Georgescu–Roegen, point out the uncounted costs of economic growth and the theoretical reasons why growth must stop.[10] We have already seen (chapter 5) that exponential growth in a finite world must eventually stop. What is not yet known is when and how growth will slow or end. These matters are complex, and serious discussion of them has only recently begun.[11] For the present, industrial leaders can be expected to press for energy to continue expansion of industrial output.

In support of the basic aims for survival and continued expansion, industry will probably urge relaxation of environmental standards, expansionist monetary and fiscal policy (even at the expense of inflation), and high priority for industrial fuel allocations.

The Energy-Consuming Public

This category includes all of us. We have under our direct control the two largest end uses of energy — the automobile and home heating (see chapter 11). It is not surprising that the first federal policies for energy conservation were directed at these two uses.

The goals listed at the beginning of this chapter are in the interest of every citizen. Unfortunately, few people seem to understand the ways in which these goals are related to energy policy. This lack of public understanding is being compounded by the persistent presentation of the points of view of industry and government in the public media. While these presentations are usually true as far as they go, many options do not get mentioned.

The only expression of grass roots opinion on energy related matters that has resulted in legislation in the last few years is in the environmental protection area. It will require some public vigilance to insure that all environmental gains are not sacrificed in the name of energy shortages. It is worth recalling that much of industry, the AEC, and most of the energy companies actively opposed the National

Environmental Policy Act, or sought to exempt themselves from it by special provision.

But the environment is only part of the story. Somehow the public must learn that issues like the highway program, mass transit, zoning and building codes, and public expenditure on research and development will determine the futue of energy supply and the fabric of their own lives.

The Government

Although we have a representative government, governmental policies do not necessarily reflect the desires of the public. Governments, like many large institutions, acquire an agenda and momentum of their own.

Historically, the energy industry has received generally favorable treatment from the government. Things have not changed much in the recent past. For example, the special energy program outlined by President Nixon on April 18, 1973, corresponds almost point-by-point with the recommendations of the American Petroleum Institute. Only on the matter of oil import quotas did the administration go against oil industry policy. The fuel shortages that occurred in the winter of 1972–73 impelled the president to end the restrictions on oil imports.

Government energy policy depends partly on history, partly on the relative strength of pressure groups, partly on public opinion, and partly on the options that are perceived. Unfortunately, it is made almost always for short- or intermediate-term goals. The following long-standing policy directions have considerable effect on the government's reaction to energy issues:

(1) Pursuit of continued exponential growth in the economy. Maintaining a fixed percentage growth rate is exponential growth (chapter 5). Although we know that such growth must eventually stop, there is no hint of any policy anticipating this certainty. In fact, it seems that government energy policy will be directed toward satisfying the demand for more energy. It is unlikely that government will seek to slow the growth rate in an effort to reduce energy consumption.

(2) Commitment to nuclear energy. The early spectacular successes with nuclear weapons technology and optimistic estimates of the future of nuclear power have produced a well-established bureaucracy in the executive branch and in Congress. Despite recent conflicts over nuclear power, these vested interests can be expected to defend the primacy of a nuclear future against all alternatives. New voices are being heard on this subject, but so far there has been little change. Consider, for example, the funding for energy research and development: for the 1969–1973 period, three fourths of all appropriations were for

nuclear sources, with the largest increases going to fusion research. Should it appear desirable to diversify, these vested bureaucratic interests will pose a problem.

(3) Fears for national security. This highly emotional issue has been intensified anew by the use of fuel supplies as a policy threat by the Arab nations. The resulting policy pressure has been for energy self-sufficiency as soon as possible. While energy self-sufficiency may be a desirable goal, it will not produce national security. Neither the world nor the United States can be secure as long as western Europe and Japan are almost entirely dependent on imported fuels.

(4) A marked preference for technological rather than institutional or social solutions to energy problems. Despite a general awareness that marked technological changes introduce large and unpredictable social changes, the government has an unvarying record of seeking technological and engineering solutions to our problems. If the public should decide against an all-nuclear energy future, they will have to make these wishes known in spite of government pressure.

The Electric Utility Industry

The electric utility industry has long been organized as a lobby in Washington and in the state capitols. Its lobbying effectiveness has been strengthened by strong public reaction to even brief interruptions of electric service. In fact, the Public Service Commissions of the states, feeling powerless to solve the larger problems of regional supply and distribution of electricity, have importuned the federal government to take action in this area.

In the past twenty-five years, the electric utility industry has seen rapid and continuous growth, accompanied by declining unit costs. Large users have been offered progressively lower rates for electric service on the grounds that the reduced unit costs meant lowered rates for all users. But we seem to have entered a new period in which further expansion no longer brings declining unit costs. Higher fuel costs and cost overruns in equipment for nuclear power plants will further increase the unit cost. Under such circumstances, these promotional policies and rate structures are no longer defensible. Declining rate block structures mean that the low volume users – who pay the highest rates – are subsidizing industry's expansion through ever higher rates.

The manager of an electric utility is in a peculiar position, however. Because user rates, rate of return on investment, and many other features of his operation are subject to public control, his only way of increasing profits is through expansion. Thus we can expect the utilities to push for an expansionary energy policy measure, even if the environment must suffer and small users must subsidize large users. The usual utility argument that it is cheaper to service large users than small users is self-serving. If rates were to be made solely on a cost-of-service basis, then they should also be a function of the user's distance from the generating station. Long ago it was decided that such a charge was inadvisable. The point is that we already violate the cost-of-service principle.

Thus the electric industry is likely to favor low fuel costs, expansionary policies, and reduced opposition from environmental groups. If energy shortages worsen, the electric utilities will seek relaxed environmental standards for utility construction and operation.

Foreign Nations

For many years the United States and other industrialized nations have relied on relatively cheap supplies of imported fuels and materials which they needed. The 20 percent of the world population in industrialized nations have for many years consumed about 80 percent of the depletable resources produced each year. Further, these supplies were often produced by U.S. companies, or those of other industrialized nations operating under foreign concessions. This state of affairs was justified — even made a source of pride in colonial days — on the grounds that such resource production added to the economies of the poor countries that were the sources. The low prices were justified on the grounds that the free marketplace was functioning.

But things are changing in the poor nations of the world. Their governments have realized that they were parting with their resources very cheaply. In an inversion of the old roles, the lesser developed countries with large unexploited resources play off the industrialized nations against one another for the best deal, much in the way that the rich nations once shopped among the poor nations for oil and minerals.

In the case of petroleum fuels, the poor nations have banded together to obtain higher prices. The Organization of Petroleum Exporting Countries (OPEC) has become a powerful force in the world search for assured fuel supplies. Should we oppose the OPEC grouping as a monopoly? If it is a monopoly, it is hard to know just what we could do about it that would not worsen world tensions.

The practical course would be to vary our energy supply options. If our energy resources were diversified, we would not feel so threatened by a cutoff of our Middle East oil supply.

Meanwhile, if the OPEC nations should nationalize their petroleum resources, the United States must react with caution. If these nations seek to purchase control of foreign oil companies' operations within their borders, their demands should be acceded to gracefully — for the alternative is seizure without payment. After nationalization is accomplished, these countries will seek to reenter the international market to sell their oil. As the world's largest customer, we will have to exercise discretion to prevent ourselves from taking unfair advantage at that time.

For the OPEC nations, nationalization of oil resources may be the only course to a better future. It is the only means whereby they can achieve an improved standard of living for their populations, and it behooves the United States to help poor nations in this effort.

PRESENT ENERGY POLICY

We *do* have an energy policy in the United States, but most of the practices that make up this policy were not thought out as part of a consistent program. Nevertheless, the conglomeration of activities, regulations, restrictions, and plans for energy supply must be the point from which any attempt at a coherent policy must start.

The Choice of Fuels

While energy was cheap, environmental effects slight, and fuel shortages not troublesome, most users had a choice of energy sources. Interfuel competition, however, applied primarily to initial choices. Once an industrial process was chosen or a furnace installed, the user was committed to a single fuel. Choice was further modified by technology — for example, steam and electric automobiles disappeared many years ago, and gasoline is the only fuel choice for current autos.

Government subsidies to some fuels further modify the market. Environmental concerns and public expenditures — on roads, for example — limit or distort the choice of fuels still more. Persistent fuel shortages will bring further limitations.

We cannot recover an unmodified free market in fuel supply any more than we can return to the days when people cut their winter fuel supply from the land on which they lived. We could attempt to return to the free market, but it would be a long and tortuous path, and we should consider the reasons why society intervened in the first place. There were often good reasons, whether or not the intervention solved the difficulties.

Government Regulation of Fuels and Energy

Scattered among 16 agencies — or 42, depending on who is counting — are a wide variety of regulatory functions of the federal government. Among the most prominent of these agencies are the Federal Power Commission (FPC), the Interstate Commerce Commission (ICC), the Atomic Energy Commission (AEC), the Environmental Protection Agency (EPA), the Civil Aeronautics Board (CAB), the Federal Aviation Administration (FAA), the Bureau of Mines, and the

Oil and Gas Division of the U.S. Geological Survey. But even these
agencies are only a part of the federal activities that help determine our
present energy policy. Agencies that are active in the transportation area
all influence fuel and energy use. Other agencies involved with housing,
agriculture, health, land use, transportation and shipping, and a host of
other government activities directly or indirectly influence energy
sources and uses.

     With the advent of fuel shortages in the early 1970s, hearings,
legislation, special task forces, and consultants appeared everywhere.
Because energy is one of the two fundamental inputs to an industrial
society, decisions of many kinds, from mining safety laws to FHA mort-
gage conditions, have impact on energy supply or consumption. There
is simply no realistic possibility of combining all energy-related activities
in one agency of the government — state or federal. One might as well
try to bring together in one agency all activities that use typewriters.

     It is clear, however, that until recently the various agencies have
paid little attention to their common relationship to energy supply and
consumption. It is this lack of coordination that many have in mind
when they conclude that the United States has no energy policy. We
share in the basic dilemma of all industrialized countries. First, we have
a great many problems and objectives which frequently come into conflict when the making and execution of policy is considered. Second,
though there may be an optimum organizational structure for each
particular problem, we can have only one organization at a time — and
whatever one we have must be a compromise that attempts to deal with
a variety of problems simultaneously. As society becomes more complex and its problems become more numerous and serious, an organizational structure's effectiveness in dealing with any given problem will
decrease. Sloganeering of the sort the energy companies and some
politicians engage in will not help under these circumstances.

     For better or worse, through a variety of government activities,
we do have our hands in the workings of the energy supply and consumption activities of society. It is almost certain that we will continue
to regulate, license, support research, and in other ways influence the
use and availability of energy. Of course these activities should have
better coordination. To that end, structures like a Council of Energy
Advisors deserve attention, but the limitations of such arrangements
should be realized. Public discussion of options and the preservation of
a wide variety of options are often the result of conflicting views.
Centralization of authority will not encourage public discussion.
Furthermore, the choice of energy policy certainly involves decisions
about employment of the nation's natural resources (public and private),
foreign policy, environmental standards and, at times, social objectives,
economic stability, conditions for workers, and the very survival of our

society. Such decisions do not belong in a coordinating group. No matter how messy it may be at times, these decisions belong to the people of the nation engaged in the political process.

Regulation also will continue, even if we should decide tomorrow to reduce it as far as possible. The difficulty of regulating a technically independent industry must still concern us. An astronomer who was serving on an advisory board of the FCC once remarked that one shouldn't stay in that kind of activity too long because sooner or later it is easy to become sympathetic with the problems of the regulated industries. That has been a persistent problem in regulatory agencies. The regulators, in the course of learning their work, come to understand that the problems of the regulated are real. When the regulated activity is also a technical one — as is the case in matters related to energy — the principal source of qualified people is the industry itself. The solution to this difficulty is not to be found in a search for unbiased men. It is likely that when you find someone who is unbiased about the oil industry, you will have also found someone that knows little or nothing about it. Such a man is an easier mark for the manipulator in industry than a person who understands oil — biases and all.

Since we are committed to continued regulation, it may be time to recognize regulatory activity as a permanent feature of all industrialized societies. Regulatory actions have more in common with judicial proceedings than with the administrative one with which they are ordinarily grouped. The time may have come to group all regulatory activities together, and separate them from both the executive and judicial branches of government. Then the government may be able to build up the kind of procedural safeguards that will escape the most serious difficulties of the regulators becoming the captives of the regulated. In the case of energy regulatory activities the grouping together of standard setting, research and development, promotional activities and regulation was tried with the AEC. This arrangement has an inherent conflict of interest in the assigned activities, and has made the AEC subject to considerable—inevitable but often undeserved—suspicion. David Lilienthal, first chairman of the AEC, concluded that the arrangement did not work, and has long advocated the separation of AEC activities.[12]

OPTIONS FOR NATIONAL ENERGY POLICY

It has been pointed out that our energy problems do not yet represent an absolute resource shortage. We could, if we chose, mount a massive effort to supply our present needs and those of the next few decades through conventional sources. But a choice for massive exploitation of traditional fuels — besides having a fearful price — will only deplete these resources all the sooner. We would then have the same problems with a smaller base of resources to solve them.

When considering our options — and we can cover only a few of the possibilities here — we must remember that future generations will have to live with the consequences of policies chosen in the next few years. Choosing policies for short-term advantage could be disastrous if the long-term results are ignored.

Institutional Options

A coordinating and advisory body is needed at the level of the Executive Office of the President. It could be a statutory group, one set up by executive order, or one located within the existing structure (for example, within the Office of Management and Budget), but it should be required to report periodically to the Congress and the public on the state of energy resources, research, achievement of policy goals and the like. A Department of Energy and Resources could be useful — and there is, in Canada, an example of this arrangement worthy of study — but much energy-related activity has been handled by the Department of Interior, and that has not solved our problems.

The most difficult organizational problems arise in connection with regulatory activities, which must be well separated from the action programs of government. The possible options range from a facelifting of present regulatory agencies, to the establishment of new, separate regulatory agencies, to the more dramatic step of instituting a separate branch of government, coequal with the present branches, which would implement all regulatory efforts, including those for energy matters. With several different kinds of regulatory activities proceeding under one set of leaders, it might be possible to construct the kind of procedural safeguards that have characterized the courts including the right of appeal.

In the Congress, progress on energy matters depends upon finding ways to change the jealously guarded fiefdoms of the congressional committees. At present, more than twelve committees claim jurisdiction over various energy issues. These jurisdictions often overlap. As a practical matter, it might be possible to abolish the Joint Atomic Energy Committee and replace it with a Joint Energy Committee. This is a minimum measure. More desirable measures will have to wait for resolution of some of Congress's longstanding archaic practices. Congressional reform has been sought for many years, but with little success.

Litigation surrounding power plant siting has revealed a longstanding institutional shortcoming of our court system. With opposing litigants presenting expert testimony on matters of considerable complexity, the normal protagonist procedures of the court are inadequate.

The courts need some means of obtaining third-party expert information. Such a procedure would frequently bring evidence into the court which is widely known in the technical community — and relevant to the question at issue — but not introduced by the contending parties for reasons of their own.

These institutional suggestions have been made many times. If we are really to seek energy for policy, we must recall the goals of society and seek the institutional changes conducive to achieving those goals. One of the clearest messages heralded by the energy shortage is that change is coming.

We should seriously consider direct public control of fuel resources and major facilities for energy conversion. There is considerable experience with varying degrees of public control in many countries, including the socialist countries. The lessons from these arrangements in times of energy shortage are not yet clear, but it appears that central control is no assurance against the development of energy shortages nor does it guarantee efficiency.

The record of government operation in the United States is more encouraging. The TVA has its weaknesses, but it is a success by nearly any standards in a program that would have been hard to execute with a private industrial operation. Similarly, the many municipal utilities show no particular disadvantage compared to privately owned utilities. Perhaps we should set up several large public energy corporations, modeled on TVA, to test the success of public operation of energy supply and to provide a standard against which the performance of the energy companies can be measured. We think it is at least time to apply public utility control to the energy industry. But our own mythology gets in the way: the word nationalization has evil connotations to many.

Legislative and Regulatory Strategies

Legislative measures can be instituted to bring a reduction in energy use without changing basic living patterns, and without aiming to lessen growth. But such measures can only buy a few more years (chapter 11). Some time to solve our problems would be welcome, *if* the time is actually employed to seek solutions, and not — as is usually the case — simply used to forget the basic problem for a while.

Measures could be taken to accelerate supply and production of presently used fuels and energy. But this would be foolish for the production of fossil fuels, since the handwriting of change is already on the wall. Expanding fossil fuel production would be justified only as a part of a program to seek new energy resources, with the fossil fuels used to alleviate short-term shortages.

The most promising strategy would be to mount a variety of programs designed to produce energy from a wide range of sources, especially on-site sources, such as solar home heating, and to institute research into those sources which still most be proven feasible. Measures to encourage less use of energy (such as tax incentives to individuals) could be very helpful. Prohibitory measures should be taken with caution, but it may be necessary to limit the size of automobiles, since it appears that appeals to the auto industry have but limited effect.

For regulatory agencies, it is time to consider using the rate-making power as part of an overall energy policy. Recent studies indicate that the elasticity of the demand for electricity is considerable, and it would thus be possible to use the rate structure to inhibit growth in demand. At least it is time to end promotional practices and rate structures, unless it can be proven that such practices will bring a reduction in unit cost.

Technical Options

The United States is heading toward commitment to a nuclear future, but the option for more varied approaches is still open. The vision of a nuclear utopia has long since been discredited, and the director of Oak Ridge National Laboratory now calls it (approvingly) "a Faustian bargain."

We have discussed many alternative energy sources. The public image of many of these sources is somewhat distorted. The public has heard that breeder reactors are almost here — and almost safe — and that other energy sources are futuristic stuff. Meanwhile, amateurs are heating hot water and homes with local solar energy conversion, farmers are constructing methane generators which operate on animal wastes, hot steam geothermal generation of electricity is succeeding in California and Italy, and modern windmills are doing very well in Australia and Denmark. None of these sources is any more likely to solve all our problems than is the breeder reactor, but the technology is understood and operating. The principal problems are with cost and engineering, which is quite a different thing from MHD, thermionic, or thermo-electric power generation where much basic work remains to be done.

For those energy sources whose principal problems are cost and engineering design, the space program is a model. The space program was an engineering success. Consider where we might be in energy development if we invested billions of dollars each year for a decade on solar energy. If that is unconvincing, consider the reverse case. Where would we be in space if we had spent a million or two each year in the 1960s?

Energy, Environment and Planning

In the end it comes down to what we want. Until goals are established, planning for the future is not possible. It becomes, in the words of the OECD planning conference in Bellagio, Italy, "an effort to make the inherently bad . . . more efficiently bad."[13] The United States has a strong technical base. When we have the goal, the energy limitations on it, if any, can be discovered. If there are none, the goal can be met.

REFERENCES

1. B. C. Netschert, "The Energy Company: A Monopoly Trend in the Energy Markets," *Science and Public Affairs* 27 (1971): 13–17.
2. Ibid., pp. 13–17.
3. American Petroleum Institute, *Statement of Policy: Energy* (New York: November 1972).
4. Congressional Record, July 19, 1972, H6707–16.
5. Economic Report of the President, prepared by the Council of Economic Advisors, various years.
6. W. W. Heller, "Coming to Terms with Growth and the Environment," in *Energy, Economic Growth, and the Environment,* ed. S. H. Schurr (Baltimore: Johns Hopkins Press, 1972), pp. 3–29.
7. National Petroleum Council, *U.S. Energy Outlook* (Washington, D.C., 1972), 134 p.
8. R. A. Buschman, "Presidential Address" (Address delivered at the Texas Mid-Continent Oil and Gas Association, Houston, Texas, October 10, 1972, mimeographed, 8 p.
9. J. A. Lieberman, in *Energy and Public Policy – 1972* (New York: The Conference Board, 1972), p. 14.
10. E. J. Mishan, *The Costs of Economic Growth* (New York: Praeger, 1967). N. Georgescu-Roegen, *The Entropy Law and the Economic Process* (Cambridge, Mass.: Harvard University Press, 1971).
11. American Academy of Arts and Sciences, "The No-Growth Society," *Daedelus,* Fall 1973.
12. D. Lilienthal, *Change, Hope and the Bomb* (Princeton, N.J.: Princeton University Press, 1963).
13. Quoted in E. Jantsch, *Technological Planning and Social Futures* (New York: John Wiley & Sons, 1972), 256 p.

SUGGESTED READING

Congressional Quarterly, *Energy Crisis in America.* Washington: Congressional Quarterly, Inc., 1972.
Fabricant, N., and Hallman, R. M. *Toward a Rational Power Policy.* New York: George Braziller, 1971.
Murphy, J. J., ed. *Energy and Public Policy – 1972.* New York: The Conference Board, 1972.
National Petroleum Council. *U.S. Energy Outlook.* Washington: National Petroleum Council, 1972.

Schurr, S. H., ed. *Energy, Economic Growth, and the Environment.* Baltimore: Johns Hopkins Press, 1972.

U.S. Congress, Senate, *Council on Energy Policy,* Hearings before the Senate Committee on Commerce. Washington: GPO, 1973.

CHAPTER 14

Return to The Future

Upon this gifted age, in its dark hour,
Rains from the sky a meteoric shower
Of facts . . . they lie unquestioned, uncombined.
Wisdom enough to leech us of our ill
Is daily spun; but there exists no loom
To weave it into fabric. . . .

Edna St. Vincent Millay

A man, viewed as a behaving system, is quite simple. The apparent
complexity of his behavior over time is largely a reflection of the
complexity of the environment in which he finds himself.

Herbert Simon

If we are to take any hand in the future, to aim at any goal, we must first recognize the patterns imposed on us by the present and the past. If we wish to know how much we need of energy or resources, we should first understand in which direction we are going.

At present, the universal aim is continued growth. Rich and poor nations alike strive for increased industrialization, more goods, more specialization, and — to drive the whole process — more energy. One would suppose that this universal aim of nations implied great satisfaction with the course of history, seeing it as a steady improvement in the human condition.

But is the present better than the past? In chapter 4 we indicated that evidence on this point is mixed. Many people are better off than ever before, living in conditions of material abundance that were available only to monarchs and priests a few centuries ago. But world population has increased so vastly that there are also more people — larger absolute numbers of persons — living in abject poverty than at any time in the past. But since many are living in relative freedom from hunger and disease and fear, we view history, especially recent history, as progress.

The continuing growth and industrialization of modern times has generated a litany sanctioning inequalities and injustices even while taking pride in the increased numbers of the well-to-do. The goal of industrial society was to have enough for everyone — to have freedom from hunger, disease, fear; and an opportunity for each individual to search for satisfaction.

Most industrialized countries can now achieve these goals, but although inequalities continue, they show no signs of slackening their growth or sharing their excess with the poor of the world. In some respects, the rich industrialized nations have achieved their growth at the expense of the poor nations.

A group of distinguished British scientists summarizes the problem this way:[1]

> The principal defect of the industrial way of life with its ethos of expansion is that it is not sustainable. Its termination within the lifetime of someone born today is inevitable — unless it continues to be sustained for a while longer by an entrenched minority at the cost of imposing great suffering on the rest of mankind.

We shall have growth for a while yet, perhaps for a long while in the poor nations of the world, but the industrialized nations must prepare to end the kind of growth that is achieved through use of ever more energy. We will not consider how the privileged few might maintain their position against the destitute many.

The question at hand is energy. We need to know the minimum amount needed and how to get it, and how much more can be counted on as a long-range supply. If our civilization is to be more than a brief and aberrant experiment among civilizations, this long-range supply must not encounter obvious limits for at least a millennium.

PREDICTING FUTURE ENERGY USE

As the public media began giving increased attention to fuel shortages and the energy crisis, graphs showing the amount of energy used in the recent past began to appear. On these same graphs were projections showing how much energy their author thought we would use in the future.

The simplest of these projections are just what they appear to be — extrapolation of past totals into the future. For some quantity that has been growing linearly (that is, adding a fixed amount each year) such a technique would be satisfactory providing that the same forces that were active in the past continue into the future, and providing that no limitations are encountered. With nonlinear growth — for example, the exponential growth that has characterized energy consumption for many years — a simple method is to linearize the graph and extrapolate as before. For exponential growth, a plot on a logarithmic scale will provide a linear graph for projection (see figure 14–3 for such a graph). But such techniques are guaranteed to fail when past trends and relationships change, or take new directions. This basic weakness constitutes an advantage if the basic forces causing growth are not understood, and do not change. In such cases, gross projections of totals may be more accurate than more complex methods.

Most projections of energy use are made from models of some sort. The most common type of projection divides energy use (or supply) into a number of categories and sectors and projects each of these separately. Totals are obtained by recombining the categorical estimates. In this approach — sometimes called the building block approach — assumptions are made about the behavior of variables that are assumed to effect the level of future energy use. Among these variables are increases in gross national product and population, fuel prices in relation to prices of other commodities, availability of fuels, and technological change. Even with this small number of variables, models of considerable complexity can result, and there may be difficult questions about the quantitative behavior of the variables considered.

Figure 14–1 presents twenty-six estimates of energy use forecast for the year 1980. The estimates are from many sources and represent a wide variety of methods and models. If the estimates are separated and compared according to the year in which they were made, none differs from other contemporary forecasts by as much as a factor of 2. The trend in recent years toward higher values for the 1980 estimates is clearly seen. With one exception, forecasts made as recently as 1972 show nearly as much scatter as ones made earlier. This probably reflects differences in the assumed effect of related variables and their future magnitude. In any case, comparison of actual energy use with the forecasts strongly suggests that, despite the method used, earlier forecasts reflect the usage of the late 1950s and early 1960s, and later forecasts strongly reflect the increased energy use experienced in the late 1960s.

One forecast in figure 14–1 predicts a range of possible values for 1980. This is not a measure of uncertainty in the usual sense. Such a forecast is a contingency forecast, that is, one which tests several values

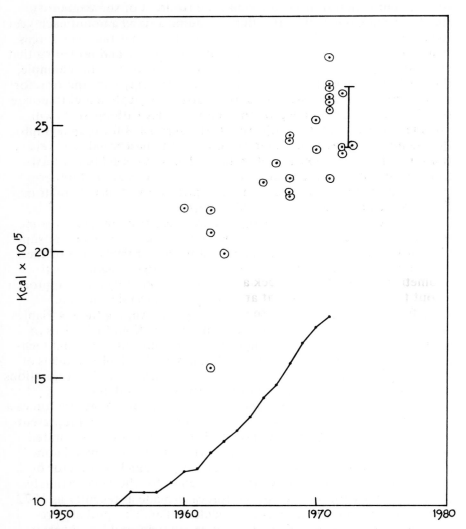

Figure 14–1. A published forecast of energy use. Twenty-six forecasts of U.S. energy use for 1980, compared with actual energy use. Forecasts are plotted according to their year of publication. Sources: U.S., Congress, House, Committee on Interior and Insular Affairs, *Energy "Demand" Studies: An Analysis and Appraisal* (Washington, D.C., 1972); Battelle Memorial Institute, *A Review and Comparison of Selected United States Energy Forecasts* (Washington, D.C., 1969); U.S., Department of the Interior, *United States Energy Through the Year 2000* (Washington, D.C., 1972); Shell Oil Company, *The U.S. Energy Position* (Shell Oil Co., 1971).

of the related variables (GNP growth rates, technology changes, population growth, and so on) and estimates the results of the various combinations. Such estimates are sometimes requested by policymakers to
assess the effects of various policy changes.

Figure 14–2 presents thirteen forecasts of energy use for the
year 2000. As might be expected, these forecasts vary more than do
those for 1980. The trend toward higher estimates reflects the recent
acceleration in energy use. This suggests that — as in the 1980 forecasts — recent experience is the most heavily weighted.

The matter of estimates of future consumption cannot be
treated here with the depth needed. At present, extensive efforts are
underway to provide more reliable estimates. These efforts should be
encouraged, but with the understanding that forecasts can become self-
fulfilling prophecies. A considerable amount of skepticism is warranted,
even required, until the conceptual problems are solved, if indeed they

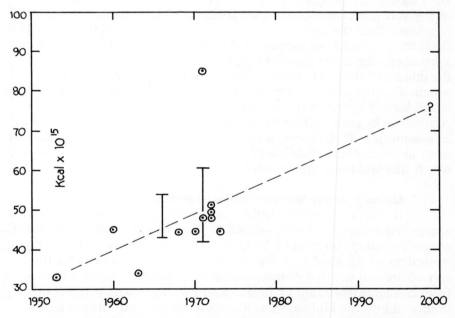

Figure 14–2. Thirteen forecasts of U.S. energy use for the year 2000. Forecasts are
plotted according to their year of publication. Trend line is suggestive only. Sources:
U.S., Congress, House, Committee on Interior and Insular Affairs, *Energy "Demand"
Studies: An Analysis and Appraisal* (Washington, D.C., 1972); Battelle Memorial
Institute, *A Review and Comparison of Selected United States Energy Forecasts*
(Washington, D.C., 1969); U.S., Department of the Interior, *United States Energy
Through the Year 2000* (Washington, D.C., 1972); Shell Oil Company, *The U.S.
Energy Position* (Shell Oil Co., 1971).

ever can be. Meanwhile, the work should continue, for one cause of the shortage of electrical generating capacities in the early 1970s was that future needs were underestimated at the time new capacity was planned.

ENERGY NEEDS OF THE FUTURE WORLD

Throughout this book we have concentrated on fuels and energy supply for the United States. But we in the United States cannot operate as if the remainder of the world will fit smoothly into whatever plans we choose. Policies of other nations are of crucial importance to our fuel supply (and for our supply of other mineral resources as well). Internal policies of other nations are made with their own needs in mind, not ours, and to begin to estimate the future for the United States requires a hard look at the future situation for the world. Figure 14–3 shows very clearly that changes are in store. Without projections of any sort it is clear that the past course of development must and will be altered. Even the optimistic estimates in figure 14–3 demonstrate that fossil fuels, which have supplied the bulk of the world's energy for three generations, are inadequate to supply the world's needs much beyond the middle of the next century. But projections of past experience assume that the present imbalances in distribution of goods and services which leave 80 percent of the world's population at poverty level will continue. The poor nations of the world are not willing to accept such an assumption. If allowance is made for their attempts at rapid improvement in the material standard of living for their citizens, and the energy which that will take, the crunch for energy becomes even clearer.

Minimum Energy Requirements for a Satisfactory Life

It is easy enough to declare an absolute per capita minimum for energy requirements. For thousands of years people lived at a personal energy consumption level of 2500 to 3000 kcal per day — the energy equivalent of the food they hunted and gathered. With the advent of agriculture and the first domestic animals, per capita energy use grew from this level to 10,000 to 15,000 kcal per day, where it remained until well into the Middle Ages. But these limits are of little interest today — although much of the world has yet to exceed them — because we cannot, at present population levels, recover those past conditions even if we should wish to do so.

We know of only one effort to estimate the minimum energy necessary to provide a satisfactory life. Everett Hafner has produced such an estimate.[2] For production of food, 300 watts' continuous expenditure is allowed, or about 6200 kcal per day. In the light of the

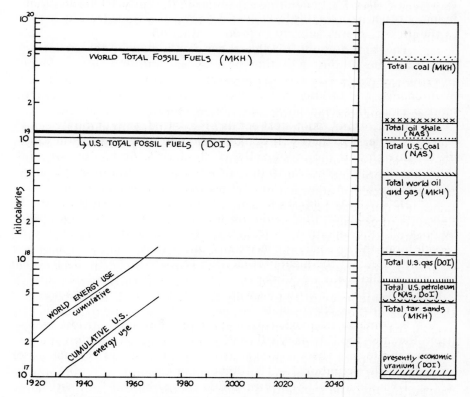

Key: DOI: estimate in U.S., Department of Interior, *United States Energy, A Summary Review* (Washington, D.C., 1972).

MKH: estimate in M.K. Hubbert, "Energy Resources for Power Production," in International Atomic Energy Agency Symposium on Environmental Aspects of Nuclear Power Stations (Vienna, 1971).

NAS: National Academy of Sciences, Man, Materials, Environment: A Report to the National Commission on Materials Policy (Washington, D.C., 1973).

Figure 14–3. Cumulative world and U.S. energy use is compared to total fossil fuel resources and totals of some of the component resources. These estimates include submarginal resources not now exploitable. Note that nearly 90 percent of total fossil fuel resources are coal. Other sources: U.S. energy use: S.H. Schurr and B.C. Netschert, *Energy in the American Economy, 1850–1975* (Baltimore: Johns Hopkins Press, 1960); U.S., Department of the Interior, *United States Energy Through the Year 2000* (Washington, D.C., 1972); World Energy use: J. Darmstadter et al., *Energy in the World Economy* (Baltimore: Johns Hopkins Press, 1971).

food-energy relations described in chapter 6, this energy subsidy would be approximated by 1920s levels in the United States food system, but in many other nations this level would represent a considerable increase of the present energy subsidy to food production.

The same amount, 6200 kcal per day, is allowed for shelter. Hafner assumes a housing lifetime of ten years, and thus this level would represent 30 man-years of effort to provide for original construction, maintenance, and utilities. Since houses customarily provide for two or more persons, this seems like a plausible amount.

For clothing, 2065 kcal per day is allotted. This amount seems generous, at least in theory. It could be thought of as one person working for three months to produce the raw materials and another working three months each year just to provide a wardrobe for a single person. Our present clothing energy expenditures do not exceed this amount.

Hafner allows 4130 kcal per day for transportation. At present transport efficiencies, this would mean an average of 14 miles per day by bus or 17 miles per day by train (or even 92 miles per day by bicycle), but the one-man-one-car transportation system could not be accommodated. At the higher efficiencies that are theoretically possible, the mileage allotment would rise to 50 miles per day by public transport. Clearly, Hafner's estimates would work only if we could revise our present practices in city design.

Beyond the basic necessities are many things: education, recreation, the arts, and the many other ways of seeking satisfaction and meaning in life. For these leisure activities, Hafner allows as much as for food and shelter combined — 12,400 kcal per day.

To summarize Hafner's minimum energy budget for a satisfactory life:

Food	6,200 kcal/day
Housing	6,200 kcal/day
Clothing	2,065 kcal/day
Transportation	4,130 kcal/day
Leisure	12,400 kcal/day
Total	30,995 kcal/person/day

This total of about 31,000 kcal per day is not the only such budget that could be devised. By contrast, present per capita energy use in the United States is about six times as large as in the Hafner minimum. Clearly, more work is needed in this area to find out, even theoretically, what is required for a livable society.

How Much Energy Does the World Need?

At what levels of energy consumption is life tolerable for everyone? When that question is answered, we must redirect our pattern of energy use so that the desirable level of energy consumption can be reached by everyone. There are extensive political disputes about how much we should assist the poor countries in reaching a higher standard of living. If the rich industrialized countries adopt policies for growth and energy use which foreclose the supply of energy, then arguments about assistance for the poor of the world are just ritualized words. So, on at least two accounts we need to take the above question seriously: first, because our aspirations as human beings and as a nation depend on the possibility of an opportunity for a better world; and second, because a world in which a majority of the population has no chance of achieving a decent standard of living is, almost without question, a world ripe for intolerable conflict.

Figure 14–4 summarizes some of the possibilities. Future population levels used in calculating figure 14–4 represent the medium projection of the United Nations. It is interesting that actual world energy consumption crossed the Hafner minimum in the early 1960s. The future increases in Hafner's minimum were meant to reflect only future population increase. Thus the actual world increases indicate the expanding average per capita usage more than population growth (just as is the case in the United States, where three-fourths of the growth in energy use represents per capita increases). In many areas of the world the expansion in per capita energy use reflects the improved conditions under which many more people live. Thus we should not be surprised to find energy use increasing faster than population in poor nations, for it accompanies any improvement in their standard of living.

But the matter is quite different for the industrialized nations. As we tried to show in chapter 11, much of the increase in per capita energy consumption reflects an elaboration of standard of living for people already well off even by United States standards. Some of this increase, such as the continuing enlargement of auto engines, appears absolutely pointless. The endless expansion of per capita energy consumption by the well-to-do must stop. This need not result in an end to social improvement (as some have suggested) or repression of individual choice. A program to inhibit growth in per capita usage by those with an adequate standard of living could include some or all of the following measures: 1) Increased energy prices to reflect the true costs of energy production – including the environmental costs. 2) An end to tax subsidies to the energy industry. This would be reflected in increased energy prices, and thereby the consumer would be offered a clearer choice of how much energy he wishes to purchase. 3) The choice of rate structures for electricity, gas, and possibly other fuels to provide increased costs for large users whether residential, commercial or industrial. In principle, rapidly escalating rate structures for large users can be chosen to obtain any decrease in usage desired. 4) Tax incentives or government assistance programs to encourage expenditures for

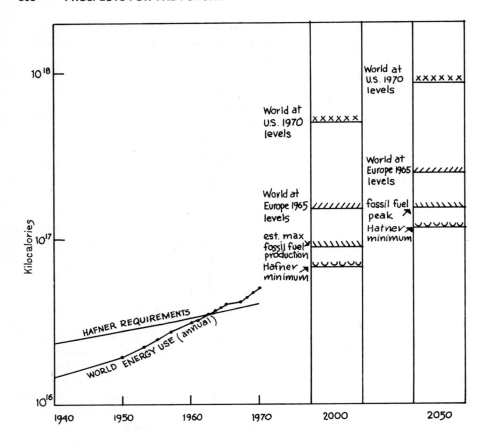

Figure 14-4. Comparison of actual world energy use and requirements of the Hafner minimum. Projections for the years 2000 and 2050 were calculated on the basis of medium United Nations population estimates. World requirements at the per capita use levels of Europe, 1965 and the United States, 1970 were calculated on the basis of the same population projections. Estimated maximum fossil fuel levels are shown for comparison. Sources: S.H. Schurr and B.C. Netschert, *Energy in the American Economy, 1850-1975* (Baltimore: Johns Hopkins Press, 1960); U.S., Department of the Interior, *United States Energy Through the Year 2000* (Washington, D.C., 1972); J. Darmstadter, *Energy in the World Economy* (Baltimore: Johns Hopkins Press, 1971).

energy conservation (such as better insulation, fewer energy-intensive industrial practices, and the like). 5) Direct regulation or control of expanding energy uses which are unresponsive to other measures (for example, the growing size of automobiles). 6) Promotion of low-energy options for transportation and a halt to subsidies for energy-consumptive transportation. This would require mass transit and efforts at urban

redesign. Urban rebuilding will take time, but the present growth rate of urban populations suggests our urban areas will nearly double in the next thirty years, providing an opportunity to improve many items.
7) Tax incentives or direct subsidies to encourage the installation of non-fuel energy systems (such as solar space and hot water heating, windmills, garbage burners, methane generators from garbage, and so on).

Some of the above measures do place restrictions on people, but we must learn, sooner or later, that restriction accompanies a technologically complex society. There is ample individual choice remaining in the above measures. Only the first two items are regressive. If they interfere with social gains, the situation can be remedied with tax or subsidy measures. Maintaining false prices for energy is not the best road to social improvement. Many European countries have done at least as well as the United States in promoting a better standard of living for the poor, although European energy prices have usually been higher than ours.

The question of how much energy the world needs thus cannot be answered directly. Figure 14–4 shows some possibilities for the years 2000 and 2050, based upon the median estimates for world population on those dates. While the undeveloped nations of the world struggle with their many problems, the advanced nations can and should strive to inhibit further growth in per capita energy use. There seems to be no technical reason why energy cannot be supplied at any of the levels shown.

A Middle Class World

The larger estimates of energy needs in figure 14–4 imply a middle class world on the average. It does not necessarily mean a drably uniform distribution. With an average energy use at the level of 1965 Europe, considerable diversity would be possible, with the lowest energy use levels still offering an adequate standard of living.

All of this should not be taken to suggest that we can achieve these levels in fifty or even one hundred years. The poor nations face staggering problems, of which energy supply is far from the most pressing. Glenn Seaborg, Nobel laureate and former chairman of the Atomic Energy Commission, gives a good example of the proportions of their difficulties by noting that just in the next decade they face the problem of providing new jobs for 300,000 people each week. To do this he suggests their best strategy may be more labor-intensive and less capital-intensive (and energy-intensive) industrial development, including more labor-intensive agriculture.[3] Labor-intensive industries and agriculture can be just as productive as the more energy-intensive kinds (see chapter 6). But if the advanced nations continue blindly to increase their energy consumption, they will eventually foreclose the chances of the poor nations.

The Ultimate Limits to Energy Use

The ultimate limits to the admittedly finite capacities of the earth have been a subject of fascination and dispute at least since the time of Malthus, 150 years ago. We know well enough that the limits are there, but the attempts to specify the earliest limits the world might encounter have been inconclusive. It is easy to specify some limits that cannot be exceeded. For example, when the production and transport of fuel to its final use requires more energy than is originally available in the fuel, we will have reached one of these limits. Similarly, when the flux of man's energy use approaches the flux of solar energy driving the physical phenomena of the planet, we will be in serious difficulty. Energy use at this level in a few centuries could be predicted on the basis of simple extrapolations of the growth of the past century and a half. But it seems quite clear that we will not continue to that particular fate (such an extrapolation would include a world population more than 100 times as large as the present one). Figure 14–3 presents this view of limits for the fossil fuels. It summons up the vision of the cumulative energy use of the world colliding with the fossil fuel limits. But long before that could occur, costs, difficulties of extraction, pollution loads, and other problems will cause a lessening in the use of fossil fuels.

We must conclude that, for the present, the dispute about what limitations we will first encounter for total energy use is not resolvable. In earlier chapters we have tried to display the extent of this dispute as it relates to climate modification, pollution loading and other possible limits. Limits do exist, and any prudent person would do well to anticipate the worst — and be pleasantly surprised if the larger limits turn out to be correct. The distant future, about which we can estimate little, will probably be better off if we adopt that strategy. It seems unlikely, on the basis of past experience, that we will encounter ultimate limits in a great cataclysm.

The argument about limits to energy use (and other ultimate limits to growth, for that matter) should be watched closely. For anyone outside the narrow circle of anointed experts, the technical issues are difficult or impossible to unravel — depending, as they often do, upon fine technical points or complicated models. Nevertheless, there are several common forms of argument against which anyone can be on guard. Those who argue that there are no real limits often erect a "straw man" limit and then knock it down to prove that there are no limits. One expert, for example, points out that at one hundred times the present level of energy consumption, we would only be using, and releasing, 0.4 percent of the solar energy budget.[4] But this is more energy than drives all the winds and circulation of the atmosphere, and it would be released in highly concentrated areas — not uniformly over the surface of the earth. We cannot say whether this level of energy use would be intolerable, but the argument above does not prove anything at all. Similar overstatements and unsupportable arguments are offered by the prophets of impending doom — with similar assurance. Until these arguments about limits can be resolved (which may take a very long time), we are forced to plan a strategy in the absence of complete information. In such cases, the only sane strategy is a conservative one. The penalty for overestimating the supplies is so great that erring by underestimating the size of the energy supply is a safe, if inconvenient, alternative to disaster. As long as innovation continues with this strategy in mind, there is no reason why social goals need be limited by the availability of energy. A world operating at average 1965 European levels (or even 1970 United States levels) of energy use should be more than comfortable. There is no technical reason why such a strategy cannot proceed. If the world's institutions cannot adapt to these conditions, we are probably undone.

THE LONG-RANGE SUPPLY OPTIONS

In chapters 7, 8, and 9 we outlined in some detail the present status and future prospects for the main energy sources. Those matters will not be repeated here, but it is appropriate to make a summary comparison of our future technical options and estimate how those options might serve us in a future more distant than the 10 to 50 year periods for which estimates are most often made. As indicated above, precise estimates of future levels of use or need are not yet possible, but we do know that world energy consumption will continue to increase for some time and that decisions made in the next few decades may have consequences that extend for several thousand years into the future. In these cases, we must make the best evaluation we can despite the uncertainties.

One message from figure 14–3 is that the world will change its main source of fuel or its growth pattern or both. From the point of view of energy supply, there are several options. Because of the fundamentality of energy as a primary input to modern society, the choice among these options is vastly more than a simple engineering or technical choice. Upon this choice, and several others, may depend the very texture of future society. Nevertheless, we must postpone such speculation for yet another moment to summarize some of what has been said along the way about the technical alternatives.

Coal and Other Hydrocarbons

As we have tried to demonstrate, large-scale dependence on liquid petroleum and natural gas is even now, before the peak of world production, coming to a close. It will not do so with the clanging discontinuity implied by simple extrapolation of the cumulative use lines on figure 14–3 — at least not on technical or economic grounds, for the enterprises that manufacture a host of materials from petroleum and natural gas can and will pay higher prices. Even among fuel users, those not easily shifted away from petroleum and natural gas will have to pay higher prices. Cumulative world and United States energy use is likely to pass beyond the limits on the right of figure 14–3 not by exhausting them in succession, but by diverting the remaining supply into the uses which can bear the highest prices.

But the situation for coal is somewhat different. We are still so far from the coal limits — or, more accurately, so early in the total production curve — that we could shift the world to a coal-based economy and continue past growth rates for a few decades, or perhaps for a few centuries, before encountering stringent limits based on availability alone. Table 14–1, which summarizes the future options briefly, shows several reasons why this is not an attractive idea. First, the pollutants associated with coal are troublesome. This pollution is not beyond hope of technological control, but this effort itself will require expenditure of still more energy, and always with the guaranteed failure of achieving complete control. Second, the distribution of coal in the world is not suitable for the present distribution of political control, and the possible conflict over control of energy supplies encourages the same strains that have riddled the past with endless wars. Third, the supply of coal represents the raw material, as a substitute for oil and gas, for many kinds of manufactured chemicals and other goods. We may very well wish to expand (or we may have to expand) our use of coal during the transition to a new mix of energy supplies, but it should be with the understanding that it is only a temporary measure.

Breeder Reactors

For many years the United States has set its hopes for long-range energy supply on the breeder reactor. Problems have arisen and been solved, only to have others arise. Meanwhile the early estimates of cost have doubled and then doubled again. It should be stated here that there are no technical problems that are clearly beyond solution, but there are problems about which there is vigorous dispute. These disputes — between men of considerable understanding of what they are talking about — usually revolve about whether solutions will be too costly in money or dislocation of society or both.

Starting with the observation that the present generation of burner reactors cannot be sustained in the long run without the un-imaginable destruction inherent in pursuing ever lower grade uranium ores (and perhaps not even then), we can summarize the main questions remaining about breeder reactors. First are questions about safety. The penalties for a major accident are great. While no accident rate can ever be reduced to zero, nagging fears about the safety of present and pro-jected plans persist. Second, the storage of nuclear wastes and radio-active materials from abandoned plants will be a problem for thousands of years. We are unsure that we can or should make such a commitment on behalf of future society. Third, the widespread availability of plu-tonium from breeders endangers society with purposeful damage from the maniacal fringe. Even nations from time to time display a kind of madness. Widespread production of plutonium, in the opinion of some, could plunge us into a nuclear nightmare.

It is too early to say the final word on the breeder because the extensive experience that might resolve some of the uncertainties is not available. It would be foolish to discontinue work on breeder re-actors at this time or until there are other assured energy sources. It would be even more foolish to place sole reliance, or even primary reliance, on breeder technology until there is a resolution of the present disputes.

Fusion and Solar Conversion

By placing these two possibilities side by side the extremes of the options open to us can be shown. Although table 14–1 summarizes the facts, several points require emphasis. Perhaps because direct solar conversion and nuclear fusion are often talked of as options for the distant future, the idea is often conveyed that they present equally dif-ficult and possibly unsolvable technical questions. As we explained in chapter 8, the fundamental problems of a sustained, controlled fusion reaction are far from solved. Until there is a workable laboratory scheme, all of the engineering problems cannot be specified in detail. But since the operating conditions for a fusion reaction can be speci-fied, some engineering analysis has been done and the problems appear staggering although not beyond the range of possible solution. Resource problems may arise in connection with the engineering solutions, even if the basic problems of sustained fusion reaction are solved.

The situation for solar conversion is quite different. There are no basic research problems to be solved, nor do complex engineering difficulties remain. The only problem with solar energy conversion is that it is thought to be too expensive. Both basic research and engineer-ing improvements could be of great help in reducing the cost, but even at the present cost it may become economically competitive, depending on how high conventional energy costs (including environmental costs)

Table 14-1. Long-range Energy Sources

	Supply Available	World Distribution	Environmental Problems		Basic Research Required	Engineering Development Needed	Scarce Resource Requirements
			Pollutants[1]	Land Use			
Coal	5×10^{19} kcal	Spotty. Some areas with little or none.	SO_x, CO_x, NO_x, particulates trace elements	Extensive and possibly destructive from mining, power stations, and storage	None[2]	Cheaper methods of gasification and liquefaction	None
Breeder Reactors	Very large	Widespread (but some areas with very low grade ores)	Radiation release from accidents, transport, or storage	Extensive for mining, processing, and storage and disposal of waste	None	Several large scale engineering improvements needed. Especially for transport and storage safety.	None
Fusion Reactors (^{2}H-^{2}H type)	Very large[3]	Widespread (requires ocean access)	None; but plant and/or coolant may become radioactive	Uncertain, probably less than above	Several unsolved and possibly unsolvable problems	Many difficult engineering problems	Niobium or[3] several other scarce minerals have been suggested by some designers
Local Solar Conversion	Very large	Everywhere	None	Minimal	None	Engineering for cost reduction for converters[4]	None
Central Solar Conversion	Very large	Everywhere	None	Extensive, probably larger than breeders or fusion; but not destructive	None	Engineering for cost reduction for converters and energy storage[4]	None

1. All methods except local solar conversion generate thermal pollution. Nuclear reactors have a larger heat disposal problem than coal-fired power plants. The amount from fusion reactors and central solar converters is not certain until the technology is specified, but could be largest of all.

2. Engineering and perhaps some basic research associated with removal of pollutants are required, especially for SO_x. It is not clear whether new research and new methods or better engineering of existing methods are required. These problems apply to oil as well as coal.

3. If fusion reactors of the lithium-deuterium type are developed, rather than the deuterium-deuterium type, lithium resources may be sharply limiting for fusion power.

4. Photovoltaic conversion would be more attractive if large cost reduction (by 10 to 100) could be obtained. Some could come from large-scale industrial production of solar cells, but research and engineering breakthroughs may be needed. New or improved energy storage methods are needed if solar conversion to electricity is undertaken.

rise. It is probable that solar energy costs could be reduced simply from mass production savings in unit cost.

As table 14–1 shows, there are two kinds of direct solar energy conversion in question. Local conversion for space heating and hot water heating is done now — more widely in other countries than in the United States. it has been shown to be competitive with residential electric heating at 1970 energy prices in places as far north as Boston. Its competitive position will only improve as energy prices increase,[5] even if there are no cost reductions for solar heating units. Experience suggests that, by putting such conversion units into mass production, price can be reduced by a factor of 2 to 5.

For central solar conversion the engineering problems associated with energy storage need work, but even without dramatic progress there, we could use the energy to produce hydrogen, which is a satisfactory, and environmentally clean, fuel. Roger Schmidt of Honeywell, appearing before the House Science and Astronautics subcommittee, estimated that within ten years costs for solar units will be about one thousand dollars per kilowatt of installed electric capacity. This is about twice the present cost of burner reactors, and the breeders will cost even more. For 1973, estimates of the cost of the prototype breeder reactor were two thousand dollars per kilowatt (about double the early 1972 estimates).[6]

There are two less obvious advantages of direct conversion of solar energy. First, it is a low technology option. The poor nations, which often have limited technical capacities, could use this energy source without dependence on the technology of the advanced countries. Second, since the land area involved in solar conversion (of the central station type) is proportional to the energy wanted, there is a built-in warning system for society when energy use begins to get on toward the misty, but real, ultimate limits. By contrast, a successful fusion reactor, located on the sea bottom (more science fiction than plan at the moment), is out of sight and out of mind. In that case, the past suggests that the first notice of too much energy use will come from nature — possibly in the form of disastrous change.

Finally, fusion energy represents the conditions on the sun. We have no real idea how difficult or undesirable it might be to transfer those conditions to the earth even on a small scale (if you can call the world's energy supply a small scale). But the sun is its own fusion reactor and solar energy rains down upon all of us. If it is a little more work to collect it, or even a little more expensive, at least we know what we are doing. From a functional point of view, we will be taking a lesson from the green plants. We will photosynthesize, although not with chlorophyll.

If we, as authors, have a bias, it is for solar energy. We state it without shyness for the reasons outlined above. The level of work on this energy source is expanding, but should be expanded still faster. Work on fusion should continue as well, but the clear priority for direct solar conversion should be made clear. At a more distant time in the future, society may find it advantageous to use all of the above sources for special applications, and it would be foolish to discard the options until some insoluble problem is encountered in the technical work. But it is even more foolish to burden the same distant future with endless streams of nuclear waste if we need not, or to wait upon fusion, like Mr. Micawber, confident that "something will turn up."

Diversity for the Future
We have pointed out that future options should be left open, even if there are unsolved technical problems with some of the options. Remembering the value of diversity to survival in natural systems, we should plan our future energy supplies to include some of the smaller sources — wind, falling water, geothermal sources, waste burning, biological sources, and so on — in the places where they are available and appropriate. Because some of these smaller sources are local, they do not require the large-scale complexity of the proposed giant nuclear complexes, for example. If the ever increasing complexity of society is not a mortal danger (as some have warned), neither is it an attractive feature to be sought after. Choosing simple technologies when possible and aiming for simplicity of technical means is not a retreat to the past. Choices for simplicity, and maintenance of diversity, could and should be the hope for a more satisfying and understandable world of the future.

Change continues, but we should not look to the business world, especially the energy companies, for leadership. With their horizontal and vertical control of the main sources of fuel (chapter 13) we cannot expect them to urge new choices. The competitive market of classical economics has long since vanished from the energy field and even inter-fuel competition is vanishing before the wave of mergers and expansion. The industry seeks to reduce what remaining risks it faces through public subsidy. General Electric suggests subsidies may be needed to make breeder reactors "competitive," and the AEC obligingly puts money in its budget in the event that it becomes necessary to pay such subsidies.[6]

Energy and the Environment
Along the way we have said much about the environmental risks and uncertainties associated with energy use. In a larger sense,

there are only two things to do with unwanted byproducts of society's activities: we will either reuse our pollutants or live with them diluted into the environment around us.

For energy and fuel use, there are two classes of pollutants — the various chemical and radioactive materials, and heat. For the first class, technical means can convert air pollution to solid waste or otherwise capture the unwanted residual, but it does not go away. If we cannot reuse it, we must store it or dump it somewhere. The second item, heat, will be produced and released as the inevitable consequence of energy use. Where and under what circumstances it is released will determine whether and when it becomes a problem. Ultimately — if growth in energy use continues — it will become a problem; first on a local or regional basis, and later on a worldwide scale. It should be high on our priority list to learn, as accurately as possible, when and under what circumstances these problems may beset us.

There are other environmental difficulties. Amount of land used for fuel production and energy conversion and distribution is already a problem in some areas. Such conflicts in land use can be expected to worsen as long as the growth in energy use continues. More than land use is at stake. The attractiveness of our surroundings is also involved. Oil refineries, strip mines, power lines or electric utilities are not attractive neighbors, yet more and more of us will find one of these next door as energy grows.

Any program that lessens the growth rate in energy use, that saves energy, or makes possible a satisfactory life without escalating energy use will be reflected in the diminution of the above problems.

Energy for Simplicity and Elegance

We cannot now conclude for doomsday or utopia. The future holds uncertainty and change — and neither more nor less can be said at present.

At the end of his life, Immanuel Kant said that he was still plagued by three questions. They were: What may I know? What may I hope? and What ought I to do? At the profound level that Kant meant these questions, we cannot answer, but in a narrower context we can make some response.

We know that the fossil fuels will diminish in quantity and will eventually cease to be used as fuels. With adequate work we can know when. We know that growth in the production of goods will cease at some time. We can know (but do not at present) when we must prepare for that time. We know that world energy use will level off or decline at some time in the future. We can know — more accurately than at present — when and to what extent. We know that there is no escape from our problems through increased efficiency. We know we will change. We can know how to make those changes in ways that will economize on energy use and still maintain a satisfactory life.

We may hope for a livable world without a warning and a threat from every look at the near future. We may hope for levels of energy use that make the opportunity for a decent standard of living for everyone a reality. If these hopes can be realized, we may then hope for our individual, private visions of a better world.

What we ought to do is to talk frankly and unashamedly about our hopes for the future — to anyone who will listen. What we ought to do is to seek simplicity and economy of means in the face of complexity. We ought to learn from the past but not seek to return to it. We ought to hold the aims of our own lives to ourselves and not surrender our dreams to the imperatives of faceless experts. For energy specifically, we ought to seek help from the solar energy falling upon us, but not rule out other options for our future.

We — your authors — were trained as scientists. The finest achievements of science have been marked by simplicity and elegance. It has never been the goal of science to find just any explanation of the phenomena of the world around us. The explanations that have enriched understanding are the simple ones, whose very economy of means, exhibit the elegance of which we speak. The world does not now have the option of discarding technology. Innovation must continue — more in institutions, perhaps, than in things — but it need not generate ever more complexity and growth. If the innovation is guided by the search for simplicity and economy of means in solving our problems, we may yet find it possible for individual life to be dignified and satisfying — for everyone.

REFERENCES

1. "Blueprint for Survival," *The Ecologist* 2 (1972): 1–43.
2. E. Hafner, *An Energy Budget,* mimeographed (Hampshire College, 1971).
3. G. T. Seaborg, "Science, Technology and Development: A New World Outlook," *Science* 181 (1973): 13–19.
4. P. Sporn, "Possible Impacts of Environmental Standards on Electric Power Availability and Costs," in *Energy, Economic Growth, and the Environment,* ed. S. Schurr (Baltimore: Johns Hopkins Press, 1972), pp. 69–88.
5. R. A. Tybout and G. O. G. Löf, "Solar House Heating," *Natural Resource Journal* 10 (1970): 268–326.
6. R. Gillette, "One Breeder for the Price of Two?," *Science* 182 (1973): 38.

APPENDIX A

1. UNITS AND CONVERSION FACTORS

Energy

kcal = kilocalorie = 10^3 calories; kwh = kilowatt-hour = 10^3 watt-hours

1 watt-hour = 10^{-3} kwh

1 calorie* = 10^{-3} kcal

1 Q = 10^{18} BTU = 2.52×10^{17} kcal

1 therm = 10^5 BTU = 2.52×10^4 kcal

*Note: The term Calorie used in discussions of food is equal to the kilo-calorie of physics used in the table on the following page.

Power

kw = kilowatt = 10^3 watts; HP = horsepower; kcal/s = kilocalorie per second

1 kcal/s = 4.186 kw = 5.615 HP

1 HP = 0.178 kcal/s = 0.7455 kw

1 kw = 0.239 kcal/s = 1.341 HP

1 megawatt = 10^6 watts = 10^3 kw

Length

m = meter; cm = centimeter; mi = mile; ft = ft = foot; in = inch; km = kilometer

1m = 39.37 in = 3.281 ft

1 cm = 10^{-2} m

1 ft = .3048 m

1 m = 2.54×10^{-2} m

1 km = 10^3 m

1 mi = 1.609×10^3 m

Area

1 m^2 = 10^4 cm^2 = 10.76 ft^2

1 cm^2 = 10^{-4} m^2

1 in^2 = 6.452×10^{-4} m^2

1 km^2 = 10^6 m^2

1 mi^2 = 2.59×10^6 m^2

1 ft^2 = 0.0929 m^2

1 hectare = 10^4 m^2 = 2.471 acres

1 acre = 4.047×10^3 m^2

Table A–1. Conversion Table for Common Energy Units

$\downarrow$ From To $\rightarrow$	Kilocalorie	Kilowatt-hour	Joule	Erg	BTU	Mev
Kilocalorie	1	1.162×10^{-3}	4.184×10^3	4.184×10^{10}	3.967	2.612×10^{16}
Kilowatt-hour	860.4	1	3.60×10^6	3.60×10^{13}	3.413×10^3	2.247×10^{19}
Joule	2.39×10^{-4}	2.778×10^{-7}	1	10^7	9.48×10^{-4}	6.242×10^5
Erg	2.39×10^{-11}	2.778×10^{-14}	10^{-7}	1	9.48×10^{-11}	6.242×10^{12}
BTU (British Thermal Unit)	0.252	2.93×10^{-4}	1.055×10^3	1.055×10^{10}	1	6.584×10^{15}
Mev	3.829×10^{-17}	4.45×10^{-20}	1.602×10^{-13}	1.602×10^{-6}	1.519×10^{-16}	1

Volume

1 m³ = 35.31 ft³ = 10³ liters
1 liter = 1.057 quarts = 10⁻³ m³
1 U.S. gallon = 3.785 liters
1 in³ = 16.39 × 10⁻⁶ m³
1 ft³ = 0.02832 m³
1 barrel = 42 U.S. gallons = 0.159 m³
1 acre-ft = 4.356 × 10⁴ ft³ = 1233.5 m³
1 imperial gallon = 4.546 liters = 4.546 × 10³ m

Mass and Weight

kg. = kilogram; gm = gram; lb = pound; oz = ounce
1 kg = 1000 gm = 2.205 lbs
1 gm = 10⁻³ kg
1 oz = 28.35 gms
1 lb = 0.4536 kg = 16 oz
1 ton = 2000 lbs = 907.2 kg
1 long ton = 1016 kg = 2240 lbs
1 metric ton = 100 kg

Temperature

°C = degrees Celsius (or centigrade); °K = degrees Kelvin;
°F = degrees Fahrenheit
0.0°C = 32°F = 273° K
conversion   °C = 5/9 (°F − 32) = °K − 273
              °F = 9/5 °C + 32
              °K = °C + 273

2. HEAT VALUES OF COMMON FUELS

Average values of energy (heat) content of fuels used in this book are as follows:

1 metric ton coal = 7.06 × 10⁶ kcal
1 ton coal   = 6.60 × 10⁶ kcal
1 barrel oil   = 1.46 × 10⁶ kcal
1 gallon gasoline = 3.48 × 10⁴ kcal
1 cubic foot gas = 261 kcal

Actual heat content of fuels varies according to the grade, type of refinery product and chemical composition. This table gives some average heat values for common fuels. Actual heat values vary from deposit to deposit because of differences in chemical composition and kind of processing, so that even these values should be considered as typical rather than exact.

bituminous coal	1 ton = 6.60×10^6 kcal
anthracite coal	1 ton = 6.35×10^6 kcal
lignite	1 ton = 3.0×10^6 kcal
peat	1 ton = 2.6×10^6 kcal
gasoline	1 gallon = 3.13×10^4 kcal
diesel oil (includes #1 and #2 fuel oil)	1 gallon = 3.43×10^4 kcal
kerosene (includes jet fuel)	1 gallon = 3.40×10^4 kcal
heating oil #3	1 gallon = 3.53×10^4 kcal
#4	1 gallon = 3.65×10^4 kcal
#5	1 gallon = 3.74×10^4 kcal
#6 (includes residual)	1 gallon = 3.83×10^4 kcal
refinery gas (still gas)	1 cubic foot = 378 kcal
natural gas	1 cubic foot = 261 kcal
propane	1 cubic foot = 635 kcal
butane	1 cubic foot = 821 kcal

Photosynthesis and Respiration

Factors Affecting the Rate of Photosynthesis

Many things, including carbon dioxide concentration, temperature, light, nutrients, and water, may limit the amount of energy photosynthesis can store.

All other conditions being favorable, most plants will photosynthesize more rapidly if the ambient concentration of CO_2 is increased. On a bright, warm, windless day when adequate moisture and mineral nutrients are available, CO_2 becomes a strongly limiting factor.

Tropical soils are often poor in quality and low in essential nutrients. Light, too, is at a premium because of the dense growth. Far to the north and south, low temperatures restrict photosynthesis to the point where plants barely maintain themselves, even though the long days of summer are very long indeed.

Light penetrates the ocean to a depth of only 20 or 30 meters, clamping a firm upper limit on the productivity of the seas. Within the limits imposed by light, the temperature, nutrients, and the turnover of waters determine the actual rate of photosynthesis in the sea.

Finally, in arid regions water restricts photosynthesis. Most of the adaptations that permit desert plants to survive in their stern habitat also insure that growth, metabolism, and gaseous exchange will be minimal.

Photosynthesis and Respiration:
Energy Storage and Release

In their net results, photosynthesis and respiration are exactly opposite processes. In photosynthesis, energy is stored, carbon dioxide is reduced to carbohydrate, and oxygen is released: $6CO_2 + 12H_2O$ + energy $\rightarrow C_6H_{12}O_6 + 6H_2O + 6O_2$. (The balanced equation must be written showing water on both sides because all the liberated oxygen comes from water.) In respiration, energy is released, carbohydrate is oxidized to carbon dioxide, and oxygen is consumed: $C_6H_{12}O_6 + 6O_2 \rightarrow 6CO_2 + 6H_2O$ + energy. The intermediate steps in the two processes are dissimilar, however. They occur in different subcellular structures where all the necessary enzymes and reactants are efficiently packaged: photosynthesis takes place in chloroplasts and respiration occurs in mitochondria.

Both processes involve the passage of electrons from molecule to molecule along an electron transport chain. Powered by sunlight, electrons gain energy and move "uphill" in photosynthesis, thus escaping from molecules that hold them very tightly. When such a molecule loses an electron it becomes a strong oxidizing agent — strong enough even to oxidize water, which is what happens in photosynthesis. (Water is hydrogen that has been burned. To reverse the burning process is no small achievement.) At other steps along the electron transport chain, energetic molecules called ATP are built. These molecules, along with others bearing the hydrogen from the splitting of water, move into the Calvin cycle where their energy becomes stored in the chemical bonds of carbohydrates.

In respiration, electrons move "downhill," losing energy at each step until they ultimately react with molecular oxygen and hydrogen ions to form water. The energy yielded up by the electrons along their path from carbohydrate to water is used to build more ATP molecules, which provide the chemical energy for most of the synthetic and maintenance work done by the cell as well as for cellular movement (kinesis). If the energy of the glucose molecule were released all at once, most of it would be wasted as heat. (For constructive purposes, an explosion is not nearly so useful as a controlled fire.) The step-wise process assures that the major part of the energy will be channeled into useful cellular work.

Two biochemical cycles operate in conjunction with the electron transport chains. In the Calvin cycle of photosynthesis, three molecules of a 5-carbon sugar called ribulose–1, 5–diphosphate combine with three molecules of carbon dioxide. These three 6-carbon molecules split immediately to yield six molecules of a 3-carbon sugar called 3–phosphoglycerate. The cycle progresses through a number of steps until five of the 3–carbon molecules are rearranged to regenerate the original carbon dioxide acceptors: three molecules of ribulose–1, 5–diphosphate. One molecule of 3–phosphoglycerate remains, its synthesis achieved through three turns of the cycle (or one turn of the cycle for three carbon dioxide acceptor molecules). This molecule is the starting point for the synthesis of sugars, amino acids, and many other compounds. Before Calvin's work on the chemistry of photosynthesis, most people believed that glucose was the primary product of the process. Although Calvin showed that this is not strictly true, we are still approximately correct in representing glucose as the end product because much of the 3-phosphoglycerate is rapidly converted to glucose, which then serves as the major fuel for most cells.

Two types of respiration operate to release energy from glucose. The first, called anaerobic respiration or glycolysis, is thought to be the more primitive pathway because it does not utilize free oxygen and could therefore have occurred under the postulated conditions of early life in an oxygen-free atmosphere. The end product of anaerobic respiration in microorganisms is usually ethyl alcohol — a product which man exploits to both his joy and his sorrow. Although anaerobic respiration allowed life to develop in a rudimentary way, the process is woefully inefficient as a means of recovering the energy of the glucose molecule. About 90 percent of the potential energy of glucose remains locked in the end products of anaerobic respiration.

When free oxygen became available to living cells, another biochemical cycle evolved that could extract the remaining energy from the products of glycolysis. This is the familiar Krebs (or citric acid, or tricarboxylic acid) cycle, named for the pioneering biochemist who postulated its existence in 1937. A 2-carbon fragment of glucose enters the cycle by combining with a 4-carbon acceptor molecule. As the cycle turns, two molecules of CO_2 are released, hydrogen ions and electrons are shuttled off down the electron transport chain, and the original acceptor molecule is regenerated.

Where, now, is the energy of the glucose molecule? About 40 percent has been lost as heat (although even this is not a total loss, as it represents the source of body heat for warm blooded animals and permits life to reach the epitome of complexity represented by birds and mammals). The other 60 percent of the energy resides in the phosphate bonds of ATP. The process of glycolysis yields two molecules of ATP directly and six more through the electron transport chain, for a total of 8 ATPs per glucose molecule. The preparation of the glycolytic product for entrance into the Krebs cycle yields an additional six molecules of ATP. Each turn of the cycle then results in the formation of 12 ATPs, which gives a total of 24 per glucose molecule because two turns are necessary to account for each original glucose. All this yields 38 ATPs from the complete oxidation of one molecule of glucose: 38 ATPs ready to migrate from the mitochondrion to all parts of the cell, to accomplish work, to bring about change, to make things happen, by the transfer of their energy to something else.

Chronology of Events in the History of Man and Energy

	1,700,000 B.C.	First Ice Age begins. Several varieties of erect, man-like primates exist.
Before	500,000	Man begins to use fire.
Before	13,000	Domestication of the dog.
	9,000	Beginnings of agriculture.
	8,000	Last retreat of the continental ice sheet.
	7,000	First sickles, found in Palestine.
	6,000	Domestication of goats, pigs, sheep, cattle, oxen.
	4,000	Domestication of the horse.
	3,500	Wheel invented, probably in Mesopotamia.
	3,000	Man learns to smelt metal and make bronze.
	1,000	Beginning of iron technology. Domestication of the camel.
	300	Waterwheels in Greece.
	200	Modern harness invented in China.
	100	Horizontal shaft waterwheel produces 0.3 kilowatts power.
	27	Book by Vitruvius describes watermills, steam jets, and machines in general.
A.D.	300	Vertical shaft waterwheel produces 2 kilowatts power.
	500	Waterwheels come to Europe.
	650	First windmills. Modern horse harness reinvented in Europe.
	852	Coal burned in an English monastery.
	900	Whale oil used for lighting.

1239	Coal used as fuel by smiths and brewers.
1300	First coal used in home heating.
1404	First giant cannon, in Austria.
1500	Tide mills in the Netherlands; windmills used to drain submerged lands and maintain them.
1600	Versailles water works produces 56 kilowatts power.
1606	First known experimental steam engine built by Della Porta.
1673	Huygens builds internal combustion engine run on gunpowder.
1690	Papin designs the first piston engine.
1693	Leibnitz states the law of conservation of potential and kinetic energy.
1712	Newcomen builds first steam pumping engine.
1740	Improvements in iron technology.
1765	Modern steam engine conceived by Watt.
1789	Coulomb's work in electrostatics.
1820–1860	Work of Oersted, Ampere, Faraday, and Maxwell in electricity. Principles of thermodynamics worked out by Carnot and Clausius.
1857	First oil well drilled in Pennsylvania.
1866	Transatlantic cable laid.
1876	Otto designs four-stroke internal combustion engine.
1882	First incandescent lighting, New York.
1895	Roentgen discovers X-rays.
1896	Becquerel discovers radioactivity.
1898	Tsiolkovski works out principles of rocket flight.
1903	First flight of Wright brothers.
1920	First scheduled public radio broadcast, Pittsburgh.
1926	Goddard fires first rockets with liquid propellant.
1941	First jet plane flight.
1942	Fermi starts first atomic reactor in Chicago.
1945	First nuclear explosion, Alamogordo, New Mexico.
1945	Uranium bomb dropped on Hiroshima; plutonium bomb, on Nagasaki.
1952	First hydrogen bomb explosion.

1954   Launching of first atomic-powered submarine,
            Nautilus. First nuclear power plant put into
            service near Moscow, U.S.S.R.
1957   Sputnik I, first artificial satellite. First nuclear
            power plant in U.S., Shippingport, Penn-
            sylvania.
1969   Man lands on the moon.

APPENDIX D

Calculation of Energy in the Food System

Numerical data for the energy analysis of the food system are shown in Table D-1. Sources of these data, the assumptions behind the analysis, and some comments on methods are in the notes to Table D-1. The following discussion of omissions and duplications serves to set limits on the accuracy of the results.

There are other functional systems of society for which similar energy analyses may be desirable (housing, transportation, clothing, and recreation immediately come to mind). As energy becomes a scarce and expensive commodity, calculation of energy requirements is likely to become an essential ingredient of policy formation. The calculations are straightforward.

OMISSIONS AND DUPLICATIONS FOR
FOOD SYSTEM ENERGY VALUES

Several omissions, duplications, and overlaps have already been mentioned. A little closer attention to these values will provide some idea of how complete the values given in table D-1 are and allow a crude estimate of the numerical reliability of the conclusions.

On the farm the direct fuel usage may be overstated by the amount of fuel used by the farmer's household, which, by our approach, would not be chargeable to the food system. Similarly the personal use of electricity may be included in some of the data we have used and should be excluded. But about 10 percent of the total acreage farmed is held by corporate farms for which the electrical use is not included in

Table D-1. Energy Use in the U.S. Food System (all × 10^{12} kcal)

	1940	1947	1950	1954	1958	1960	1964	1968	1970	Notes
On Farm										
Fuel (direct use)	70.0	136.0	158.0	172.8	179.0	188.0	213.9	226.0	232.0	1,2,3
Electricity	0.7	32.0	32.9	40.0	44.0	46.1	50.0	57.3	63.8	2,4
Fertilizer	12.4	19.5	24.0	30.6	32.2	41.0	60.0	87.0	94.0	2,5
Agric. Steel	1.6	2.0	2.7	2.5	2.0	1.7	2.5	2.4	2.0	2,6
Farm Mach.	9.0	34.7	30.0	29.5	50.2	52.0	60.0	75.0	80.0	2,7
Tractors	12.8	25.0	30.8	23.6	16.4	11.8	20.0	20.5	19.3	8
Irrigation	18.0	22.8	25.0	29.6	32.5	33.3	34.1	34.8	35.0	9
Subtotal	124.5	272.0	303.4	328.6	356.3	373.9	440.5	503.0	526.1	
Processing Industry										
Food Prod. Indst.	147.0	177.5	192.0	211.5	212.6	224.0	249.0	295.0	308.0	1,2,10
Food Proc. Mach.	0.7	5.7	5.0	4.9	4.9	5.0	6.0	6.0	6.0	11
Paper Packaging	8.5	14.8	17.0	20.0	26.0	28.0	31.0	35.7	38.0	12
Glass Cont.	14.0	25.7	26.0	27.0	30.2	31.0	34.0	41.9	47.0	13
Steel Cans & Alum.	38.0	55.8	62.0	73.7	85.4	86.0	91.0	112.2	122.0	14
Transport (Fuel)	49.6	86.1	102.0	122.3	140.2	153.3	184.0	226.6	246.9	15
Trks & Trls (Mfg)	28.0	42.0	49.5	47.0	43.0	44.2	61.0	70.2	74.0	16
Subtotal	285.8	407.6	453.5	506.4	542.3	571.5	656.0	787.6	841.9	
Commercial and Home										
Comm. Refrig. & Cooking	121.0	141.0	150.0	161.0	176.0	186.2	209.0	241.0	263.0	17,1
Refrig. Mach. (Home & Comm.)	10.0	24.0	25.0	27.5	29.4	32.0	40.0	56.0	61.0	18,2
Home Refrig. & Cooking	144.2	184.0	202.3	228.0	257.0	276.6	345.0	433.9	480.0	17,1
Subtotal	275.2	349.0	377.3	416.5	462.4	494.8	594.0	730.9	804.0	
Total	685.5	1028.6	1134.2	1251.5	1361.0	1440.2	1690.5	2021.5	2172.0	

1. All figures for use of electricity have been converted to fuel input values using the average efficiency values for power plants given by Summers.[6] Self-generated electricity was converted to fuel inputs at an efficiency of 25 percent after 1945 and 20 percent before that year.

2. Purchased material in this analysis was converted to energy of manufacture according to the following values which were derived from the literature or calculated. In doubtful cases we have made what we believe to be conservative estimates:

steel (including fabricated and castings)	1.7×10^7 kcal/ton	natural gas	0.26×10^3 kcal/ft^3
aluminum (including castings and forgings)	6.0×10^7 kcal/ton	petroleum wax	2.2×10^6 kcal/ton
		gasoline and diesel engines	3.4×10^6 kcal/engine
		electric motors over 1 hp.	45×10^3 kcal/motor
copper and brass (alloys, millings, castings and forgings)	1.7×10^6 kcal/ton	ammonia	2.7×10^7 kcal/ton
		ammonia compounds	2.2×10^6 kcal/ton
paper	5.5×10^6 kcal/ton	sulfuric acid and sulfur	3×10^6 kcal/ton
plastics	1.25×10^6 kcal/ton	sodium carbonate	4×10^6 kcal/ton
coal	6.6×10^6 kcal/ton	other inorganic chemicals	2.2×10^6 kcal/ton
oil and gasoline	1.5×10^6 kcal/bbl		

3. Direct fuel use on farms — Expenditures for petroleum and other direct fuels on farms were obtained from Statistical Abstracts and Census of Agriculture data. A special survey of fuel use in farms in the 1964 Census of Agriculture was used for that year, and to determine mix of fuel products used. By comparing expenditures for fuel in 1964 with actual fuel use, the apparent unit price for this fuel mix was calculated. Using actual retail prices and price indices from Statistical Abstracts and the ratio of actual prices paid to retail prices in 1964, we derived the fuel quantities used in other years. Changes in the fuel mix used (primarily the recent trend toward more diesel tractors) may understate the energy in this category slightly in years since 1964 and overstate slightly in years before 1964. For example, Schurr and Netschert, using different methods, estimate a figure 10 percent less for 1955 than that given here.[7] On the other hand, some retail fuel purchases appear to be omitted from all these data for all years. Perelman, using different data, calculates 270×10^{12} kcal energy usage from tractors alone.[8]

4. Electricity use on farms — Data on monthly usage on farms from Report of the Administrator, Rural Electrification Administration, U.S. Department of Agriculture. Totals calculated from annual farm usage × number of farms × fraction electrified. Some non-agricultural uses included which may overstate the totals slightly for years before 1955. Nevertheless, the totals are on the conservative side. A survey of on-farm electricity usage published by the Holt Investment Advisory, May 18, 1973 reports per farm usage 30–40 percent higher than that given here, thus suggesting that our totals may be much too small. The discrepancy probably arises from the fact that the largest farm users are included in business and commercial categories (and excluded from the U.S.D.A. tabulations used).

5. Fertilizer — Direct fuel use by fertilizer manufacturers was added to the energy required for manufacture of raw materials purchased as inputs for fertilizer manufacture. There is allowance for the following: ammonia and related compounds, phosphatic compounds, phosphoric acid, muriate of potash, sulfuric acid and sulfur. No allowance for other inputs (of which phosphate rock, potash and "fillers" are the largest), packaging or capital equipment. Source: Census of Manufactures various years.

6. Agricultural Steel — Source: Statistical Abstracts, various years. Converted to energy values according to note 2.

7. Farm Machinery (except tractors) — Source: Census of Manufactures. Totals include direct energy use and steel, aluminum, copper, brass, alloys and engines converted according to note 2.

(continued)

8. Tractors – Numbers of new tractors were derived from Statistical Abstracts and Census of Agriculture Data. Direct data on energy and materials use for farm tractor manufacture was collected in Census of Manufactures data for 1954 and 1947 (in later years these data were merged with other data). For these years energy consumption was calculated as for farm machinery. A figure of 2.65×10^6 kcal/tractor horsepower was derived (e.g. 1954 data 23.6×10^{12} total energy used/315,000 sales/28.7 average tractor h.p. in 1954). This figure was used to calculate energy use in tractor manufacture in more recent years to take some account of the continuing increase in tractor size and power. It probably is a slight understatement of the energy in tractor manufacture in more recent years.

9. Irrigation energy – Source: Acres irrigated were taken from U.S. Statistical Abstracts for various years. Converted to energy use at 10^6 kcal/acre irrigated. This is an intermediate between two values cited by Pimentel and associates.[3]

10. Food Processing Industry – Source: Census of Manufactures. Direct fuel inputs only. No account taken for raw materials other than agricultural products, except for those items (packaging and processing machinery) accounted for in separate categories.

11. Food Processing Machinery – Source: Census of Manufactures various years. Items included are the same as for farm machinery (note 1).

12. Paper Packaging – Source: Census of Manufactures various years. In addition to direct energy use by the industry, energy values were calculated for purchased paper, plastics and petroleum wax, according to note 2. Proportions of paper products having direct food usage were obtained from Containers and Packaging, U.S. Department of Commerce. (The values given include only proportional values from Standard Industrial Classifications 2651 [1/2], 2653 [1/2], 2654 [all].)

13. Glass Containers – Source: Census of Manufactures various years. Direct energy use and sodium carbonate (converted according to note 2) were the only inputs considered. Proportions of containers assignable to food is taken from Containers and Packaging, U.S. Department of Commerce. Understatement of totals may be more than 20 percent in this category.

14. Steel and Aluminum Cans – Source: Census of Manufactures various years. Direct energy use, steel and aluminum inputs were included. Proportion of cans for food use has been nearly constant at 82 percent of total production, (Containers and Packaging, U.S. Department of Commerce).

15. Transportation Fuel Usage – Trucks only are included in totals given. After subtracting trucks used solely for personal transport (all of which are small trucks) 45 percent of all remaining trucks and 38 percent of trucks larger than pickup and panel trucks are engaged in hauling food and/or agricultural products in 1967. These proportions were assumed to hold for earlier years as well. Comparison with ICC analyses of Class I motor carrier cargoes suggest this is a reasonable assumption. Total fuel usage for trucks was apportioned according to these values. Direct calculation from average mileage per truck and average mi/gallon produces agreement within ± 10 percent for 1967, 1963 and 1955. There is some possible duplication with the direct fuel use on farms, but it cannot be more than 20 percent considering on-farm truck inventories. On the other hand, inclusion of rail, water, air and transport of fertilizer, machinery, packaging and other inputs transportation energy could raise these figures by 30–40 percent if ICC commodity proportions apply to all transportation. Sources: Census of Transportation 1963, 1967. Statistical Abstracts, ICC Freight Commodity Statistics, Class I Motor Carrier, various years.

16. Trucks and Trailers – Using truck sales numbers and the proportions of trucks engaged in food and agriculture obtained in note 15 above, the energy values were calculated at 75×10^6 kcal/trucks for manufacturing and delivery energy.[9] The results were checked against Census of Manufactures data for 1967, 1963, 1958, and 1939 by proportioning motor vehicles categories between automobiles and trucks. These checks suggest our estimates are too small by a small amount. Trailer manufacture was estimated by the proportional dollar value to truck sales (7 percent). Since a larger fraction of aluminum is used in trailers than in trucks, these energy amounts are probably conservative. Automobiles and trucks used for personal transport in the food system are omitted. Totals here are probably

significant but we know of no way to estimate them at present. Sources: Statistical Abstracts, Census of Manufactures, Census of Transportation, various years.

17. Commercial and home refrigeration and cooking — Data for 1960–68 (1970 extrapolated) is from *Patterns of Energy Consumption in the United States*.[10] For earlier years sales and inventory in-use data for stoves and refrigerators were compiled by fuel and converted to energy from average annual use figures from Edison Electric Institute and American Gas Association values, various years.

18. Refrigeration machinery — Source: Census of Manufactures. Direct energy use was included. Steel, aluminum, copper and brass were included. A few items produced under this SIC category for some years perhaps should be excluded for years prior to 1958, but other inputs, notably electric motors, compressors and other purchased materials should be included.

our data and which understate the direct fuel usage. Other estimages of these two categories are much higher (notes 3 and 4 of the table).

There is no allowance for food exported, which has the effect of overstating the energy used in our own food system. For the years prior to 1960 the United States was at times a net importer of food, at times an exporter, and at times near balance in this activity. But during this period the net flow of trade was never more than a few percent of total farm output, and hence the energy estimates were not affected much. Since 1960 net exports have increased to about twenty percent of the gross farm product. The items comprising the vast majority of the exports have been rough grains, flour, and other plant products with very little processing. Imports include more processed food than exports and represent energy expenditure outside the United States. Thus the overestimate of energy input to the food system might be 5 percent with an upper limit of 15 percent.

The items omitted are more numerous. Fuel losses from the wellhead or mineshaft to end use total 10 to 12 percent. This would represent a flat addition of 10 percent or more to the totals, but we have not included this item because it is not customarily charged to end uses.

We have computed transport energy for trucks only. Considerable food is transported by train and ship, but these items were omitted because they are small compared to the consumption of truck fuel. Small amounts of food are shipped by air, and, although air shipment is energy-intensive, the amount of energy consumed appears small. We have traced support materials until they could no longer be assigned to the food system. Some transportation energy consumption is not charged in the transport of these support materials. These omissions are numerous and hard to estimate, but it would be difficult to increase the food system's totals by more than one or two percent.

A more serious understatement of energy usage occurs with respect to vehicle usage (other than freight transport) on farm business, food related business in industry and commercial establishments, and in the supporting industries. A special attempt to estimate this category for 1968 suggests that this category of energy usage amounts to about 5 percent of the food system energy totals. Unfortunately, reliable data for this estimate are not available and the estimate would be subject to nearly 100 percent uncertainty. Since the category is real, we must be satisfied to suggest that 1 to 10 percent should be added to the totals on this account.

Waste disposal is related to the food system, at least in part. Whether to charge the energy use to the food system is a matter of opinion. We have chosen not to do so, but if one-half of the waste disposal activity is taken as food-related, about 2 percent must be added to the food system energy totals.

In addition, we have not included parts and maintenance energy for machinery, vehicles, buildings, and the like, or lumber for farm, industry or packaging uses. These miscellaneous activities would not constitute a large addition in any case. But we have also excluded construction. Building and replacement of farm structures, food industry structures, and commercial establishments are all directly part of the food system. Construction of roads is in some measure related to the food system, since nearly half of all trucks transport food and agricultural items. Even home construction could be charged in part to the food system since space, appliances and plumbing are in part a consequence of the food system. New construction has constituted about 10 percent of the gross national product in recent years. If 10 percent of housing, of institutional construction (for institutions with food service) and 10 percent of highway construction is charged to the food system, the total is about 10 percent of the total construction in 1970. If total energy consumption divides in the same way that gross national product does (which overstates energy use in construction), the addition to the total of the table would be about 10 percent or 200×10^{12} kcal. This is a crude and highly simplified calculation but does provide an estimate of the amounts of energy involved. It is hardly worth doing a more precise calculation until one is able to specify more exactly the way in which energy for construction is to be apportioned.

The energy used to generate the highly specialized seed and animal stock has been excluded because there is no easy way to estimate it. Pimentel and associates estimate 1,800 kcal are required to produce one pound of hybrid corn seed.[3] But in addition to this amount, some energy use should be included for all the schools of agriculture, agricultural experiment stations, the far-flung network of county agricultural agents (one local agent said he travelled over 50,000 automobile miles per year in his car), the U.S. Department of Agriculture and the wide ranging agricultural research program that enables man to stay ahead of the new pest and disease threats to our highly specialized food production system. These are extensive activities and there are no useful data available; nevertheless we cannot see how more than a few percent could be added to the totals on table D–1.

Finally, we have made no attempt to include the amount of private automobile usage which constitutes the delivery system from retailer to home, nor other food-related uses of private autos. Rice reports 4.25×10^{15} kcal for the energy cost of autos in 1970,[11] and shopping constitutes 15.2 percent of all automobile usage.[12] If only half of the shopping is food related, 320×10^{12} kcal of energy use is at stake here. Between 8 and 15 percent should be added to the totals of Table D-1, depending on just how one wishes to apportion this item.

From the above it is clear that it is hard to take an approach that might calculate any smaller totals but depending upon point of view, the totals could be much larger. If we accumulate the larger estimates from the above paragraphs, as well as the reductions, the total could be enlarged by 30 to 35 percent, especially for recent years. As it is, the values for energy use in the food system from table D-1 account for 12.8 percent of the total U.S. energy use in 1970. This does seem to present a more accurate picture of the present state of affairs than the value of two percent or so usually credited to agriculture.

REFERENCES

1. *Statistical Abstract of the United States,* 1973.
2. *Historical Statistics of the United States* (Washington, D.C., 1960). 182.
3. D. Pimentel et al., "Food Production and the Energy Crisis," *Science* 182 (1973): 443–449.
4. N. Georgescu-Roegen, *The Entropy Law and the Economic Process* (Cambridge, Mass.: Harvard University Press, 1971), 301.
5. M. Slesser, "How Many Can We Feed?," *The Ecologist,* 3 (1973): 216–220
6. C. M. Summers, "The Conversion of Energy," *Scientific American* 224 (1971): 148–163.
7. S. H. Schurr and B. C. Netschert, *Energy in the American Economy, 1850–1975* (Baltimore: Johns Hopkins Press, 1960), p. 774.
8. M. J. Perelman, "Farming with Petroleum," *Environment* 14 (1972): 10.
9. A. B. Makhijani and A. J. Lichtenberg, *An Assessment of Energy and Materials Utilization in the U.S.A.,* Memorandum no. ERL-M310 (revised) (Berkeley: University of California, 1971).
10. U.S., Office of Science and Technology, Executive Office of the President, *Patterns of Energy Consumption in the United States,* prepared by Stanford Research Institute, January 1972.
11. R. A. Rice, "System Energy and Future Transportation," *Technology Review,* (1972): 32–36.
12. Federal Highway Administration, *Nationwide Personal Transportation Study,* Report No. 1, 1971. As reported in *Energy Research and Development,* Hearings before the Committee on Science and Astronautics, May, 1972, p. 151.

Synthesis of Fuels and Chemicals from Coal

Coal is an intricate network of carbon rings in which the carbon is combined with hydrogen in approximately a 1:1 ratio. Coal also contains varying amounts of nitrogen, oxygen, and sulfur, as well as other minerals. Thus many materials can be obtained from coal. Coke, the standard fuel for metallurgy, is obtained by heating coal in the absence of air. The process typically yields about 3/4 ton of coke (essentially pure carbon) for each ton of coal. A variety of byproducts is recovered, including ammonia, coal tar, and coal gas. Coal gas is not desirable as fuel for general heating because of its low energy content, but it is used to fire the coking ovens, and on purification it yields such products as benzene, toluene, and methane. The yield of coal tar is about 3 percent of the weight of the coal. It provides material for the complex petrochemical industry, which produces, among other things, the coal tar dyes. More than 150 compounds have been isolated from coal tar and identified.

By providing a source of hydrogen and varying the conditions of temperature and pressure, gaseous or liquid fuel can be made from coal. When heated coal reacts with steam the following reactions occur, representing the first step in gasification:

$$C + H_2O + 32{,}457 \text{ cal} \rightarrow CO + H_2$$
$$CO + H_2O \rightarrow CO_2 + H_2 + 7{,}838 \text{ cal}$$
$$C + 2H_2 \rightarrow CH_4 + 21{,}854 \text{ cal}$$

In the second step the mixture of gases is cleaned to eliminate ammonia, CO_2, and oxides of sulfur. A mixture of CO, CH_4, and H_2 remains. This mixture may be used at the site of production for generating electricity, or its energy value may be increased by further reaction with hydrogen and a catalyst to give synthetic natural gas: $3H_2 + CO \rightarrow CH_4 + H_2O$.

The initial step in production of liquid fuel by the Fischer-Tropsch process also involves reacting heated coal with steam. The CO formed is then hydrogenated in the presence of one or more catalysts — usually iron, but sometimes also nickel, cobalt, copper, rubidium, zinc oxide, or others:

$$C + H_2O \rightarrow CO + H_2$$

$$nCO + 2nH_2 \xrightarrow{\text{catalyst}} C_nH_{2n} + nH_2O$$

$$nCO + (2n + 1)H_2 \xrightarrow{\text{catalyst}} C_nH_{2n+2} + nH_2O$$

The yield of hydrocarbons represents about two-thirds of the CO that entered the reaction. Typically, about half of this is in the gasoline fraction and the remainder is a variety of products including methane, a mixture of alcohols, and hydrocarbons of high molecular weight.

The Bergius process, developed in Germany during World War I for the production of aviation gasoline, yields a ton of gasoline for every 1.5 to 2 tons of coal. Here, finely ground coal is mixed with tar or oil and reacted with hydrogen under high temperature and pressure in the presence of a catalyst. The chemistry of this process resembles the chemistry of the Fischer-Tropsch process.

Glossary

AEC (Atomic Energy Commission): a five member commission established after World War II to supervise and promote uses of nuclear energy.

aerobic: occurring in the presence of free oxygen. An aerobic organism requires free oxygen for respiration.

albedo: ratio of the radiation reflected from an object to the total radiation incident upon it, often expressed as a percent.

alpha rays: radiation emitted during some nuclear reactions and consisting of charged particles which are composed of two protons and two neutrons. An alpha particle is identical with the nucleus of a helium atom.

anaerobic: occurring in the absence of air or free oxygen. Anaerobic respiration is sometimes called fermentation.

API (American Petroleum Institute): a trade organization of which most major oil companies are members.

asphalt: a semi-solid mixture of hydrocarbons, usually formed as a result of evaporation of volatile constituents of petroleum.

atomic nucleus: the positively charged core of an atom, with which is associated almost the entire atomic mass but only a minute fraction of the atomic volume.

atmosphere: the gaseous envelope surrounding a celestial object. Earth's atmosphere (the air) is a mixture of gases, vapors, and suspended particles with a mass less than 0.0001 percent of the total mass of the earth.

barrel: a liquid volume measure equal to 42 gallons, commonly used in expressing quantities of petroleum and petroleum products.

biochemical oxygen demand (BOD): a measure of the oxygen needed to oxidize all the organic material in a body of water.

biomass: the total mass (or weight) of all organisms in a habitat or area.

biosphere: the zone of air, land, and water at the surface of the earth that is occupied by living organisms.

breeder reactor: a nuclear reactor which creates more fissionable fuel than it consumes.

burner reactor: a nuclear reactor that produces almost no nuclear fuel.

calorie: originally, the amount of heat energy required to raise the temperature of 1 gram of water $1°$ C. Because this quantity varies with the temperature of the water, the calorie has been redefined in terms of other energy units. One calorie is equal to 4.2 joules. The relationship of the calorie to other units of energy is given in Appendix A.

carbohydrate: an organic compound consisting of a chain of carbon atoms to which hydrogen and oxygen are attached in a ratio of 2 to 1. Carbohydrates include sugars, starch, glycogen, cellulose, some plant gums, and other minor compounds.

Celsius: a temperature scale based on the freezing and boiling points of water ($0°$ and $100°$, respectively). Its abbreviation is C. The name Celsius has replaced the name Centigrade in most scientific usage.

chain reaction: a reaction in which one of the necessary agents is itself produced so as to perpetuate the reaction. In a nuclear fission chain reaction, a neutron causes the fission of a nucleus, resulting in release of more neutrons which, in turn, cause other fissions.

chemical energy: the energy involved in chemical reactions (the recombination of constituent atoms of reacting substances into different substances). Release of chemical energy involves rearrangement of outer orbital electrons.

cirrus clouds: thin, wispy clouds composed of ice crystals which exist at altitudes where the temperatures are below freezing. They are almost always found at least four miles high in the tropics, although they may be near the ground in polar areas.

coke: the standard fuel for metallurgical processes, obtained by heating coal in the absence of air. Volatile material and moisture are driven off during the coking process, leaving an almost smokeless fuel.

conduction: the process by which energy is transferred directly from molecule to molecule. It is the way in which electricity travels through a wire or heat moves from a warm body to a cool one when the two bodies are placed in contact.

continental shelf: the submerged shelf of land sloping gradually from the exposed edge of a continent. It is usually defined as those areas where the water is less than 200 meters (600 feet) deep.

convection: the transfer of heat by the circulation of a liquid or gas.

converter reactor: a nuclear reactor which creates substantial amounts of nuclear fuel, but less than it consumes.

Council of Economic Advisors (CEA): three persons appointed by the President to provide advice on economic matters. The term is sometimes used to refer to both the advisors and their staff. The CEA accumulates the data and prepares an annual economic report to the Congress.

cumulus clouds: low clouds composed of water droplets, the familiar billowed heaps with flat bases and tufted tops.

curie: a measure of radioactivity. One curie is the quantity of a radioactive substance which undergoes 3.7×10^{10} nuclear disintegrations per second. This is the activity of one gram of radium.

DNA: deoxyribonucleic acid, the carrier of genetic information in cells.

efficiency: the ratio of output to input of energy or power. For a process involving heat, efficiency is related to the initial and final temperatures of the system.

electricity: a form of energy having chemical, radiant, and magnetic effects. It is a property of the basic particles of matter. A current of electricity is created by the flow of charged particles.

electromagnetic radiation: energy emitted in the form of radiowaves, heat, light, etc. from atoms and molecules that are undergoing internal change. It generates a set of alternating electric and magnetic fields and is propagated through space at a rate of 300,000 kilometers per second.

electromagnetic spectrum: the range of electromagnetic radiations, from low frequency radiowaves to high frequency gamma rays.

electron: an elementary particle with a rest mass of 9.1×10^{-28} grams, bearing either a positive or negative electric charge. Negative electrons orbit the atomic nucleus; their transfer or rearrangement between atoms underlies all chemical reactions. Either negative or positive electrons (sometimes called positrons) may be emitted from atomic nuclei during nuclear reactions; they are then called beta particles and they are the constituents of beta rays.

electron volt: a unit of energy representing the charge of an electron falling through a potential difference of one volt. It is equal to 1.6×10^{-12} erg.

energy: the capacity to do work. A quantity which is conserved, although it may be exchanged among bodies and transformed from one form to another, or interconverted with mass.

energy conversion: the transformation of energy from one form to another.

erg: a unit of energy or work, defined as the amount of work done by a force of one dyne (one gram-centimeter per $\sec^2$) acting through a distance of one centimeter.

evapotranspiration: the conversion of water from liquid to gaseous form, through both evaporation from soil, bodies of water, and other objects and evaporation (transpiration) from leaves of plants.

exponential growth: type of growth illustrated by the compound interest law. A useful characteristic of an exponential growth rate is that the "doubling time," or the length of time required for the growing thing to double in size, is constant.

fast neutron: high energy neutron. Fast neutrons are utilized in the fast breeder reactor both to produce nuclear fissions and to transform fertile material (e.g. ^{238} U) into fissionable nuclear fuel.

Federal Power Commission (FPC): a five member commission whose members are appointed by the President and serve staggered terms. It licenses hydroelectric projects; has jurisdiction over interstate commerce involving sale of electric energy and natural gas.

fission: see *nuclear fission*

fixation (of nitrogen): the conversion of atmospheric nitrogen to ammonia or other compounds that can be used by plants. Carbon dioxide is also "fixed" into carbohydrates by green plants.

food chain: a series of organisms dependent on one another for food (more accurately called a food web). Most food chains begin with plants or microorganisms and end with the largest carnivores.

fossil fuel: any naturally occurring fuel of an organic nature, such as coal, oil shale, natural gas, or crude oil.

free market: the ideal market of classical economics. It is characterized by many sellers and many buyers, each having such small influence on the price and operation of the market that their individual actions do not affect price or market conditions.

fuel cell: a device for converting the energy released in a chemical oxidation reaction directly into electrical energy.

fusion: see *nuclear fusion.*

gamma rays: very energetic electromagnetic radiation released as a result of transition from one energy level to another within an atomic nucleus. Gamma rays are frequently emitted during nuclear reactions.

gasification (of coal): the conversion of coal to a gaseous fuel.

geothermal energy: the heat energy available in the rocks, hot water, and steam in the earth's subsurface.

GNP (Gross National Product): the total market value of the goods and services produced, before the deduction of depreciation and other allowances for capital consumption. A widely used measure of economic activity.

gravitational energy: the predominant form of energy in the universe, resulting from the universal attraction existing between all material bodies. The force of attraction varies directly with the product of the masses of the two bodies and inversely with the square of the distance between them.

greenhouse effect: the warming of the lower atmosphere and the surface of the earth due to the absorption and reradiation of infrared radiation by the carbon dioxide and water vapor in the atmosphere.

green revolution: increase in agricultural productivity resulting from use of the new high-yielding "miracle grains."

half-life: the time required for half of a substance to undergo disintegration or reaction or some other process that removes it from the sample. By analogy with exponential growth, the half-life represents the rate of exponential shrinking.

heat: a form of kinetic energy, whose effects are produced by the vibration, rotation, and general motions of molecules.

heat engine: an engine in which heat is transformed into mechanical energy.

heat pump: a refrigeration machine that is used for heating rather than cooling. Expanding refrigeration fluid removes heat from a large heat source; the fluid is then compressed, and the heat resulting from compression is discharged to a heat exchanger next to the surroundings to be heated.

heat sink: the medium or location to which waste heat is discharged and where, hopefully, it is dissipated without producing undesirable environmental effects.

horizontal integration: the control by one company or industry grouping of a number of related or substitutable products. In the energy industry this would be characterized by control of more than one fuel or energy source.

hydrocarbon: a compound containing only carbon and hydrogen. The fossil fuels are predominantly hydrocarbons, with varying amounts of organic compounds of sulfur, nitrogen, and oxygen, and some inorganic material.

hydrosphere: all the water on the surface of the earth, including oceans and seas, lakes, rivers, and underground water.

infrared: the portion of the electromagnetic spectrum associated with phenomena of heat. Infrared means "below the red;" infrared radiation is less energetic than visible light, which occupies the adjacent portion of the spectrum.

ion: an electrically charged atom or group of atoms.

ionization: the addition of electrons to or removal of electrons from atoms or molecules.

ionizing radiation: radiation which causes ionization by impartinf energy to atoms or molecules.

isotope: one of the possible forms of a chemical element, differing from other forms in the number of neutrons in the nucleus. Isotopes of an element usually have the same chemical properties but somewhat different physical properties as a result of their different atomic weights.

Kelvin: a temperature scale whose degrees are quantitatively equal to degrees on the Celsius scale, but whose zero point is the "absolute zero" of temperature at which all molecular motion theoretically ceases. On the Kelvin scale the freezing point of water is approximately $273°$ and the boiling point approximately $373°$.

kilo-: a prefix used in the metric system meaning one thousand.

kilowatt: a unit of power, commonly used as the commercial measure of electric power. It is equivalent to 1000 watts or 1000 joules per second.

kilowatt hour: a measure of energy or work equal to that done by one kilowatt acting for one hour.

kilovolt: a unit of electric potential difference, equal to 1000 volts. In the transmission of electricity, voltage is very roughly analogous to pressure in the transmission of fluids.

kinetic energy: energy of motion.

latent heat: the amount of heat energy released when a gas is condensed to a liquid or a liquid is changed to a solid without change of temperature, expressed in calories per gram. Heat energy is stored as latent heat in the water vapor of the atmosphere.

lignite: a brownish-black coal in which the alteration of organic material has proceeded farther than in peat but not as far as in bituminous coal.

liquefaction (of coal): the conversion of coal into liquid hydrocarbons and related compounds by hydrogenation.

liquefied natural gas (LNG): natural gas that has been liquefied by cooling to about $-140°$ C. In this form, it occupies a relatively small volume and can be transported economically by ocean tanker.

liquefied petroleum gas (LPG): a mixture of gaseous hydrocarbons, principally propane and butane, which can be liquefied under moderate pressure at normal temperatures.

lithosphere: the solid outer crust of the earth.

magnetohydrodynamics (MHD): the science related to phenomena arising from the motion of electrically conducting fluids in the presence of electric and magnetic fields. A technique for generating electricity directly by moving liquids or gases through a magnetic field.

mass defect: the difference between the mass of an atomic nucleus (or atom) calculated as the summation of the masses of its constituent particles and the actual mass, which is always less since some mass is converted to energy during the formation of the nucleus. The mass defect of an isotope is often expressed as the mass defect per nucleon.

mega-: a prefix meaning one million.

megawatt: the unit of power equal to 10^6 watts,

mesosphere: the region of the atmosphere extending from about 50 to 80 kilometers above the earth, characterized by rapidly decreasing temperature as altitude increases.

Mev: million electron volts, a unit of energy commonly used to express energy involved in nuclear reactions (see **electron volt**).

micro-: a prefix meaning one millionth.

microclimate: the conditions of temperature, humidity, wind, etc. immediately surrounding an organism or in a particular habitat.

milli-: a prefix meaning one thousandth.

moderator: a material, for example graphite or water, used to control the rate of fission in a nuclear reactor. By slowing down neutrons to speeds at which they tend not to be absorbed by nonfissionable nuclei, the moderator prevents quenching of the chain reaction.

mutation: a change in the genetic material, or DNA, of a cell. The change may be caused by ionizing radiation, various chemicals or physical factors, or a random "mistake" in the synthesis of the DNA.

National Environmental Policy Act (NEPA): an act passed in 1970 requiring that the environmental impact of most large projects and programs be considered. Among its important provisions is one requiring a detailed statement of environmental impact of and alternatives to a project to be submitted to the government before the project can begin.

National Petroleum Council (NPC): an advisory group to the executive branch on petroleum related matters. The appointed members are most often from the oil and gas industry.

natural gas: a mixture of gaseous hydrocarbons, chiefly methane, which occurs in reservoirs in the earth.

natural gas liquids: hydrocarbons other than methane recovered during the processing of natural gas, including LPG and natural gasoline.

natural monopoly: certain goods, and especially services, for which multiple sellers are thought to be wasteful or not in the public interest. Telephone service, mass transit, and those services referred to as public utilities are usually natural monopolies.

neutron: an elementary particle with approximately the mass of a proton but without any electric charge. It is one of the constituents of the atomic nucleus. It is frequently released during nuclear reactions and, on entering a nucleus, can cause nuclear reactions including nuclear fission.

non-symbiotic nitrogen fixation: the fixation of nitrogen by free-living organisms in the soil or in water.

nuclear energy: energy released as particulate or electromagnetic radiation and heat during reactions of atomic nuclei.

nuclear fission: the splitting of large atomic nuclei into two or more new nuclear species, with the release of large amounts of energy.

nuclear fusion: the process by which small atomic nuclei join together with the release of large amounts of energy.

nucleon: a proton or neutron, one of the particles comprising the atomic nucleus.

nucleus: see *atomic nucleus*.

oil shale: a sedimentary rock containing solid organic matter from which oil can be obtained when the rock is heated to a high temperature.

OPEC (Organization of Petroleum Exporting Countries): a confederation of nations (including Venezuela and a number of Middle Eastern and North African nations) whose purpose is developing common policies in the marketing of petroleum.

ozone: a form of molecular oxygen containing three atoms of oxygen per molecule. Ozone is deadly to life, but bands of ozone high in the atmosphere absorb lethal ultraviolet radiation and thus protect life on earth.

petroleum refinery: a plant that converts crude petroleum into the many petroleum fractions (asphalt, fuel oil, gasoline, etc.). Usually this conversion is accomplished by fractional distillation.

photochemical reaction: a chemical reaction brought about by light; one which derives the necessary energy from light. See **photosynthesis.** Photochemical reactions play a major role in the formation of smog.

photon: a quantum of electromagnetic energy having properties of both a wave and a particle, but without mass or electric charge.

photosynthesis: a photochemical reaction by which carbon dioxide is reduced (fixed) to carbohydrate in the presence of chlorophyll. The process by which green plants utilize solar energy to convert carbon dioxide and water into new biomass.

plasma: the "fourth state of matter," existing at temperatures high enough to strip all electrons away from atomic nuclei. The plasma is a gaseous mixture of atomic nuclei, electrons, protons, and neutrons. This state of matter is common in the stars; it must be achieved on earth in order to obtain useful energy from nuclear fusion.

plutonium: a manmade fissionable element (nuclear fuel) created by bombarding uranium-238 with neutrons in a reactor.

pollution: the accumulation of wastes or byproducts of human activity. Pollution occurs when wastes are discharged in excess of the rate at which they can be degraded, assimilated, or dispersed by natural processes. Although the concept of pollution is generally understood in terms of human processes, there are many examples of "natural" pollution, including pollution from volcanic eruptions and natural oil seeps.

potential energy: energy which a body possesses because of its position with respect to another body, or relative to other parts of itself. More generally, potential energy is energy in any form not associated with motion; thus the energy stored in chemical bonds is potential energy.

power: the rate at which energy is expended or work is done.

primary fuels: those fuels providing original energy, as contrasted to secondary energy sources and fuels such as electricity or hydrogen. At present primary fuels are all fossil fuels except for small amounts of uranium. For capture of continuous natural energy processes such as wind or falling water there is no primary fuel.

primary producers: organisms (green plants or certain bacteria) which produce organic compounds through photosynthesis or chemosynthesis.

prime mover: a machine that converts food, fuel, or force to work or power.

proton: a positively charged elementary particle having a mass of about 1.7×10^{-24} grams, roughly 1840 times as great as the mass of an electron. Protons are constituents of atomic nuclei and are emitted in some nuclear reactions.

public utility: a business performing some public service and subject to special government regulation. Electric, water, and sewer service are examples. (See also **natural monopoly**.)

pumped storage: an arrangement in which water is pumped into a storage reservoir when a surplus of electricity is being generated; during times of peak demand for electricity, this water is then used for the generation of electricity as in any hydroelectric power plant.

rad: a unit of measurement of the absorbed dose of ionizing radiation. It corresponds to an energy transfer of 100 ergs per gram of irradiated object.

radiation: the process by which energy in the form of electromagnetic radiation is emitted from matter. Also, the electromagnetic or particulate rays that are emitted from atoms or molecules as they undergo internal change.

radioactivity: the spontaneous decomposition of an atom accompanied by the release of energy.

radioisotope: a radioactive isotope of a chemical element.

reactor: a device in which nuclear fission is sustained in a self-supporting chain reaction.

rem: a unit of measurement of absorbed dose of ionizing radiation by human tissue. It is usually equivalent to a rad, except in the case of very energetic alpha rays, when a dose of one rad may correspond to 10 or 20 rem. The relationship between the rad and the rem depends on characteristics of the radiation.

reserves: the amount of a fuel or other mineral resource known to exist and expected to be recoverable by existing techniques and under existing economic conditions.

resources: in the restricted sense, the estimated total quantity of a fuel or other mineral in the ground, including prospective undiscovered reserves and material that cannot be recovered under existing conditions.

respiration: the process by which an organism oxidizes energy-yielding organic compounds to obtain the energy necessary for other life processes.

roentgen: a unit of measure of X radiation or gamma radiation; it measures exposure to radiation, rather than the absorbed dose. One roentgen is equivalent to the amount of radiation that imparts 87.8 ergs of energy to one gram of dry air.

sensible heat: heat that affects the temperature of the material (as opposed to **latent heat**).

slow neutron: a low energy neutron, sometimes called a thermal neutron. The energy of a slow neutron is about 0.025 electron volts, in contrast to the energy of a **fast neutron**, which may exceed 1000 electron volts. Slow neutrons are very efficient in causing fission of uranium-235. Nuclear power plants now in operation are designed to use slow neutrons to sustain the fission reaction.

smog: term used broadly to mean polluted air. There are various types of smog which are produced from certain classes of pollutants under specific meteorologic conditions. Photochemical smog results from photochemical reactions involving hydrocarbons and oxides of nitrogen, common constituents of polluted air.

solar cell: a device which converts solar radiation to a current of electricity.

solar constant: the average intensity of solar radiation striking the atmosphere. The solar constant is measured on a plane perpendicular to the path of the radiation. Its value is 1.36 kilowatts per square meter.

solar spectrum: the total distribution of electromagnetic radiation emitted from the sun, minus those wavelengths that are absorbed by the solar atmosphere.

stratosphere: the region of the atmosphere extending from about kilometers above the earth to 50 kilometers. It contains the layers of ozone which absorb the most energetic ultraviolet rays of the sun, and it is the region where high-flying aircraft fly.

strip mining: the mining of coal by removing covering material (the overburden) and "stripping" away the entire underlying coal seam. Other forms of coal mining are underground or deep mining, in which large vacant "rooms" are left underground, and auger mining in which coal is drilled out of seams exposed along the side of a mountain

symbiotic nitrogen fixation: the fixation of nitrogen by bacteria living in nodules in the roots of leguminous plants.

tar sands: sedimentary rocks which contain viscous, heavy petroleum that cannot be recovered by conventional methods of petroleum production.

Tennessee Valley Authority (TVA): a quasi-governmental corporation whose board of directors is appointed by the President. It provides navigable channels and flood control for the Tennessee River and some of its tributaries; produces and disposes of electric power; produces and improves fertilizer.

temperature: the intensity of heat. The temperature of a body is proportional to the average kinetic energy of the molecules of which it is composed. Various properties of a body change when its temperature changes, and these changes are the bases for different temperature scales.

thermionic device: a device which converts heat into electricity by "boiling" electrons from a hot metal surface and condensing them on a cooler surface.

thermodynamics: the science dealing with the relationship of heat and mechanical energy, and the conversion of one into the other.

thermodynamics, laws of: the first law of thermodynamics states that heat can be converted into work or work into heat. There is a constant relationship between the two quantities which is known as the mechanical equivalent of heat: one calorie equals about 4.2 joules. The second law of thermodynamics states that when a free exchange of heat takes place between two bodies, the heat is always transferred from the warmer to the cooler body.

thermoelectric device: a device based on the thermoelectric effect. If metals at two different temperatures are placed in contact, there is a difference in electric potential between the two and a current of electricity will flow.

thermosphere: the upper region of the atmosphere, characterized by temperatures which may reach $1500°$ K. It is sometimes called the ionosphere because it contains bands of ionized gases and free electrons. The aurora borealis (northern lights) is a phenomenon of the lower thermosphere.

threshold: the level of a stimulus required to produce an effect.

transpiration: loss of water vapor from leaves and other exposed parts of plants.

transuranium: beyond uranium. Nuclei of uranium contain 92 protons, more than any other naturally occurring element. However, elements with a greater number of protons can be created by bombarding nuclei of the heavier elements with subatomic particles. Thus plutonium, with 94 protons in the nucleus, is formed when the nucleus of a uranium atom absorbs a neutron and emits two electrons; the loss of the two negative electrons increases the positive charge of the nucleus by 2.

troposphere: the layer of the atmosphere nearest the ground, where most of the phenomena of weather originate.

ultraviolet: the portion of the electromagnetic spectrum lying between the range of visible light and X rays.

U.S. Geological Survey (USGS): a large bureau within the Department of the Interior which includes most of the professional geologists of the government. Among its many activities is the supervision of oil and gas production on public lands through the Oil and Gas division.

vertical integration: the control by one company of the various stages of a commodity from primary production, through processing and marketing, to final consumers.

volt: a unit of electromotive force or electric potential difference. A potential difference must exist across a conductor in order for a current of electricity to flow, and if other factors are held constant, the greater the voltage is, the greater is the current that will flow. A volt is the potential difference that exists across a conductor which carries a current of one ampere and dissipates thermal energy at the rate of one watt.

voltage: difference of potential measured in volts.

watt: a unit of power. It is the rate of energy use or conversion when one joule of energy is used or converted per second. (A joule is about 0.25 calories.)

work: the transfer of energy from one body to another; or the energy itself, in the process of transfer. Work and energy are measured in the same units.

X rays: very energetic electromagnetic radiation. Their emission is commonly associated with changes in energy levels of electrons near the atomic nucleus.

Index